Essential Japanese Grammar

A Comprehensive Guide to Contemporary Usage

MASAHIRO TANIMORI
ERIKO SATO

TUTTLE Publishing

Tokyo | Rutland, Vermont | Singapore

The Tuttle Story: "Books to Span the East and West"

Most people are surprised to learn that the world's largest publisher of books on Asia had its beginnings in the tiny American state of Vermont. The company's founder, Charles E. Tuttle, belonged to a New England family steeped in publishing. And his first love was naturally books—especially old and rare editions.

Immediately after WW II, serving in Tokyo under General Douglas MacArthur, Tuttle was tasked with reviving the Japanese publishing industry, and founded the Charles E. Tuttle Publishing Company, which thrives today as one of the world's leading independent publishers.

Though a westerner, Charles was hugely instrumental in bringing knowledge of Japan and Asia to a world hungry for information about the East. By the time of his death in 1993, Tuttle had published over 6,000 books on Asian culture, history and art—a legacy honored by the Japanese emperor with the "Order of the Sacred Treasure," the highest tribute Japan can bestow upon a non-Japanese.

With a backlist of 1,500 titles, Tuttle Publishing is more active today than at any time in its past—inspired by Charles' core mission to publish fine books to span the East and West and provide a greater understanding of each.

Published by Tuttle Publishing, an imprint of Periplus Editions (HK) Ltd.

www.tuttlepublishing.com

Copyright © 2012 by Masahiro Tanimori

Library of Congress Cataloging-in-Publication Data

Tanimori, Masahiro, 1958–
 Essential Japanese grammar : a comprehensive guide to contemporary usage / Masahiro Tanimori, Eriko Sato.
  p. cm.
 ISBN 978-4-8053-1117-2 (pbk.)
1. Japanese language—Grammar. 2. Japanese language—Textbooks for foreign speakers—English. 3. Japanese language—Self-instruction. I. Sato, Eriko, 1962– II. Title.
PL685.T365 2011
495.6'82421—dc23
                    2011019340

ISBN 978-4-8053-1117-2

Distributed by

North America, Latin America & Europe
Tuttle Publishing
364 Innovation Drive
North Clarendon, VT 05759-9436 U.S.A.
Tel: 1 (802) 773-8930; Fax: 1 (802) 773-6993
Email: info@tuttlepublishing.com
Web: www.tuttlepublishing.com

Japan
Tuttle Publishing
Yaekari Building, 3rd Floor, 5-4-12 Osaki,
Shinagawa-ku, Tokyo 141 0032
Tel: (81) 3 5437-0171; Fax: (81) 3 5437-0755
Email: sales@tuttle.co.jp Web: www.tuttle.co.jp

Asia Pacific
Berkeley Books Pte. Ltd.
61 Tai Seng Avenue #02-12, Singapore 534167
Tel: (65) 6280-1330; Fax: (65) 6280-6290
Email: inquiries@periplus.com.sg
Web: www.periplus.com

First edition
16 15 14 13 12   10 9 8 7 6 5 4 3 2 1
1111MP

Printed in Singapore

CONTENTS

PART TWO
DICTIONARY OF USAGE

PREFACE

Just as a word among countless words can bring a sentence to life, it is our hope that readers of this book will see the grammar of Japanese come alive within its pages and discover the essence of the language while moving farther along on the path to its mastery.

Essential Japanese Grammar is a complete revision, greatly enlarged and enhanced, of the *Handbook of Japanese Grammar* (Tuttle Publishing, 1994). It is intended to be a thorough grammar reference and self-study guide for language learners who wish to study Japanese seriously or refresh their understanding of the language. This book consists of two parts. Part I lists essential grammatical notions including parts of speech, sentence constructions, conjugation forms, speech styles, and accentuation rules. Part II lists essential words and functional elements that are useful for communication, both spoken and written. The items in each part are alphabetically ordered and are related to other items in the same part and across the two parts through extensive cross-referencing. Each entry in both parts comprises a brief English glossary, a clear explanation, and helpful example sentences. Readers can master the usage of each item through these explanations and examples, expand their knowledge through the cross-references, and thus improve their communicative skills. Furthermore, the appendices provide word lists for certain selected categories, which may be of use not only to students but also teachers of Japanese as well as linguists who study the Japanese language.

Essential Japanese Grammar presents a number of unique features. First, grammatical terminology has been kept to a minimum so that extensive prior knowledge of grammar is not required. Different grammarians use different grammar terms, but this book adopts the terms that are most accessible and easy to comprehend for English-speaking learners. For example, the *ta* that is regarded as an auxiliary verb (*hojo dōshi*) in Japanese traditional grammar is called a verb suffix in this book. Our intention has been that the terminology be readily graspable by readers and that the explanations as to how and why words or phrases function as they do be as straightforward as possible.

Second, this book offers abundant example sentences, with a view to illustrating concretely and comprehensively how and where the key word or phrase may be used within a sentence. It is hoped this will enable readers to better understand Japanese sentence structure and have fun creating new sentences by assembling the verbal elements. The example sentences—consisting of Japanese characters followed by *romaji* and the English translation—are designed to make Japanese sentence structure evident, by allowing easy comparison of the positions of Japanese words with their Romanization and English equivalents. Occasionally, this means that the English translation will be somewhat stilted, when the English deliberately reflects the Japanese structural pattern. The authors have also made every effort to include both everyday and interesting usages in the example sentences and to offer a range of nuances of particular Japanese words or phrases, so as to keep readers engaged. Included among the various styles and forms are informal words, plain style, polite style, spoken style, written style, and even young people's slang.

Third, the authors have tried to reveal aspects of grammar that may not be found in comparable grammar books. For example, the section on adjectival nouns includes those that take *no* instead of *na* when modifying nouns. In addition, this book presents the description of the honorific systems in accordance with the latest version of the "Guidelines for Honorific Expressions," which were revised by the Japanese government's Council for Cultural Affairs in 2007. Also worth noting in Part I is a section called English Preposition Equivalents, where English prepositions are listed first, with typical example sentences illustrating the different ways in which they may be expressed in Japanese. This unique treatment of English prepositions is intended to help learners solve an often ticklish problem when navigating between the two languages. Another special section, called Accents, explains how differently Japanese words or phrases are accented from English words or sentences.

Furthermore, the Japanese particle *ga,* which is famous for its trickiness, is explained in a very different way to show better how it differs from the similarly tricky particle *wa.* Part II includes some words newly created by young people as well as some that have started to be used unconventionally by young people, like the prefix *cho* and the suffixes *ppoi* and *ru.* It also includes very old words or phrases that are still utilized in modern Japanese, like *zaru o enai* and *zu ni.* Care is taken to explain how some words may imply the speaker's negative emotion, or be risky to use in friendly conversation.

The authors hope this book will enable its users to make great strides in mastering the Japanese language.

Finally, the authors extend special thanks to the staff of the Tuttle Publishing, especially to Calvert Barksdale, for his valuable suggestions and for his patience in editing this book.

PART ONE

Japanese Grammar: An Overview

INTRODUCTION

Although the Japanese language includes a large volume of Chinese vocabulary and utilizes more than 2,000 Chinese characters in common written forms, Japanese is quite different from standard Chinese in its grammatical structure and is in fact closer to Korean in this regard. As you might expect, Japanese grammar is extremely different from that of English.

Word order and particles

English and Japanese show a number of asymmetries in terms of their sentence structures. First, the basic word order in English is subject-verb-object, whereas in Japanese it is subject-object-verb. Second, the subject cannot be absent in English even if it is understood, whereas Japanese speakers make every effort to omit the subject (as well as the object) if it is understood. Third, the word order is rigid in English in most cases but can be very flexible in Japanese. For example, if a sentence in Japanese has a subject noun, an object noun, and a verb, the subject and the object can switch places as long as the verb remains at the end of the sentence. For instance, the English sentence *Ben invited Lisa* can be either *Ben-ga Lisa-o shōtaishita* or *Lisa-o Ben-ga shōtaishita* in Japanese. These sentences mean the same thing because the subject noun is marked by the subject particle *ga* and the object noun is marked by the object particle *o* in both of the Japanese sentences, regardless of their positions within the sentence. Notice that there are no English counterparts for *ga* and *o*. On the other hand, the particles that mark items other than subjects and objects in Japanese usually do have English counterparts. For example, *Nichiyōbi ni ikimasu* means '(I will) go (there) on Sunday.' The particle *ni* in the Japanese sentence corresponds to *on* in English. However, the latter is considered a *pre*position, whereas the former is a *post*position. This demonstrates an additional asymmetrical aspect between the two languages. The Japanese word order can be schematically represented as below, where [P] stands for a particle:

[NOUN]+[P] [NOUN]+[P] ... [NOUN]+[P] [VERB]

Japanese particles do not just express the grammatical functions of words and phrases within a sentence. They also include focus particles, which express information beyond the sentence, such as the speaker's views, attitudes, and perspectives. For example, *Katakana mo kakimasu* means someone writes katakana in addition to at least one different type of characters. *Katakana dake kakimasu* means someone writes just katakana. *Katakana nado kakimasu* means someone writes katakana and other types of characters. As this shows, particles can express contextual information in Japanese. Particles can also express specificity, which in English is conveyed by articles such as *a* and *the*. For example, *inu wa asoko ni imasu* means 'The dog is over there,' but *inu ga asoko ni imasu* means 'There is a dog over there.' The particle *wa* definitely marks the item as already known by the speaker and the listener, although the major function of the particle *wa* in such a sentence is to clarify the sentence's topic. Again, there are no English counterparts for these particles.

Verb morphology

English verbs conjugate based on the number and the person of the subject, as in *I eat, she eats*, and *they eat*. On the other hand, Japanese verbs do not change form based on the number or person. In fact, nouns do not have a singular/plural distinction either. Japanese verbs change form based on tense and polarity (whether they are affirmative or negative) as well as what follows them (e.g. suffixes, particles, auxiliaries, nouns, and sentence-ending predicates). For example, *tabe* is the shortest pronounceable form of the verb 'to eat' and does not itself bear any information about the tense. However, *tabe-ru* means 'will eat' or 'eat (regularly),' *tabe-ta* means 'ate,' and *tabe-nakat-ta* means 'did not eat.' Japanese verbs can be followed by additional verb suffixes or auxiliary verbs, creating a long verb phrase, which sounds like one long word. For example, *tabe-sase-ta* means 'made someone eat,' *tabe-sase-rare-ta* means 'was made to eat,' *tabe-sase-rare-nakat-ta* means 'was not made to eat.' These examples demonstrate that Japanese verb morphology is highly agglutinating, allowing a long sequence of suffixation within the same phonological unit. Interestingly, Japanese adjectives show some verbal nature in that they also conjugate according to tense and polarity. For example, *taka* is the stem of the adjective *taka-i* 'expensive,' but *taka-i* means not just 'expensive' but also 'is expensive' if used as a sentence predicate. Just like verbs, adjectives change form depending on the tense and polarity: *taka-kat-ta* means 'was expensive' and *taka-ku-na-kat-ta* means 'was not expensive.'

Counters

One linguistic item present in Japanese but not in English is the counter. Counters are placed after numerals in order to express the quantity or amount of people and things, and the choice of counters varies depending on the shape, size, and type of the item. For example, *-hiki* is the counter used for small-to-medium-size animals such as cats and dogs; *-nin* is the counter used for people; *-hon* is the counter used for long cylindrical-shaped items such as pencils and wine bottles; and *-satsu* is the counter used for bound items such as books and magazines. To illustrate, *go-nin no hito* means 'the five people'; *go-hiki no inu* means 'the five dogs'; *go-hon no pen* means 'the five pens'; and *go-satsu no zasshi* means 'the five magazines.' English has some unit words for measurement such as *pieces*, *slices*, and *cups*, as in *five pieces of cake, five slices of pizza,* and *five cups of milk,* but the quantity of countable items such as dogs and books does not require any unit words.

Honorifics

The Japanese language has rich and extensive honorific systems that express respect, humility, courteousness, politeness, and refinement. These systems govern speech styles through the choices of suffixes, prefixes, (pro)nouns, verbs, adjectives, and phrases that are determined based on the relationship among the speaker, the listener, and the third party with respect to the social grouping and the social hierarchy. The Japanese honorific systems are most dominantly manifested in verb forms. For example, the following sentences all mean 'Did (you) read (it)?': *Yonda no* (addressed to one's brother); *Yomimashita ka* (addressed to one's colleague); and *O-yomi-ni narimashita ka* (addressed to one's teacher). English does not have such verbal prefixes, suffixes, and auxiliary verbs used for expressing politeness or respect. Although English does have some honorific systems, including titles such as *Mr.* and *Mrs.* and some auxiliary verbs such as *could* and *would*, politeness is mostly expressed by elaborating on a statement through the addition of kind comments or brief explanations.

In the following sections of Part 1, we list alphabetically the parts of speech, essential constructions, and grammatical functions in Japanese, describing each item and giving example sentences that illustrate its usage.

ACCENTS

The Japanese and English accentuation systems are considerably different. Accents are manifested by stress in English, whereas they are manifested by pitch in Japanese. In standard Japanese, there are two pitch values, high and low, which apply to moras. A mora is a syllable-like timing unit that corresponds to a single kana like あ (a) and か (ka) or a kana with a small kana to express palatalized sounds as in きゃ (kya), ジェ (je), or ヴァ(va). Each mora usually contains a vowel, but a single kana ん (n) and a single small character っ (a part of double consonants) also count as moras although they do not include any vowel sound, and a prolonged vowel counts as two moras. Moras show how many beats a word has, and moras are the bearers of pitch values in Japanese. For example, the Japanese word *yūbinkyoku* ゆうびんきょく has six moras, ゆ, う, び, ん, きょ, and く, and each is either high or low in pitch, as shown by H (high pitch) and L (low pitch) below:

ゆうびんきょく
yu u bi n kyo ku
L HHL L L

Pitch can affect word meanings. For example, *hashi* means 'chopsticks' if pronounced with the HL pitch pattern, but means 'bridge' or 'edge' if pronounced with the LH pitch pattern:

はし	はし	はし
ha shi	**ha shi**	**ha shi**
H L	L H	L H
'chopsticks'	'bridge'	'edge'

If we add a particle, for example *ga*, all of the above three words become distinct:

はしが	はしが	はしが
ha shi ga	**ha shi ga**	**ha shi ga**
H L L	L H L	L H H
'chopsticks'	'bridge'	'edge'

Evidently some part of the pitch information, namely the position of the pitch fall, if any, is usually specific to individual lexical items when pronounced separately. For example, *hashi* 'chopsticks' has a pitch fall right after the first mora; *hashi* 'bridge' has a pitch fall right after the second mora; and there is no pitch fall for *hashi* 'edge.' Although the pitch patterns must be conditioned in each morphological context, the ultimate pitch values of all moras in any chunked phrase (phrase flexibly cut off) conform to the following two generalizations in standard Japanese, where chunked phrases mean sound-based units recognized by native speakers to which prosodic properties such as accentuation and phrase boundaries apply.

1. In each chunked phrase, the first mora and the second mora are always different in pitch.

2. There can be only one part (a mora or sequence of moras) that is pronounced with a high pitch in each phrase. Once the pitch is lowered, the pitch does not rise in the same chunked phrase. Accordingly, if you hear a pitch rise, it will be the signal of the beginning of a new chunked phrase, or is the result of sentential intonation such as question intonation. As mentioned above, the pitch patterns are conditioned by morphological contexts. For example, the verb *kaku* (to write) in the dictionary form has a pitch fall after the first mora (*kaku* HL) and no pitch rise, but its *masu* form, *kakimasu*, has a pitch rise after the initial mora and a pitch fall after the third mora (*kakimasu* LHHL). However, the above two generalizations still hold regardless of the morphological complexity of phrases.

Therefore, each chunked phrase in standard Japanese including loanwords takes one of the following three patterns: the High-Low pattern; the Low-High pattern; the Low-High-Low pattern. This is illustrated with some nouns below:

1. High-Low pattern

The initial mora is in high pitch, but the following mora(s) is (are) in low pitch.

X X(. . . X)
H L(. . . L)

Examples:

いのち	バニラ	ギター	テキスト	ポーランド
i no chi	ba ni ra	gi ta a	te ki su to	po o ra n do
H L L	H L L	H L L	H L L L	H L L L L
'life'	'vanilla'	'guitar'	'text'	'Poland'

2. Low-High pattern

The initial mora is in low pitch, but the following mora(s) is (are) in high pitch. After adding some particles such as *ga* and *wa*, some nouns maintain the high pitch until the end of the phrase (a), but others drop the pitch right after the final mora of the word (b), or after the second final mora when the final mora is a special one like '人,' '⊃,' or a prolonged part of a vowel.

a. Words that do not cause a pitch fall
   XX(. . . X)+(ga)
   LH (. . . H)+(H)

   Examples:

はな(が)	えんぴつ(が)	バイオリン(が)	カリフォルニア(が)
ha na (ga)	e n pi tsu (ga)	ba i o ri n (ga)	Ka ri fo ru ni a (ga)
L H (H)	LH H H (H)	L HH H H (H)	L HH HHH (H)
'nose'	'pencil'	'violin'	'California'

b. Words that cause a pitch fall after the word-final mora
   XX(. . . X)+(ga)
   LH (. . . H)+(L)

   Examples:

はな(が)	おとこ(が)	あかるい(が)	じゅうにがつ(が)
ha na (ga)	o to ko (ga)	a ka ru i (ga)	ju u ni ga tsu (ga)
L H (L)	L H H (L)	L H HH (L)	L HH H H (L)
'flower'	'man'	'bright'	'December'

3. Low-High-Low pattern

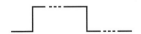

The initial mora is in low pitch, the second mora is in high pitch, and some of the following mora(s) may be in high pitch, but at some point in the sequence, the pitch drops and the rest of the mora(s) remain(s) in low pitch.

   X X(. . . X)X(. . . X)
   L H(. . . H)L(. . . L)

Examples:

こころ	あんない	ストライク	トランペット	アンサンブル
ko ko ro	**a n na i**	**su to ra i ku**	**to ra n pe t to**	**a n sa n bu ru**
L H L	L H H L	L H H L L	L H H H L L	L H H L L L
'heart'	'guiding'	'strike'	'trumpet'	'ensemble'

Note that pitch patterns differ depending on the geographic area in Japan. Also, pitch patterns can change over time. For example, an increasing number of young people are favoring the Low-High pattern, and some words (e.g. gitā 'guitar') are acquiring an additional pitch pattern (the Low-High pattern).

Also note that when creating compound words, the pitch pattern of each word in the compound words may vary widely.

Examples:

こくさい	うこう	いき	でんしゃ
kokusai	**kuu ko o**	**i ki**	**den sha**
L H H H	L H H H	L H	L H H
'international'	'airport'	'bound for'	'train'

↓

こくさいくうこう
kokusai kuu ko o   →   こくさいくうこういき
L H H H H L L L   **kokusai kuu ko o i ki**
'an international airport'   L H H H H H H HH H
                                               'bound for an international airport'

↓

こくさいくうこういきのでんしゃ
kokusai kuu ko o i ki no den sha
L H H H H H H H H H H H H H H
'a train bound for the international airport'

↓

こくさいくうこうのでんしゃ
kokusai kuu ko o no den sha
L H H H H L L L L L H H
'a train at the international airport'

ADJECTIVAL NOUNS

Adjectival nouns describe the properties of people and things just as adjectives do. They do not conjugate like adjectives (→ See Adjectives.) but pattern very similarly to nouns in a variety of contexts. Most adjectival nouns are *na*-type. They are followed by *na* when occurring before a noun that they modify (e.g. *shizuka na resutoran* 'a quiet restaurant'). However, some are *no*-type, requiring *no* instead of *na* in the same context, just like ordinary nouns (e.g. *byōki no hito* 'a sick person'). A large number of adjectival nouns were derived from Sino-Japanese vocabulary, i.e. Japanese vocabulary that was borrowed from Chinese or made of Chinese morphemes, but there are many adjectival nouns that were derived from Western words and onomatopoeias. (→ See Appendix 1 for the list of common adjectival nouns.)

1. Used as noun modifiers

- Followed by *na*

  綺麗な庭　***kirei na*** niwa　　　　　a beautiful garden

  健康な子ども　***kenkō na*** kodomo　　a healthy child

  無茶な話し　***mucha na*** hanashi　　an unreasonable story

  無駄な出費　***muda na*** shuppi　　　wasteful expenses

  デリケートな肌　***derikēto na*** hada　delicate skin

  ハンサムな人　***hansamu na*** hito　　a handsome person

  彼は親切な人ですね。　*Kare wa **shinsetsu na** hito desu ne.*
  He is a kind person, isn't he?

  それは深刻な問題です。　*Sore wa **shinkoku na** mondai desu.*
  It is a serious problem.

- Followed by *no*

  本当の話し　***hontō no*** hanashi　　　a true story

  公の事実　***ōyake no*** jijitsu　　　　a public fact

  ピカピカの靴　***pikapika no*** kutsu　shiny shoes

  パサパサの髪　***pasapasa no*** kami　dry hair

- Followed by *na* or *no*

  平等な立場　***byōdō na*** tachiba　　　equal footing

  平等の権利　***byōdō no*** kenri　　　　equal rights

2. Used as predicates

Adjectival nouns can be used as a sentence predicate, being followed by the linking verb *da/desu*, which takes a different form depending on the tense and whether affirmative or negative: for example, *datta, ja nai, ja nakatta, deshita, ja arimasendeshita,* and *ja nakatta desu.* (→ See Linking verb *da/desu.*)

あの辞書は便利だ。でも，これは便利じゃない。
*Ano jisho wa **benri da**. Demo, kore wa benri ja nai.*
That dictionary is handy. However, this one is not.

鈴木さんは昨日ちょっと静かだった。
*Suzuki san wa kinō chotto **shizuka datta**.*
Mr. Suzuki was a little quiet yesterday.

高田さんはいつも元気です。*Takada san wa itsumo **genki desu**.*
Mr. Takada is always in good spirits.

あの学生はまじめじゃありません。*Ano gakusei wa **majime ja arimasen**.*
That student is not very serious (studious).

メアリーさんは綺麗で，親切な人です
*Mearī san wa **kirei de**, shinsetsu na hito desu.*
Mary is a pretty and kind person.

3. Followed by a predicative phrase

Adjectival nouns may be used with a variety of sentence-final predicative phrases. In such cases, adjectival nouns are followed by a linking verb (*da* or its variants), *na, no,* or nothing depending on whether they are *no*-type or *na*-type and depending on the nature of the predicative phrase.

■ Followed by *da*

この辺りは安全だそうだ。*Kono atari wa **anzen da sō da**.*
They say that this neighborhood is safe.

このアパートはあまり静かじゃないそうです。
*Kono apāto wa amari **shizuka ja nai sō desu**.*
I heard that this apartment is not very quiet.

→ See *sō da* <hearsay>.

■ Followed by *na*

このレストランはおいしいスープで有名なんです。
*Kono resutoran wa oishii sūpu de **yūmei na n desu**.*
This restaurant is famous for delicious soup.

高橋さんはもう95歳ですが，とても健康なようです。
*Takahashi san wa mō 95 sai desu ga, totemo **kenkō na yō desu**.*
Ms. Tanaka is already 95 years old, but she seems to be very healthy.

田中教授はあの論文にとても批判的なようでした。
*Tanaka kyōju wa ano ronbun ni totemo **hihanteki na yō deshita**.*
Professor Tanaka appeared to be very critical of that paper.

日本の地下鉄は便利なはずだ。 *Nihon no chikatetsu wa **benri na hazu da**.*
The subways in Japan are supposed to be convenient.

→ See *no da*, *yō da* <*conjecture*>, and *hazu da*.

- Followed by *no*

  このプログラムは最悪のようだ。 *Kono puroguramu wa **saiaku no yō da**.*
  This program appears to be the worst.

  彼女は今独身のはずです。 *Kanojo wa ima **dokushin no hazu desu**.*
  I'm sure she is single now.

→ See *yō da* <*conjecture*> and *hazu da*.

- Directly followed by a predicative phrase

  この地区は安全そうだ。 *Kono chiku wa **anzen sō da**.*
  This area seems to be safe.

  あの人は病気かもしれない。 *Ano hito wa **byōki kamoshirenai**.*
  That person may be sick.

  伊藤さんの家庭はとても裕福らしいです。
  *Itō san no katei wa totemo **yūfuku rashii desu**.*
  Mr. Ito's family seems to be very wealthy.

  あそこは静かだろう。 *Asoko wa **shizuka darō**.*
  That place is probably quiet.

→ See *sō da* <*conjecture*>, *kamoshirenai*, *rashii* <*conjecture*>, and *darō*.

4. Used as nouns

Some adjectival nouns can function as nouns, and can be placed before a particle, conjoined with a noun, or used as a part of a compound noun.

- Placed before a particle

  私はもっと自由が欲しい。 *Watashi wa motto **jiyū ga** hoshii.*
  I want more freedom.

  あまりの無駄は避けなければならない。
  *Amari no **muda wa** sakenakereba naranai.*
  We have to avoid too much waste.

あまり無茶を言わないでください。 *Amari **mucha o** iwanaide kudasai.*
Please don't talk too much nonsense.

- ■ Conjoined with a noun

  自由と責任は両方必要です。 ***Jiyū** to sekinin wa ryōhō hitsuyō desu.*
  Both freedom and responsibilities are needed.

- ■ Being a part of a compound noun

  自由経済 ***jiyū** keizai* free market economy

  安全対策を怠らないようにしてください。
  ***Anzen** taisaku o okotaranai yōni shite kudasai.*
  Please do not neglect safety measures.

5. Used as adverbs

Adjectival nouns (*na*-type and *no*-type) can be followed by the particle *ni* and function as adverbs, describing the manner of actions.

この写真はきれいに撮れています。
*Kono shashin wa **kirei ni** torete imasu.*
This photograph is taken beautifully.

自由に決めてください。 ***Jiyū ni** kimete kudasai.*
Please make a decision freely.

妻はいつも靴をピカピカに磨いてくれます。
*Tsuma wa itsumo kutsu o **pikapika ni** migaite kuremasu.*
My wife always polishes my shoes till they are shiny.

6. Used as a complement

Na-type and *no*-type adjectival nouns can express the result of some changes conveyed by *suru* and *naru*. (→ See *suru* and *naru*.) In this case, they take the adverbial form followed by *ni*, as discussed in the above section. Note that some of them may also be followed by *to* in this context, when they occur before *naru*.

彼は私たちに親切にしてくれました。
*Kare wa watashi tachi ni **shinsetsu ni** shite kuremashita.*
He treated us kindly.

彼女はとてもきれいになりました。
*Kanojo wa totemo **kirei ni** narimashita.*
She became very beautiful.

あの事件は公に(**or** と)なりました。
*Ano jiken wa **ōyake ni** (**or to**) narimashita.*
That incident became public.

囚人は自由になりました。　*Shūjin wa **jiyū ni** narimashita.*
The prisoner became free.

手をきれいにしておきなさい。　*Te o **kirei ni** shite okinasai.*
Keep your hands clean.

→ See *oku.*

高橋さんの家族はばらばらになってしまった。
*Tahahashi san no kazoku wa **barabara ni** natte shimatta.*
Mr. Takahashi's family got scattered about.

→ See *shimau.*

7. Additional types of adjectival nouns

It is also possible to consider nouns that are followed by *taru* and *to shita*, when modifying a noun, as adjectival nouns, although they are typically used in a formal spoken/written context and may not have all the functions that are available for *na*-type or *no*-type adjectival nouns. (→ See Appendix 1.)

***dōdō taru** shōri* 堂々たる勝利	a splendid victory
***rekizen taru** jijitsu* 歴然たる事実	an obvious fact
***danko taru** ketsui* 断固たる決意	a firm decision
***dōdō to shita** kōshin* 堂々とした行進	a march in grand style
***hirobiro to shita** shinshitsu* 広々とした寝室	a roomy bedroom
***bakuzen to shita** setsumei* 漠然とした説明	a vague explanation

社長は淡々とした口調で話しました。
*Shachō wa **tantan to shita** kuchō de hanashimashita.*
The company president spoke in a cool tone.

彼は歴然たる事実を否定した。　*Kare wa **rekizen taru jijitsu** o hitei shita.*
He denied an evident fact.

Adjectival nouns of this type are followed by *to* rather than *ni* when functioning as adverbs.

社長は淡々と話しました。
*Shachō wa **tantan** to hanashimashita.*
The company president spoke coolly.

ADJECTIVES

Adjectives in Japanese are also called *I*-adjectives because they all end in the syllable *i* when placed before a noun, as a prenominal modifier, as in *takai doresu* 'an expensive dress.' We often need to distinguish them from adjectival nouns, including so-called *Na*-adjectives, based on their syntactic properties. Adjectives describe the property of people and things. They can be used as a prenominal modifier (e.g. *takai doresu*) or as a sentence predicate (e.g. *Kono doresu wa takai* 'This dress is expensive.') just like verbs. Adjectives in Japanese conjugate depending on the tense, polarity (affirmative or negative), or the function they play in the sentence. Their conjugation pattern is very regular, and there is only one irregular case (*ii* 'good,' which conjugates like *yoi* for historical reasons). There are some auxiliaries and suffixes that create new adjective-like words by following other words, and they doubtlessly follow the conjugation and derivation patterns of *I*-adjectives (*tai*, *nai*, and *rashii*). (→ See Appendix 2 for a list of common adjectives.)

1. Dictionary form

The dictionary form of adjectives is the form they take before the noun they modify. The dictionary form of all adjectives ends in the suffix *i*.

Dictionary Form
takai 'expensive'
tanoshii 'pleasant'
warui 'bad'
omoi 'heavy'
ii 'good'

Dictionary forms can end a sentence in an informal context, and can be followed by *desu* (the polite linking verb) in a polite context. (Note that the dictionary form of adjectives cannot be followed by *da*. → See *no da*.)

■ Placed before a noun

私はとても高いカメラを買いました。
*Watashi wa totemo **takai kamera** o kaimashita.*
I bought a very expensive camera.

■ Placed at the end of a sentence (can be followed by *desu*)

日本の魚はおいしい。 *Nihon no sakana wa **oishii**.*
Japanese fish are delicious.

今日は忙しいか。
*Kyō wa **isogaii ka**.* (talking to one's subordinate or insiders)
Are you free today?

この料理は大変おいしいです。 *Kono ryōri wa taihen **oishii** desu.*
This dish is very tasty.

来週の日曜日は忙しいですか。 *Raishū no Nichiyōbi wa **isogashii** desu ka.*
Are you busy next Sunday?

今日はとても暑いですね。 *Kyō wa totemo **atsui** desu ne.*
It's very hot today, isn't it?

■ Placed at the end of a clause

Desu is not allowed at the end of a clause when followed by other items, although some types of clauses allow it (e.g. direct quotation clause, the clause with *kara,* and the clause with *ga*).

この中古車が安いと思います。 *Kono chūkosha ga **yasui** to omoimasu.*
I think this used car is cheap.

彼女にどれがいい(の)か尋ねよう。 *Kanojo ni dore ga **ii** (no) ka tazuneyō.*
I will ask her which is good.

田中さんは「面白いです。」と言いました。
*Tanaka san wa "**Omoshiroi** desu." to iimashita.*
Mr. Tanaka said, "It is interesting."

高いですが，いい物ですから買います。
***Takai** desu ga, ii mono desu kara kaimasu.*
It's expensive, but I'll buy it because it is a good item.

■ Followed by a predicative phrase

天気予報によればあしたは寒いでしょう。
*Tenki yohō ni yoreba ashita wa **samui** deshō.*
According to the weather forecast it will probably be cold tomorrow.

この食べ物は古いかもしれない。
*Kono tabemono wa **furui** kamo shirenai.*
This food may be stale.

2. *Ku-*form

The *ku-*form of adjectives is made by replacing the final *i* of the adjective in the dictionary form with *ku*. The *ku-*form of *ii* 'good' is *yoku*. The *ku-*form can serve as an adverb. Accordingly, it can be used with verbs such as *suru* 'to do' and *naru* 'to become' to express some changes. (→ See *suru* and *naru*.) The *te-*forms and *nai*-forms of adjectives can be easily created by adding *te* and *nai* respectively at the end of an adjective in the *ku*-form. To make a polite negative form, *arimasen* (the polite negative form of *aru*) or *nai desu* can be added at the end of the *ku*-form. (*Nai desu* is less formal than *arimasen*, but commonly used in conversations.)

Dictionary Form	Ku-Form
takai 'expensive'	*takaku*
tanoshii 'pleasant'	*tanoshiku*
warui 'bad'	*waruku*
omoi 'heavy'	*omoku*
ii 'good'	*yoku*

- Used as adverbs

  私たちは今日楽しく午後を過ごしました。
  *Watashi tachi wa kyō **tanoshiku** gogo o sugoshimashita.*
  We spent this afternoon pleasantly.

  彼はいつも忙しく動き回っています。
  *Kare wa itsumo **isogashiku** ugokimawatte imasu.*
  He is always busily moving about.

- Describing a change

  彼女は美しくなりました。 *Kanojo wa **utsukushiku** narimashita.*
  She became beautiful.

  私は髪を長くしました。 *Watashi wa kami o **nagaku** shimashita.*
  I grew my hair.

  私を悲しくさせないでください。 *Watashi o **kanashiku** sasenaide kudasai.*
  Please don't make me sad.

- Used to form polite negative predicates

  私の家は駅からそんなに遠くありません。
  *Watashi no ie wa eki kara sonna ni **tōku** arimasen.*
  My house is not so far from the train station.

  私の家は駅からそんなに遠くないです。
  *Watashi no ie wa eki kara sonna ni **tōku** nai desu.*
  My house is not so far from the train station.

  試合の結果は良くありませんでした。
  *Shiai no kekka wa **yoku** arimasen deshita.*
  The results of the game were not good.

試合の結果は良くなかったです。
*Shiai no kekka wa **yoku** nakatta desu.*
The results of the game were not good.

■ Followed by a particle

写真は大きくはなりましたが，良くはなりませんでした。
*Shashin wa **ōkiku wa** narimashita ga, **yoku wa** narimasen deshita.*
The photo became bigger, but did not become better.

写真は大きくもなりましたし，良くもなりました。
*Shashin wa **ōkiku mo** narimashita shi, **yoku mo** narimashita.*
The photo became bigger, and also became better.

これは高くはないが，あまり良く(も)ない。
*Kore wa **takaku wa** nai ga, amari **yoku mo** nai.*
This is not expensive, but it's not so good.

3. *Nai*-form

The *nai*-form of adjectives is made by adding *nai* at the end of an adjective in the *ku*-form. (→ See *Ku*-form above.) The *nai*-forms conjugate like *i*-adjectives. The *nai*-form is the negative counterpart of adjectives in the dictionary form. It can be placed in positions where adjectives in the dictionary form can be placed, and has a non-past form and the past form.

Dictionary Form	*Ku*-Form	*Nai*-Form (non-past)	*Nai*-Form (past)
takai 'expensive'	*takaku*	*takakunai*	*takakunakatta*
tanoshii 'pleasant'	*tanoshiku*	*tanoshikunai*	*tanoshikunakatta*
warui 'bad'	*waruku*	*warukunai*	*warukunakatta*
omoi 'heavy'	*omoku*	*omokunai*	*omokunakatta*
ii 'good'	*yoku*	*yokunai*	*yokunakatta*

今日はあまり寒くないですね。昨日も寒くなかったですね。
*Kyō wa amari **samuku nai** desu ne. Kinō mo **samuku nakatta** desu ne.*
Today isn't very cold, is it? It wasn't cold yesterday, either, right?

悪くないと思います。 ***Waruku nai** to omoimasu.*
I think it is not bad. (I don't think it is bad.)

あまり難しくない本を買った方がいいです。
*Amari **muzukashiku nai** hon o katta hō ga ii desu.*
It would be better for you not to buy a book that is not very difficult.

彼女の言うことは正しくないでしょう。
*Kanojo no iu koto wa **tadashiku nai** deshō.*
Probably what she says is not right.

4. *Ta*-form

The *ta*-form of adjectives can be created by replacing the final syllable *i* of adjectives in the dictionary form with *katta*. For a negative *ta*-form, replace *i* with *ku nakatta*.

Dictionary Form	Ta-Form (affirmative)	Ta-Form (negative)
takai 'expensive'	*takakatta*	*takakunakatta*
tanoshii 'pleasant'	*tanoshikatta*	*tanoshikunakatta*
warui 'bad'	*warukatta*	*warukunakatta*
omoi 'heavy'	*omokatta*	*omokunakatta*
ii 'good'	*yokatta*	*yokunakatta*

The *ta*-form is actually the plain affirmative past form. The *ta*-form of adjectives also expresses past states or the state that has continued until the time of speech.

今日はとても寒かったですね。 *Kyō wa totemo **samukatta** desu ne.*
It was (*or* has been) cold today, wasn't (*or* hasn't) it?

→ See *ta* for additional example sentences with adjectives in the *ta*-form.

5. *Te*-form

The *te*-form of adjectives is made by adding *te* at the end of an adjective in the *ku*-form. (→ See *Ku*-form under Adjectives.)

Dictionary Form	Ku-Form	Te-Form (affirmative)	Te-Form (negative)
takai 'expensive'	*takaku*	*takakute*	*takakunakute*
tanoshii 'pleasant'	*tanoshiku*	*tanoshikute*	*tanoshikunakute*
warui 'bad'	*waruku*	*warukute*	*warukunakute*
omoi 'heavy'	*omoku*	*omokute*	*omokunakute*
ii 'good'	*yoku*	*yokute*	*yokunakute*

Adjectives in the *te*-form can be used to non-emphatically list properties in the same sentence. Depending on the situation, they can express reasons, causes, conditions, or contrastive properties.

> この問題はむずかしくて私にはできません。
> *Kono mondai wa **muzukashikute** watashi ni wa dekimasen.*
> **This problem is so difficult that I can't solve it.**

→ See *te* for additional examples with adjectives in the *te*-form.

6. *Ba*-form

The *ba*-form of adjectives is made by replacing *i* at the end of an adjective in the dictionary form with *kereba*. The negative counterpart can be created by adding *nakereba* at the end of an adjective in the *ku*-form.

Dictionary Form	Ku-Form	Ba-Form (affirmative)	Ba-Form (negative)
takai 'expensive'	*takaku*	*takakereba*	*takakunakereba*
tanoshii 'pleasant'	*tanoshiku*	*tanoshikereba*	*tanoshikunakereba*
warui 'bad'	*waruku*	*warukereba*	*warukunakereba*
omoi 'heavy'	*omoku*	*omokereba*	*omokunakereba*
ii 'good'	*yoku*	*yokereba*	*yokunakereba*

This form expresses a present, past, or future condition.

> 天気が悪ければ延期しましょう
> *Tenki ga **warukereba** enki shimashō.*
> **If the weather is bad, let's postpone it.**

> あなたの助けがなければできませんでした。
> *Anata no tasuke ga **nakereba** dekimasen deshita.*
> **Without your help, I couldn't have done it.**

> 休みたければこの部屋を使ってください。
> ***Yasumidakereba*** *kono heya o tsukatte kudasai.*
> **If you want to rest, please use this room.**

→ See *ba* for additional examples with adjectives in the *ba*-form.

7. *Tara*-form

This form expresses a present, past, or future condition.

The *tara*-form of adjectives can be created by adding *ra* at the end of the adjectives in the *ta*-form. The negative counterpart is made by adding *nakattara* at the end of the adjectives in the *ku-form*.

Dictionary Form	*Tara*-Form (affirmative)	*Tara*-Form (negative)
takai 'expensive'	*takakattara*	*takakunakattara*
tanoshii 'pleasant'	*tanoshikattara*	*tanoshikunakattara*
warui 'bad'	*warukattara*	*warukunakattara*
omoi 'heavy'	*omokattara*	*omokunakattara*
ii 'good'	*yokattara*	*yokunakattara*

安かったら絶対それを買います。 ***Yasukattara*** *zettai sore o kaimasu.*
If it were cheap, I'm sure I would buy it.

もっと安かったら絶対それを買ったのに。
*Motto **yasukattara** zettai sore o katta noni.*
If it had been much cheaper, I would have bought it.

高くなかったらそれを買うかもしれません。
Takaku nakattara *sore o kau kamo shiremasen.*
If it is not expensive, I may buy it.

→ See *tara* for additional examples with adjectives in the *tara*-form.

8. Root

The root of an adjective is the form you get after dropping *i* at the end of the dictionary form. The root of an adjective can be directly followed by some suffixes, auxiliary verbs, and predicative phrases such as *garu*, *sugiru*, and *sō da*. (→ See *garu*, *sugiru*, and *sō da* <conjecture>.)

みんなうれしがっています。 *Minna **ureshi**gatte imasu.*
It looks like everybody feels happy.

外は寒そうです。 *Soto wa **samu** sō desu.* **It seems cold outside.**

このパソコンは使うには古すぎます。
*Kono pasokon wa tsukau ni wa **furu**sugimasu.*
This personal computer is too old to use.

Adjective roots can be combined with nouns, verbs in the combining forms, or another adjective to form a compound word.

DICT. FORM	ROOT	COMPOUND WORD
甘い (sweet) *amai*	甘 *ama*	甘苦い *ama-nigai* (bitter-sweet)
古い (old) *furui*	古 *furu*	古新聞 *furu-shinbun* (an old newspaper)
早い (fast) *hayai*	早 *haya*	早とちり *haya-tochiri* (jumping to a wrong conclusion)
重い (heavy) *omoi*	重 *omo*	重荷 *omo-ni* (a heavy load)
寒い (cold) *samui*	寒 *samu*	寒気 *samu-ke* (a chill)
高い (high) *takai*	高 *taka*	高望み *taka-nozomi* (aiming too high)
うれしい (happy) *ureshii*	うれし *ureshi*	うれし涙 *ureshi-namida* (tears of joy)
悪い (bad) *warui*	悪 *waru*	悪ふざけ *waru-fuzake* (a mischievous act)
安い (cheap) *yasui*	安 *yasu*	安物 *yasu-mono* (a cheap article)

ADVERBS

Adverbs express the manner of the action expressed by the verb in a sentence. Adverbs are typically placed right after the topic phrase or right before the verb, but can also take some other positions between phrases or at the beginning of a sentence. Adverbs may not be placed at the end of the sentence.

- 私はほとんど肉を食べません。
  *Watashi wa **hotondo** niku o tabemasen.*
- 私は肉をほとんど食べません。
  *Watashi wa niku o **hotondo** tabemasen.*
- ほとんど私は肉を食べません。
  ***Hotondo** watashi wa niku o tabemasen.*

  I eat little meat.

- 毎日私はたくさん漢字を覚えます。
  ***Mainichi** watashi wa **takusan** kanji o oboemasu.*
- 毎日私は漢字をたくさん覚えます。
  ***Mainichi** watashi wa kanji o **takusan** oboemasu.*
- 毎日たくさん私は漢字を覚えます。
  ***Mainichi takusan** watashi wa kanji o oboemasu.*
- 私は毎日たくさん漢字を覚えます。
  *Watashi wa **mainichi takusan** kanji o oboemasu.*
- 私は毎日漢字をたくさん覚えます。
  *Watashi wa **mainichi** kanji o **takusan** oboemasu.*

  I memorize a lot of kanji every day.

Some adverbs can be followed by *no* to modify nouns.

ほとんどの日本人は刺身を食べます。
***Hotondo no Nihonjin** wa sashimi o tabemasu.*
Almost all the Japanese people eat sashimi.

私は毎日たくさんの漢字を覚えます。
*Watashi wa mainichi **takusan no kanji** o oboemasu.*
I memorize a lot of kanji every day.

Adverbs may also be derived from adjectives, adjectival nouns, nouns (+ particles), or verbs.
→ See Appendix 3 for a list of common adverbs.

1. Adjective root + *ku*

hayaku	早く	early, fast, quickly, rapidly
hidoku	ひどく	badly, severely, terribly
kuwashiku	詳しく	in detail
mijikaku	短く	briefly
sugoku	すごく	terribly, awfully
umaku	うまく	well, cleverly, deliciously, smoothly

Note that young people often use *sugoi* (the dictionary form) as an adverb without converting it into an adverb form, but such a use of this adjective is considered slang.

アルバイトをしてすごい疲れた。
*Arubaito o shite **sugoi** tsukareta.*
I worked at a part time job and got terribly tired.

→ See also Adjectives.

2. (Adjectival) nouns

asatte	明後日	day after tomorrow
ashita	明日	tomorrow
gūzen	偶然	by chance, by accident
ima	今	now, at present
kinō	昨日	yesterday
kondo	今度	next time, this time, some other time
kyō	今日	today
ototoi	おととい	the day before yesterday
raigetsu	来月	next month
raishū	来週	next week
saikin	最近	recently
tokubetsu	特別	especially, particularly
totsuzen	突然	suddenly, abruptly, unexpectedly
zenbu	全部	all
zettai	絶対	absolutely, surely

3. Adjectival nouns + *ni*

gutaiteki ni	具体的に	concretely, definitely
hontō ni	本当に	really, truly

jiyū ni	自由に	**freely**
jōzu ni	上手に	**skillfully**
kantan ni	簡単に	**easily**
omo ni	主に	**chiefly, mainly**

→ See also Adjectival nouns.

4. Mimetic words and onomatopoeias

Japanese has a large inventory of words that describe items by sound-symbolically representing their sound, action, movement, appearance, or inner state, and they are categorized into mimetic words and onomatopoeias. Mimetic words describe the manner, action, state, and appearance of people and things. Onomatopoeias describe the sounds associated with the actions and movement of people, animals, and things. Some mimetic words and onomatopoeias can also represent psychological states of people. Mimetic words and onomatopoeias are used as adverbs in a sentence, optionally followed by the particle *to*, or as verbs by being combined with the verb *suru* 'to do.'

男たちががやがや（と）話していた。
*Otoko tachi ga **gayagaya (to)** hanashite ita.*
The guys were talking loudly.

蛇がにょろにょろ（と）近づいてきた。
*Hebi ga **nyoronyoro (to)** chikazuite kita.*
The snake slithered toward me.

彼女はこつこつ（と）働く。　*Kanojo wa **kotsukotsu (to)** hataraku.*
She works diligently.

姉は今日プンプンしています。　*Ane wa kyō **punpun** shite imasu.*
My older sister is in a bad mood (in a fume) today.

5. Additional types of adverbs

There are some groups of phrases that can pattern like adjectival nouns, being followed by *taru* or *to shita*. (→ See Adjectival nouns and Appendix 1.) They can function as adverbs, being followed by *to*.

彼は意見を堂々と述べた。　*Kare wa iken o **dōdō to** nobeta.*
He stated his opinion fearlessly.

彼は淡々とそれを受けた。　*Kare wa **tantan to** sore o uketa.*
He took it coolly.

AUXILIARY VERBS & ADJECTIVES

Some verbs and adjectives also function as auxiliary verbs and auxiliary adjectives, respectively.

1. Auxiliary verbs

Auxiliary verbs follow verbs in the combining form or in the *te*-form, or adjectives in the root form. The resulting form conjugates as a verb.

- Following verbs in the combining form

  食べすぎました。 *Tabesugimashita.* **I overate.**

  もう7時ですから食べ始めましょう。
  *Mō shichiji desu kara **tabe-hajimemashō**.*
  It is already 7 o'clock, so let's start eating.

- Following verbs in the **te**-form

  お金を使ってしまいました。 *Okane o **tsukatte shimaimashita**.*
  I used the money (regrettably).

  母はよく私の洋服を作ってくれます。
  *Haha wa yoku watashi no yōfuku o **tsukutte kuremasu**.*
  My mother often makes clothes for me.

- Following adjectives in the root form

  このかばんは高すぎます。 *Kono kaban wa **takasugimasu**.*
  This bag is too expensive.

2. Auxiliary adjectives

Auxiliary adjectives follow verbs in the combining form or in the *te*-form. The resulting form conjugates as an adjective does.

- Following verbs in the combining form

  すしは食べやすいですが, ハンバーガーは食べやすくありません。
  *Sushi wa tabe**yasui** desu ga, hanbāgā wa **tabeyasuku arimasen**.*
  Sushi is easy to eat, but hamburgers are not easy to eat.

  あの先生は話しにくいです。 *Ano sensei wa **hanashinikui** desu.*
  That teacher is hard to talk with.

■ Following verbs in the **te**-form

私の車を買ってほしいのですが。

*Watashi no kuruma o **katte hoshii** no desu ga.*

I want you to buy my car, but . . .

CLAUSES

Clauses are just like sentences, having a subject and a predicate as well as tense-specification, and can be a statement or a question. However, unlike sentences, clauses are not used as a main sentence but as a part of one, by modifying or completing the meaning of a variety of parts in the main sentence. They can be an adjectival clause, an adverbial clause, a quotation clause, or a nominalized clause.

I. ADJECTIVAL CLAUSES

Just as adjectives can modify a noun, clauses can modify a noun. In English such clauses are placed after the noun they modify, and often are introduced by a relative pronoun such as *which, when, where, who, whom,* and *that*. For example, the clause in brackets in each of the following two sentences modifies the underlined noun:

> <u>The student</u> *[who(m) Mr. Smith saw ___ yesterday] was tall.*
> *Tom did not receive <u>the notice</u> [that students can use the university's printer for free].*

As you can see, the adjectival clause in the first sentence has a gap, which is indicated by the underline: there should be a noun after the verb *saw*, but it is missing, and the gap in fact corresponds to the noun being modified (*the student*). Such adjectival clauses with a gap are called relative clauses. Their function is to qualify nouns. By contrast, such a gap does not exist in the adjectival clause in the second sentence above, but the information expressed in the adjectival clause is absolutely needed for completing the meaning of the noun (*the notice*). Without it, we will not know what notice is being referred to. Such gapless adjectival clauses needed for completing the meaning of a noun are called noun complement clauses.

Unlike in English, adjectival clauses in Japanese, regardless of whether they are relative clauses or noun complement clauses, are placed before the noun that they modify rather than after them. Furthermore, no relative pronouns are needed in Japanese adjectival clauses, as you can see in the following two sentences, which are equivalent to the above two English sentences:

スミスさんが昨日見た学生は背が高かった。
[Sumisu san ga kinō mita] <u>gakusei</u> wa se ga takakatta.

トムは大学の学生はプリンターがただで使えるというお知らせを受
け取らなかった。
Tomu wa [daigaku no gakusei wa purintā ga tada de tsukaeru to iu] <u>*o-shirase*</u>
o uketoranakatta.

Additional characteristics of these adjectival clauses are described below.

1. Relative clauses

Relative clauses end in verbs and adjectives in the plain form, nouns followed
by *no,* or adjectival nouns followed by *na* or *no*. Note that the particle *wa* is not
allowed within a relative clause unless needed for contrasting some item. The
subject marker *ga* can optionally be replaced by *no* in a relative clause. Furthermore, particles that are expected to be present for the modified noun are often
missing in Japanese relative clauses. In the following examples, relative clauses
are in brackets and the modified noun is underlined.

- Ending in adjectival nouns followed by *na*

  母が好きな食べ物はてんぷらです。私の好きな食べ物はラーメンです。
  [Haha ga suki na] <u>*tabemono*</u> *wa tenpura desu. [Watashi no suki na]* <u>*tabe-*</u>
  <u>*mono*</u> *wa rāmen desu.*
  **The food that my mother likes is tempura. The food that I like is ramen
  noodles.**

- Ending in nouns followed by *no*

  両親が中国人の学生はクラスの25％をしめている。
  [Ryōshin ga Chūgokujin no] <u>*gakusei*</u> *wa kurasu no ni jū go pāsento o shime-*
  teiru.
  **The students whose parents are Chinese constitute 25 percent of the stu-
  dents in the class.**

- Ending in (adjectival) nouns followed by *datta, ja nai*, or *ja nakatta*

  学生が必要だった教材は漢字の辞書だった。
  [Gakusei ga hitsuyō datta] <u>*kyōzai*</u> *wa kanji no jisho datta.*
  The teaching material that the students needed was a kanji dictionary.

- Ending in verbs and adjectives in the dictionary form

  お金がほしい人はよく株に投資します。
  [Okane ga hoshii] <u>*hito*</u> *wa yoku kabu ni tōshi shimasu.*
  People who want (more) money often invest in stocks.

  あなたが行くところに私も行きたいです。
  [Anata ga iku] <u>*tokoro*</u> *ni watashi mo ikitai desu.*
  I also want to go to the place you go to.

奥さんが先生をしている人は太郎さんです。
[Okusan ga sensei o shite iru] <u>hito</u> *wa Tarō san desu.*
The person whose wife is a teacher is Taro.

私が買いたい車は四駆(or 4WD)です。
[Watashi ga kai-tai] <u>kuruma</u> *wa yon ku* (or *yon daburu dī*) *desu.*
The car that I want to buy is a four-wheel drive.

私が仕事を辞める理由は秘密です。
[Watashi ga shigoto o yameru] <u>riyū</u> *wa himitsu desu.*
The reason I will quit my job is a secret.

太郎さんが愛する女の人は洋子さんです。
[Tarō san ga aisuru] <u>onna no hito</u> *wa Yōko san desu.*
The woman (whom) Taro loves is Yoko.

あしたここに来る人は太郎さんです。
[Ashita koko ni kuru] <u>hito</u> *wa Tarō san desu.*
The person who will come here tomorrow is Taro.

向こうにいる女の子はだれですか。
[Mukō ni iru] <u>onna no ko</u> *wa dare desu ka.*
Who is the girl that is over there?

私が泊まる部屋は三階です。　*[Watashi ga tomaru]* <u>heya</u> *wa san kai desu.*
The room (where) I'm staying is on the third floor.

これは私が漢字を覚える方法です。
[Kore wa watashi ga kanji o oboeru] <u>hōhō</u> *desu.*
This is the way I learn kanji.

飛行機が着く時間を教えて下さい。
[Hikōki ga tsuku] <u>jikan</u> *o oshiete kudasai.*
Tell me the time the airplane will arrive.

彼がいっしょに行く人は太郎さんです。
[Kare ga isshoni iku] <u>hito</u> *wa Tarō san desu.*
The person with whom he will go is Taro.

私が今要るものはパソコンです。
[Watashi ga ima iru] <u>mono</u> *wa pasokon desu.*
What I need now is a personal computer.

彼が言うことはいつも難しいです。
[Kare ga iu] <u>koto</u> *wa itsumo muzukashii desu.*
What he says is always difficult.

駅に行く道を教えてくれませんか。
[Eki ni iku] <u>michi</u> *o oshiete kuremasen ka.*
Won't you tell me the way to the train station?

('The way to the train station' is 'the way that leads to the train station' in Japanese.)

- Ending in verbs and adjectives in the *nai*-form

ムスリム が/の 食べない食べ物は豚肉です。
[Musurimu ga/no tabenai] <u>tabemono</u> wa butaniku desu.
The food Muslims do not eat is pork.

私は読まない本がたくさんあります。
Watashi wa [yomanai] <u>hon</u> ga takusan arimasu.
I have many books that I don't read.

私は子供が読まない本をほかの子供にあげます。
Watashi wa [kodomo ga yomanai] <u>hon</u> o hoka no kodomo ni agemasu.
I'll give other children the books that my child doesn't read.

だれも行かない所に行きたいです。 *[Dare mo ikanai]* <u>tokoro</u> ni ikitai desu.
I want to visit a place nobody goes to.

太郎さんが合わない人はボスです。
[Tarō san ga awanai] <u>hito</u> wa bosu desu.
The person (whom) Taro is not compatible with is his boss.

お酒を飲まない人は太郎さんです。
[Osake o nomanai] <u>hito</u> wa Tarō san desu.
The person who does not drink sake is Taro.

彼が来ない理由はよく分かりません。
[Kare ga konai] <u>riyū</u> wa yoku wakarimasen.
The reason he does not come is unknown.

彼がぜんぜん話さない人は太郎さんです。
[Kare ga zenzen hanasanai] <u>hito</u> wa Tarō san desu.
The person to whom he does not talk at all is Taro.

旦那さんが仕事をしない人は洋子さんです。
[Danna san ga shigoto o shinai] <u>hito</u> wa Yōko san desu.
The person whose husband does not work is Yoko.

失敗しないいい方法がありますか。 *[Shippai shinai ii]* <u>hōhō</u> ga arimasu ka.
Is there any good way not to fail?

あなたが要らないものをください。 *[Anata ga iranai]* <u>mono</u> o kudasai.
Give me what you do not need.

彼がしないことを代わりにします。
[Kare ga shinai] <u>koto</u> o kawari ni shimasu.
I will do instead of him what he does not do.

- Ending in verbs and adjectives in the *ta*-form

私の買った車はハイブリッドカーです。
[Watashi no katta] <u>kuruma</u> wa haiburiddo kā desu.
The car I bought is a hybrid car.

私はあなたが昨日買った本を読みたいです。

Watashi wa [anata ga kinō katta] <u>hon</u> *o yomitai desu.* (The subject of *katta* is *anata*.)

I want to read the book that you bought yesterday.

私は昨日買った本をもう読みました。

Watashi wa [kinō katta] <u>hon</u> *o mō yomimashita.* (The subject of *katta* is omitted.)

I've already read the book that I bought yesterday.

あなたが行った所に私も行きたいです。

[Anata ga itta] <u>tokoro</u> *ni watashi mo ikitai desu.*

I also want to go to the place you went to.

太郎さんが愛した女の人は洋子さんでした。

[Tarō san ga aishita] <u>onna no hito</u> *wa Yōko san deshita.*

The woman (whom) Taro loved was Yoko.

おとといここに来た人は太郎さんでした。

[Ototoi koko ni kita] <u>hito</u> *wa Tarō san deshita.*

The person who came here the day before yesterday was Taro.

さっきここにいた女の子はだれですか。

[Sakki koko ni ita] <u>onna no ko</u> *wa dare desu ka.*

Who is the girl that was here a short while ago?

私が予約したホテルはまあまあ安いホテルです。

[Watashi ga yoyaku shita] <u>hoteru</u> *wa māmā yasui hoteru desu.*

The hotel I booked is a relatively cheap one.

彼女が離婚した理由は旦那さんのDVです。

[Kanojo ga rikon shita] <u>riyū</u> *wa danna san no dībui desu.*

The reason she divorced is her husband's domestic violence.

これが私が漢字を覚えた方法です。

Kore ga [watashi ga kanji o oboeta] <u>hōhō</u> *desu.*

This is the way I learned kanji.

あなたと初めて会った日を覚えています。

[Anata to hajimete atta] <u>hi</u> *o oboete imasu.*

I remember the day when I met you for the first time.

奥さんが最近亡くなった人は太郎さんです。

[Okusan ga saikin nakunatta] <u>hito</u> *wa Tarō san desu.*

The person whose wife recently died is Taro.

太郎さんがいっしょに旅行に行った人は花子さんです。

[Tarō san ga isshoni ryokō ni itta] <u>hito</u> *wa Hanako san desu.*

The person with whom Taro went for a trip is Hanako.

私が最近買ったものは電子ブックリーダーです。
[Watashi ga saikin katta] <u>mono</u> *wa denshi bukku rīdā desu.*
What I bought recently is an electronic book reader.

彼が話したことはためになりました。
[Kare ga hanashita] <u>koto</u> *wa tame ni narimashita.*
What he said was useful.

2. Noun complement clauses

The predicates in noun complement clauses are in the plain form, but they may be followed by *to to iu*, which is the combination of the particle *to* (quotation marker) and the verb *iu* 'to say.' (→ See *to, to iu*.) Unlike in relative clauses, the topic particle is allowed in noun complement clauses. In the following example sentences, noun complement clauses are in brackets and the noun that they complement are underlined.

- Ending in predicates in the plain form

  すみません，三時に友達と会う約束があるんですが。
  Sumimsen, sanji ni [tomodachi to au] <u>yakusoku</u> *ga aru n desu ga.*
  Sorry, I have an appointment to meet my friend at three.

  彼が成功する望みはない。　*[Kare ga seikō suru]* <u>nozomi</u> *wa nai.*
  There is no hope that he will succeed.

  彼は諦める様子がない。　*Kare wa [akirameru]* <u>yōsu</u> *ga nai.*
  He shows no sign of giving up.

  彼はそのことを知らない様子です。
  Kare wa [sono koto o shiranai] <u>yōsu</u> *desu.*
  It looks like he does not know it.

  だれにも言わない約束ですよ。　*[Dare ni mo iwanai]* <u>yakusoku</u> *desu yo.*
  That's a promise not to tell it to anybody, all right?

  そこには生物が存在しない可能性が高い。
  [Soko ni wa seibutsu ga sonzai shinai] <u>kanōsei</u> *ga takai.*
  The possibility that living things do not exist there is strong.

  彼は諦めた様子がなかった。　*Kare wa [akirameta]* <u>yōsu</u> *ga nakatta.*
  He showed no sign of having given up.

  デモで人が一人殺された事実は消えない。
  [Demo de hito ga hitori korosareta] <u>jijitsu</u> *wa kienai.*
  The fact that a person was killed in the demonstration does not vanish.

- Ending in *to iu*

  東京に着いたという知らせを受けた。　*[Tokyō ni tsuita **to iu**]* <u>shirase</u> *o uketa.*
  (I) received the notice that says (he) arrived there.

彼のポジションはどうなる（の）かという疑問をもった。
*[Kare no pojishon wa dō naru (no) ka **to iu**] <u>gimon</u> o motta.*
I raised the question of what would happen to his position.

II. ADVERBIAL CLAUSES

Adverbial clauses are created by conjoining a clause and some conjunctional particle or a clause-end phrase, which may include nouns, and they are optionally added to a sentence to provide additional information such as time, reasons, causes, purposes, manners, contrast, conflict, etc. Some adverbial clauses (e.g. those formed by conjunctional particles such as *node, ga,* and *kara*) optionally or conditionally allow *desu/masu* style, but others do not. (→ See *node, ga,* and *kara* for more details.)

- Time

  歯をみがくときに，顔も洗います。
  Ha o migaku toki ni, *kao mo araimasu.*
  When I brush my teeth, I also wash my face.

  → See also *toki, mae, ato,* and *aida.*

- Reason

  彼が来るのでここで待っています。
  ***Kare ga kuru node** koko de matte **imasu**.*
  I am waiting here because he is coming.

  私がしますから，どうぞ休んで下さい。
  ***Watashi ga shimasu kara**, dōzo yasunde **kudasai**.*
  I will do it for you, so please take a rest.

  太郎さんは来ませんから，もう行きましょう。
  ***Tarō san wa kimasen kara**, mō ikimashō.*
  Let's go now because Taro will not come.

  雨が降りますから，傘を貸しましょう。
  ***Ame ga furimasu kara** kasa o kashimashō.*
  I will lend you an umbrella because it will rain.

  私はもう一つ買いましたから，どうぞこれを使ってください。
  ***Watashi wa mō hitotsu kaimashita kara**, dōzo kore o tsukatte **kudasai**.*
  I bought another one, so please use this (= I'll give you this).

  兄は背が高いからバスケットボールを始めた。
  ***Ani wa se ga takai kara** basukettobōru o hajimeta.*
  My big brother started basketball because he is tall.

  → See also *node* and *kara.*

■ Cause

彼が帰ったので，ここは私一人です。
Kare ga kaetta node, koko wa watashi hitori desu.
Because he went home, I am alone here.

彼女が来ないのでつまらないです。
Kanojo ga konai node tsumaranai desu.
I am bored because she does not come.

面倒ですからしません。 *Mendō desu kara shimasen.*
It's tedious, so I won't do it.

→ See also *node* and *kara*.

■ Purpose

電車に間に合うように早く行きましょう。
Densha ni maniau yō ni hayaku ikimashō.
Let's go early so that we can catch the train.

電車に遅れないように早く行きましょう。
Densha ni okurenai yō ni hayaku ikimashō.
Let's go early so that we may not miss the train.

→ See also *yō da* <*resemblance*>.

■ Manner

彼 が/のやったようにしてみてください。
Kare ga/no yatta yō ni shite mite kudasai.
Please try doing it as he did.

こぼさないように運んでください。 *Kobosanai yō ni hakonde kudasai.*
Please carry them without spilling.

→ See also *yō da* <*resemblance*>.

■ Contrast

私はそこへ行きましたが，彼は来ませんでした。
Watashi wa soko e ikimashita ga, kare wa kimasen deshita.
I went there, but he didn't.

この会社はエンジンを作るが，車を作らない。
Kono kaisha wa enjin o tsukuru ga, kuruma o tsukuranai.
This company manufactures engines but does not manufacture cars.

この会社はハイブリッドカーを作らないが，電気自動車を作る。
Kono kaisha wa haiburiddo kā o tsukuranai ga, denki jidōsha o tsukuru.
This company does not manufacture hybrid cars but manufactures electric cars.

この会社はかつてバイクだけを作ったが，今は車も作っている。
Kono kaisha wa katsute baiku dake o tsukutta ga ima wa kuruma mo
tsukutte iru.
This company once manufactured only motorbikes but now also manufactures cars.

→ See also *ga*.

■ Concession

父が何を言っても，兄は全然聞かない。
Chichi ga nani o itte mo, ani wa zenzen kikanai
No matter what my father says (to him), my brother does not listen.

だれが何と言おうが気にしない。 *Dare ga nan to iō ga ki ni shinai.*
Whoever may say whatever, I don't care.

→ See also *temo/demo* and *ga*.

■ Transition

私は外で食べますが，あなたもいっしょに行きませんか。
Watashi wa soto de tabemasu ga anata mo isshoni ikimasen ka.
I will eat out, but won't you come with me?

私は行きますが，あなたはどうしますか。
Watashi wa ikimasu ga anata wa dō shimasu ka.
I will go, but what will you do?

私は行きませんが，あなたはどうしますか。
Watashi wa ikimasen ga anata wa dō shimasu ka.
I will not go, but what will you do?

→ See also *ga*.

III. QUOTATION CLAUSES

Certain verbs such as 'to think,' 'to know,' 'to say,' and 'to ask' require a statement or a question to complete their meanings. Such statements and questions can be called quotation clauses because they can be quoted in speaking, hearing, reading, writing, or even in thinking. Quotation clauses can express either a declarative quotation or an interrogative quotation. Declarative quotation clauses are marked by the particle *to,* and interrogative quotation clauses are marked by *ka*. The predicates in a quotation clause must be in the plain form, and *masu/desu* forms are not allowed unless in a direct quotation. The topic particle *wa* can be used in quotation clauses.

1. Declarative quotation clauses

Declarative quotation clauses are followed by the particle *to*. Direct quotations can be marked by a pair of quotation markers—「 and 」—and followed by *to*. The declarative quotation clauses are in angle brackets in the following example sentences.

私は彼女は彼と結婚すると思います。
Watashi wa "kanojo wa kare to kekkon suru to" omoimasu.
I think that she will marry him.

あそこはたぶん静かだと思います。
"Asoko wa tabun shizuka da to" omoimasu.
I think it is probably quiet over there.

医者は「大丈夫ですよ。」と言いました。
Isha wa "'Daijōbu desu yo.' to" iimashita.
My doctor said, "You will be okay."

彼女はそれを知らないと思います。
"Kanojo wa sore o shiranai to" omoimasu.
I think she doesn't know that. (I don't think she knows that.)

2. Interrogative quotation clauses

Interrogative quotation clauses end in either *ka* or *ka dōka*. *Ka dōka* means 'whether or not' and is allowed only for *yes-no* questions. (→ See Yes-no questions under Questions.) In interrogative quotations, *ka (dō ka)* follows a predicate in plain form, a clause followed by *no*, or (adjectival) nouns. The interrogative quotation clauses are in brackets in the following example sentences.

■ Ending in (adjectival) nouns + ***ka (dō ka)***

薬の名前は何か聞いてください。
*[Kusuri no namae wa nani **ka**] kiite kudasai.*
Please ask what is the name of the medication.

あの学生はまじめか（どうか）知っていますか。
*[Ano gakusei wa majime **ka (dō ka)**] shitte imasu ka.*
Do you know whether (or not) that student is serious?

これは抗生物質か（どうか）聞いてください。
*[Kore wa kōseibusshitsu **ka (dō ka)**] kiite kudasai.*
Please ask whether (or not) it is an antibiotic.

■ Ending in predicates + ***ka (dō ka)***

石田さんは来るか（どうか）知っていますか。
*[Ishida san wa kuru **ka (dō ka)**] shitte imasu ka.*
Do you know whether Mr. Ishida is coming?

あの人は誰だか当ててみてください。
*[Ano hito wa dare da **ka**] atete mite kudasai.*
Please guess who that man is.

山田さんは何を専攻にするか決めましたか。
*Yamada san wa [nani o senkō ni suru **ka**] kimemashita ka?*
Ms. Yamada, have you decided what you will major in?

あのレストランはケータリングができるか（どうか）調べてください。
*[Ano resutoran wa kētaringu ga dekiru **ka (dō ka)**] shirabete kudasai.*
Please check whether (or not) that restaurant can cater.

■ Ending in *no ka (dō ka)*

林さんの誕生日はいつなのか教えてください。
*[Hayashi san no tanjōbi wa itsu na **no ka**] oshiete kudasai.*
Please let me know when Mr. Hayashi's birthday is.

あなたが元気なのか（どうか）いつも考えていました。
*[Anata ga genki na **no ka (dō ka)**] itsumo kangaete imashita.*
I was always wondering whether (or not) you are well.

行くのかどうか早く決めなさい。 *[Iku **no ka dō ka**] hayaku kimenasai.*
Quickly decide whether you will go or not.

IV. NOMINALIZED CLAUSES

Clauses can be nominalized by being followed by the unsubstantial noun *koto* or the particle *no* and placed in a position where nouns are usually placed in a sentence. The predicate in nominalized clauses is in the plain form. If a nominalized clause is placed before *da/desu*, only *koto* should be used, and *no* should not be used because the sequence of *no da* or *no desu* might be interpreted as a predicative phrase. (→ See *no da*.) In the following examples, nominalized clauses are in brackets.

漢字を覚える こと/の はとても難しいです。
*[Kanji o oboeru **koto/no**] wa totemo muzukashii desu.*
Learning kanji is very difficult.

何をする こと/の が好きですか。
*[Nani o suru **koto/no**] ga suki desu ka.*
What do you like to do?

食べる こと/の と寝る こと/の が好きです。
*[Taberu **koto/no**] to [neru **koto/no**] ga suki desu.*
I like eating and sleeping.

勉強しない こと/の はいけないことです。
*[Benkyō shinai **koto/no**] wa ikenai koto desu.*
Not studying is a bad thing.

彼が来ない こと/の を知りませんでした。
*[Kare ga konai **koto/no**] o shirimasen deshita.*
I did not know that he will not come.

彼が参加した こと/の は心強いです。
*[Kare ga sanka shita **koto/no**] wa kokorozuyoi desu.*
It is encouraging that he has joined.

勝手にあなたがした こと/の が問題です。
*[Katte ni anata ga shita **koto/no**] ga mondai desu.*
The problem is that you did it at your own discretion.

彼がイギリスに行った こと/の を知っていますか。
*[Kare ga Igirisu ni itta **koto/no**] o shitte imasu ka.*
Do you know that he has gone to England?

私の趣味はインターネットをすることです。
*Watashi no shumi wa [Intānetto o suru **koto**] desu.*
My hobby is surfing the Internet.

私の短所はコンピューターができないことです。
*Watashi no tansho wa [konpyūtā ga dekinai **koto**] desu.*
My weak point is that I can't operate a computer.

問題は彼が会を脱退したことです。
*Mondai wa [kare ga kai o dattai shita **koto**] desu.*
The problem is that he left the club.

COMPARISONS

It is relatively easy to form comparative and superlative sentences in Japanese because the adjectives, adjectival nouns, and adverbs do not change their forms. What is needed is to add appropriate adverbial phrases or adverbs (e.g. *Lisa yori* 'than Lisa' and *ichiban* 'the most') so that the sentences can be understood as comparisons or superlatives.

1. Comparatives

To make the simplest comparative sentence, just add a phrase with *yori* 'than.' (→ See *yori*.) When asking a question comparing two items, list two items using the particle *to*, and use the interrogative word *dochira*, *dochira no hō*, or *dotchi* 'which one' to form a question. (→ See *dochira* and *hō*.) A typical answer includes *hō*, which clarifies the fact that you are answering the question that compares two items.

> 高橋さんは山田さんよりやさしいです。
> *Takahashi san wa Yamada san **yori** yasashii desu.*
> **Mr. Takahashi is kinder than Mr. Yamada.**

> りんごとバナナとどちらの方が好きですか。
> *Ringo to banana to **dochira no hō** ga suki desu ka.*
> **Which one do you like better, apples and bananas?**

> バナナの方が好きです。 *Banana no **hō** ga suki desu.*
> **I like bananas better.**

> 田中君と山田君とどちらの方がよく勉強しますか。
> *Tanaka kun to Yamada kun to **dochira no hō** ga yoku benkyō shimasu ka.*
> **Between Mr. Tanaka and Mr. Yamada, which one studies harder?**

> この方があれより私にはいいです。
> *Kono **hō ga** aore **yori** watashi ni wa ii desu.*
> **This is better than that for me.**

> あのゲーム機の方が新しいタイプです。
> *Ano gēmuki no **hō** ga atarashii taipu desu.*
> **That game machine is a newer type.**

2. Superlatives

The superlative is made by adding *mottomo* or its informal equivalent, *ichiban*, before the predicate. (→ See *mottomo* and *ichiban*.) *De*, *no uchi de*, or *no naka de* can be used to specify the group or the list based on which the comparison is made. (→ See *uchi de*.) Interrogative words such as *doko* and *dare* can always be used. However, if the items are not people or locations, *dore* is required when the items are listed, but *nani* is used when the group is specified.

日本でもっとも高い山は富士山です。
*Nihon de **mottomo** takai yama wa Fuji san desu.*
The highest mountain in Japan is Mt. Fuji.

太郎さんが三人のうちでいちばんイケメンです。
*Tarō san ga san nin no uchi de **ichiban** ikemen desu.*
Taro is the cutest of the three.

このアパートの中でどれがいちばんいいと思いますか。
*Kono apāto no naka de dore ga **ichiban** ii to omoimasu ka.*
Which do you think is the best of these apartments?

クラスでだれが一番背が高いですか。
*Kurasu de dare ga **ichiban** se ga takai desu ka.*
Who is the tallest in the class?

食べ物では何が一番好きですか。
*Tabemono de wa nani ga **ichiban** suki desu ka.*
Among foods, what do you like the best?

バナナとりんごとオレンジでは，どれが一番好きですか。
*Banana to ringo to orenji de wa, dore ga **ichiban** suki desu ka.*
Among bananas, apples, and oranges, which one do you like the best?

3. Equivalent degree comparison

To onaji kurai/gurai, which literally means 'to the extent of similarity,' is used in a sentence with an affirmative predicate. To negate such sentences, *hodo...nai* is used. (→ See *kurai* and *hodo*.)

カタカナはひらがなと同じくらい覚えるのがむずかしい。
*Katakana wa hiragana **to onaji kurai** oboeru no ga muzukashii.*
Katakana are as difficult as hiragana to learn.

私は彼ほど賢くありません。
*Watashi wa kare **hodo** kashikoku arimasen.*
I am not as clever as he.

私は兄ほどよく勉強しません。
*Watashi wa ani **hodo** yoku benkyō shimasen.*
I do not study as hard as my big brother.

CONDITIONALS

We can express statements with conditions by creating a conditional clause that ends in *to, tara, ba,* or *nara.*

1. *To*

To can follow verbs, adjectives, and the linking verb in the dictionary form, in the *nai*-form, or in the polite non-past form (*-masu, -masen,* and *desu*) and creates a conditional clause to express some situation where one event is always followed by another event (generic condition). In this case, the main clause must express something that always happens, and may not express the speaker's volitional action, requests, suggestions, permissions, commands, or desires. (→ See *to* for additional examples.)

> 3に5をたすと8になります。
> *San ni go o tasu to hachi ni narimasu.*
> **If we add 3 and 5, we get 8.**

> 眠いと本が読めません。
> *Nemui to hon ga yomemasen.*
> **If I'm sleepy, I cannot read a book.**

> スミスさんが来ると田中さんはいつもいなくなります。
> *Sumisu san ga kuru to Tanaka san wa itsumo inaku narimasu.*
> **When Mr. Smith comes, Mr. Tanaka always disappears.**

2. *Tara*

The *tara*-form of verbs, adjectives, and the linking verb can be created just by adding *ra* after their *ta*-form. (→ See *Tara*-form under Verbs.) The conditional clause with *tara* is similar to the one with *to* discussed above, in that the event/state expressed in the conditional clause must precede the event/state expressed in the main clause. However, unlike the case of *to*, conditional clauses with *tara* allow their main clause to express not only automatic consequences but also the speaker's intentions, desires, requests, suggestions, invitations, permissions, commands, or conjectures. Accordingly, *tara*-conditionals are more versatile than *to*-clauses.

> スミスさんが来たら田中さんはいつもいなくなります。
> *Sumisu san ga kitara Tanaka san wa itsumo inaku narimasu.*
> **When Mr. Smith comes, Mr. Tanaka always disappears.**

スミスさんが来たら帰りましょう。
Sumisu san ga kitara kaerimashō.
If/When Mr. Smith comes, let's leave.

無事空港に着いたら電話を下さい。
Buji kūkō ni tsuitara denwa o kudasai.
When you have safely arrived at the airport, call me.

家に 帰ったらメールをく下さい。
Ie ni kaettara mēru o kudasai.
When you have arrived home, send me an e-mail.

勝手にこれを見たらいけません。
*Katteni kore o **mitara** ikemasen.*
If you see this without permission, it's no good. (You must not see this without permission.)

京都に行ったらどこを見ようか。
Kyōto ni ittara doko o miyō ka.
When we visit Kyoto, what spot shall we see?

家に帰ったら野球の試合を見たいです。
Ie ni kaettara yakyū no shiai o mitai desu.
When (After) I go home, I want to see the baseball game.

3. *Ba*

The *ba*-forms of verbs and adjectives are created by adding *(r)eba* and *kereba* to their respective roots. (→ See *Ba*-form under Verbs and under Adjectives.) The *ba*-form of the linking verb *da* is *nara ba*. (→ See Linking verb *da/desu*.) *Ba*-conditionals allow their main clause to be a command, a request, or a suggestion, just like *tara*-conditionals, but *ba*-conditionals have some restrictions that *tara*-conditionals do not have. When the main clause expresses a command, a request, or a suggestion, the predicate in the *ba*-conditional clause must express a state rather than an action, as you can see in the contrast between the following two sentences.

つまらなければ帰りましょう。
Tsumaranakereba kaerimashō.
If it is boring, let's leave.

＊スミスさんが来れば帰りましょう。(Ungrammatical)
Sumisu san ga kureba kaerimashō.
(Intended reading: If Mr. Smith comes, let's leave.)

4. *Nara*

Nara can directly follow (adjectival) nouns (with particles), but it also follows a clause followed by *no* or *n*. (→ See *nara* for more details.) The conditional clause with *nara* defines the basis of the statement, meaning *if . . .* or *if you are talking about . . .* . Unlike the conditionals with *to*, *tara*, and *ba*, which require the event/state in the main clause to follow the event/state in the conditional clause, the *nara*-clause does not restrict the temporal order between the two events/states. For example, the action expressed in the main clause can follow or precede the action expressed in the *nara*-clause, and the predicates in the *nara*-clause can be in the past tense or in the non-past tense. For this reason, *nara*-clauses cannot be used for expressing temporal condition, where a certain time sequence between two actions is the main issue. The *nara*-clause is most convenient when you evaluate facts and make suggestions, plans, and speculations based on some assumptions or existing knowledge.

買い物なら渋谷がいいでしょう。
*Kaimono **nara** Shibuya ga ii deshō.*
If you are interested in shopping, Shibuya would be a good place.

あなたが行かないなら彼はキャンセルするでしょう。
*Anata ga ikanai **nara** kare wa kyanseru suru deshō.*
If you're not going, I guess he will cancel it.

あなたが行くなら私も行きたいです。
*Anata ga iku **nara** watashi mo ikitai desu.*
If you're going, I want to go, too.

東京に行くなら割引切符がありますよ。
*Tōkyō ni iku **nara** waribiki kippu ga arimasu yo.*
If you're going to Tokyo, I recommend a good discount ticket.

東京に行く(の)なら新幹線がいいですよ。
*Tokyo ni iku (no) **nara** Shinkansen ga ii desu yo.*
If you're going to Tokyo, you should take the Shinkansen.

彼女がそこへ行ったなら彼も行ったでしょう。
*Kanojo ga soko e itta **nara**, kare mo itta deshō.*
If she had gone there, he would have gone there, too.
(If it is true that she went there, I guess he went there, too.)

あなたがそこへ行ったなら，私も行ったのに。
*Anata ga soko e itta **nara**, watashi mo itta noni.*
If you had gone there, I would have gone, too, but . . .

CONJOINING

Words, phrases, clauses, and sentences are conjoined by particles, specific conjunctional forms, phrases, and conjunctional words.

1. Conjunctional particles for nouns and nominalized verbs

Words and phrases can be conjoined or listed by conjunctional particles such as *to*, *ya*, *mo*, and *ka*. (→ See *ka*, *mo*, *to*, and *ya*.)

私はテニスとスキーとスケートが得意です。
*Watashi wa tenisu **to** sukī **to** sukēto ga tokui desu.*
I am good at tennis, skiing, and skating.

暇なときは新聞や雑誌を読みます。
*Hima na toki wa shinbun **ya** zasshi o yomimasu.*
When I'm free, I read things such as newspapers and magazines.

彼女は日本語も中国語も話します。
*Kanojo wa Nihongo **mo** Chūgokugo **mo** hanashimasu.*
She speaks Japanese and also Chinese (both Japanese and Chinese).

コーヒーか紅茶を飲みたい。 *Kōhī **ka** kōcha o nomitai.*
I want to drink coffee or tea.

食べるのと飲むのと寝るのと，どれが一番好きですか。
*Taberu no **to** nomu no **to** neru no **to**, dore ga ichiban suki desu ka.*
Eating, drinking, and sleeping, which one do you like the best?

食べる(の)か飲む(の)か寝る(の)か早く決めてください。
*Taberu (no) **ka** nomu (no) **ka** neru (no) **ka** hayaku kimete kudasai.*
Please quickly decide on whether you'll eat, drink, or go to bed.

2. *Te*-forms

The *te*-form can be used to conjoin verbs and adjectives in the same sentence. They may be sequentially ordered, in a cause-result relationship, or in contrast. In addition, they may express simultaneous actions or various states.

家へ帰って寝た方がいい。 *Ie e **kaette** neta hō ga ii.*
You had better go back home and sleep.

あなたに会えてとてもうれしいです。
*Anata ni **aete** totemo ureshii desu.*
I could meet you and I am very glad. (I am very glad to meet you.)

母が料理をして父が皿を洗います。
Haha ga ryōri o shite chichi ga sara o araimasu.
My mother cooks, and my father does the dishes.

彼は働きすぎて病気になった。 *Kare wa hatarakisugite byōki ni natta.*
He overworked and became sick.

あの車は高くて買えません。 *Ano kuruma wa takakute kaemasen.*
That car is expensive, and so I can't buy it. (That car is too expensive for me to buy.)

この刺身は新しくておいしいですよ。
Kono sashimi wa atarashikute oishii desu yo.
This raw fish is fresh and delicious.

彼は背が高くて素敵です。 *Kare wa se ga takakute suteki desu.*
He is tall and nice.

母は病気で寝ています。 *Haha wa byōki de nete imasu.*
My mother is sick and sleeping. (My mother is sick in bed.)

今日は雨で蒸し暑い。 *Kyō wa ame de mushiatsui.*
Today is rainy and sultry.

彼は冷静で賢明な人です。 *Kare wa reisei de kenmei na hito desu.*
He is a calm and earnest man.

電車に遅れてどうしたんですか。 *Densha ni okurete dō shita n desu ka.*
What did you do after you missed the train?

たくさん漢字を覚えてやっと新聞が読めるようになりました。
Takusan kanji o oboete yatto shinbun ga yomeru yō ni narimashita.
I learned many kanji, and so finally I've become able to read newspapers.

頭が痛くて今日は早めに帰ろうかと思う。
Atama ga itakute kyō wa hayame ni kaerō ka to omou.
I have a headache, so I think I'll go home a little earlier.

彼女はちょっときれいでいいなと思う。
Kanojo wa chotto kirei de ii na to omou.
She is somewhat pretty, so I think she is nice.

いつも音楽を聴いて本を読みます。
Itsumo ongaku o kiite hon o yomimasu.
I always read books while listening to music.

3. Combining forms

The combining form can be used to list actions and events just as *te*-forms do, but this usage of the combining form is mainly found in formal speech contexts or in written forms. Writers may purposely mix the *te*-form and combining form in the same sentence for a rhetorical reason.

- 私は丘に立って海を眺めてそのことを考えて泣きました。
  *Watashi wa oka ni **tatte** umi o **nagamete** sono koto o **kangaete** naki-mashita.*
- 私は丘に立ち，海を眺め，そのことを考えて泣きました。
  *Watashi wa oka ni **tachi**, umi o **nagame**, sono koto o **kangaete** nakimashita.*

I stood on a hill, watched the sea, thought of it and cried.

日本は戦後復興し，経済発展を成功させた。
*Nihon wa sengo **fukkō shi**, keizai hatten o seikō saseta.*
Japan rebuilt itself after the war and has accomplished successful economic development.

彼女は子供を失い，ひどく悲しんでいた。
*Kanojo wa kodomo o **ushinai**, hidoku kanashinde ita.*
She lost her child and was terribly grieved.

太郎さんがいつもご飯を作り，花子さんが皿洗いをする。
*Tarō san ga itsumo gohan o **tsukuri**, Hanako san ga sara arai o suru.*
Taro always cooks meals, and Hanako washes the dishes.

4. Conjunctional particles for clauses

■ Temporal adverbial clauses

Some temporal nouns (e.g. *aida, ato, mae, toki, uchi* and *tabi*) and conjunctional particles (e.g. *nagara*) can create temporal adverbial clauses/phrases. (→ See Adverbial clauses under Clauses.)

赤ちゃんが寝ている間に，私はメールをチェックします。
*Akachan ga nete iru **aida ni**, watashi wa mēru o chekku shimasu.*
I check emails while the baby is sleeping.

テレビを見ながら勉強してはいけません。
*Terebi o mi**nagara** benkyō shite wa ikemasen.*
It's not good to study while watching TV.

■ Conditional clauses

Conjunctional particles such as *ba, tara, to*, and *nara* can create conditional clauses. (→ See *ba, nara, tara, to*, and Conditionals.)

先生に聞けば分かりますよ。 *Sensei ni kike**ba** wakarimasu yo.*
If you ask your teacher, you'll understand it.

合格したらすぐに教えてくださいよ。
*Gōkaku shi**tara** suguni oshiete kudasai yo.*
Please let me know immediately if you pass (the exam).

押すと開きます。 *Osu **to** akimasu.* If you push it, it opens.

中国に行くならビザをとらなくてはいけませんよ。
*Chūgoku ni iku **nara** biza o toranakute wa ikemasen yo.*
If you are going to China, you need to get a visa.

■ Adverbial clauses for contrast/conflict

Conjunctional particles such as *ga, noni,* and *keredomo* connect sentences that are in contrast or conflict. (→ See *ga, keredo(mo),* and *noni*.)

雪が降っているのに出かけたんですか。
*Yuki ga futte iru **noni** dekaketa n desu ka.*
Did you go out even though it was snowing?

この本はちょっと難しいけれど面白い。
*Kono hon wa chotto muzukashii **keredo** omoshiroi.*
This book is a bit difficult, but interesting.

■ Adverbial clauses for reasons

Conjunctional particles such as *kara* and *node* connect clauses that are in a cause-result relationship. (→ See *kara, node,* and *tame ni*.)

今日は雨が降るかもしれませんから，傘を持っていってください。
*Kyō wa ame ga furu kamoshiremasen **kara**, kasa o motte itte kudasai.*
It might rain today, so please bring an umbrella.

私は要らないのでどうぞ使ってください。
*Watashi wa iranai **node** dōzo tsukatte kudasai.*
I do not need it, so please use it.

5. Sentence-conjunctional words

Sentence-conjunctional words are placed at the beginning of a sentence, and show the relationship between the previous sentence and the following sentence.

daga だが **but, however** (written language, formal speech)

dakara だから **and so, therefore, that's why** (informal)

demo でも **but, however** (informal)

dewa では **then, if so** (informal form is *ja*)

keredo(mo) or kedo けれど(も) *or* けど **but** (informal)

nande ka to iu to 何でかというと **because** (informal)

naze ka to iu to なぜかというと **because** (less informal than above)

nazenara(ba) なぜなら(ば) **because** (written language, formal speech)

shikashi しかし **but** (written language, formal speech)

shitagatte 従って **and so, therefore, that's why** (written language, formal speech)

sorekara それから **and, and then, after that, since then**

soreni それに **moreover, besides**

sorede それで **and, and then** (informal)

soshite そして **and, and then** (less informal than above)

(→ See *daga, dakara, demo <conjunction>, dewa, keredo(mo), nazena-raba, shikashi, sorekara, soreni, sorede,* and *soshite.*)

偶然道で田中さんに会いました。それで，一緒に食事をしました。
*Gūzen michi de Tanaka san ni aimashita. **Sorede**, issho ni shokuji o shi-mashita.*
I happened to meet Mr. Tanaka on the street. And then we had a meal together.

昨日あなたに何度も電話をかけました。けれど出ませんでした。
*Kinō anata ni nando mo denwa o kakemashita. **Keredo** demasen deshita.*
I telephoned you many times yesterday. But there was no answer.

DEMONSTRATIVES

Demonstratives can be used to refer to things in terms of their physical location relative to the speaker and the listener in their visual domain. They can function as pronouns, adjectives, adverbs, or adjectival nouns, indicating for example which items, locations, directions, types, and manners are meant. For instance, for referring to a book near the speaker, the demonstrative pronoun *kore* or the demonstrative adjective and a common noun, *kono hon*, is used. For referring to a book near the listener but far from the speaker, *sore* or *sono hon* is used. For referring to a book that is far from both the speaker and the listener, *are* or *ano hon* is used. For asking which book, *dore* or *dono hon* is used. (→ See *are*, *dore*, *kore*, and *sore*.) *Kore*, *sore*, *are*, and *dore* can be used for things and animals. For people, use the demonstrative adjectives *kono*, *sono*, *ano*, and *dono* along with a common noun, as in *kono hito* 'this person' or *kono gakusei* 'this student' (although the people in a photo or picture can be referred to by demonstrative pronouns). For referring to other notions, use the demonstratives listed in the following table.

	Close to the speaker	Close to the listener but far from the speaker	Far from both the speaker and the listener	Question
Things and animals	*kore*	*sore*	*are*	*dore*
Location	*koko*	*soko*	*asoko*	*doko*
Direction (polite)	*kochira*	*sochira*	*achira*	*dochira*
Direction (informal)	*kotchi*	*sotchi*	*atchi*	*dotchi*
Type	*konna*	*sonna*	*anna*	*donna*
Manner	*kō*	*sō*	*ā*	*dō*

これは何ですか。
Kore wa nan desu ka.
What is this?

あの人はだれですか。
Ano hito wa dare desu ka.
Who is that person over there?

これは亡くなった本田さんですか。
Kore wa nakunatta Honda san desu ka. (pointing at a man in a photo)
Is this the late Mr. Honda?

あそこに車がありますね。あれは私のです。
Asoko ni kuruma ga arimasu ne. Are wa watashi no desu.
There is a car over there, right? That's mine.

ちょっとあっちに行ってよ。
Chotto atchi ni itte yo.
Please just go away.

山田さんはどちらからですか。
Yamada san wa dochira kara desu ka.
Where are you from, Mr. Yamada?

こんな鞄がほしかったんです。
Konna kaban ga hoshikatta n desu.
I wanted to get this kind of bag.

ここはこうしてください。
Koko wa kō shite kudasai.
Please make this part this way.

彼はどんな人ですか。
Kare wa donna hito desu ka.
What kind of person is he?

HONORIFICS

The first step to make your speech polite is to use the *desu*/*masu* style. *Desu* is the polite counterpart of the linking verb *da*. *Masu* is the polite suffix used for verbs. In addition, you can use a variety of prefixes, suffixes, lexical items, and constructions to be applied to nouns, adjectival nouns, adjectives, and verbs. The usage of honorific forms is conditioned by the notions of in-group and out-group. An in-group includes one's family, close friends, and those who work in the same company or institution. An out-group includes the others. Depending on the function, honorific forms are categorized into five forms: respectful forms, humble forms, courteous forms, polite forms, and refined forms. The respectful form is used to elevate the stature of the person or the person's in-group members (insiders) to whom or about whom the speaker is talking, or used to upgrade or value that person's belongings. The humble form is used to humbly or modestly express the speaker's or the speaker's in-group member's actions or states. The courteous form is used to show the speaker's courteous attitude toward his clients or customers in business contexts. The polite form is usually used for any out-group members (outsiders), but its purpose is merely to make the expressions and utterances sound polite rather than elevate the stature of the addressee. The beautifying form is used just as grace words.

I. FOR NOUNS

1. The prefixes *o* and *go*

The honorific prefixes *o* and *go* can be attached at the beginning of a noun to express respect to the person with whom the item is associated or to express humility of the speaker with whom the item is associated. In some cases, *o* is used regardless of the item's association with a person (e.g. *o-kome* 'rice' and *o-kane* 'money'). The basic rule is to use *o* before a native Japanese word and *go* before a Sino-Japanese word (a word of Chinese origin), but there are numerous exceptions.

- The prefix *o*

o-dekake	お出かけ	**going out** (relating to the other person)
o-hana	お花	**flower**
	お鼻	**a nose**
o-kaeri	お帰り	**going back, welcome home** (relating to the other person)
o-kāsan	お母さん	**mother** (of the other person)

o-kuruma	お車	a car (of the other person)
o-naka	お腹	the belly
o-namae	お名前	the name (of the other person)
o-miyage	お土産	a souvenir
o-tōsan	お父さん	father (of the other person)
o-umare	お生まれ	birth (of the other person)
o-kome	お米	rice
o-mise	お店	a shop

■ The prefix *go*

go-jitaku	ご自宅	a house (of the other person)
go-jūsho	ご住所	address (of the other person)
go-kekkon	ご結婚	marriage (of the other person)
go-seikō	ご成功	success (of the other person)
go-shujin	ご主人	husband (of the other person)

■ The prefix *o* used for a Sino-Japanese word

o-cha	お茶	tea
o-chawan	お茶碗	a rice bowl
o-denwa	お電話	a telephone
o-futon	お布団	bedclothes
o-heya	お部屋	a room
o-kanjō	お勘定	counting money, check
o-keshō	お化粧	makeup
o-nimotsu	お荷物	baggage
o-rei	お礼	thanks
o-saifu	お財布	a purse, a wallet
o-satō	お砂糖	sugar
o-shokuji	お食事	a meal
o-sōji	お掃除	cleaning, sweeping
o-sushi	お寿司	sushi
o-ryōri	お料理	a dish
o-yasai	お野菜	vegetables

■ The prefix *o* used for a loanword

o-toire	おトイレ	**a toilet**
o-zubon	おズボン	**pants, slacks**
o-sōsu	おソース	**sauce**
o-bīru	おビール	**beer**

2. Honorific suffixes *san* and *sama*

Proper nouns and common nouns associated with people's positions and relationships can be followed by suffixes such as *san* or *sama* to show respect or politeness to the person. These suffixes should never be used after the speaker's name. The suffix *san* can be added at the end of a proper name (family name or given name), kin terms, or professional titles. It can also be used in set phrases, following nouns that express concepts. The suffix *sama* is the more respectful and formal version of the suffix *san*.

Tanaka san	田中さん	**Mr. (Ms.) Tanaka**
Tarō san	太郎さん	**Taro**
oji san	おじさん	**uncle or an oldish gentleman**
oba san	おばさん	**aunt or an oldish lady**
kachō san	課長さん	**the chief of a section**
otsukare san	お疲れさん	**tiredness (You may be tired, thank you.)**
gokurō san	ご苦労さん	**hardship (I made you work hard, thank you. (The set phrases for thanking somebody after finishing a job.))**
Yamada sama	山田様	**Mr. (Ms.) Yamada**
o-kyaku sama	お客様	**customer or visitor**
dochira sama	どちら様	**who**
donata sama	どなた様	**who**

3. Honorific pronouns and interrogatives

Pronouns and interrogative words have specific honorific forms. Note that *kochira, sochira, achira,* or *dochira* can be used for people and things in addition to locations.

ORDINARY PRONOUN	POLITE PRONOUN	MEANING
kore (noun)	*kochira*	**this**
	kochira (sama)	**this person**

kono (prefix)	*kochira no*	this
kotchi	*kochira*	this direction/area
sore	*sochira*	it, the thing
	sochira (sama)	the person there, you
sono (prefix)	*sochira no*	near the other person, your
sotchi	*sochira*	area of the other person, you
are (noun)	*achira*	that
	achira (sama)	that person
ano (prefix)	*achira no*	that
atchi	*achira*	that direction/area
dore, doko	*dochira*	which one, where
	dochira (sama)	who
dono, doko no (prefix)	*dochira no*	which, where
dotchi	*dochira*	which direction, where

「どちらになさいますか。」「こちらにいたします。」
*"**Dochira** ni nasaimasu ka." "**Kochira** ni itashimasu."*
"Which will you choose?" "I'll take this."

ご紹介します。こちらが本田太郎さんです。
*Goshōkai shimasu. **Kochira** ga Honda Tarō san desu.*
Let me introduce (someone to you). This is Taro Honda.

どちら様でしょうか。 ***Dochira** sama deshō ka.* Who are you?

II. FOR ADJECTIVAL NOUNS AND ADJECTIVES

The prefixes *o* and *go* can be used for adjectival nouns and adjectives just as they are used for nouns.

最近はお忙しいですか。 *Saikin wa **o**-isogashii desu ka.*
Have you been busy lately?

お肌がおきれいですね。 ***O**-hada ga o-kirei desu ne.* Your skin is pretty.

ご立派です。 ***Go**-rippa desu.* You are great.

ピアノがお上手ですね。 *Piano ga **o**-jōzu desu ne.*
You are good at the piano.

III. FOR VERBS

The honorific system most extensively applies to verbs through verbal suffixes, constructions, and specific lexical items.

1. *(R)areru* (respectful)

The verb suffix *(r)areru* can be used to create the respectful form of verbs. (→ See Respectful form under Verbs for how to create this form.) Note that the honorific form of *iru* (to be) becomes *orareru*, made from *oru* (the equivalent of *iru*). In addition, many commonly used verbs have their specific respectful forms, which can be used instead of their respectful forms with *(r)areru*.

この本は山田先生が書かれたのですか。
*Kono hon wa Yamada sensei ga **kakareta** no desu ka.*
Did Professor Yamada write this book?

あなたもいっしょに食べられますか。（召し上がりますか）
*Anata mo issho ni **taberaremasu** ka. (**meshiagarimasu** ka)*
Will you eat together, too?

先生は今日は来られません。（いらっしゃいません）
*Sensei wa kyō wa **koraremasen**. (**irasshaimasen**)*
The teacher isn't coming today.

よかったら見られますか。（ご覧になりますか）
*Yokattara **miraremasu** ka. (**go-ran ni narimasu** ka)*
Will you see it if you'd like to?

そろそろお食事にされますか。（なさいますか）
*Sorosoro o-shokuji ni **saremasu** ka. (**nasaimasu** ka)*
Will you have a meal soon?

社長は今部屋におられますか。（いらっしゃいますか）
*Shachō wa ima heya ni **o-raremasu** ka. (**irasshaimasu** ka)*
Is the president in his room now?

2. *O/go . . . suru* (humble)

For expressing the speaker's action that can affect the other person, form a humble phrase by using the verb in the combining form, preceded by *o* and followed by the verb *suru*. The verb *suru* can be replaced by *itasu*, which is the courteous version of *suru*. If your action does not affect the other person at all, as in 'I clean my room,' such a construction should not be used.

電話をお借りいたします。
*Denwa o **o-kari itashimasu**. (humbly and courteously speaking)*
I'd like to use your telephone.

When using a *suru*-verb, put *o* or *go* before *suru* depending on the noun.

東京をご案内します。*Tōkyō o **go-annai shimasu**.*
I'll guide you around Tokyo.

喜んでご協力します。 *Yorokonde **go-kyōryoku shimasu**.*
I'm pleased to cooperate with you.

少しご質問いたします。
*Sukoshi **go-shitsumon itashimasu**.* (humbly and courteously speaking)
I'd like to ask you something.

3. *O/go . . . nasaru/ni naru/desu* (respectful)

For expressing the addressee's action, you can use a noun or a verb with the prefix *o* or *go* and *nasaru*, *ni naru*, or *desu*. *Nasaru* is a slightly irregular *u*-verb, and its modern *masu*-form is *nasaimasu* rather than *nasarimasu*. Note that when you reply to a question in this construction, do not use a respectful form because it is improper for you to respect yourself. Use a humble and/or courteous version of the verbs.

- *O/go* + noun (action) + *nasaru*

  「お部屋でインターネットをご利用なさいますか。」「はい利用いたします。」
  *"O-heya de intānetto o **go-riyō nasaimasu** ka." "Hai, **riyō itashimasu**."*
  "Will you make use of the Internet in your room?" "Yes, I will."

  社長が今ご到着なさいました。
  *Shachō ga ima **go-tōchaku nasaimashita**.*
  The president (of the company) has just arrived.

  「そろそろお食事(に)なさいますか。」「はい、いたします。」
  *"Sorosoro **o-shokuji (ni)nasaimasu** ka." "Hai, itashimasu."*
  "Will you be having a meal soon?" "Yes, I will."

- *O/go* + noun + *ni naru*

  「お部屋でインターネットをご利用になりますか。」「はい，利用いたします。」
  *"O-heya de intānetto o **go-riyō ni narimasu** ka." "Hai, riyō itashimasu."*
  "Will you make use of the Internet in your room?" "Yes, I will."

  社長が今ご到着になりました。
  *Shachō ga ima **go-tōchaku ni narimashita**.*
  The president (of the company) has just arrived.

- *O* + verb in the combining form+ *ni naru*

  「お呼びになりましたか。」「はい，お呼びいたしました。」
  "O-yobi ni narimashita ka." "Hai, o-yobi itashimashita."
  "Did you call me?" "Yes, I did."

  「明日はお出かけになりますか。」「いえ，いたしません。」
  *"Ashita wa **o-dekake ni narimasu** ka." "Ie, itashimasen."*
  "Are you going out tomorrow?" "No, I'm not."

- *O/go* + noun + *desu*

社長が今ご到着です。 *Shachō ga ima **go-tōchaku desu**.*
The president (of the company) has just arrived.

「ご主人は今お留守ですか。」「はい，留守でございます。」
*"Go-shujin wa ima **o-rusu desu ka**." "Hai, rusu de gozaimasu."*
"Is your husband away from home now?" "Yes, he is."

先生は明日までご出張です。 *Sensei wa ashita made **go-shutchō desu**.*
The teacher is away on business till tomorrow.

4. Honorific verbs

There are some verbs that are used as respectful verbs, humble verbs, or courteous verbs.

- Respectful Verbs

RESPECTFUL VERB	PLAIN FORM	MEANING
ご存知だ *go-zonji da*	知っている *shitte iru*	to know
いらっしゃる *irassharu*	いる/行く/来る *iru, iku, kuru*	to stay, go, come
召し上がる *meshiagaru*	食べる *taberu*	to eat
なさる *nasaru*	する *suru*	to do
おっしゃる *ossharu*	言う *iu*	to say
ご覧になる *goran ni naru*	見る *miru*	to see

- Humble Verbs

HUMBLE VERB	PLAIN FORM	MEANING
存じている *zonjite iru*	知っている *shitte iru*	to know
伺う *ukagau*	行く，来る，尋ねる *iku, kuru, tazuneru*	to go, to come, to inquire
頂く *itadakuu*	食べる，もらう *taberu, morau*	to eat, receive
申し上げる *mōshiageru*	言う *iu*	to say

拝見する	見る	
haiken suru	*miru*	**to see**
差し上げる	あげる	
sashiageru	*ageru*	**to give**

■ Courteous Verbs

COURTEOUS VERB	PLAIN FORM	MEANING
申す	言う	
mōsu	*iu*	**to say**
致す	する	
itasu	*suru*	**to do**
参る	行く, 来る	
mairu	*iku, kuru*	**to go, come**
でござる	だ	
de gozaru	*da*	**to be**
ござる	ある	
gozaru	*aru*	**to exist**
おる	いる	
oru	*iru*	**to be, stay**
(... て)おる	(... て)いる	
(... te) oru	*(... te) iru*	**to be doing ...**

Note that both the courteous verb *mairu* and the humble verb *ukagau* can mean 'to come' and 'to go,' but when the speaker speaks just courteously to the listener without showing the respect to the person who is talked about, only the former can be used and the latter cannot be used. In Japanese the speaker's in-group members are usually not the target of respectful verbs. Thus, *mairimasu* in the following sentence cannot be replaced by *ukagaimasu*:

今から叔父の所に参ります。 *Ima kara oji no tokoro ni **mairimasu**.*
I'm now going to call at my uncle's house.

Also note that replacing *te imasu* with *te orimasu* makes the statement sound courteous.

存じております	知っています	
zonjite orimasu	*shitte imasu*	**to know**

INTERROGATIVES

Interrogatives are words used for asking content questions. Interestingly, interrogatives can also be used to create indefinite pronouns when combined with a particle such as *ka, mo,* and *demo.*

I. INTERROGATIVES USED IN CONTENT QUESTIONS

The following are some examples of interrogative words in Japanese.

誰	*dare*	who
どう	*dō*	how
どちら	*dochira*	which way, who' (honorific)
どこ	*doko*	where
どなた	*donata*	who (honorific)
どんな	*donna*	what kind of
どの	*dono*	which
どのくらい or どのぐらい	*donokurai* or *donogurai*	how much (any sorts of measurement)
どうして	*dōshite*	why, how
いくら	*ikura*	how much (price)
いつ	*itsu*	when
なに	*nani*	what
なぜ	*naze*	why

Interrogative words can be created with counters, particles, and nouns.

何時に行きますか。 ***Nanji** ni ikimasu ka.*
What time are you going there?

学生は何人いますか。 *Gakusei wa **nannin** imasu ka.*
How many students are there?

どの人が田中さんですか。 ***Dono hito** ga Tanaka san desu ka.*
Which person is Mr. Tanaka?

どんな人が来ましたか。 ***Donna hito** ga kimashita ka.*
What kind of person came?

どのように書けばいいですか。 ***Dono yō ni*** *kakeba ii desu ka.*
How should I write it?

どれだけ飲めばいいですか。 ***Dore dake*** *nomeba ii desu ka.*
How much should I drink?

II. INTERROGATIVES USED IN INDEFINITE PRONOUNS

By adding some particle at the end of interrogatives, we can create useful pronouns with quantificational meanings such as 'some,' 'no,' 'all,' and 'any.' (→ See Interrogatives for the list of interrogative words.) These morphological/syntactic processes are not completely productive, and have many exceptions.

1. Interrogative + *ka* (some/any)

By adding the particle *ka* at the end of an interrogative noun, we can create an indefinite pronoun that shows the existence of some item without specifying its identity. (→ See *ka*.)

彼は何かが欠けている。 *Kare wa **nanika** ga kakete iru.*
He is missing something in himself.

どこかで会いませんか。 ***Dokoka*** *de aimasen ka.*
Shall we meet somewhere?

だれかと付き合っているのですか。 ***Dareka*** *to tsukiatte iru no desu ka.*
Are you seeing someone?

昨日はだれかに会いましたか。 *Kinō wa **dareka** ni aimashita ka.*
Did you see someone yesterday?

2. Interrogative + *mo* + . . . *nai* (no)

By adding the particle *mo* after an interrogative noun and its associated particle and placing it in a negative sentence, we can create a negative pronoun that shows the absence of some kind of thing. Note that the particle *ga* and *o* must be deleted if they are followed by *mo*. (→ See *mo*.)

このことは誰にも話してはいけません。
*Kono koto wa **dare ni mo** hanashite wa **ikemasen**.*
You must not talk about this matter with anyone.

夏休みはどこにも行きませんでした。
*Natsuyasumi wa **doko ni mo** ikimasen deshita.*
I did not go anywhere during the summer vacation.

昨日は誰も来ませんでした。 *Kinō wa **dare mo** kimasen deshita.*
No one came yesterday.

3. Interrogative + *mo* (every/all)

By adding the particle *mo* at the end of an interrogative noun and using it in an affirmative sentence, we can create a universal pronoun that refers to all of some kind of thing. (→ See *mo*.)

> この会社ではだれもがライバルだ。
> *Kono kaisha de wa **daremo** ga raibaru da.*
> **In this company, everyone is my rival.**

> 彼女はいつもニコニコしている。
> *Kanojo wa **itsumo** nikoniko shite iru.*
> **She is always smiling.**

4. Interrogative + *demo* (free-choice 'any')

By adding *demo* after an interrogative word plus its associated particle other than *ga* or *o*, we can create a free-choice indefinite pronoun. (→ See *demo*.) In an informal conversational context, *demo* may be replaced by *datte*. (→ See *datte*.)

> ATM はどこにでもありますよ。
> *Ei-tī-emu wa **doko ni demo** arimasu yo.*
> **ATMs can be found in anywhere.**

> そんなことは誰でも知っていますよ。
> *Sonna koto wa **dare demo** shitte imasu yo.*
> **Anyone knows such a thing.**

> 誰だって持ってるよ。 ***Dare datte** motteru yo.*
> **Anyone has (it).**

LINKING VERB (*DA/DESU*)

Da is often considered to be a Japanese linking verb and is usually translated as *am*, *is*, or *are* in English. However, *da* is not really a word, unlike these English words. *Da* cannot stand by itself, and must directly follow a word or phrase. This is because *da* is historically derived from the combination of the particle *de* and the verb *aru*. (→ See *de aru*.) All forms in the table below have alternative forms that were created based on *de aru*: for example, *de atta*, *de arō*, *de atta de arō*, *de ari*. It is used to express the identity or the state (including the location) of people and things by following a noun, a noun plus a particle, or an adjectival noun. *Da* is in the plain non-past affirmative form, and *desu* is its polite counterpart.

Their other conjugated forms as well as those combined with other commonly used grammatical items are summarized in the following table.

		Affirmative	Negative
Non-past *am, are, is* *am not, are not, is not*	Plain	…だ …*da*	…じゃない …*ja nai*
	Polite	…です …*desu*	…じゃないです …*ja nai desu* or …じゃありません …*ja arimasen*
Past/Perfect *was, were, has been* *was not, were not,* *have not been*	Plain	…だった …*datta*	…じゃなかった …*ja nakatta*
	Polite	…でした …*deshita*	…じゃなかったです …*ja nakatta desu* or …じゃありませんでした …*ja arimasen deshita*
Presumptive present *will (not) be*	Plain	…だろう …*darō*	…じゃないだろう …*ja nai darō*
	Polite	…でしょう …*deshō*	…じゃないでしょう …*ja nai deshō*
Presumptive past/perfect *may (not) have been*	Plain	…だっただろう …*datta darō*	…じゃなかっただろう …*ja nakatta darō*
	Polite	…だったでしょう …*datta deshō*	…じゃなかったでしょう …*ja nakatta deshō*

Te-form ...and	--	...で ...*de*	...じゃなくて ...*ja nakute*
Tara-form	--	...だったら ...*dattara*	...じゃなかったら ...*ja nakattara*
Tari-form	--	...だったり ...*dattari*	...じゃなかったり ...*ja nakattari*
Ba-form	--	...ならば ...*nara ba*	...じゃなければ ...*ja nakereba*

■ *ja*

じゃ *ja* in the above table, except the last three, can be replaced by では *dewa*.

■ *desu*

Although *da* does not follow adjectives, *desu* (the polite counterpart of *da*) can follow adjectives in a sentence-predicate position regardless of the tense and polarity (affirmative/negative) to add politeness, as in *takai desu* 'is expensive,' *takakatta desu* 'was expensive,' *takaku nai desu* 'is not expensive,' and *takaku nakatta desu* 'was not expensive.' (→ See also Adjectives.)

■ *deshō*

Although *darō* (the plain present presumptive linking verb) does not follow adjectives, *deshō* (the polite counterpart of *darō*) can follow adjectives in a sentence-predicate position regardless of the tense and polarity (affirmative/negative), as in *takai deshō* 'is probably expensive,' *takakatta deshō* 'was probably expensive,' *takaku nai deshō* 'is not expensive,' and *takaku nakatta deshō* 'was probably not expensive.'

■ *deshita*

Deshita (the past counterpart of *desu*) is also used as a part of a polite negative past form of verbs, following *masen*, as in *ikimasen deshita* 'did not go.'

■ *nara*

Nara (the front part of the *ba*-form) can follow adjectives in a clause-predicate position regardless of the tense and polarity (affirmative/negative), as in *takai nara* 'if (it) is expensive,' *takaku nai nara* 'if (it) is not expensive,' *takakatta nara* 'if (it) was expensive,' and *takaku nakatta nara* 'if (it) was not expensive.'

NUMBERS & COUNTERS

There are two number systems in Japanese: the Chinese system and the native Japanese system. The following table shows how the numbers from 1 to 10 are pronounced in Japanese.

	Chinese System	Native Japanese System
0	rei	--
1	ichi	hitotsu
2	ni	futatsu
3	san	mittsu
4	shi	yottsu, yon
5	go	itsutsu
6	roku	muttsu
7	shichi	nanatsu, nana
8	hachi	yattsu
9	kyū, ku	kokonotsu
10	jū	tō

Note that the number phrases listed in the native Japanese system in principle refer to the number of some objects, except for *yon* and *nana*. Although the Japanese system is still frequently used, it goes up to 10. Thus, in business, administrative, or academic contexts, the Chinese system is predominantly used. However, *shi* 'four' is often replaced by *yon*, as in *yon kai* 'fourth floor,' because *shi* also means 'death' in Japanese and considered to be a bad-luck number. *Shichi* 'seven' is also often replaced by *nana*, as in *nana ji* 'seven o'clock' as *shichi ji* and *ichi ji* sound similar and confusing.

The following table shows the pronunciation of the numbers from 11 to 20.

11	jūichi	16	jūroku
12	jūni	17	jūshichi, jūnana
13	jūsan	18	jūhachi
14	jūshi, jūyon	19	jūkyū, jūku
15	jūgo	20	nijū

Jūyon and *jūnana* in the above table are exceptionally created by attaching a Chinese word to a native Japanese word.

The following table shows the multiples of 10, 100, 1,000, and 10,000. Notice many irregular sound changes with the multiples of 100 (*hyaku*, *byaku*, and *pyaku*) and 1,000 (*sen* and *zen*.)

10	*jū*	100	*hyaku*	1,000	*sen, issen*	10,000	*ichiman*
20	*nijū*	200	*nihyaku*	2,000	*nisen*	20,000	*niman*
30	*sanjū*	300	*sanbyaku*	3,000	*sanzen*	30,000	*sanman*
40	*yonjū*	400	*yonhyaku*	4,000	*yonsen*	40,000	*yonman*
50	*gojū*	500	*gohyaku*	5,000	*gosen*	50,000	*goman*
60	*rokujū*	600	*roppyaku*	6,000	*rokusen*	60,000	*rokuman*
70	*nanajū*	700	*nanahyaku*	7,000	*nanasen*	70,000	*nanaman*
80	*hachijū*	800	*happyaku*	8,000	*hassen*	80,000	*hachiman*
90	*kyūjū*	900	*kyūhyaku*	9,000	*kyūsen*	90,000	*kyūman*

To express the quantity or the amount of items, the Japanese use a counter after the number for counting almost everything, and the counter varies depending on the shape, size, and type of the item being counted. For example, the counter for birds and rabbits is *wa* and the counter for medium-size animals like dogs and cats is *hiki*. The counter for flat items like paper and towels is *mai*, and the counter for mechanical items like cars is *dai*. The number phrases can be placed in a variety of places, but the most neutral position is right after the item. If the associated particle is *ga* or *o*, the number phrase tends to be placed after the particle. These counters can be followed by the suffix *me* to show the place in an order. For example, *2 dai me* means 'the second (mechanical item).' Some counters such as *ji* 'o'clock' exclusively specify the position in an order even without the suffix *me*. Also note that many counters cause minor sound changes or exceptional pronunciations when combined with numerals. For example, the counter *hiki* is pronounced as *hiki*, *piki* or *biki* depending on the number that precedes it.

1 匹	*ippiki*	6 匹	*roppiki*
2 匹	*nihiki*	7 匹	*nanahiki*
3 匹	*sanbiki*	8 匹	*happiki, hachihiki*
4 匹	*yonhiki*	9 匹	*kyūhiki*
5 匹	*gohiki*	1 0 匹	*jippiki* or *juppiki*

→ See Appendix 4 for the list of common counters and their pronunciations.

■ After the noun (+ particle)

鳥が二羽います。 **Tori ga ni wa** imasu. There are two birds.

犬が一匹と,鳥とうさぎが二羽ずついます。
Inu ga ippiki to **tori to usagi ga ni wa** zutsu imasu.
There are one dog, two birds, and two rabbits.

家の前に車が二台停まっています。
Ie no mae ni **kuruma ga ni dai** tomatte imasu. (or **ni dai kuruma ga**)
Two cars are parked in front of the house.

ここにペンが二本と紙が二枚あります。
Koko ni **pen ga ni hon** to **kami ga ni mai** arimasu. (or ni hon pen to ni mai kami ga)
Here are two pens and two sheets of paper.

毎日コーヒーを二杯飲みます。
Mainichi **kōhī o ni hai** nomimasu. (or ni hai kōhī o)
I drink two cups of coffee every day.

駅までタクシーで二十五分かかります。
Eki made **takushī de ni jū gofun** kakarimasu. (or ni jū gofun takushī de)
It takes twenty-five minutes to reach the train station by taxi.

■ Before the noun, followed by **no**

三人の学生が欠席です。 **San nin no gakusei** ga kesseki desu.
Three students are absent.

右から三番目の席に座って下さい。
Migi kara **san banme no seki** ni suwatte kudasai.
Please be seated in the third seat from the right.

■ In a question

Nani (what) becomes nan before counters. The first consonant of a counter tends to become voiced when preceded by nan just as when preceded by san 'three.'

一週間に本を何冊ぐらい読みますか。
Isshūkan ni **hon o nan satsu** gurai yomimasu ka.
About how many books do you read in a week?

ゲームソフトを何個持っていますか。
Gēmu sofuto o nan ko motte imasu ka.
How many game software titles do you have?

休みは一ヶ月に何日ありますか。
Yasumi wa ikkagetsu ni **nan nichi** arimasu ka.
How many days off do you have in a month?

NOUNS

Nouns refer to people, things, and concepts, and can be placed in the subject or object position of a sentence or can be followed by particles. Nouns include proper nouns, common nouns, pronouns, and others. Japanese nouns have no gender/number distinctions. Case is specified by particles.

1. Proper nouns

Proper nouns include personal names and place names. Personal names are often followed by suffixes such as *san* and *sama* in Japanese. (→ See Honorifics.)

> 私は山田です。こちらは田中さんです。
> *Watashi wa **Yamada** desu. Kochira wa **Tanaka** san desu.*
> **I'm Yamada. This person is Mr. Tanaka.**

> 上海とニューヨークに行きます。 ***Shanhai** to **Nyūyōku** ni ikimasu.*
> **I will go to Shanghai and New York.**

2. Common nouns

Common nouns refer to a class of items and can be preceded by demonstrative adjectives such as *kono* 'this' and *sono* 'that.' They can be accompanied by quantify/amount phrases.

> この猫はかわいいですね。 *Kono **neko** wa kawaii desu ne.*
> **This cat is cute, isn't it?**

> 学生が二人来ました。 ***Gakusei** ga futari kimashita.*
> **Two students came.**

> 砂糖を少し下さい。 ***Satō** o sukoshi kudasai.*
> **Please give me a little bit of sugar.**

3. Nouns created from verbs

Some verbs in the combining form can function as nouns. (→ See Combining form under Verbs.) For example, the verb *hajimeru* means 'to begin,' and its combining form, *hajime*, can serve as a noun that means 'the beginning.' The same applies to auxiliary verbs. For example, the verb and auxiliary verb combination, *nomi-sugiru*, means 'to overdrink' or 'drink excessively,' and its combining form, *nomi-sugi*, can function as a noun that means 'overdrinking.' See Appendix 6 for an extensive list of nouns made of verbs in the combining form.

行きはバスで帰りはタクシーです。
Iki wa basu de *kaeri* wa takushī desu.
I go by bus and come back by taxi.

お生まれはどこですか。 *O-umare* wa doko desu ka.
Where were you born?

助けは要りません。 *Tasuke* wa irimasen.
I do not need your help.

彼は勉強よりも遊びが好きです。
Kare wa benkyō yori mo **asobi** *ga suki desu.*
He prefers playing to studying.

4. Nouns created from adjectives

The roots of some adjectives alone or the roots of some adjectives followed by the suffix *-sa* or *-mi* can serve as nouns all by themselves.

<u>Adjective</u>	<u>Noun</u>
akai 赤い to be red	*aka* 赤 red
fukai 深い to be deep	*fukasa* 深さ depth (of a pool)
	fukami 深み depth (of a thought)
shiroi 白い to be white	*shiro* 白 white
takai 高い to be high	*takasa* 高さ height
tanoshii 楽しい to be pleasant	*tanoshimi* 楽しみ pleasure

5. Compound nouns

Two nouns can be joined to form a compound noun.

- Multiple simple nouns
  jikoku hyō　　　時刻表　　**a timetable**

  gijutsu kakushin　技術革新　**technological innovation**

  nichi bei kankei　日米関係　**Japan-U.S. relations**

- Verb in the combining form + noun
  wasuremono　忘れ物　**forgotten item**

  deguchi　　　出口　　**exit, way out**

- Adjective root + noun
  chikamichi　近道　**shortcut**

- Noun + verb in the combining form
  hana-mi　花見　**flower viewing**

- Multiple verbs in the combining form
  hiki-dashi 引き出し **drawer**

- Adjective root + verb in the combining form
  yasu-uri 安売り **bargain sale**

- Noun + verb in the combining form
  ki-naga 気長 **leisurely attitude**

- Multiple adjective roots
  hoso-naga 細長 **slenderness**

- Repeating nouns
  hito-bito 人々 **people**

6. Personal pronouns

Japanese pronouns do not change form depending on the case, because the case is expressed by case particles such as *ga* and *o*. Plural pronouns are specified by some suffixes such as *tachi* or *ra*.

	<u>Singular</u>	<u>Plural</u>
1st person, gender neutral	*watashi,* *watakushi*	*watashitachi,* *watakushitachi*
1st person, masculine	*boku, ore*	*bokutachi, oretachi*
2nd person, gender neutral	*anata, kimi*	*anatatachi, kimitachi*
3rd person, masculine (sing.) or gender neutral (plur.)	*kare*	*karera*
3rd person, feminine	*kanojo*	*kanojora*

Watashi or *watakushi* can be used by both male and female, but *watakushi* sounds more formal than *watashi*. *Ore* and *boku* are used only by males, and *ore* sounds informal and rough, whereas *boku* sounds neutral. *Kimi* is used by superiors to refer to their subordinates. Note that personal pronouns are usually omitted in Japanese when understood from the context. For example, using *anata* 'you' when the speaker knows the person's name gives a very cold or distant impression. Thus, 'I love you' can be expressed just by *Suki desu* without any pronoun. When one wants to say 'you,' the name of the person, his/her position, or his/her occupation followed by the polite suffix *san* is commonly used instead of pronouns such as *anata*. For example, if you want to ask Mr. Smith "Is it yours?," you can say "*Kore wa Sumisu san no desu ka*" although he (*Sumisu* 'Mr. Smith') is the person you are talking to.

7. Demonstrative pronouns (→ See Demonstratives.)

PARTICLES

Particles are short elements that follow words, phrases, clauses, or sentences. Particles themselves do not conjugate but express the role of the items they follow or connect them with another part of the sentence.

I. PARTICLE TYPES

It is possible to classify particles into case particles, focus particles, conjunctional particles, and sentence-final particles.

1. Case particles

Case particles usually follow nouns and express the function of the noun in the sentence or in the phrase. More specifically, they express the relationship between nouns, or between a noun and a verb or an adjective. Case particles include *ga, o, ni, no, de, e, kara, made, to, ya*, and *ka*. (→ See *ga, o, ni, no, de, e, kara, made, to, ya*, and *ka*.)

父が弟を叱りました。 *Chichi **ga** otōto **o** shikarimashita.*
My father scolded my little brother.

私の友達の妹が来ました。 *Watashi **no** tomodachi **no** imōto **ga** kimashita.*
My friend's younger sister came (here).

2. Focus particles

Focus particles follow words and another particle in order to focus on the entity denoted by the word and express sentence-external information such as the speaker's knowledge, understanding, mood, attitude, and perspective. Focus particles include *wa, mo, bakari, sae, demo, dake, shika, shi*, and *koso*. (→ See *wa, mo, bakari, demo, dake, shika, shi*, and *koso*.)

カラオケにはよく行きます。居酒屋にもよく行きます。
*Karaoke ni **wa** yoku ikimasu. Izakaya ni **mo** yoku ikimasu.*
I go to karaoke very often. I also go to *izakaya* very often.

一万円しかありません。 *Ichiman'en **shika** arimasen.*
I have only 10,000 yen.

3. Conjunctional particles

Conjunctional particles follow phrases and clauses and conjoin verbs and adjectives or create adverbial phrases/clauses. Conjunctional particles include *te, tari, tara, to, ka, ba, node, noni, kara,* and *ga.* (→ See *te, tari, tara, to, ka, ba, node, noni, kara,* and *ga.*)

昨日は食べて飲んで寝ました。 *Kinō wa tabete nonde nemashita.*
I ate, drank, and slept yesterday.

明日の天気はどうかわかりませんが、たぶん晴れると思います。
Ashita no tenki wa dō ka wakarimasen ga, tabun hareru to omoimasu.
I'm not sure about tomorrow's weather, but I think that it will probably be fine.

タバコは身体に悪いのでやめました。
Tabako wa karada ni warui node, yamemashita.
Cigarettes are not good for health, so I quit.

4. Sentence-final particles

Sentence-final particles are placed at the end of a sentence and specify the function of the sentence or show the speaker's mood, attitude, or subtle implications. Sentence-final particles include *ka, ne, yo,* and *na.* (→ See *ka, ne, yo,* and *na.*)

いいですか。 *Ii desu ka.* (question) **Is it okay?**

あの人はきれいですね。
Ano hito wa kirei desu ne. (seeking agreement)
That person is pretty, isn't she?

これは駄目ですよ。 *Kore wa dame desu yo.* (emphasis)
This one is not good.

雨は降るかな。 *Ame wa furu kana.* (speculation)
I wonder whether it will rain.

II. ENGLISH PREPOSITION EQUIVALENTS

Common English prepositions are generally expressed by post-positional particles, nouns, or compound phrases in Japanese. Compound phrases fall into three types: Noun + Particle; Particle + Verb/Adjective; and Particle + Particle.

■ Compound Phrase (Noun + Particle)

Compound phrases in the Noun + Particle type may also be preceded by another particle, and their ending particle may be dropped or changed depending on the function of the phrase within the sentence.

うちの猫はいつもソファーとテーブルの間で寝ている。
Uchi no neko wa itsumo sofā to tēburu no aida de nete iru. (between)
My cat is always sleeping between the sofa and the table.

- Compound Phrase (Particle + Verb/Adjective)

  Compound phrases in the Particle + Verb/Adjective type may look like verb/adjective phrases in a variety of forms or like adverbial phrases.

  抗がん剤に関する研究発表が多かった。
  *Kōganzai **ni kansuru** kenkyū happyō ga ōkatta.* (about)
  There was much research presentation about an antineoplastic drug.

- Compound Phrase (Particle + Particle)

  Compound phrases in the Particle + Particle type simply consist of multiple particles.

  12月29日までに出してください。
  *Jū ni gatsu ni jū ku nichi **made ni** dashite kudasai.* (by)
  Please submit (it) by December 29th.

1. About

- ***ni tsuite*** or ***ni kanshite*** について or に関して regarding, concerning

  そのことについては心配しなくていいです。
  ***Sono koto ni tsuite** wa shinpai shinakute ii desu.*
  You don't need to worry about it.

  この件に関して質問があったらメールをください。
  ***Kono ken ni kanshite** shitsumon ga attara mēru o kudasai.*
  If you have any questions about this matter, please e-mail to me.

- ***ni tsuite no*** or ***ni kansuru*** についての or に関する regarding, concerning

  憲法九条に関するさまざまな議論がある。
  ***Kenpō kyūjō ni kansuru** samazamana giron ga aru.*
  We have a variety of discussions about Article 9 of the Constitution.

  (*"Kenpō kyūjō ni kansuru"* modifies the noun *giron*.)

- ***koro*** or ***goro*** 頃 near in time

  来年の今頃は結婚しています。
  *Rainen no **ima goro** wa kekkon shiteimasu.*
  I'll be married about this time next year.

2. Above

- ***no ue de/ni*** の上 で/に higher than

  今私たちは雲の上にいます。
  *Ima watashi tachi wa **kumo no ue ni** imasu.*
  We are above the clouds now.

- *ijō* 以上 to a greater degree than

  私のテストの点は平均以上です。
  *Watashi no tesuto no ten wa **heikin ijō** desu.*
  My test scores are above average.

3. Across

- *o yokogitte* を横切って crossing from one side to the other side of

  お婆さんが道路を横切って歩いていますよ。
  *Obāsan ga **dōro o yokogitte** aruite imasu yo.*
  An old woman is walking across the road.

- *no mukō de/ni* の向こう で/に on the opposite side of, over

  市役所はあの銀行の向こうにあります。
  *Shiyakusho wa ano **ginkō no mukō ni** arimasu.*
  The city office is on the other side of/over that bank.

4. After

- *(no) ato de/ni* (の)後 で/に in the time/order that follows

  仕事の後でお茶を飲もう。 ***Shigoto no ato de** ocha o nomō.*
  Let's have tea after work.

  買い物をした後で映画を見よう。 *Kaimono o **shita ato de** eiga o miyō.*
  Let's see a movie after shopping.

  あなたの後でけっこうです。 ***Anata no ato de** kekkō desu.*
  After you is fine.

5. Along

- *ni sotte* or *o* に沿って or を parallel to the length of

  通りに沿って桜の木が植えてあります。
  ***Tōri ni sotte** sakura no ki ga uete arimasu.*
  There are cherry trees planted along the street.

  私は時々海岸を散歩します。
  *Watashi wa tokidoki **kaigan o** sanpo shimasu.*
  I sometimes take a walk along the beach.

- *o* を from one end to the other end of

  この通りを行くと大きな交差点がある。
  ***Kono tōri o** iku to ōkina kōsaten ga aru.*
  Go along this street, and you will find a large crossroads.

6. Among

- *no naka de/ni* の中 で/に in the middle of, being one of

  三冊の中でこれがいちばん好きです。
  San satsu no naka de kore ga ichiban suki desu.
  I like this best among the three books.

- *no aida de/ni* の間 で/に in the group of

  それはすでに私たちの間で議論された。
  Sore wa sude ni watashi tachi no aida de giron sareta.
  It has already been discussed among us.

7. Around

- *no mawari de/ni* の周り で/に on all sides of

  駅の周りに居酒屋がたくさんあります。
  Eki no mawari ni izakaya ga takusan arimasu.
  There are a lot of *izakaya* (Japanese-style bars) around the train station.

8. At

- *ni* に at, on, in (time)

  月曜日に来ます。その日の三時に会いましょう。
  Getsuyōbi ni kimasu. Sono hi no sanji ni aimashō.
  I'll come on Monday. Let's meet at three on that day.

  昨日夜中に宿題をしました。 *Kinō yonaka ni shukudai o shimashita.*
  I did my homework at midnight yesterday.

- *ni* に place of existence or presence

  日曜日は家にいます。 *Nichiyōbi wa ie ni imasu.*
  I stay at home on Sundays.

- *ni* に cause of some feeling

  あの事故には驚いた。 *Ano jiko ni wa odoroita.*
  I was surprised at that accident.

- *ni* に arriving point

  今駅に着きました。 *Ima eki ni tsukimashita.*
  I arrived at the train station just now.

- *de* で place where an action is performed

  この電気製品は秋葉原の店で買いました。
  Kono denki seihin wa Akihabara no mise de kaimashita.
  I bought this electrical appliance at a store in Akihabara.

■ *de* で place where an event is held

今晩彼の家でパーティーがあります。
*Konban kare no **ie de** pātī ga arimasu.*
There will be a party at his house tonight.

9. Before

■ *(no) mae ni* (の)前に at the time that precedes

私は朝食と夕食(の)前に犬と散歩をします。
*Watashi wa **chōshoku to yūshoku no mae ni** inu to sanpo o shimasu.*
I take a walk with my dog before breakfast and supper.

遊びに行く前にすることがあります。
***Asobi ni iku mae ni** suru koto ga arimasu.*
I have something to do before I go to play.

■ *no mae de/ni* の前 で/に in front of

大勢の前で話すのは苦手です。
*Ōzei **no mae de** hanasu no wa nigate desu.*
I'm bad at speaking before a lot of people.

10. Behind

■ *no ushiro de/ni* の後ろ で/に in the back of

黄色い線の後ろに下がって下さい。
*Kiiroi **sen no ushiro ni** sagatte kudasai.*
Please step back behind the yellow line.

■ *no ura de/ni* の裏 で/に at the back of

駐車場は建物の裏にあります。
*Chūshajō wa **tatemono no ura ni** arimasu.*
The parking lot is behind the building.

■ *yori okurete* より遅れて later than

飛行機は予定より30分遅れて着きました。
*Hikōki wa **yotei yori san jippun okurete** tsukimashita.*
The airplane arrived 30 minutes behind schedule.

11. Below

■ *no shita de/ni* の下 で/に in/on a lower place than

真っ赤な太陽が水平線の下に沈んだ。
*Makkana taiyō ga **suiheisen no shita ni** shizunda.*
The crimson sun went below the horizon.

■ *ika de/ni* 以下 で/に less than

気温は零下五度以下になるでしょう。
*Kion wa **reika go do ika ni** naru deshō.*
The temperature will go below five degrees below zero.

12. Beside

■ *no soba de/ni* のそば で/に near

学校のそばにおいしいラーメン屋があります。
Gakkō no soba ni oishii rāmen'ya ga arimasu.
There is a delicious Chinese vermicelli shop beside our school.

13. Besides

■ *ni kuwaete* に加えて in addition to

地震に加えて火事も起こった。
Jishin ni kuwaete kaji mo okotta.
Besides the earthquake, fires also occurred.

■ *no hoka ni* のほかに except

これのほかにお金はもうありません。
Kore no hoka ni okane wa mō arimasen.
I have no more money besides this.

14. Between

■ *. . . to . . . no aida de/ni* ⋯と⋯の間で/に between (of space)

コンビニは交番と郵便局の間にあります。
*Konbini wa **kōban to yūbinkyoku no aida ni** arimasu.*
The convenience store is between the police box and the post office.

■ *. . . kara . . . no aida de/ni* ⋯から⋯の間で/に between (of time)
二時から三時の間に電話かメールを下さい。
Niji kara sanji no aida ni denwa ka mēru o kudasai.
Please call me or send me an e-mail between two and three o'clock.

15. By

■ *de/o tsukatte* で/を使って by a method or a means

タクシーで行きましょう。 *Takushī de ikimashō.* Let's go by taxi.

インターネットを使って情報を集めます。
Intānetto o tsukatte jōhō o atsumemasu.
I gather information by (way of) the Internet.

- *made ni* までに within the limit of time/by a deadline

  来週水曜日までに書類を提出しなければなりません。
  Raishū Suiyōbi made ni shorui o teishutsu shinakereba narimasen.
  I have to hand in the paper by next Wednesday.

  五時までに戻ります。 *Go ji made ni modorimasu.* **I'll be back by five.**

- *no soba de/ni* のそば で/に near

  トイレは出口のそばにあります。
  Toire wa deguchi no soba ni arimasu.
  The restroom is by the exit.

- *ni (yotte)* に(よって) the agent in a direct passive sentence

  私は父に叱られた。 *Watashi wa chichi ni shikarareta.*
  I was scolded by my father.

  デモは軍隊によって抑えられた。
  Demo wa guntai ni yotte osaerareta.
  The demonstration was suppressed by the troops.

  The use of *ni yotte* is not appropriate for expressing everyday-life incidents, the direct involvement of the speaker, or how of the speaker is affected by the action. (→ See *rareru*.)

16. During

- *no aida* or *jū* の間 or 中 throughout the whole period of

  夏休みの間外国にいます。 *Natsu yasumi no aida gaikoku ni imasu.*
  I'll be abroad during the vacation.

- *no aida ni* の間に at some time within a period of

  留守の間に誰か来ましたか。 *Rusu no aida ni dareka kimashita ka.*
  Did anyone call on me during my absence?

17. Except

- *igai wa/ni* 以外 は/に except

  雨の日以外は歩いて行きます。 *Ame no hi igai wa aruite ikimasu.*
  I walk there except on rainy days.

18. For

- *ni* に indirect object

  母の日にお母さんに何を買ってあげましたか。
  Haha no hi ni okāsan ni nani o katte agemashita ka.
  What did you buy for your mother on Mother's day?

- *ni* に purpose

  毎朝散歩に行きます。 *Maiasa **sanpo ni** ikimasu.*
  I go for a walk every morning.

- *ni* に occasion

  誕生日に電子辞書をもらった。 ***Tanjōbi ni** denshi jisho o moratta.*
  I was given an electronic dictionary for my birthday.

- *kan* or *no aida* 間 or の間 period of time

  二年間日本にいます。 ***Ni nen kan** Nihon ni imasu.*
  I've been (*or* I'll be) in Japan for two years.

- *no tame ni* のために benefit of someone/something

  彼女のために誕生日パーティーをします。
  ***Kanojo no tame ni** tanjōbi pātī o shimasu.*
  We'll give a birthday party for her.

- *e* or *ni* へ or に destination or direction

  出張で九州の博多に出かけます。
  *Shutchō de **Kyūshū no Hakata ni** dekakemasu.*
  I'm leaving for Hakata in Kyushu on business.

- *ni totte* にとって the item to which the situation applies

  漢字を覚えるのは私にとってちょっとむずかしい。
  *Kanji o oboeru no wa **watashi ni totte** chotto muzukashii.*
  It is a little difficult for me to learn kanji.

- *ni wa* には someone for whom some state is excessive

  このハイビジョン液晶テレビは私には高すぎる。
  *Kono hai bijon ekishō terebi wa **watashi ni wa** takasugiru.*
  This high-definition liquid crystal television is too expensive for me.

- *de* で price

  新しい本を二千円で買って千円で売りました。
  *Atarashii hon wo **ni sen en de** katte **sen en de** urimashita.*
  I bought a new book for two thousand yen and sold it for one thousand yen.

19. From

- *kara* から starting point

  新幹線のぞみは博多駅から出ます。
  *Shinkansen Nozomi wa **Hakata eki kara** demasu.*
  The Shinkansen *Nozomi* starts from Hakata station.

■ *kara* から a time something starts

百貨店は十時から開いている。 *Hyakkaten wa **jū ji kara** aite iru.*
The department store is open from ten o'clock on.

■ *kara* から material

酒は米から作られる。 *Sake wa **kome kara** tsukurareru.*
Sake is made from rice.

20. In

■ *ni* に at some time during

私は夏に富士山に登ります。
*Watashi wa **natsu ni** Fuji san ni noborimasu.*
I'll climb Mt. Fuji in the summer.

■ *ni* に place of existence

私の兄はアメリカにいます。 *Watashi no ani wa **Amerika ni** imasu.*
My brother is in the U.S.

■ *de* で a place where an action is performed

私は放課後図書館で勉強します。
*Watashi wa hōkago **toshokan de** benkyō shimasu.*
I study in the library after school.

■ *de* で a place where an event is held

会議はこの部屋で開かれます。
Kaigi wa kono heya de hirakaremasu.
The meeting will be held in this room.

祇園祭は京都の四条であります。
*Gion matsuri wa **Kyōto no Shijō de** arimasu.*
The Gion festival is held in Shijo in Kyoto.

日本語の授業はどの教室でありますか。
*Nihongo no jugyō wa **dono kyōshitsu de** arimasu ka.*
In which classroom will the Japanese lesson be given?

■ *no naka de/ni* の中 で/に within an enclosed space

パスポートは鞄の中にしまってます。
*Pasupōto wa kaban **no naka ni** shimattemasu.*
I keep my passport in my bag.

水槽の中でイルカとアシカが泳いでいます。
***Suisō no naka de** iruka to ashika ga oyoide imasu.*
Dolphins and sea lions are swimming in the fish tank.

- **de** で a method or a means

  これは漢字でどう書きますか。 *Kore wa* **kanji de** *dō kakimasu ka.*
  How do you write this in kanji?

- **ni** に a direction in which an action is done or something is

  このバスは新宿方面に行きます。
  Kono basu wa **Shinjuku hōmen ni** *ikimasu.*
  This bus goes in the direction of Shinjuku.

  駅はあの方向にあります。 *Eki wa* **ano hōkō ni** *arimasu.*
  The train station is in that direction.

- **ni oite** において description more limited or specific in meaning, in terms of

  A社の製品は品質において先を行っている。
  Ei sha no seihin wa **hinshitsu ni oite** *saki o itteiru.*
  The products of company A are ahead in terms of quality.

  (When modifying a noun, *oite* becomes *okeru*.)

  インターネットにおける個人情報の保護は困難だ。
  Intānetto ni okeru kojin jōhō no hogo wa konnan da.
  The protection of personal information on the Internet is difficult.

21. Into

- **no naka e** の中へ toward the inside of

  猫がこたつの中へ入ってきた。
  Neko ga **kotatsu no naka e** *haitte kita.*
  A cat came into the *kotatsu* (a Japanese table with an electric heater).

- **ni** に a result of a change

  この文を日本語に直して下さい。
  Kono bun o **Nihongo ni** *naoshite kudasai.*
  Please put (translate) this sentence into Japanese.

22. Near

- **no chikaku de/ni** の近く で/に close to

  駅の近くに安いホテルはありますか。
  Eki no chikaku ni yasui hoteru wa arimasu ka.
  Are there any cheap hotels near the train station?

  家の近くで交通事故がありました。
  Ie no chikaku de kōtsū jiko ga arimashita.
  There was a traffic accident near my house.

23. Of

- *no* の belonging to, in relation to

  私は部屋の窓をふきました。 *Watashi wa heya no mado o fukimashita.*
  I wiped the windows of my room.

  私はそのクラブのメンバーです。
  *Watashi wa **sono kurabu no menbā** desu.*
  I am a member of the club.

- *no* の semantic subject/object of a noun expressing action

  その俳優の演技は好評です。 *Sono **haiyū no engi** wa kōhyō desu.*
  The acting of the actor is well received.

  この意味の説明はむずかしすぎる。
  ***Kono imi no setsumei** wa muzukashisugiru.*
  The explanation of this meaning is too difficult.

- *no* の apposition

  私は神戸の街が好きです。 *Watashi wa **Kōbe no machi** ga suki desu.*
  I like the city of Kobe.

- *de* で cause

  お祖父さんは癌で死にました。*Ojīsan wa **gan de** shinimashita.*
  My grandfather died of cancer.

24. On

- *ni* に at the time of

  原稿は何曜日にできますか。 *Genkō wa **nanyōbi ni** dekimasu ka.*
  On what day of the week will the manuscript finished?

- *ni/de* に/で on the surface of

  壁にきれいな掛け軸があります。 ***Kabe ni** kirei na kakejiku ga arimasu.*
  There is a beautiful hanging scroll on the wall.

  天井に蠅が止まっている。 ***Tenjō ni** hae ga tomatte iru.*
  There is a fly on the ceiling.

- *de* で place of action or event

  1番ホームで待っています。 ***Ichiban hōmu de** matte imasu.*
  I'll be waiting on Platform No.1.

- *ni* に place of presence

  トイレは2階と4階にあります。
  *Toire wa **ni kai to yon kai ni** arimasu.*
  The washrooms are on the second and fourth floors.

■ *no ue de/ni* の上 で/に on the horizontal surface of

枝の上にアゲハ蝶が止まっている。
Eda no ue ni ageha chō ga tomatte iru.
A swallow-tailed butterfly perches on the branch.

砂糖と塩はテーブルの上にあります。
Satō to shio wa tēburu no ue ni arimasu.
Sugar and salt are on the table.

多くの日本人は畳の上で死にたいと言います。
Ōku no Nihonjin wa tatami no ue de shinitai to iimasu.
Many Japanese say they want to die on a tatami mat.

25. Onto

■ *no ue e/ni* の上 へ/に toward the surface of

猫が魚をねらってテーブルの上に飛び上がった。
Neko ga sakana o neratte tēburu no ue ni tobiagatta.
The cat jumped onto the table aiming for the fish.

26. Over

■ *no ue de/ni* の上 で/に in a higher position

その海峡の上に大きな橋ができた。
Sono kaikyō no ue ni ōkina hashi ga dekita.
A big bridge has been built over the strait.

■ *yori takaku* より高く higher than

あの気球は雲より高く飛んでいる。
Ano kikyū wa kumo yori takaku tonde iru.
That balloon is flying over the clouds.

■ *o koete* を越えて from one side to the other side of

泥棒が塀を越えて逃げた。 *Dorobō ga hei o koete nigeta.*
A thief ran away over the fence.

■ *no mukō de/ni* の向こう で/に on the other side of

彼女はあのビルの向こうに住んでいます。
Kanojo wa ano biru no mukō ni sunde imasu.
She lives on the other side of that building.

■ *yori ōku/ōi* より 多く/多い more than

百枚より多くDVDを持っています。
Hyaku mai yori ōku dī bui dī o motte imasu.
I have over one hundred DVDs.

27. Since

- **kara** or **irai** から or 以来 from a point in past time

  先週の日曜日から病気で寝ています。
  *Senshū no **Nichiyōbi kara** byōki de nete imasu.*
  I've been sick in bed since last Sunday.

  彼女と最後に会ってから二年になります。
  *Kanojo to **saigo ni atte kara** ni nen ni narimasu.*
  It is two years since I saw her last.

- **no toki kara** の時から from a point in past time

  私たちは子供の時からの親友です。
  *Watashi tachi wa **kodomo no toki kara** no shin'yū desu.*
  We've been good friends since we were children.

28. Through

- **o tōtte** を通って in one side and out the other side of

  電車が長いトンネルを通って出てきた。
  *Densha ga **nagai tonneru o tōtte** detekita.*
  A train came out through the long tunnel.

- **no aida** の間 from the beginning to the end of

  冬の間北海道でスキーができます。
  ***Fuyu no aida** Hokkaidō de sukī ga dekimasu.*
  We can ski in Hokkaido through the winter.

- **made** まで up to and including

  月曜日から土曜日まで働く会社員もいます。
  *Getsuyōbi kara **Doyōbi made** hataraku kaishain mo imasu.*
  Some office workers work from Monday through Saturday.

29. Throughout

- **no aida zutto** の間ずっと from start to finish

  私は学生時代の間ずっとアルバイトをしました。
  *Watashi wa **gakusei jidai no aida zutto** arubaito o shimashita.*
  I worked part-time throughout my school days.

- **no aida jū** の間中 from start to finish

  兄は食事の間中マンガを読んでいた。
  *Ani wa **shokuji no aida jū** manga o yonde ita.*
  My big brother was reading a comic book throughout the mealtime.

30. To

- *ni* に indirect object

  先生にお歳暮を送ります。**Sensei ni** *oseibo o okurimasu.*
  I'll send my teacher an *oseibo* **(a year-end gift).**

- *ni* or *e* or *made* に or へ or まで destination or direction

  九州から東北まで新幹線で行けます。
  Kyūshū kara **Tōhoku made** *Shinkansen de ikemasu.*
  You can go by Shinkansen from Kyushu to Tohoku.

- *made* まで the end of a period of time

  私は十時から六時まで働きます。
  Watashi wa jū ji kara **roku ji made** *hatarakimasu.*
  I work from ten to six.

31. Toward

- *no hō e* の方へ in the direction of

  彼が駅の方へ歩いて行くのを見ました。
  Kare ga **eki no hō e** *aruite iku no o mimashita.*
  I saw him walk toward the train station.

32. Under

- *no shita de/ni* の下 で/に in or to a lower place than

  テーブルの下にゴキブリがいます。
  Tēburu no shita ni *gokiburi ga imasu.*
  There is a cockroach under the table.

- *miman de/ni* 未満 で/に less than

  十八才未満の人は入れません。
  Jū hassai miman no *hito wa hairemasen.*
  People under eighteen may not enter.

  (As explained above, *no* must replace *de* and *ni*.)

33. Until

- *made* まで up to

  夜中まで本を読んでいました。
  Yonaka made *hon o yonde imashita.*
  I'd been reading books till midnight.

  書類はあしたまで準備できません。
  Shorui wa **ashita made** *junbi dekimasen.*
  The paper will not be ready till tomorrow.

34. With

■ **to (issho ni)** と(一緒に) accompanied by

あなたと一緒に行きたいです。 **Anata to issho ni** ikitai desu.
I want to go with you.

■ **de/ o tsukatte** で/を 使って means or method

黒のボールペンで申込書を記入して下さい。
*Kuro no **bōrupen de** mōshikomisho o kinyū shite kudasai.*
Please fill out the application form with a black ballpoint pen.

このナイフを使って切れば4つに分けるのは簡単です。
*Kono **naifu o tsukatte** kireba yottsu ni wakeru no wa kantan desu.*
It's easy to divide it into four pieces if you cut it with this knife.

■ **de** で cause

昨日は風邪で寝ていました。 *Kinō wa **kaze de** nete imashita.*
I was in bed with a cold yesterday.

■ **no aru** のある having a characteristic of

彼はユーモアのある人です。 *Kare wa **yūmoa no aru** hito desu.*
He is a man with a sense of humor.

■ **no tsuita** の付いた attached, possessing

赤いラベルの付いた商品がバーゲン品です。
***Akai raberu no tsuita** shōhin ga bāgen hin desu.*
The items with red labels are bargains.

■ **de** で material for covering

富士山は冬の間雪で覆われている。
*Fuji san wa fuyu no aida **yuki de** ōwarete iru.*
Mt. Fuji is covered with snow during winter.

35. Within

■ **nai de/ni** or **no naka de/ni** 内 で/に or の中 で/に inside

政府内に反対意見がある。 ***Seifunai ni** hantai iken ga aru.*
There are contrary opinions within the government.

心の中であなたの無事を祈っています。
***Kokoro no naka de** anata no buji o inotteimasu.*
I pray for your safety within myself.

■ **inai de/ni** 以内 で/に not beyond the limits of, less than a particular
distance or time

最近収入以内で暮らせないです。 *Saikin **shūnyū inai de** kurasenai desu.*
Recently I cannot live within my income.

注文の本は24時間以内に発送される。
*Chūmon no hon wa **ni jū yo jikan inai ni** hassō sareru.*
Books on order are sent out within 24 hours.

大学から5キロ以内にアパートを探したいです。
*Daigaku kara **gokiro inai ni** apāto o sagashitai desu.*
I want to find an apartment within a five-kilometer distance.

36. Without

- ■ *nai de* or *zu ni* ないで or ずに not doing something specified, without doing something

朝ごはんを食べないでクラスに行きました。
*Asagohan o **tabenai de** kurasu ni ikimashita.*
I went to the class without eating breakfast.

私は音楽を聴かないで勉強すると逆に効率が悪い。
*Watashi wa **ongaku o kikanai de** benkyō suru to gyakuni kōritsu ga warui.*
Studying without listening to music is less efficient for me.

私たちはゆっくり観光ができずに移動しました。
*Watashitachi wa **yukkuri kankō ga dekizu ni** idō shimashita.*
We moved without having enough time to do sightseeing.

- ■ *nashi de* なしで not having or including something

コーヒーは砂糖なしで飲まれますか。
*Kōhī wa **satō nashi de** nomaremasu ka.*
Will you drink coffee without sugar?

あなたなしでは生きられないです。
*Anata **nashi de** wa ikirarenai desu.*
I can't live without you.

PREDICATIVE PHRASES

Sentences often end in predicative phrases such as *sō da* 'they say that . . . ,' *hazu da* 'it is supposed to be the case that . . . ,' and *kamoshirenai* 'it is possible that . . . ,' to show the speaker's sureness, attitude, or implications. The verbs and adjectives that precede them are usually in the dictionary, *nai-*, or *ta-* form. Nouns and adjectival nouns that precede them are followed by the conjugated form of *da* (*da, ja nai, datta, ja nakatta,* etc.), *na, no,* or nothing.

明日は林さんの誕生日だそうだ。
*Ashita wa Hayashi san no tanjōbi **da sō da.***
I heard (*or* hear) that tomorrow is Mr. Hayashi's birthday.

失業率が下がったそうだ。
*Shitsugyōritsu ga sagatta **sō da.***
They say that the unemployment rate has decreased.

東京の地下鉄は便利なはずだ。
*Tōkyō no chikatetsu wa benri **na hazu da.***
Subways in Tokyo are supposed to be convenient.

田中さんは明日ここに来るはずです。
*Tanaka san wa ashita koko ni kuru **hazu desu.***
Mr. Tanaka is supposed to come here tomorrow.

胃がんかもしれません。
Igan kamoshiremasen.
I may have stomach cancer.

石田さんは来ないかもしれない。
*Ishida san wa ko**nai kamoshirenai.***
Mr. Ishida might not come.

→ See also *beki da, hazu da, kamoshirenai, rashii <conjecture>, sō da <hearsay>,* and *yō da <conjecture>.*

QUESTIONS

Question sentences can be easily formed from statement sentences without changing the word order in Japanese.

1. Yes-no questions

To form a simple yes-no question, you can just place the question particle *ka* at the end of a statement sentence. (→ See *ka*.)

> 明日はテストがあります。
> *Ashita wa tesuto ga arimasu.*
> **There is a test tomorrow.**

> 明日はテストがありますか。
> *Ashita wa tesuto ga arimasu ka.*
> **Is there a test tomorrow?**

The answers to questions often drop understood nouns. When the answer is negative, *chigaimasu* 'to differ' is more commonly used than *sō dewa arimasen* 'it is not so.'

> 「明日はテストがありますか。」「はい、あります。」
> *"Ashita wa tesuto ga arimasu ka." "Hai, arimasu."* (Repeat the verb.)
> **"Is there a test tomorrow?" "Yes, there is."**

> 「明日は休みですか。」「はい、そうです。／いえ、違います。」
> *"Ashita wa yasumi desu ka." "Hai soo desu./ Ie, chigaimasu."*
> **"Is tomorrow your day off?" "Yes, it is./ No, it isn't."**

2. Content questions

To ask a content question, put an interrogative word at the place where you expect an answer to be, and add the question particle *ka*. (→ See Interrogatives.)

> 「明日は誰が来ますか。」「明日はビルさんが来ます。」
> *"Ashita wa **dare** ga kimasu ka." "Ashita wa Biru san ga kimasu."*
> **"Who will come here tomorrow?" "Bill will come here tomorrow."**

> 昨日はレストランで何を食べましたか。
> *Kinō wa resutoran de **nani** o tabemashita ka.*
> **What did you eat at the restaurant yesterday?**

いつもどこで勉強していますか。
*Itsumo **doko** de benkyō shite imasu **ka**.*
Where do you always study?

3. Embedded questions

Verbs such as *shiru* 'to know' and *kiku* 'to ask' can select a question sentence as their complement clause to complete their meanings. (→ See Quotation clauses under Clauses.) If a complement clause is a yes-no question, the particle *ka, ka dōka, or no ka* can be used. If it is a content question, *ka* or *no ka* can be used.

明日テストがあるか(どうか)知っていますか。
***Ashita tesuto ga aru ka (dō ka)** shitte imasu ka?*
Do you know whether (or not) we have a test tomorrow?

田中さんはいつテストがある(の)か知っていますか。
*Tanaka san wa **itsu tesuto ga aru (no) ka** shitte imasu ka.*
Mr. Tanaka, do you know when we'll have a test?

何をすればいい(の)か教えてください。
***Nani o sure ba ii (no) ka** oshiete kudasai.*
Please let me know what I should do.

REQUESTS

There are many different ways to form a request sentence. Some of them are listed below, starting with simple request sentences followed by more elaborate request sentences.

- Verbs in the *te*-form + *kudasai*

  This is a polite form, but it is actually perceived as a command. Thus, it is not appropriate to use this form to one's superior. However, it can be appropriately used for giving permission or requesting something that the speaker cannot do.

  暑いので，窓を開けて下さい。
  Atsui node, mado o akete kudasai. (command)
  It's hot. Please open the window.

  「入ってもいいですか。」「はい，どうぞ。入って下さい。」
  "Haittemo ii desu ka." "Hai, dōso. Haitte kudasai." (giving permission)
  "Can I come in?" "Yes, please come in."

  すみませんが，ちょっとこれを教えて下さい。
  Sumimasen ga, chotto kore o oshiete kudasai. (requesting what the speaker cannot do.)
  Excuse me, please teach it to me for a while.

- Verbs in the *te*-form + *kuremasu ka*

  (あなたは)(私を)手伝ってくれますか。
  (Anata wa)(watashi o) Tetsudatte kuremasu ka.
  Literal meaning: Do you give me a favor by your doing it?
  Actual meaning: Will you help me?

- Verbs in the *te*-form + *moraemasu ka*

  Moraeru is the potential form of *morau*.

  (私は)(あなたに)手伝ってもらえますか。
  (Watashi wa)(anata ni) Tetsudatte moraemasu ka.
  Literal meaning: Can I get a favor from you by your doing it?
  Actual meaning: Can I get you to help me?

- Verbs in the *te*-form + *kudasaimasu ka*

  Kudasaru is the respectful counterpart of *kureru*. Its *masu*-form is not *kudasarimasu* but *kudasaimasu*.

（あなたは）（私を）手伝ってくださいますか。
*(Anata wa)(watashi o) Tetsudatte **kudasaimasu ka**.*
Literal meaning: Will you give me a favor by your doing it?
Actual meaning: Will you please help me?

■ Verbs in the *te*-form + *kudasaimasen ka*

（あなたは）（私を）手伝ってくださいませんか。
*(Anata wa)(watashi o) Tetsudatte **kudasaimasen ka**.*
Won't you please help me?

■ Verbs in the *te*-form + *itadakemasu ka*

Itadakeru is the potential form of the humble verb *itadaku,* which is the humble version of *morau.*

（私は）（あなたに）手伝っていただけますか。
*(Watashi wa)(anata ni) Tetsudatte **itadakemasu ka**.*
Literal meaning: Could I get a favor from you by your doing it?
Actual meaning: Could I get you to help me?

■ Verbs in the *te*-form + *itadakemasen ka*

（私は）（あなたに）手伝っていただけませんか。
*(Watashi wa)(anata ni) Tetsudatte **itadakemasen ka**.*
Couldn't I get you to help me?

■ Verbs in the *te*-form + *kudasaimasen deshō ka*

（あなたは）（私を）手伝ってくださいませんでしょうか。
*(Anata wa)(watashi o) Tetsudatte **kudasaimasen deshō ka**.*
Couldn't you possibly help me?

■ Verbs in the *te*-form + *itadakemasen deshō ka*

（私は）（あなたに）手伝っていただけませんでしょうか。
*(Watashi wa)(anata ni) Tetsudatte **itadakemasen deshō ka**.*
Couldn't I possibly get you to help me?

■ *Dōka* + verbs in the *te*-form + *kudasaimasen/itadakemasen deshō ka*

The adverb *dōka* enhances the degree of elaboration and politeness.

どうか手伝ってくださいませんでしょうか。
*Dōka tetsudatte **kudasaimasen deshō ka**.*
Couldn't you possibly help me?

どうか手伝っていただけませんでしょうか。
*Dōka tetsudatte **itadakemasen deshō ka**.*
Couldn't I possibly get you to help me?

VERBS

Unlike in English, Japanese verbs do not conjugate based on the person or the number of the subject and must be placed at the end of a sentence. Japanese verbs change forms based on tense, polarity (affirmative or negative), and what is following them (e.g. nouns, predicative phrases, and particles). The non-past affirmative plain form is called the dictionary form because it is the form used for listing verbs in dictionaries. Some examples of Japanese verbs in the dictionary form are *taberu* 'to eat,' *miru* 'to watch,' *nomu* 'to drink,' and *oyogu* 'to swim.'

I. CONJUGATION CLASSES

All Japanese verbs are classified into two types of regular verbs (*ru*-verbs and *u*-verbs) and irregular verbs. See Appendix 5 for an extensive list of verbs.

1. *Ru*-Verbs

Ru-verbs are the verbs whose dictionary forms end in the syllable る *ru*, and their conjugated forms are created by dropping the final *ru* and adding some suffix or particle. For example, *taberu* 'to eat' is a *ru*-verb, and other forms of this verb all have *tabe*, which is *taberu* minus *ru*. The following are some examples of the forms of the verb *taberu*:

> *taberu* (dictionary form, plain affirmative non-past)
> *tabenai* (*nai*-form, plain negative non-past form)
> *tabemasu* (*masu*-form, polite affirmative non-past form)
> *tabereba* (*ba*-form, conditional form)
> *tabero, tabeyo* (command form)
> *tabeyō* (volitional form)

In fact, all *ru*-verbs end in a sequence of *iru* or *eru*, so they are also called *iru*-verbs or *eru*-verbs. *Taberu* 'eat' is an *eru*-ending *ru*-verb, and *kariru* 'borrow' is an *iru*-ending *ru*-verb. (→ See the list of *ru*-verbs (both *eru*-ending and *iru*-ending) in Appendix 5.)

2. *U*-Verbs

U-verbs are the verbs whose dictionary form ends in one of nine syllables, which are う *u*, く *ku*, ぐ *gu*, す *su*, つ *tsu*, む *mu*, ぬ *nu*, ぶ *bu*, and る *ru*, and their conjugated forms are created by dropping the final *u* and adding some suffix or particle. For example, *hanasu* 'to talk' is an *u*-verb, and other forms of this verb all have *hanas,* which is *hanasu* minus *u.* The following are some examples of the forms of the verb *hanasu.*

> *hanasu* (dictionary form, plain affirmative non-past)
>
> *hanasanai* (*nai*-form, plain negative non-past form)
>
> *hanashimasu* (*masu*-form, polite affirmative non-past form)
>
> *hanaseba* (*ba*-form, conditional form)
>
> *hanase* (command form)
>
> *hanasō* (volitional form)

As some *u*-verbs can end in *iru* or *eru,* just like *ru*-verbs, one cannot tell whether a verb is a *ru*-verb or an *u*-verb just by looking at its dictionary form if it ends in an *iru* or *eru* sequence. For example, *kaeru* 'to change' is a *ru*-verb, but *kaeru* 'to return' is an *u*-verb. Thus, you must remember whether a verb is a *ru*-verb or an *u*-verb if a verb ends in *iru* or *eru.* By contrast, if a verb doesn't end in *iru* or *eru,* it is always an *u*-verb, unless it is an irregular verb. It is helpful to know that most verbs that end in *iru* or *eru* are *ru*-verbs, and only a handful of them are *u*-verbs.

- *U*-verbs that end with *iru*

hairu	入る	to enter
hashiru	走る	to run
kiru	切る	to cut (*kiru* (着る) 'to wear' is a *ru*-verb)
shiru	知る	to know
iru	要る	to need (*iru* (いる) 'to be' is a *ru*-verb)

- *U*-verbs that end with *eru*

keru	蹴る	to kick
shaberu	しゃべる	to speak, chat
suberu	滑る	to slip, slide
kaeru	帰る	to go back, come back (*kaeru* (変える) 'to change' is a *ru*-verb)
neru	練る	to elaborate, knead (*neru* (寝る) 'to go to bed' is a *ru*-verb)

3. Irregular Verbs

There are only two irregular verbs in Japanese, which are:

> *kuru* 来る to come
>
> *suru* する to do, perform various actions, be in some state

The following are some examples of the forms of the verb *kuru*.

kuru (dictionary form, plain affirmative non-past form)
konai (*nai*-form, plain negative non-past form)
kimasu (*masu*-form, polite affirmative non-past form)
kureba (*ba*-form, conditional form)
koi (command form)
koyō (volitional form)

The following are some examples of the forms of the verb *suru*.

suru (dictionary form, plain affirmative non-past form)
shinai (*nai*-form, plain negative non-past form)
shimasu (*masu*-form, polite affirmative non-past form)
sureba (*ba*-form, conditional form)
shiro, seyo (command form)
shiyō (volitional form)

There are several slightly irregular verbs (e.g. *irassharu* 'to exist, be, go, come,' *kudasaru* 'to give,' *gozaru* 'to exist,' *nasaru* 'to do,' *ossharu* 'to say,' and *aru* 'to exist, be,') but they are basically regular verbs with only minor sound changes and do not count as irregular verbs.

II. VERB FORMS

1. Dictionary form

The dictionary form is in fact the plain non-past affirmative form, but it is commonly called 'dictionary form' because it is the form used for listing verbs in most dictionaries in Japan. The dictionary forms of verbs always end with the vowel *u,* as in:

Ru-verbs	*U*-verbs	Irregular verbs
taberu 'eat'	*kaku* 'write'	*suru* 'do'
miru 'see'	*oyogu* 'swim'	*kuru* 'come'
	kau 'buy'	
	toru 'take'	
	katsu 'win'	
	hanasu 'speak'	
	yomu 'read'	
	shinu 'die'	
	tobu 'fly'	

Dictionary forms can end sentences in informal conversations, followed by some sentence-ending particle or uttered with a certain contextually appropriate intonation. However, this form is also needed before a certain predicative phrases, nouns, or particles even in polite/formal conversational contexts. (→ See also *ru* for example sentences with the dictionary form.)

2. *Nai*-form

The *nai*-form is the plain non-past negative form, and thus it is the negative counterpart of the dictionary form. The *nai*-form of verbs is created by replacing the final *ru* of a *ru*-verb and the final *u* of an *u*-verb with *nai* and *anai*, respectively. However, if the verb is an *u*-verb that ends in a sequence of two vowels, as in *kau* 'to buy' and *iu* 'to say,' the final *u* is replaced by *w*, and then *anai* is added. The *nai*-form of the irregular verbs *suru* and *kuru* are *shinai* and *konai*, respectively. Also note that *ts* in a verb that ends in *tsu* (e.g. *katsu*) becomes *t* after replacing the final *u* with *anai* as shown below.

Dictionary Form	Nai-Form
Ru-verbs	
taberu 'eat'	*tabenai*
miru 'see'	*minai*
U-verbs	
kaku 'write'	*kakanai*
oyogu 'swim'	*oyoganai*
kau 'buy'	*kawanai*
toru 'take'	*toranai*
katsu 'win'	*katanai*
hanasu 'speak'	*hanasanai*
yomu 'read'	*yomanai*
shinu 'die'	*shinanai*
tobu 'fly'	*tobanai*
Irregular verbs	
suru 'do'	*shinai*
kuru 'come'	*konai*

Nai is a verb suffix, but it bears a superficial resemblance to an adjective (*i*-adjective), and thus the *nai*-form conjugates just like an adjective. For example, the *ta*-form, *te*-form, *ba*-form, and *tara*-form of *nai*-form are -*nakatta*, -*nakute* (or -*nai de*), -*nakereba*, and -*nakattara*, respectively.

Like the dictionary forms, the *nai*-form can end sentences in informal conversation, followed by some sentence-ending particle or uttered with a certain contextually appropriate intonation, but it is also needed before a certain predicative phrases, nouns, or particles even in polite/formal conversational contexts. (→ See *nai* for example sentences with *nai*-forms.)

3. Combining form (Pre-*masu* form)

The combining form of a verb is commonly known by its nickname, pre-*masu* form, because it is the form found before the polite suffix *masu*. It is actually the shortest pronounceable verb form that can be combined with numerous kinds of items to form a new word or phrase. It is also called the conjunctive form because we can list verbs in this form in a sentence. The combining form can be created by dropping the final *ru* of a *ru*-verb and by replacing the final *u* of an *u*-verb with *i*. The combining form of the irregular verbs *suru* and *kuru* are *shi* and *ki*, respectively. Also note that *ts* in a verb that ends in *tsu* and *s* in a verb that ends in *su* become *ch* and *sh* after replacing the final *u* with *i*, as shown in the following table.

Dictionary Form	Combining Form
Ru-verbs	
taberu 'eat'	*tabe*
miru 'see'	*mi*
U-verbs	
kaku 'write'	*kaki*
oyogu 'swim'	*oyogi*
kau 'buy'	*kai*
toru 'take'	*tori*
katsu 'win'	*kachi*
hanasu 'speak'	*hanashi*
yomu 'read'	*yomi*
shinu 'die'	*shini*
tobu 'fly'	*tobi*
Irregular verbs	
suru 'do'	*shi*
kuru 'come'	*ki*

The combining form can be used to list verbs in a sentence, just like the *te*-form. (→ See Conjoining.) The combining form can function as a noun (e.g. *hajime* 'the beginning') or a part of a noun (e.g. *tabemono* 'food') in some cases. (→ See Nouns created from verbs under Nouns, and see Appendix 6.) It can also combine with numerous suffixes (e.g. *masu* and *tai*), particles (e.g. *ni*), auxiliary verbs (e.g. *sugiru*), and auxiliary adjectives (e.g. *nikui*). (→ See also *masu*, *tai*, *ni*, *sugiru*, and *nikui*.)

4. *Masu*-form

The verb that ends the main sentence is usually in the *masu*-form in a neutral/polite speech context. For this reason, *masu* is often considered a polite suffix. *Masu* follows verbs in the combining form. (→ See Combining form under Verbs.) *Masu* is in fact in the polite non-past affirmative form of verbs, expressing future or habitual actions, to mean 'will do' or 'do/does.' The variations of *masu* include the following:

masen	Polite non-past negative: will not do, do not do
mashita	Polite past/perfect affirmative: did, have done, used to do
masen deshita	Polite past/perfect negative: did not do, have not done
mashō	Polite volitional: will do, let me/us do

→ See *masu* for example sentences with *masu*-forms.

5. *Te*-form

The *te*-form is made by adding the suffix *te* to the combining form of a verb, but the *te*-form of most *u*-verbs undergoes extensive euphonic changes. First, the suffix *te* becomes *de* for the verbs whose dictionary forms end in *mu, nu, bu,* or *gu*. Second, the syllable *ki* or *gi* at the end of the combining form becomes a simple vowel *i* for the verbs whose dictionary forms end in *ku* or *gu*. Third, the syllable *mi, ni,* or *bi* at the end of the combining form becomes a syllabic nasal *n* for the verbs whose dictionary forms end in *mu, nu,* or *bu*. Fourth, the syllable *ri* or *chi* at the end of the combining form as well as the syllable *i* not preceded by a consonant but occurring at the end of the combining form must be deleted and its position must be filled by doubling the consonant *t* of the suffix *te* for the *u*-verbs whose dictionary form ends in *ru, tsu,* or *u* not preceded by a consonant. There is one exception: the *te*-form of the verb *iku* 'to go' is *itte*, rather than *iite*. These are illustrated in the following table. The negative *te*-form of a verb can be created by replacing *nai* in its *nai*-form with *nakute* (e.g. *tabenakute*) or by adding *de* to its *nai*-form (e.g. *tabenai de*). Which negative *te*-form should be used depends on the context. (→ See *nai de* and *nakute*.)

Dictionary Form	Combining Form	Te-Form (aff.)	Te-Form (neg.) . . . nakute	Te-Form (neg.) . . . nai de
Ru-verbs				
taberu 'eat'	tabe	tabete	tabenakute	tobanai de
miru 'see'	mi	mite	minakute	minai de
U-verbs				
kaku 'write'	kaki	kaite	kakanakute	kakanai de
iku 'go'	iki	itte	ikanakute	ikanai de
oyogu 'swim'	oyogi	oyoide	oyoganakute	oyoganai de
kau 'buy'	kai	katte	kawanakute	kawanai de
toru 'take'	tori	totte	toranakute	toranai de
katsu 'win'	kachi	katte	katanakute	katanai de
hanasu 'speak'	hanashi	hanashite	hanasanakute	hanasanai de
yomu 'read'	yomi	yonde	yomanakute	yomanai de
shinu 'die'	shini	shinde	shinanakute	shinanai de
tobu 'fly'	tobi	tonde	tobanakute	tobanai de
Irregular verbs				
suru 'do'	shi	shite	shinakute	shinai de
kuru 'come'	ki	kite	konakute	konai de

The verbs in the *te*-form can be used to list verbs in a sentence in order to specify actions in succession, a reason or cause, an action simultaneous with the main action, and a contrastive action. They can also be followed by auxiliary verbs (e.g. *oku*), auxiliary adjectives (e.g. *hoshii*), and particles (e.g. *wa* and *bakari*). (→ See *te* for example sentences with *te*-forms.)

6. *Ta*-form

The *ta*-form is actually the plain past/perfect affirmative form. The *ta*-form of verbs can be easily created by replacing the final vowel *e* in the *te*-form with the vowel *a*. (→ See *te*-form under Verbs.) Its negative counterpart can be easily made by replacing *nai* at the end of their *nai*-form with *nakatta*.

Dictionary Form	Te-Form	Ta-Form (aff.)	Ta-Form (neg.)
Ru-verbs			
taberu 'eat'	tabete	tabeta	tabenakatta
miru 'see'	mite	mita	minakatta

Dictionary Form	*Te*-Form	*Ta*-Form (aff.)	*Ta*-Form (neg.)
U-verbs			
kaku 'write'	*kaite*	*kaita*	*kakanakatta*
iku 'go'	*itte*	*itta*	*ikanakatta*
oyogu 'swim'	*oyoide*	*oyoida*	*oyoganakatta*
kau 'buy'	*katte*	*katta*	*kawanakatta*
toru 'take'	*totte*	*totta*	*toranakatta*
katsu 'win'	*katte*	*katta*	*katanakatta*
hanasu 'speak'	*hanashite*	*hanashita*	*hanasanakatta*
yomu 'read'	*yonde*	*yonda*	*yomanakatta*
shinu 'die'	*shinde*	*shinda*	*shinanakatta*
tobu 'fly'	*tonde*	*tonda*	*tobanakatta*
Irregular verbs			
suru 'do'	*shite*	*shita*	*shinakatta*
kuru 'come'	*kite*	*kita*	*konakatta*

The *ta*-form of verbs expresses past actions or events, completion of an action or movement, a lasting state as the result of an action or movement, and experiences at some undefined time. The *ta*-form can end sentences in informal conversations, followed by some sentence-ending particle or uttered with a certain contextually appropriate intonation. However, this form is also needed before a certain predicative phrases, nouns, or particles even in polite/formal conversational contexts. (→ See *ta* for example sentences with *ta*-forms.)

7. *Ba*-form

The *ba*-form of a verb can be created by replacing the final *ru* of a *ru*-verb and the final *u* of an *u*-verb with *reba* and *eba*, respectively. The *ba*-form of the irregular verbs *suru* and *kuru* are *sureba* and *kureba*, respectively. The negative *ba*-form can be created by replacing *nai* at the end of their *nai*-form with *nakereba*.

Dictionary Form	*Ba*-Form (aff.)	*Ba*-Form (neg.)
Ru-verbs		
taberu 'eat'	*tabereba*	*tabenakereba*
miru 'see'	*mireba*	*minakereba*

Dictionary Form	*Ba*-Form (aff.)	*Ba*-Form (neg.)
U-verbs		
kaku 'write'	kakeba	kakanakereba
oyogu 'swim'	oyogeba	oyoganakereba
kau 'buy'	kaeba	kawanakereba
toru 'take'	toreba	toranakereba
katsu 'win'	kateba	katanakereba
hanasu 'speak'	hanaseba	hanasanakereba
yomu 'read'	yomeba	yomanakereba
shinu 'die'	shineba	shinanakereba
tobu 'fly'	tobeba	tobanakereba
Irregular verbs		
suru 'do'	sureba	shinakereba
kuru 'come'	kureba	konakereba

The *ba*-form can provide a variety of conditional clauses, just like the *tara*-form, but the *tara*-form is more frequently used in conversation. In addition, some commands, requests, and suggestions that are possible with *tara*-forms are not always compatible with *ba*-forms. (→ See *ba* and Conditionals for example sentences with *ba*-forms.)

8. *Tara*-form

The *tara*-form of verbs can be easily created by adding *ra* to their *ta*-form, regardless of whether it is affirmative or negative. In fact, the consonant *t* in *tara* includes the meaning of completion. (→ See *Ta*-form under Verbs.)

Dictionary Form	*Tara*-Form (aff.)	*Tara*-Form (neg.)
Ru-verbs		
taberu 'eat'	tabetara	tabenakattara
miru 'see'	mitara	minakattara
U-verbs		
kaku 'write'	kaitara	kakanakattara
iku 'go'	ittara	ikanakattara
oyogu 'swim'	oyoidara	oyoganakattara
kau 'buy'	kattara	kawanakattara

Dictionary Form	*Tara*-Form (aff.)	*Tara*-Form (neg.)
toru 'take'	*tottara*	*toranakattara*
katsu 'win'	*kattara*	*katanakattara*
hanasu 'speak'	*hanashitara*	*hanasanakattara*
yomu 'read'	*yondara*	*yomanakattara*
shinu 'die'	*shindara*	*shinanakattara*
tobu 'fly'	*tondara*	*tobanakattara*
Irregular verbs		
suru 'do'	*shitara*	*shinakattara*
kuru 'come'	*kitara*	*konakattara*

The *tara*-form is used to create a conditional clause that means 'if,' 'when,' or 'after.' (→ See *tara* and Conditionals for example sentences with verbs in the *tara*-form.)

9. Potential form

The potential form of a verb can be created by replacing the final *ru* of a *ru*-verb and the final *u* of an *u*-verb with *rareru* and *eru*, respectively. The potential substitute of the verb *suru* 'to do' is the verb *dekiru* and the potential form of *kuru* 'to come' is *korareru* or *koreru*. Note that a growing number of Japanese speakers are replacing the final *ru* of *ru*-verbs with *reru* rather than with *rareru*. The potential form of verbs can conjugate like *ru*-verbs.

Dictionary Form	Potential Form	Potential Form with *masu*
***Ru*-verbs**		
taberu 'eat'	*tabe(ra)reru*	*tabe(ra)remasu*
miru 'see'	*mi(ra)reru*	*mi(ra)remasu*
***U*-verbs**		
kaku 'write'	*kakeru*	*kakemasu*
oyogu 'swim'	*oyogeru*	*oyogemasu*
kau 'buy'	*kaeru*	*kaemasu*
toru 'take'	*toreru*	*toremasu*
katsu 'win'	*kateru*	*katemasu*
hanasu 'speak'	*hanaseru*	*hanasemasu*
yomu 'read'	*yomeru*	*yomemasu*

Dictionary Form	Potential Form	Potential Form with *masu*
shinu 'die'	*shineru*	*shinemasu*
tobu 'fly'	*toberu*	*tobemasu*
Irregular verbs		
suru 'do'	*dekiru*	*dekimasu*
kuru 'come'	*ko(ra)reru*	*ko(ra)remasu*

Verbs in the potential form express one's potential and ability, meaning 'be able to do. . . .' The understood direct objects of verbs in the potential form or potential verbs (e.g. *wakaru*) are usually marked by *ga* rather than by *o*. (→ See *rareru* for example sentences with verbs in the potential form, and see Spontaneous-potential verbs under Verbs for examples.)

10. Passive form

The passive form of verbs is created by replacing the final *ru* of a *ru*-verb and the final *u* of an *u*-verb with *rareru* and *areru*, respectively. However, if the verb is an *u*-verb that ends in a sequence of two vowels, as in *kau* 'to buy' and *iu* 'to say,' the final *u* is replaced by *w*, and then *areru* is added. The passive form of the irregular verbs *suru* and *kuru* are *sareru* and *korareru*, respectively. Also note that *ts* in a verb that ends in *tsu* (e.g. *katsu*) becomes *t* after replacing the final *u* with *areru* as shown below. The passive form of verbs can conjugate like *ru*-verbs. Note that the passive form and the potential form of *ru*-verbs and the irregular verb *kuru* 'to come' are exactly the same. (→ See Potential form under Verbs.)

Dictionary Form	Passive Form	Passive Form with *masu*
Ru-verbs		
taberu 'eat'	*taberareru*	*taberaremasu*
miru 'see'	*mirareru*	*miraremasu*
U-verbs		
kaku 'write'	*kakareru*	*kakaremasu*
sawagu 'make a noise'	*sawagareru*	*sawagaremasu*
kau 'buy'	*kawareru*	*kawaremasu*
toru 'take'	*torareru*	*toraremasu*
katsu 'win'	*katareru*	*kataremasu*
hanasu 'speak'	*hanasareru*	*hanasaremasu*
yomu 'read'	*yomareru*	*yomaremasu*

Dictionary Form	Passive Form	Passive Form with *masu*
shinu 'die'	*shinareru*	*shinaremasu*
hakobu 'carry'	*hakobareru*	*hakobaremasu*
Irregular verbs		
suru 'do'	*sareru*	*saremasu*
kuru 'come'	*korareru*	*koraremasu*

Not only transitive verbs but also intransitive verbs such as *kuru* 'to come' can be in the passive form (*korareru*), because they can be used in adversative passive sentences. (→ See *rareru* for example sentences with verbs in the passive form.)

11. Respectful form

One way to create a verb in the respectful form is to add *rareru* or *areru*, exactly in the same way as in the passive form. (→ See Passive form under Verbs.) Thus, the respectful form with *(r)areru* is exactly the same as the passive form. In addition, the potential form of *ru*-verbs and the irregular verb *kuru* 'to come' are also exactly the same as their respectful form with *rareru*. Thus, the interpretation of some verbs with *rareru* depends on the context. (→ See *rareru*.) Verbs in the respectful form with *rareru* can be used to describe the action of the person to whom a respect is due. (→ See Honorifics for example sentences with verbs in the respectful form.)

12. Command form

The command form of a verb can be created by replacing the final *ru* of a *ru*-verb and the final *u* of an *u*-verb with *ro* (or *yo*) and *e*, respectively. The command form of *suru* 'to do' is *shiro* or *seyo*, and the command form of *kuru* 'to come' is *koi*. The negative command form can be created by adding *na* at the end of the verbs in the dictionary form.

Dictionary Form	Command Form (aff.)	Command Form (neg.)
***Ru*-verbs**		
taberu 'eat'	*tabero, tabeyo*	*taberuna*
miru 'see'	*miro, miyo*	*miruna*
***U*-verbs**		
kaku 'write'	*kake*	*kakuna*
oyogu 'swim'	*oyoge*	*oyoguna*
kau 'buy'	*kae*	*kauna*

Dictionary Form	Command Form (aff.)	Command Form (neg.)
toru 'take'	*tore*	*toruna*
katsu 'win'	*kate*	*katsuna*
hanasu 'speak'	*hanase*	*hanasuna*
yomu 'read'	*yome*	*yomuna*
shinu 'die'	*shine*	*shinuna*
tobu 'fly'	*tobe*	*tobuna*
Irregular verbs		
suru 'do'	*shiro, seyo*	*suruna*
kuru 'come'	*koi*	*kuruna*

The command form expresses a strong and emphatic command if used at the end of a sentence, and thus its use in conversation is not advised unless the speaker wants to sound rough. (→ See *ro* for example sentences with verbs in the command form.)

13. Volitional form

The volitional form of a verb can be created by replacing the final *ru* of a *ru*-verb and the final *u* of an *u*-verb with *yō* and *ō*, respectively. The volitional form of *suru* 'to do' is *shiyō*, and the volitional form of *kuru* 'to come' is *koyō*. The polite version can be created by adding *mashō* at the end of the verb in the combining form.

Dictionary Form	Volitional Form	Volitional Form (polite)
Ru-verbs		
taberu 'eat'	*tabeyō*	*tabemashō*
miru 'see'	*miyō*	*mimashō*
U-verbs		
kaku 'write'	*kakō*	*kakimashō*
oyogu 'swim'	*oyogō*	*oyogimashō*
kau 'buy'	*kaō*	*kaimashō*
toru 'take'	*torō*	*torimashō*
katsu 'win'	*katō*	*kachimashō*
hanasu 'speak'	*hanasō*	*hanashimashō*
yomu 'read'	*yomō*	*yomimashō*

Dictionary Form	Volitional Form	Volitional Form (polite)
shinu 'die'	*shinō*	*shinimashō*
tobu 'fly'	*tobō*	*tobimashō*
Irregular verbs		
suru 'do'	*shiyō*	*shimashō*
kuru 'come'	*koyō*	*kimashō*

The volitional form expresses the speaker's volition. When used at the end of a sentence, it means either 'I will do . . .' or 'Let's do. . . .' (→ See *(y)ō* for additional usage of the volitional form.)

14. Causative form

The causative form of verbs is created by replacing the final *ru* of a *ru*-verb and the final *u* of an *u*-verb with *saseru* and *aseru*, respectively. However, if the verb is an *u*-verb that ends in a sequence of two vowels, as in *kau* 'to buy' and *iu* 'to say,' the final *u* is replaced by *w*, and then *aseru* is added. The causative form of the irregular verbs *suru* and *kuru* are *saseru* and *kosaseru*, respectively. Also note that *ts* in a verb that ends in *tsu* (e.g. *katsu*) becomes *t* after replacing the final *u* with *aseru* as shown below. The causative form of verbs can conjugate like *ru*-verbs. However, this causative form can occasionally be simplified by removing *er* from the causative suffix *(s)aseru*, yielding *(s)asu*. In this case, the output causative verb is an *u*-verb. These two types of causative forms are shown below.

Dictionary Form	Causative Form: *(s)aseru*	Simplified Causative Form: *(s)asu*
Ru-verbs		
taberu 'eat'	*tabesaseru*	*tabesasu*
miru 'see'	*misaseru*	*misasu*
U-verbs		
kaku 'write'	*kakaseru*	*kakasu*
oyogu 'swim'	*oyogaseru*	*oyogasu*
kau 'buy'	*kawaseru*	*kawasu*
toru 'take'	*toraseru*	*torasu*
katsu 'win'	*kataseru*	*katasu*
hanasu 'speak'	*hanasaseru*	*hanasasu*
yomu 'read'	*yomaseru*	*yomasu*

Dictionary Form	Causative Form: (s)aseru	Simplified Causative Form: (s)asu
shinu 'die'	shinaseru	shinasu
tobu 'fly'	tobaseru	tobasu
Irregular verbs		
suru 'do'	saseru	sasu
kuru 'come'	kosaseru	kosasu

The causative verbs express the idea of making or letting someone or something do some action. (→ See (s)aseru for how to use verbs in the causative form.)

15. Causative passive form

The causative passive form is the passive form of the causative form. Thus, it can be created by replacing the final ru of a ru-verb and the final u of an u-verb with saserareru and aserareru, respectively. However, if the verb is an u-verb that ends in a sequence of two vowels, as in kau 'to buy' and iu 'to say,' the final u is replaced by w, and then aserareru is added. The causative passive form of the irregular verbs suru and kuru are saserareru and kosaserareru, respectively. Also note that ts in a verb that ends in tsu (e.g. katsu) becomes t after replacing the final u with aserareru as shown below. The causative passive form of verbs can conjugate like ru-verbs. However, this form can occasionally be simplified by removing er from the causative passive suffix (s)aserareru when the verb is an u-verb other than su-ending u-verb. Even in this case, the output causative verb is a ru-verb. These two types of causative passive forms are shown below.

Dictionary Form	Causative Passive Form: (s)aserareru	Simplified Causative Passive Form: (s)asareru
Ru-verbs		
taberu 'eat'	tabesaserareru	--
miru 'see'	misaserareru	--
U-verbs		
kaku 'write'	kakaserareru	kakasareru
oyogu 'swim'	oyogaserareru	oyogasareru
kau 'buy'	kawaserareru	kawasareru
toru 'take'	toraserareru	torasareru
katsu 'win'	kataserareru	katasareru
hanasu 'speak'	hanasaserareru	--

Dictionary Form	Causative Passive Form: *(s)aserareru*	Simplified Causative Passive Form: *(s)asareru*
yomu 'read'	*yomaserareru*	*yomasareru*
shinu 'die'	*shinaserareru*	*shinasareru*
tobu 'fly'	*tobaserareru*	*tobasareru*
Irregular verbs		
suru 'do'	*saserareru*	--
kuru 'come'	*kosaserareru*	--

This form means 'to be made to do. . . .' The enforcer (the person who makes someone else do something) is marked by *ni*.

私は時々社長に日曜日も働かされます。
*Watashi wa tokidoki **shachō ni** Nichiyōbi mo **hatarakasaremasu**.*
I am made to work by the company president even on Sundays at times.

妻に高い物を買わされて困っています。
***Tsuma ni** takai mono o **kawasarete** komatte imasu.*
I am in trouble because I was forced by my wife to buy something expensive.

III. VERB TYPES

Different verbs have different semantic or syntactic properties. Verbs differ in terms of the type of items they need to have to complete their meanings and the kind of particles they need to have to mark them.

1. Transitive and intransitive verbs

Verbs that can take a direct object are called transitive verbs. Direct objects are marked by the particle *o* in Japanese. For example, the verb *tateru* 'to build' is a transitive verb because it can take a direct object that is marked by *o*, as in *Uchi o tatemashita* '(I) built a house.' By contrast, verbs that cannot take a direct object are called intransitive verbs. For example, the verb *kaeru* 'to go back' is an intransitive verb. Although this verb can be used with the same noun, *uchi* 'house,' the latter is marked by *ni* rather than by *o* when used with the verb *kaeru*, so the verb *kaeru* is not a transitive verb but an intransitive verb.

去年うちを建てました。 *Kyonen **uchi o tatemashita**.*
I built a house last year.

３時にうちに帰りました。 *Sanji ni **uchi ni kaerimashita**.*
I returned to my house at three.

The direct object of an English verb is also the direct object of an equivalent Japanese verb in most cases, but not in some cases. For example, in the following examples, the understood direct objects in English sentences are not marked by *o*.

> 「きのうポールに会いましたか。」「会いませんでした。」
> *"Kinō Pōru **ni** aimashita ka." "Aimasen deshita."*
> **"Did you meet Paul yesterday?" "I didn't meet (him)."**

> 「私はゴルフができません。」「私もできません。」
> *"Watashi wa gorufu **ga** dekimasen." "Watashi mo dekimasen."*
> **"I cannot play golf." "I can't play (it), either."**

> 電車に乗りました。 *Densha **ni** norimashita.* **I took a train.**

> 太郎は花子と結婚しました。 *Taroo wa Hanako **to** kekkon shimashita.*
> **Taro married Hanako.**

Interestingly, English has some pairs of verbs such as 'to raise' and 'to rise,' which are semantically related but syntactically different in that one is a transitive verb and the other is an intransitive verb. Japanese has numerous such pairs. (→ See the extensive list of transitive/intransitive pairs in Appendix 5.) For example, compare the following two sentences, one of which has a transitive verb, *kowasu*, and the other has an intransitive verb, *kowareru*:

> 父のカメラをこわしました。 *Chichi no kamera **o** kowashimashita.*
> **I broke my father's camera.**

> 父のカメラがこわれました。 *Chichi no kamera **ga** kowaremashita.*
> **My father's camera broke.**

2. Verbs of giving and receiving

Giving and receiving can be expressed by three verbs in Japanese: *ageru* 'to give,' *kureru* 'to give,' and *morau* 'to receive.' All of them have their honorific counterparts, which are *sashiageru*, *kudasaru*, and *itadaku*, respectively. The choice of the verbs of giving and receiving depends on who the giver and the receiver are and what the relationship between the giver and the receiver is. As a result, the giver and receiver are often omitted in conversations, because the choice of verbs can clarify who is who. These verbs are also used as auxiliary verbs following another verb in the *te*-form in the same sentence, showing who received the benefit from whose action. (→ See *ageru, sashiageru, kureru, kudasaru, morau,* and *itadaku.*)

■ Giving

The verb *kureru* means 'to give,' but the receiver of the item must be the speaker, or must be the speaker's insider when the giver is his outsider.

If the giver is the speaker's insider, the receiver must be closer to the speaker than the giver. However, in a question sentence, the second person can be the receiver.

太郎は私に本をくれました。 *Tarō wa watashi ni hon o **kuremashita**.*
Taro gave me a book.

太郎は私の弟に本をくれました。
*Tarō wa watashi no otōto ni hon o **kuremashita**.*
Taro gave my brother a book.

叔父は母にお金をくれました。 *Oji wa haha ni okane o **kuremashita**.*
My uncle gave my mother money.

「太郎はあなたに本をくれましたか。」「はい，くれました。」
*"Tarō wa anata ni hon o **kuremashita** ka." "Hai, **kuremashita**."*
"Did Taro give you a book?" "Yes, he did."

In all other contexts, *ageru* is used.

私はあなたに本をあげます。 *Watashi wa anata ni hon o **agemasu**.*
I'll give you a book.

私は太郎に本をあげます。 *Watashi wa Tarō ni hon o **agemasu**.*
I'll give Taro a book.

花子は太郎に本をあげました。 *Hanako wa Tarō ni hon o **agemashita**.*
Hanako gave Taro a book.

「あなたは太郎に本をあげましたか。」「はい，あげました。」
*"Anata wa Tarō ni hon o **agemashita** ka." "Hai, **agemashita**."*
"Did you give Taro a book?" "Yes, I did."

「花子は太郎に本をあげましたか。」「はい，あげました。」
*"Hanako wa Tarō ni hon o **agemashita** ka." "Hai, **agemashita**."*
"Did Hanako give Taro a book?" "Yes, she did."

However, in a formal context, *kureru* and *ageru* are replaced by *kudasaru* and *sashiageru*, respectively.

よかったらこれをくださいますか。 *Yokattara kore o **kudasaimasu** ka.*
Will you give me this, if you don't mind?

先生にお菓子を差し上げました。 *Sensei ni okashi o **sashiagemashita**.*
I gave my teacher some sweets.

■ Receiving

The verb *morau* means 'to receive.' Thus, the subject noun denotes the receiver. The only condition is that the receiver must be closer to the speaker than to the giver. The giver is marked by the particle *kara* or *ni* when the verb is *morau*.

私は太郎 に/から 本をもらいました。
Watashi wa Tarō ni/kara hon o **moraimashita**.
I received a book from Taro.

Morau is replaced by *itadaku* when the giver is someone to whom the speaker wishes to show respect.

よかったらこれをいただけますか。 *Yokattara kore o* **itadakemasu** *ka*.
Can I have this, if you don't mind?

3. Spontaneous-Potential verbs

Some verbs such as *mieru* 'to see,' *kikoeru* 'to hear,' *wakaru* 'to understand,' and *dekiru* 'can do' lexically include so-called "spontaneous" meaning, where any action is not done consciously or voluntarily by the speaker, but some state associated with one's potential or capability arises spontaneously without being controlled by the speaker's intention. Therefore, these verbs are not used with the potential suffix (*rareru* or *eru*), because they also include the potential meaning. (→ See *rareru* and Potential form under Verbs.) The understood direct objects of these verbs are usually marked by the particle *ga* rather than the particle *o*.

すみません。ちょっと見えません。 *Sumimasen. Chotto* **miemasen**.
Excuse me. I can't see.

足音が聞こえますか。 *Ashioto ga* **kikoemasu** *ka*.
Can you hear footsteps?

日本語が分かりますか。 *Nihongo ga* **wakarimasu** *ka*.
Do you understand Japanese?

うちの子供はまだ掛け算ができません。
Uchi no kodomo wa mada kakezan ga **dekimasen**.
Our child still cannot do multiplication.

However, there are some verbs whose objects are also marked by *ga* rather than *o*. For example, *iru* 'to need' requires the particle *ga* to mark what one needs. *Kikoeru* and *mieru* can also be considered to have a passive meaning, yielding interpretations like 'Such and such is heard or seen.'

4. *Suru*-verbs

Suru can express a variety of actions by taking various direct objects, as in *tenisu o suru* 'to play tennis.' (→ See *suru*.) In fact, a large number of Japanese verbs were formed by adding the verb *suru* to a Sino-Japanese compound noun. For example, *benkyō suru* 'to study' is a *suru*-verb. They conjugate exactly in the same way as the verb *suru*. The particle *o* may or may not intervene between the noun and *suru* depending on the noun and depending on the sentence in which it occurs. There also exist many *suru*-verbs made of foreign loans, Sino-Japanese morphemes, adverbs, and mimetic expressions.

■ Sino-Japanese compound nouns + *suru*

benkyō (study) + *suru* = *benkyō suru* 勉強する to study

renshū (practice) + *suru* = *renshū suru* 練習する to practice

ryokō (travel) + *suru* = *ryokō suru* 旅行する to travel

■ Sino-Japanese morphemes + *suru*

Unlike the *suru*-verb with a Sino-Japanese compound, the *suru*-verb with a Sino-Japanese morpheme, which consists of just one Chinese character, does not allow any particle to intervene between the morpheme and *suru*. The following are some examples of *suru*-verbs made of Sino-Japanese morphemes, where the particle that marks the noun to complete the verb meaning is specified in the parentheses:

(. . . o) aisuru (. . . を) 愛する to love

(. . . ni) bossuru (. . . に) 没する to sink under, die (in)

(. . . ni) hansuru (. . . に) 反する to be against

(. . . o) hassuru (. . . を) 発する to emit, give out, radiate

(. . . o) hossuru (. . . を) 欲する to want

(. . . ni) mensuru (. . . に) 面する to face toward

(. . . o) menzuru (. . . を) 免ずる to exempt

(. . . o) ronzuru (. . . を) 論ずる to discuss

(. . . o) sassuru (. . . を) 察する to guess

(. . . o) seisuru (. . . を) 制する to control, suppress

(. . . ni) sessuru (. . . に) 接する to come in contact (with), border

(. . . ni) taisuru (. . . に) 対する to confront, oppose

(. . . ni) tassuru (. . . に) 達する to reach

(. . . ni) tekisuru (. . . に) 適する to be suitable (for)

(. . . ni) tessuru (. . . に) 徹する to put one's heart and soul (into)

(. . . ni) zokusuru (. . . に) 属する to belong (to), be affiliated (with)

■ Foreign loans + *suru*

An increasing number of *suru* verbs with foreign loans are being created.

panku (puncture) + *suru* = *panku suru* パンクする to puncture

randebū (a rendezvous) + *suru*
  = *randebū suru* ランデブーする **to rendezvous**

sutāto (a start) + *suru* = *sutāto suru* スタートする **to start**

sutoppu (a stop) + *suru* = *sutoppu suru* ストップする **to stop**

sukurappu (scrapping) + *suru* = *sukurappu suru* スクラップする **to scrap**

- Adverbs + **suru**

  Some actions that are expressed by a single word in English might have to be expressed by a combination of an adverb and *suru*.

  gakkari (disappointedly) + *suru*
    = *gakkari suru* がっかりする **to be disappointed**

  hayaku (fast) + *suru* = *hayaku suru* 早くする **to hurry**

  yasuku (cheaply) + *suru* = *yasuku suru* 安くする **to give a discount**

  yukkuri (slowly) + *suru* = *yukkuri suru* ゆっくりする **to take a rest**

IV. VERB TENSE

Japanese verbs have two major tenses, past and non-past, but these terms might be misleading. The past tense forms, in fact, represent past and perfect. For example, *tabemashita* means 'I ate at the time' or 'I have eaten.' The non-past forms represent future and habitual actions, or actions that have not been completed in the past.

昨日はすきやきを食べました。 (past) *Kinō wa sukiyaki o tabemashita.*
I ate sukiyaki yesterday.

もうご飯を食べました。 (perfect) *Mō gohan o tabemashita.*
I've already had my meal.

私は今日はまだ食べていません。
Watashi wa kyō wa mada tabete imasen. (perfect)
I have not eaten yet today.

私は今日は食べません。 *Watashi wa kyō wa tabemasen.* (future)
I will not eat today.

毎日玄米を食べます。
Mainichi genmai o tabemasu. (habit)
I eat brown rice every day.

However, depending on the structure, the time of the event can be counter-intuitive. For example, in a temporal adverbial clause with *toki* 'at the time when . . . ,' the non-past form expresses some incomplete action either in the past or in the future, and the past form expresses some completed action either in the past or in the future. (→ See also *toki*.)

昨日出発する時に電話しました。
Kinō shuppatsu suru toki ni denwa shimashita. (a past action)
When (*or* Before) I departed, I called you yesterday.

(The speaker's phone call took place at the time when he was about to depart "in the past.")

今晩寝る時にメールします。
Konban neru toki ni mēru shimasu. (a future action)
Right before I go to bed, I will send you an e-mail tonight.

(The speaker's emailing will take place right before he will get to sleep "in the future.")

昨日出発した時に電話しました。
Kinō shuppatsu shita toki ni denwa shimashita. (a past action)
When (*or* After) I departed, I called you yesterday.

(The speaker's phone call took place right after he completed departing "in the past.")

駅に着いた時にメールします。
Eki ni tsuita toki ni mēru shimasu. (a future action)
When I have arrived at the station, I will send you an e-mail.

(The speaker's emailing will take place right after he completes his arrival at the train station "in the future.")

A similar situation can hold in a sentence with other types of adverbial clauses.

早く起きないから遅れたんだよ。
Hayaku okinai kara okureta n da yo. (a past event)
Because you didn't get up early, you were late.

そんなことを言うから、嫌われたんだよ。
Sonna koto o iu kara, kirawareta n da yo. (a past action)
Because you said such a thing, you were hated.

明日私は行かないけど，あなたは行くの。
Ashita watashi wa ikanai kedo, anata wa iku no. (a future action)
I won't go tomorrow, but are you going?

Present continuing actions are expressed by *te imasu*, whereas future and habitual actions can be expressed by non-past tense.

私は外で食べます。 *Watashi wa soto de tabemasu.* (a future action)
I will eat out.

私はまだ食べています。
Watashi wa mada tabete imasu. (a present continuing action)
I am still eating.

私はいつも日本酒を飲みます。
Watashi wa itsumo Nihonshu o nomimasu. (a habitual action)
I usually drink Japanese sake.

The verbs that do not require progressive forms in English might need to be in the *te imasu* form in Japanese.

私は東京に住みます。
Watashi wa Tōkyō ni sumimasu. (a future action)
I will live in Tokyo. (I will move to Tokyo and live there.)

私は今東京に住んでいます。
Watashi wa ima Tōkyō ni sunde imasu. (a present state)
I live in Tokyo now.

荷物を持ちます。
Nimotsu o mochimasu. (a (near) future action)
I will carry your luggage.

私は今大きな荷物を持っています。
Watashi wa ima ōkina nimotsu o motte imasu. (a present state)
I have a big bag (piece of luggage) now.

ここに大きなビルが建ちます。
Koko ni ōkina biru ga tachimasu. (a future event)
A tall building will be built here.

家の前に大きなビルが建っています。
Ie no mae ni ōkina biru ga tatte imasu. (a present state)
A tall building stands in front of my house.

PART TWO

Dictionary of Usage

achira あちら → See *are*.

ageru あげる [AUXILIARY VERB]

to do something for the benefit of

The auxiliary verb *ageru* is used after a verb in the *te*-form, and shows that the action is performed for the benefit of someone. (→ See *ageru <verb>*.) Just like the verb *ageru*, the auxiliary verb *ageru* is replaced by *sashiageru* or *yaru*, depending on the relationship between the action performer and the person who receives the benefit of the action. (→ See *sashiageru* and *yaru*. See also *kureru* and *morau*.)

この自転車を貸してあげます。 *Kono jitensha o kashite agemasu.*
I will lend you this bicycle.

(The use of the auxiliary verb *ageru* is not appropriate when the listener is the speaker's superior.)

彼にそのことを教えてあげましたか。
Kare ni sono koto o oshiete agemashita ka.
Did you (kindly) tell it to him?

彼は彼女にネックレスを買ってあげました。
Kare wa kanojo ni nekkuresu o katte agemashita.
He bought a necklace for her.

よしこさんのお母さんにクッキーを作って差し上げました。
Yoshiko san no okāsan ni kukkī o tsukutte sashiagemashita.
I made cookies for Yoshiko's mother.

ageru あげる [VERB]

to give

The verb *ageru* means 'to give,' but the recipient is usually not the speaker or the speaker's insider when the giver is his outsider. (→ See *kureru* and *morau*.) *Ageru* is replaced by *sashiageru* when the recipient is someone to whom the speaker wishes to show respect, and by *yaru* when the recipient is the speaker's subordinate in an informal context, but the utterance may sound affectionate or rude depending on the intonation. (→ See *sashiageru* and *yaru*.)

この本をあげます。*Kono hon o agemasu.* **I will give you this book.**

母にネックレスをあげました。 *Haha ni nekkuresu o agemashita.*
I gave a necklace to my mother.

よしこさんのお母さんにクッキーを差し上げました。
Yoshiko san no okāsan ni kukkī o sashiagemashita.
I gave cookies to Yoshiko's mother.

太郎はお母さんにネックレスをあげました。

*Tarō wa okāsan ni nekkuresu o **agemashita**.*

Taro gave a necklace to his mother.

aida 間 [NOUN]

in between, between, during, from . . . through . . . , among, while

Aida is a noun that denotes the location or the time between two points (in time or location), or the time during some period. It is often used with particles to create an adverbial phrase. (→ See *chū ni, jū,* and *uchi ni.*)

1. By itself, specifying the location

   間に立ってください。 ***Aida** ni tatte kudasai.*

   Please stand in between.

2. After noun + ***to*** + noun + ***no,*** specifying the location

   郵便局は駅と学校の間にあります。

   *Yūbinkyoku wa **eki to gakkō no aida** ni arimasu.*

   The post office is between the train station and the school.

   人と人の間を歩きました。 ***Hito to hito no aida** o arukimashita.*

   I walked between people.

3. After noun + ***no,*** specifying the time

   留守の間に田中さんが訪ねてきました。

   ***Rusu no aida** ni Tanaka san ga tazunete kimashita.*

   Mr. Tanaka came to see you during your absence.

4. After noun + ***kara*** + noun + ***made no***, specifying the time

   10日から15日までの間は休みます。

   ***Tōka kara jū go nichi made no aida** wa yasumimasu.*

   I'll take a vacation from the 10th through the 15th.

5. After verbs in the ***te iru*** form, specifying the time

   本を読んでいる間に眠ってしまった。

   *Hon o **yonde iru aida** ni nemutte shimatta.*

   I fell asleep while I was reading a book.

6. After adjectives in the dictionary form, specifying the time

   若い間にもっと勉強しなさい。 ***Wakai aida** ni motto benkyō shinasai.*

   Study more while you are young.

aikawarazu あいかわらず [ADVERB]

as usual, as before, still

Aikawarazu is an adverb that expresses that the given situation, state, or habit is continuing for a long time or is almost an inherent characteristic or nature of the given person or thing.

1. Used with verbs expressing habits or repeated actions

   あいかわらずたばこを吸っています。 ***Aikawarazu*** *tabako o sutte imasu.*
   I still smoke as before.

   あいかわらずサラリーマンをしています。
   Aikawarazu *sararīman o shite imasu.*
   I still work at a company as usual.

   彼はあいかわらず口をききません。 *Kare wa **aikawarazu** kuchi o kikimasen.*
   He still does not talk at all.

2. Used with adjectives or (adjectival) nouns

   あいかわらず寒いですね。 ***Aikawarazu*** *samui desu ne.*
   The weather is still cold, isn't it?

   彼はあいかわらず元気です。 *Kare wa **aikawarazu** genki desu.*
   He is well, as before.

---

amari あまり [ADJECTIVAL NOUN]

overwhelming, excessive

Amari can function as a *no*-type adjectival noun that means 'overwhelming' or 'excessive.' When used before *da/desu*, it becomes *anmari*.

   あまりの言葉にあきれてものが言えませんでした。
   Amari *no kotoba ni akirete mono ga iemasen deshita.*
   I could not say anything because of the outrageously unkind words.

   あまりの幸せに涙が止まりません。
   Amari *no shiawase ni namida ga tomarimasen.*
   I cannot stop my tears because of my overwhelming happiness.

   別れるなんてそれはあんまりだ。 *Wakareru nante sore wa **anmari** da.*
   It is too heartless of you to leave me.

---

amari あまり [ADVERB]

(not) much, (not) many, (not) enough, (not) well, (not) very, too much

Amari can function as a degree/frequency adverb when used with a negative predicate, meaning that the degree of some property is not very great. (→ See also *mettani*, *hotondo*, and *sorehodo*.) *Amari* can also be used without a negative predicate if it occurs in a conditional clause.

1. Used with negative verbs

   私はあまり食べません。 *Watashi wa **amari tabemasen**.*
   I don't eat much.

   彼のことはあまり知りません。 *Kare no koto wa **amari shirimasen**.*
   I don't know much about him.

   今あまりお金を持っていません。 *Ima **amari** okane o **motte imasen**.*
   I don't have much money now.

2. Used with negative adjectives

   天気はあまりよくありません。 *Tenki wa **amari yoku arimasen**.*
   The weather is not very good.

   会社は家からあまり遠くありません。
   *Kaisha wa ie kara **amari tōku arimasen**.*
   The company is not very far from my house.

3. Used with adjectival nouns followed by a negative linking verb

   魚はあまり好きじゃない。 *Sakana wa **amari suki ja nai**.*
   I don't like fish very much.

   父はあまり健康じゃありません。 *Chichi wa **amari kenkō ja arimasen**.*
   My father is not very healthy.

4. Used in a conditional clause

   あまりたばこを吸うと体をこわしますよ。
   ***Amari** tabako o suu to karada o kowashimasu yo.*
   If you smoke too much, you will have health trouble.

   あまり貧乏だと愛も失せます。 ***Amari** binbō da to ai mo usemasu.*
   If we are too poor, our love will vanish.

angai 案外 [ADVERB]

unexpectedly, contrary to what the speaker expected

Angai is an adverb that shows that the degree of some property or state is not to the extent that was expected, and it is usually used when the speaker was relieved after observing some situation.

1. Modifies adjectives or adjectival nouns

   私の病気は案外軽そうです。 *Watashi no byōki wa **angai karu** sō desu.*
   My illness seems less severe than I imagined.

   案外元気そうですね。よくなりましたか。
   ***Angai genki** sō desu ne. Yoku narimashita ka.*
   You look better than I thought. Have you recovered?

2. Modifies verbs

彼は日本語が案外できますね。 *Kare wa Nihongo ga **angai dekimasu** ne.*
He speaks Japanese quite well.

an no jō 案の定 [ADVERB]

as expected

An no jō is an adverb that means 'as expected,' and is usually used when one finds an unfavorable expected situation.

1. Modifies adjectives or adjectival nouns

ホテルは案の定満室で予約できませんでした。
*Hoteru wa **an no jō** manshitsu de yoyaku dekimasen deshita.*
They had no vacancy in the hotel as I had expected, so I could not book.

2. Modifies verbs

案の定彼は事業に失敗しました。
***An no jō** kare wa jigyō ni shippai shimashita.*
Sure enough, he failed in business.

ano あの → See *are*.

arakajime あらかじめ [ADVERB]

beforehand, in advance

Arakajime is used when one makes arrangements such as reservations, investigations, and notifications for some upcoming event. It is often used with a verb in the *te*-form followed by the auxiliary verb *oku*. (→ See *oku*.)

念のためにあらかじめ連絡します。
*Nen no tame ni **arakajime** renraku shimasu.*
I will give you prior notice just in case.

あらかじめ準備しておきます。 ***Arakajime** junbi shite okimasu.*
I will have it ready beforehand.

are あれ [DEMONSTRATIVE]

that one over there, those, it

Are is a demonstrative pronoun and can refer to (non-human) items that are visible for the speaker and the listener but are placed far from them. (→ See also *kore* and *sore*.) *Are* can be directly followed by particles and the linking verb. For referring to locations, use *asoko* 'over there' instead of *are*. For referring to a person, use the demonstrative adjective *ano* with a common noun such as *hito* 'person' and *gakusei* 'student.' The polite form of *are* is *achira*, which means not only 'that one' but also 'that person' or 'that direction.' *Are* can also be used anaphorically to refer to some item that is not visible to the speaker and the listener at the time of speech but is known by both of them. If only one of them knows the item, use *sore*. (→ See *sore*.)

1. *Are/asoko/achira* (demonstrative pronouns)

   「あれは何ですか。」「あれは日本の祭りです。」
   *"**Are** wa nan desu ka." "**Are** wa Nihon no matsuri desu."*
   "What's that?" "It's a Japanese festival."

   トイレはあそこにあります。 *Toire wa **asoko** ni arimasu.*
   The restroom is over there.
   Another way of saying this: *Toire wa **asoko** desu.*

   私の車はあれです。 *Watashi no kuruma wa **are** desu.* My car is that one.

   あちらに着いたら電話を下さい。 ***Achira** ni tsuitara denwa o kudasai.*
   Please call me when you get there.

   「あちらはどなたですか。」「石川さんです。」
   *"**Achira** wa donata desu ka." "Ishikawa san desu."*
   "Who is that person?" "She is Ms. Ishikawa."

2. *Ano* (demonstrative adjective)

   銀行はあの建物の隣です。 *Ginkō wa **ano** tatemono no tonari desu.*
   The bank is next to the building over there.

   あの人はだれですか。 ***Ano** hito wa dare desu ka.* Who is that person?

3. *Are/asoko/achira/ano* used anaphorically

   「あれはおかしかったですね。」「ええ，でもおもしろかったです。」
   *"**Are** wa okashikatta desu ne." "Ē, demo omoshirokatta desu."*
   "That was funny, isn't it?" "Yeah, but it was interesting."

   「あれ頼みますよ。」「あれ？あぁ，あれですね。」
   *"**Are** tanomimasu yo." "**Are**? Aa, **are** desu ne."*
   "I ask you to do that." "That? Oh, I understand what that is."

   「あれはどうなりましたか。」「あれはうまくいきました。」
   *"**Are** wa dō narimashita ka." "**Are** wa umaku ikimashita."*
   "What has become of that matter?" "It went well."

   「森谷さんは親切ですね。」「ええ，あの人は本当にいい人ですよ。」
   *"Moritani san wa shinsetsu desu ne." "Ē, **ano** hito ha hontō ni ii hito desu yo."*
   "Mr. Moritani is kind, isn't he?" "Yes, that person is truly a nice person."

4. *Are* used in idiomatic expressions
   Are + *kore* means 'all sorts of things'; 'variously.'

   あれこれやることがあります。 **Are kore** *yaru koto ga arimasu.*
   I've got lots of things to do.

   あれこれやってみましょう。 **Are kore** *yatte mimashō.*
   Let us try it in various ways.

arimasen ありません [POLITE NEGATIVE VERB]

not exist, not

Arimasen is a polite negative form of the verb *aru* 'to exist.' (→ See *aru*.) Its plain version is *nai*, which is syntactically an adjective. (→ See *nai*.) *Arimasen* is also used for making the polite negative form of the linking verb *da/desu* and adjectives. (→ See *da*.)

1. Used as the polite negative form of the verb **aru**

   私は今あまりお金がありません。
   Watashi wa ima amari okane ga **arimasen**.
   I do not have enough money now.

   この辺に郵便局はありません。 *Kono hen ni yūbinkyoku wa* **arimasen**.
   There is no post office around here.

2. Used to form a polite negative form of **da,** following **dewa** or **ja**

   その問題はあまり重要ではありません。
   Sono mondai wa amari **jūyō dewa arimasen**.
   That problem is not very important.

   これは私のかばんじゃありません。
   Kore wa watashi no **kaban ja arimasen**.
   This is not my bag.

3. Used to form a polite negative form of adjectives, following the **ku**-form

   この機械はどこも悪くありません。
   Kono kikai wa doko mo **waruku arimasen**.
   Nothing is wrong with this machine.

   外は寒くありませんでした。 *Soto wa samuku arimasen deshita.*
   It wasn't cold outside.

arimasu あります → See **aru** [VERB].

aru ある [AUXILIARY VERB]

to have been . . . ed

The auxiliary verb *aru* follows a transitive verb in the *te*-form to express the state of something (or someone) that resulted from the action denoted by the verb. The item can be marked by *ga* or *o*. However, if marked by *o*, it implies that the action was performed by the speaker. (→ See Transitive and intransitive verbs under Verbs.) If the verb is an intransitive verb, *iru* is used instead of *aru*. (→ See *iru <auxiliary verb>* and *oku*.)

> ドアが閉めてあります。 *Doa **ga** shime**te arimasu**.*
> **The door is shut. (Somebody shut it.)**

> ドアを閉めてあります。 *Doa **o** shime**te arimasu**.*
> **The door is shut. (I shut it.)**

> お茶を入れてあります。 *Ocha **o** ire**te arimasu**.* Tea is ready. (I poured it.)

> 山田さんを呼んであります。 *Yamada san o yon**de arimasu**.*
> **I have invited Mr. Yamada.**

> ドアが閉まっています。 *Doa ga shimatte **imasu**.* The door is closed.

aru ある(或る) [PREFIX]

some, a certain

Aru can be placed before a common noun to refer to some specific item without identifying it clearly.

> 彼女はある人と結婚しました。 *Kanojo wa **aru hito** to kekkon shimashita.*
> **She got married to some man.**

> ある日あるところで出会いました。 ***Aru hi aru tokoro** de deaimashita.*
> **One day we came across at some place.**

> これはある種の免疫異常です。 *Kore wa **aru shu** no men'eki ijō desu.*
> **This is a certain kind of immune system disorder.**

aru ある [VERB]

to exist

The verb *aru* literally means 'to exist.' *Nai*, *arimasu*, and *arimasen* are its conjugated forms. (→ See *nai* and *arimasen*.) *Aru* is used to express what exists in a certain location, what one has, or where people and things are. *Aru* is used for inanimate items such as buildings, things, and plants, but can also be used for abstract items such as one's schedule (e.g. classes, jobs, and appointments) and one's experiences. For animate items, the verb *iru* is used instead of *aru*. (→ See *iru <verb>*.) In either case, the item that exists is expressed by the subject noun. The latter is marked by *ga*, but when it also serves as the topic, it is marked by *wa*.

1. For inanimate items

   居間にはステレオがあります。(expressing the existence)
   *Ima ni wa sutereo ga **arimasu**.*
   There is a stereo in the living room.

   ステレオは居間にあります。(expressing the location)
   *Sutereo wa ima ni **arimasu**.*
   The stereo is in the living room.

   銀行は駅の向こうにあります。 ***Ginkō wa** eki no mukō ni **arimasu**.*
   The bank is on the other side of the train station.

   「部屋にはシャワーがありますか。」「はい, あります。」
   *"Heya ni wa **shawā ga arimasu** ka." "Hai, **arimasu**."*
   "Does the room have a shower?" "Yes, it does."

   「部屋にテレビはありますか。」「いえ, ありません。」
   *"Heya ni **terebi wa arimasu** ka." "Ie, **arimasen**."*
   "Do you have a TV in your room?" "No, I do not."

   公園には木と花ががたくさんあります。
   *Kōen ni wa **ki to hana ga** takusan **arimasu**.*
   There are a lot of trees and flowers in the park.

   (If an inanimate item is what can move by itself and stops temporarily, *iru* is used instead of *aru*.)

   よかった！まだタクシーがいる。 *Yokatta! Mada **takushī ga iru**.*
   Lucky! A taxi is still there. (A driver must be in the taxi.)

   博覧会場にロボットがいます。お客さんを接待しています。
   *Hakurankaijō ni **robotto ga imasu**. Oyakusan o settai shite imasu.*
   A robot is at the fairgrounds. It is attending to guests.

2. One's schedule

   今日はクラスが３つあります。 *Kyō wa kurasu ga mittsu **arimasu**.*
   I have three classes today.

   来週結婚式があります。 *Raishū kekkonshiki ga **arimasu**.*
   There will be a wedding ceremony next week.

3. One's experiences following a verb in the **ta**-form + **koto** + **ga**

   東京に三回行ったことがあります。
   *Tokyo ni san kai it**ta koto ga arimasu**.*
   I've been to Tokyo three times.

→ See *koto ga aru*.

---

aruiwa あるいは(或いは) [CONJUNCTION / ADVERB]

or, in other words, alternatively, perhaps

Aruiwa introduces an alternative item or idea, as a sentence-initial conjunction or as an adverb.

1. At the beginning of a sentence

   環境を保護したい。あるいはＣＯ₂を削減したい。
   Kankyō o hogo shitai. **Aruiwa** *CO₂ o sakugen shitai.*
   We want to conserve the environment. Or we want to reduce CO₂.

2. Before nouns

   東京、あるいは大阪で会を開催するのがよい。
   Tōkyō, **aruiwa** *Ōsaka de kai o kaisai suru no ga yoi.*
   It is better to hold the meeting in Tokyo or Osaka.

   (For listing choices using nouns, the particle *ka* can be used.)

   東京か、大阪か、京都に行きたい。 *Tōkyō* **ka**, *Ōsaka* **ka**, *Kyōto ni ikitai.*
   I want to go to Tokyo, Osaka, or Kyoto.

   → See *ka*.

3. Used as an adverb

   高橋さんは今いませんが，あるいは来るかもしれません。
   Takahashi san wa ima imasen ga, **aruiwa** *kuru kamo shiremasen.*
   Mr. Takahashi is not here now, but probably he may come.

---

asoko あそこ → See *are*.

---

ato 後 [NOUN]

after, later

Ato is a noun that can be used by itself to mean 'later.' It can create an adverbial phrase just by being followed by a particle, or by being followed by a particle and following a noun and *no* or following a verb in the *ta*-form. (→ See *mae*.)

1. Used independently, followed by a particle

   後で電話しましょうか。 **Ato de** *denwa shimashō ka.*
   Shall I call you later?

   その話しは後にしてください。 *Sono hanahsi wa* **ato ni** *shite kudasai.*
   Please talk about it later.

   後からそんなことを言うのはひどい。
   Ato kara *sonna koto o iu no wa hidoi.*
   It's terrible to say such a thing afterward.

   後の祭りだね。 **Ato no** *matsuri da ne.*
   It's too late. (*Lit.,* It's the festival afterward.)

2. After nouns followed by **no**

いつも食事の後でコーヒーを飲みます。
*Itsumo **shokuji no ato** de kōhī o nomimasu.*
I usually drink coffee after meals.

3. After verbs in the **ta**-form

食べ終わった後で「ごちそうさま」と言います。
*Tabeowatta **ato** de 'Gochisōsama' to iimasu.*
We say "Gochisosama" after we finish eating.

仕事が終わった後で話したいことがあります。
*Shigoto ga owatta **ato** de hanashitai koto ga arimasu.*
There is something I want to talk to you about after I finish work.

→ See also *kara, mae,* and *toki.*

---

au 合う [AUXILIARY VERB]

each other, reciprocally

The auxiliary verb *au* can follow a verb in the combining form and show that the action is bidirectional between the two parties mentioned in the sentence.

助け合うことが大切です。 ***Tasukeau** koto ga taisetsu desu.*
It is important to help each other.

その問題について話し合えば解決できると思います。
*Sono mondai ni tsuite **hanashiaeba** kaiketsu dekiru to omoimasu.*
If we talk with each other about the problem, I think we can solve it.

---

ba ば [PARTICLE]

if, when

The particle *ba* forms a conditional clause. (→ See *Ba*-form under Adjectives, Verbs, and Linking verb *da/desu* for the details about how to create the *ba*-form.) Just like the conditional clause with *tara*, the conditional clause with *ba* expresses a generic condition, temporal condition, hypothetical condition, or counterfactual condition. Just like the *tara*-clause, the main clause can be a command, a request, or a suggestion. (→ See *tara.*) However, if this is the case, the predicate in the *ba*-clause itself must express a state rather than an action. (→ See Conditionals.)

1. Verbs in the **ba-form**

あそこに行けば山田さんに会えます。
*Asoko ni **ikeba** Yamada san ni aemasu.*
If you go over there, you can see Mr. Yamada.

もっと早く来ればよかった。 *Motto hayaku kureba yokatta.*
If I had come much earlier, it would have been better. (I should have come much earlier.)

忙しくなればなかなか会えませんね。
Isogashiku nareba nakanaka aemasen ne.
If you become busy, we won't be able to meet.

2. (Adjectival) noun + **nara** (conditional form of **da**) + **ba**

   あした雨ならば行きません。 *Ashita ame naraba ikimasen.*
   I won't go if it is rainy tomorrow.

3. Adjectives in the **ba**-form

   よろしければどうぞ食べて下さい。
   Yoroshikereba dōzo tabete kudasai.
   If it is all right (If you feel like it), please eat.

   今忙しくなければお話ししたいのですが。
   Ima isogashiku nakereba ohanashi shitai no desu ga.
   If you are not busy now, I would like to talk with you.

   あなたの助けがなければできませんでした。
   Anata no tasuke ga nakereba dekimasen deshita.
   Without your help, I couldn't have done it.

4. Informal suggestions using verbs in the **ba**-form

   Ending a suggestion with a verb in the *ba*-form with a rising intonation might sound very rude or cold.

   すれば。 *Sureba.*
   Do it as you like. (I don't care even if you do it.)

   行きたければ行けば。 *Ikitakereba ikeba.*
   You are welcome to go if you want.

ba . . . hodo ば . . . ほど [ADVERBIAL PHRASE]

the more . . . the more . . .

When a verb or an adjective in the *ba*-form is directly followed by the same verb or adjective in the dictionary form with the particle *hodo*, as in *sureba suru hodo* or *hayakereba hayai hodo*, the sentence expresses that the action or the state expressed by the predicate progresses or develops according to the action or the state expressed by the . . . *ba* . . . *hodo* phrase.

1. Used with verbs

   練習すればするほどうまくなります。
   Renshū sureba suru hodo umaku narimasu.
   The more you practice, the better you can do.

2. Used with adjectives

早ければ早いほどいい。 **Hayakereba hayai hodo** ii.
The sooner, the better.

→ See also *dake*.

bāi 場合 [NOUN]

a case, an occasion

Bāi is a noun that means 'situation,' but it must be preceded by some modifier.

1. Preceded by **konna, sonna,** or **anna**

こんな場合はどうすればいいですか。
Konna bāi wa dō sureba ii desu ka.
What should I do in this case?

そんな場合は何もしなくてもいいです。
Sonna bāi wa nani mo shinakutemo ii desu.
You do not need to do anything in such a case.

2. Preceded by (adjectival) noun + **no**

緊急の場合はこのボタンを押して下さい。
Kinkyū no bāi wa kono botan o oshite kudasai.
In case of emergency, push this button.

悪天候の場合は中止します。 **Akutenkō no bāi** wa chūshi shimasu.
If the weather is bad (In case of bad weather), we will cancel it.

3. Preceded by adjectival nouns + **na/no/datta/ja nai/ja nakatta**

修理が可能な場合(は)見積もりを連絡ください。
Shūri ga **kanō na bāi** (wa) mitsumori o renraku kudasai.
If repair is possible, tell me an estimated sum.

修理が可能じゃない場合(は)リサイクルします。
Shūri ga **kanō ja nai bāi** (wa) risaikuru shimasu.
If repair is not possible, I will recycle it.

4. Preceded by verbs in the dictionary, **ta-**, or **nai**-form

申し込む場合(は)あさってまでに書類を提出してください。
*Mōshimom***u bāi** (wa) asatte madeni shorui o teishutsu shite kudasai.
If you apply, please hand in the papers by the day after tomorrow.

ホテルに泊まらない場合(は)キャンセル料が必要です。
*Hoteru ni tomara***nai bāi** (wa) kyanseruryō ga hitsuyō desu.
If you do not stay at the hotel, a cancellation charge will be demanded.

(followed by *dewa/ja nai*, meaning "is not the time to do")

今そんなことを言っている場合ではない。
Ima sonna koto o itte iru bāi dewa nai.
Now is not the time to say such matters.

bakari ばかり [PARTICLE]

only, just, always, be ready to (do), have just (done), about

The focus particle *bakari* can express excessiveness, recent actions, or approximate amount/quantity.

I. *BAKARI* (EXCESSIVE ACTIVITIES)

Bakari can follow verbs in the *te*-form or nouns (with particles) to show excessive activities or habits. The particles *ga* and *o* are usually deleted when followed by *bakari*. However, *ga*, *o*, *wa*, etc. can be preceded by *bakari*.

1. After verbs in the ***te***-form, followed by ***iru/imasu***

    彼は遊んでばかりいる。 *Kare wa asonde bakari iru.*
    He is always playing.

2. After verbs in the dictionary form, followed by ***da/desu***

    彼はいつも食べるばかりです。 *Kare wa itsumo taberu bakari desu.*
    He is always ready to eat.

3. After nouns

    彼は勉強ばかりしている。 *Kare wa benkyō bakari shite iru.*
    He is always studying.

    肉ばかり（を）食べるのは健康によくない。
    Niku bakari (o) taberu no wa kenkō ni yokunai.
    Eating only meat is not good for your health.

4. After particles

    彼女は私にばかり文句を言います。
    Kanjojo wa watashi ni bakari monku o iimasu.
    She complains only to me.

    彼女はショッピングにばかり行きます。
    Kanjojo wa shoppingu ni bakari ikimasu.
    She always goes shopping.

II. *BAKARI* (RECENT ACTIONS)

Bakari can follow verbs in the *ta*-form, to show that the action was just performed.

今ちょうどここに着いたばかりです。
*Ima chōdo koko ni tsuita **bakari desu**.*
I've just arrived here.

結婚したばかりのカップルは幸せそうですね。
*Kekkon shita **bakari** no kappuru wa shiawase sō desu ne.*
Couples that have just gotten married look very happy, don't they?

→ See also *chōdo*.

III. *BAKARI* (APPROXIMATELY)

Bakari can follow quantity/amount phrases to mean 'approximately.'

一週間ばかり留守にします。 ***Isshūkan bakari** rusu ni shimasu.*
I'll be away about a week.

一ヶ月で二キロばかり体重が増えました。
*Ikkagetsu de **ni kiro bakari** taijū ga fuemashita.*
I gained about two kilograms in one month.

→ See also *dake*.

ban 番 [NOUN]

order, turn, watching over

The noun *ban* means the order or the act of watching.

1. After verbs in the dictionary form

   次は私がカラオケで歌う番です。
   *Tsugi wa watashi ga karaoke de utau **ban** desu.*
   Now it is my turn to sing karaoke.

2. After nouns + *no*

   診察の番を待っています。 ***Shinsatu no ban** o matte imasu.*
   I am waiting my turn for a medical examination.

3. Used with *o suru*

   あなたがいない間私が荷物の番をします。
   *Anata ga inai aida watashi ga nimotsu no **ban o shimasu**.*
   I'll watch over your baggage while you are away.

ban 番 [SUFFIX]

Number . . .

The suffix *ban* follows numbers to show the order of things or the number assigned to some items. *Ichiban* means 'the first' and is used to express a superlative comparison, meaning 'the most' or 'the best.' (→ See also *ichiban* and *mottomo*.)

「部屋の番号は何番ですか。」「501番の部屋です。」
*"Heya no bangō wa **nan ban** desu ka." "**Go maru ichi ban** no heya desu."*
"What is your room number?" "It is room 501."

彼はゴルフ界では1番です。 *Kare wa gorufu kai de wa **ichi ban** desu.*
He ranks first in the golf world.

町の中で訪れるには京都が一番おもしろいでしょう。
*Machi no naka de otozureru ni wa Kyōto ga **ichi ban** omoshiroi deshō.*
Among cities Kyoto will be the most interesting to visit.

あなたが一番好きです。 *Anata ga **ichi ban** suki desu.*
I like you the best.

beki da べきだ [PREDICATIVE PHRASE]

should, ought to (do)

The unsubstantial noun *beki* and the linking verb *da* can be placed at the end of a sentence directly following a verb in the dictionary form to mean 'it should be the case that. . . .' To mean 'it should not be the case that . . . ,' keep the verb before *beki* in the dictionary form, but change *da* into negative. *Suru beki da* 'should do' tends to become *subeki da*. The phrase with *beki* can also be placed before a noun and functions as an adjective phrase. (→ See also *nakereba ikenai/nakereba naranai*.)

1. At the end of a sentence

    一生けん命はたらくべきです。 *Isshōkenmei hataraku **beki desu**.*
    You should work hard.

    あなたはもっと勉強す(る)べきです。
    *Anata wa motto benkyō su(ru) **beki desu**.*
    You should study more.

    もっと早く来るべきでした。 *Motto hayaku kuru **beki deshita**.*
    I should have come much earlier.

    そんなものを買うべきではない。 *Sonna mono o kau **beki dewa nai**.*
    You shouldn't buy such a thing.

    飲酒運転はすべきじゃありません。 *Inshu unten wa su**beki ja arimasen**.*
    You should not drink and drive.

2. Placed before a noun

    するべきことはちゃんとしなさい。 *Suru **beki koto** wa chanto shinasiai.*
    Do properly the things that you should do.

それは避けるべきことです。 *Sore wa sakeru **beki koto** desu.*
That is what we should avoid.

それは注目す(る)べき点だ。 *Sore wa chūmoku su(ru) **beki ten** da.*
That's the point we should pay attention to.

bun 分 [NOUN]

quantity/amount, part, portion, degree

Bun is used to refer to some kind of portion of something.

1. After verbs in the dictionary form
   食べる分はあります。 *Taberu **bun** wa arimasu.* **There is enough to eat.**

2. After verbs in the **ta**-form
   すでに書いた分を見せて下さい。 *Sudeni kai**ta bun** o misete kudasai.*
   Please show me what you've already written.

   残った分は取っておきます。 *Nokot**ta bun** wa totte okimasu.*
   I'll keep the portion that is left.

3. After verbs in the **nai**-form
   要らない分は返しておいて下さい。
   *Ira**nai bun** wa kaeshite oite kudasai.*
   Please return the portion you don't need.

4. After possessive particle **no**
   これは私の分です。 *Kore was watashi **no bun** desu.* **This is my share.**

cha ちゃ(ja じゃ) [CONTRACTION]

if, when

Te wa or *de wa* (the ending of verbs and adjectives in the *te*-form plus the particle *wa*) are often contracted to *cha* and *ja*, respectively, in informal conversations.

そこへ行っちゃいけません。 *Soko e **itcha** ikemasen. (itte wa)*
You must not go there.

そんなことをされちゃ困ります。
*Sonna koto o **sarecha** komarimasu. (sarete wa)*
I'll be in trouble if you do that.

お酒はもう飲んじゃだめ！ *Osake wa mō **nonja** dame! (nonde wa)*
You are not allowed to drink sake anymore!

高くちゃ買わないわよ。 ***Takakucha** kawanai wa yo. (takakute wa)*
If expensive, I won't buy it.

嫌じゃ仕方ないよ。 *Iyaja* shikata nai yo. *(iya de wa)*
If you don't like (it), there is nothing (I can do).

→ See also *tewa ikenai / dewa ikenai.*

chau ちゃう(jau じゃう) [CONTRACTION]

be going to (do), finish (doing), (do something) completely

Te shimau and *de shimau* (the ending of verbs in the *te*-form plus the auxiliary verb *shimau*) are often contracted to *chau* and *jau*, respectively, in conversations. (→ See also *shimau*.) The entire verb phrase conjugates, as in . . . *chawanai/jawanai* (*nai*-form), *chatta/jatta* (*ta*-form), *chaimasu/jaimasu* (*masu*-form).

もう帰っちゃうんですか。 *Mo **kaetchau** n desu ka.*
Are you going to leave so soon?

今日はどんどん飲んじゃいます。 *Kyō wa dondon **nonjaimasu**.*
I'm going to drink like crazy today.

彼女に悪いことをしちゃいました。
*Kanojo ni warui koto o **shichaimashita**.*
I've done wrong to her.

chittomo ちっとも [ADVERB]

(not) at all, (not) a bit

Chittomo is used with a negative predicate, meaning '(not) at all' or '(not) even a bit.' It is used in an informal context. In polite contexts, use *zenzen* or *mattaku*. (→ See also *chotto*, *mattaku*, and *zenzen*.)

ちっともかまいません。 ***Chittomo** kamaimasen.*
I don't mind it at all.

あの映画はちっともよくなかったよ。
*Ano eiga wa **chittomo** yoku **nakatta** yo.*
That movie was not good at all.

chō 超 [PREFIX]

super-, ultra-, extremely

Chō is formally a prefix used for a Sino-Japanese compound word to mean 'super' or 'ultra.' However, young Japanese have started to use it before an adjective and an adjectival noun. (→ See also *mattaku* and *zenzen*.)

1. Used for Sino-Japanese compounds

   超高感度カメラで写すと見える。
   Chōkōkando *kamera de utsusu to mieru.*
   You can see it if you photograph it with a super-sensitive camera.

2. Used for adjectives and adjectival nouns (young people's language)

   予約がとれて超ラッキーです。 *Yoyaku ga torete* **chōrakkī** *desu.*
   It is so lucky that I could reserve it.

   来てくれて超うれしいです。 *Kite kurete* **chōureshii** *desu.*
   I am so happy that you have come.

chōdai ちょうだい(頂戴) [VERB]

receive, have (dishes)

Chōdai can be an informal version of *kudasai*, used as a verb or an auxiliary verb, but it can be used in a formal context if followed by the verb *suru* 'to do.' (→ See also *kudasai*.)

1. Used by itself

   りんごを三つちょうだい。 *Ringo o mittsu* **chōdai.**
   Give me three apples.

2. After verbs in the **te**-form

   いっしょに来てちょうだい。
   Issho ni kite **chōdai.** (intimate or feminine expression)
   Please come with me.

3. Used with **suru**

   ありがたくちょうだいします。 *Arigataku* **chōdai shimasu.**
   I will receive it with gratitude.

   これをちょうだいしてもいいですか。 *Kore o* **chōdai shitemo** *ii desu ka.*
   Can I have this?

   ご馳走をおいしくちょうだいしました。
   Gochisō o oishiku **chōdai shimashita.**
   I have enjoyed my dinner very much.

chōdo ちょうど [ADVERB]

(have) just (done), exactly, precisely

The adverb *chōdo* is used with verbs, adjectives, and number phrases meaning 'just.'

1. Used with verbs in the *ta*-form, followed by *tokoro* (or *bakari*) + *da/desu*

ちょうど仕事を終えたところです。 ***Chōdo** shigoto o oeta **tokoro desu**.*
I've just finished the work.

ちょうど今着いたばかりです。 ***Chōdo** ima tsuita **bakari desu**.*
I've just arrived.

→ See also *bakari* and *tokoro*.

2. Before number + counter

ちょうど九時に来て下さい。 ***Chōdo ku ji** ni kite kudasai.*
Please come at nine sharp.

3. Used with the adjective *ii* 'good'

この車のサイズはちょうどいい。 *Kono kuruma no saizu wa **chōdo ii**.*
The size of this car is just right.

この酒はちょうどいい燗だ。 *Kono sake wa **chōdo ii** kan da.*
The temperature of this sake is just right.

chokugo 直後 [NOUN]

time immediately after some event

Chokugo is a Sino-Japanese compound noun that literally means 'immediately after.' It creates a compound phrase followed by the particle *ni*, or a modification phrase followed by *no*.

→ See also *chokuzen* and *toki*.

1. Followed by *ni*

到着(の)直後に荷物を忘れたのに気づきました。
***Tōchaku (no) chokugo ni** nimotsu o wasureta no ni kizukimashita.*
I noticed just after my arrival that I forgot my luggage.

2. Followed by *no*

開始直後の事故で中止した。 ***Kaishi chokugo no jiko** de chūshi shita.*
It was discontinued due to the accident just after the start.

chokuzen 直前 [NOUN]

time immediately before some event

Chokuzen is a Sino-Japanese compound noun that literally means 'immediately before.' It creates a compound phrase followed by the particle *ni* or a modification phrase followed by *no*. (→ See also *chokugo* and *toki*.)

1. Followed by *ni*

   出発(の)直前に財布を忘れたのに気づきました。
   ***Shuppatsu (no) chokuzen ni** saifu o wasureta no ni kidukimashita.*
   I noticed just before my departure that I forgot my wallet.

2. Followed by *no*

   試合開始直前のベルが鳴った。
   *Shiai **kaishi chokuzen no beru** ga natta.*
   A bell rang to start the match.

---

chotto ちょっと [ADVERB]

for a while, a little, really

Chotto is an adverb that applies to actions or states. It literally means 'a little bit,' but can also be used to express hesitation, to get attention, just to make one's expression soft, or to express strong negation, depending on the contexts.

1. Meaning 'a little bit'

   ちょっと待ってください。 ***Chotto matte** kudasai.*   **Please wait a minute.**

   日本語はちょっと話せます。 *Nihongo wa **chotto hanasemasu.***
   I can speak Japanese a little.

   今回のことはちょっとこたえました。
   *Konkai no koto wa **chotto kotaemashita.***
   The latest happening really hit me hard.

   あなたの言うことがちょっと分かりません。
   *Anata no iu koto ga **chotto wakarimasen.***
   I really do not understand what you say.

   ちょっと高いですが、いいですか。 ***Chotto takai** desu ga, ii desu ka.*
   It is a little bit expensive, but is it okay?

→ See also *sukoshi*.

2. Expressing hesitation

   「ここでたばこを吸ってもいいですか。」「ちょっと...」
   *"Koko de tabako o suttemo ii desu ka?" "**Chotto** ..."*
   "Is it okay to smoke here?" "Ahh ..."

3. Getting attention

   「ちょっと。」「はい、何でしょうか。」 *"**Chotto**." "Hai, nan deshō ka."*
   "Excuse me." "Yes. What do you need?"

4. Softening expressions

   ちょっとすみません。 ***Chotto** sumimasen.*   **Umm, excuse me.**

そんなことはちょっとできません。 *Sonna koto wa **chotto** dekimasen.*
I really cannot do such a thing.

→ See also *chittomo*, *mattaku*, and *zenzen*.

chū ni 中に [ADVERBIAL PHRASE]

during, within

Chū ni directly follows a noun that denotes some period of time and means 'during . . .' or 'within. . . .' It often euphonically changes to *jū ni*, but the latter has additional functions. (→ See also *aida*, *jū* and *uchi ni*.)

夏休み中にアメリカに行くつもりです。
***Natsu yasumi chū ni** Amerika ni iku tsumori desu.*
I plan to go to America during the summer vacation.

今週中に休みをどこで過ごすか決めます。
***Konshū chū ni** yasumi o doko de sugosu ka kimemasu.*
I'll decide, within this week, where to spend the vacation.

二、三日中に完成します。 ***Ni san nichi jū ni** kansei shimasu.*
I'll complete it within a few days.

da だ [LINKING VERB]

is, are, am (to be)

Da can serve as a linking verb, like the English verb 'to be,' but has additional functions. It is used to express the identity or the state of people and things when directly following a noun, a noun plus a particle combination, an adjectival noun, or a verb plus *koto/no*. However, it can also be used to loosely show relevance in the form of . . . *wa* . . . *da*. *Desu* is the polite counterpart of *da*, but unlike *da*, *desu* can also be placed after adjectives just to make it sound polite. (→ See Linking verb *da/desu*.) *Darō* is the presuming counterpart of *da*, but unlike *da*, *darō* can directly follow adjectives and verbs. (→ See also *darō*.)

1. After (adjectival) nouns

   スポーツは苦手だ。 *Supōtsu wa **nigate da**.* I hate sports.

   レストランはとても静かだった。 *Resutoran wa totemo **shizuka datta**.*
   The restaurant was very quiet.

   私の名前は佐藤健二です。 *Watashi no namae wa **Satō Kenji desu**.*
   My name is Kenji Sato.

   昨日太郎君と花子さんが欠席でした。
   *Kinō Tarō kun to Hanako san ga **kesseki deshita**.*
   Taro and Hanako were absent yesterday.

私はその決定にとても満足です。
*Watashi wa sono kettei ni totemo **manzoku desu**.*
I am very much satisfied with the conclusion.

彼は日本人ではありません。中国人です。
*Kare wa **Nihonjin dewa arimasen**. **Chūgokujin desu**.*
He is not Japanese. He is Chinese.

→ See Adjectival nouns.

2. After adjectives (only **desu**)

彼の書いた絵はとてもすばらしいです。
*Kare no kaita e wa totemo **subarashii desu**.*
The pictures he drew are quite wonderful.

昨日の講義はとても面白かったです。
*Kinō no kōgi wa totemo **omoshirokatta desu**.*
Yesterday's lecture was very interesting.

→ See Adjectives.

3. After particles

クラスは木曜日までだ。 *Kurasu wa Mokuyōbi **made da**.*
The classes continue until Thursday.

私は日本からです。 *Watashi wa Nihon **kara desu**.*
I'm from Japan.

4. After time/location expressions

Understood underlining particles must be omitted before *da/desu* in some cases, but cannot be omitted before *da/desu* in other cases. Compare the two sentences in each example.

兄は今京都です。兄は今京都にいます。
*Ani wa ima **Kyōto desu**. Ani wa ima **Kyōto ni imasu**.*
My older brother is in Kyoto now.

トイレは三階です。トイレは三階にあります。
*Toire wa **san kai desu**. Toire wa **san kai ni arimasu**.*
The restroom is on the third floor.

会議は1時からです。会議は1時からあります。
*Kaigi wa **ichi ji kara desu**. Kaigi wa **ichi ji kara arimasu**.*
The meeting is from one on.

→ See *aru* and *iru*.

5. To provide a short answer

「何を注文しましたか。」「すきやきです。」
*"Nani o chūmon shimashita ka." "**Sukiyaki desu**."*
"What did you order?" "I ordered sukiyaki."

daga だが [CONJUNCTION]

but, however, although

Daga or its polite version *desuga* can be used as a sentence-initial conjunction or as a clause-final conjunction. *Daga* is usually used in written forms, whereas *desuga* is used in both written and spoken forms. Both of them show that the following sentence/clause is in conflict, contrast, or contradiction with the preceding sentence/clause. (→ See also *dakedo, demo, ga, keredo(mo)*, and *shikashi*.) When *daga* is used as a clause-final conjunction, the clause is followed by *no* or *n*, which is a part of an extended predicate. (→ See *no da*.)

1. At the beginning of a sentence

   戦争は終わった。だが多くの命が失われた。
   Sensō wa owatta. **Daga** *ōku no inochi ga ushinawareta.*
   The war is over. However, many people lost their lives.

   漢字をたくさん勉強しました。ですがほとんど忘れました。
   Kanji o takusan benkyō shimashita. **Desuga** *hotondo wasuremashita.*
   I learned a lot of kanji. But I forgot almost all of them.

   → See also *dakedo, demo*, and *keredo(mo)*.

2. After verbs/adjectives in the dictionary, **ta-**, or **nai**-form + **no/n**

   この商品は安いのだが品質が良くない。
   Kono shōhin wa yasui **no daga** *hinshitsu ga yokunai.*
   These goods are cheap, but the quality is not good.

   彼のうちを訪ねたのだが会えなかった。
   Kare no uchi o tazuneta **no daga** *aenakatta.*
   I dropped in at his house, but I could not see him.

   高いのだがどうしても買わなければならない。
   Takai **no daga** *dōshitemo kawanakereba naranai.*
   It's expensive, but I need to buy it at any cost.

   映画は面白くなかったのですが最後まで見ました。
   Eiga wa omoshiroku nakatta **no desuga** *saigo made mimashita.*
   Although the movie wasn't interesting, I watched it to the end.

   → See also *dakedo*.

3. After (adjectival) nouns (+ **na** + **no/n**)

   彼は学生なのだが会社を起こしている。
   Kare was **gakusei (na no) daga** *kaisha o okoshite iru.*
   He is a student but started a company.

   彼は誠実なのだが能力が足りない。
   Kare was **seijitsu (na no) daga** *nōryoky ga tarinai.*
   He is sincere but lacks ability.

日本語の勉強は必要なのですが漢字がむずかしいんです。
*Nihongo no benkyō wa **hitsuyō (na no) desuga** kanji ga muzukashii n desu.*
Studying Japanese is necessary, but kanji are difficult.

dakara だから [CONJUNCTION]

so, and so, that's why, therefore, because

Dakara or its polite counterpart, *desukara*, can be placed at the beginning of a sentence or at the end of a clause, showing that the preceding sentence/clause expresses the reason or cause for the state/event expressed by the following sentence/clause. (→ See also *kara*, Conjoining, and Clauses.)

1. At the beginning of a sentence

   「事故があったそうですね。」「ええ，だから遅れました。」
   *"Jiko ga atta sō desu ne." "Ee, **dakara** okuremashita."*
   "I hear there was an accident." "Yes, that's why I was late."

   「なぜなんですか。」「ですから何度も申しましたように…。」
   *"Naze na n desu ka." "**Desukara** nandomo mōshimashita yō ni."*
   "Why is it so?" "That's so, as I explained again and again."

   → See also *sorede*.

2. At the end of a clause, after (adjectival) nouns (+ **na** + **no/n**)

   This *na no/n* appears when the speaker implicitly emphasizes the fact and connects it to the topic as its explanation. (→ See also *no da*.) When simply mentioning the reason, *na no/n dakara* becomes just *da kara*.

   あなたは学生なんだからもっと勉強しなくてはいけません。
   *Anata wa **gakusei na n dakara** motto benkyō shinakute wa ikemasen.*
   Because you are a student, you have to study more.

   これは重要なんですから忘れないで下さい。
   *Kore wa **jūyō na n desu kara** wasurenaide kudasai.*
   Because this is important, never forget it.

3. At the end of a clause, after verbs and adjectives in the dictionary, **ta-**, or **nai**-form + **no/n**

   This *no/n* appears when the speaker explanatorily talks about some topic as in the above cases. When simply mentioning the reason, *no/n dakara* becomes just *kara*.

   あしたは早く起きるんだからもう寝なさい。
   *Ashita wa hayaku oki**ru n dakara** mō nenasai.*
   Go to bed now, because you have to get up early tomorrow.

   お父さんはもう行ったんだからあなたも早く行きなさい。
   *Otōsan wa mō it**ta n dakara** anata mo hayaku ikinasai.*
   Your father has already gone, so you should hurry and go too.

もう夜も遅いんですから仕事を終わって下さい。
*Mō yoru mo osoi **n desu kara** shigoto o owatte kudasai.*
It is very late at night, so finish your job now.

dake だけ [PARTICLE]

only, just, simply, as much as, as . . . as

The focus particle *dake* follows nouns, particles, phrases, and clauses to mean 'just.' It can form an adverbial phrase, or it can end a sentence along with a linking verb *da/desu*.

1. After nouns

   あなただけを愛しています。 ***Anata dake** o aishite imasu.*
   I love only you.

   それができるのは太郎だけです。 *Sore ga dekiru no wa **Tarō dake** desu.*
   Taro is the only one who can do it.

2. After particles

   あなたとだけ話したい。 *Anata **to dake** hanashitai.*
   I want to talk just with you (alone).

   その猫は沖縄にだけいます。 *Sono neko wa Okininawa **ni dake** imasu.*
   That cat lives only in Okinawa.

3. After number + counter

   父はお金は1万円だけ残して、すべて使ってしまった。
   *Chichi wa o-kane wa **ichiman-en dake** nokoshite, subete tsukatte shimatta.*
   My father used up all of his money, leaving just 100 yen.

   コーヒーを一杯だけ飲んで、帰りました。
   *Kōhī o **ippai dake** nonde, kaerimashita.*
   He left after having just one cup of coffee.

4. After verbs/adjectives in the dictionary form and (adjectival) nouns + *na*

   明日またできるだけ早くここに来て下さい。
   *Asu mata **dekiru dake** hayaku koko ni kite kudasai.*
   Please come here again tomorrow as soon as you can.

   ほしいだけ飲んでけっこうです。 ***Hoshii dake** nonde kekkō desu.*
   You can drink as much as you want.

   好きなだけ食べて下さい。 ***Suki na dake** tabete kudasai.*
   Please eat as much as you like.

   彼は有名なだけでたいした政治家ではありません。
   *Kare wa **yūmei na dake** de taishita seijika dewa arimasen.*
   He is merely famous, and not much of a politician.

彼は勉強ができる学生なだけです。
*Kare wa benkyō ga dekiru **gakusei na dake** desu.*
He is just a student who is academically strong.

5. After verbs and adjectives in the dictionary form, followed by **da/desu**

私はここで人を待っているだけです。
*Watashi wa kokode hito o matte **iru dake desu**.*
I am only waiting for somebody here.

これは高いだけです。あまりよくありません。
*Kore wa takai **dake desu**. Amari yoku arimasen.*
This is just expensive. It's not so good.

彼は漢字が書けないだけじゃありません。カタカナも書けないんです。
*Kare wa kanji ga kake**nai dake ja arimasen**. Katakana mo kakenai n desu.*
It is not just that he cannot write kanji. He even cannot write katakana.

→ See also *bakari*.

6. After verbs and adjectives in the **nai**-form, followed by **da/desu**

彼とはあまり話をしないだけです。嫌いじゃありません。
*Kare to wa amari hanshi o shi**nai dake desu**. Kirai ja arimasen.*
I simply don't talk with him so often. I don't mean I dislike him.

言いたくないだけです。それ以上聞かないで下さい。
*Iitaku**nai dake desu**. Sore ijō kikanaide kudasai.*
I just don't want to say it. Don't ask me anymore.

7. After verbs and adjectives in the **ta**-form, followed by **da/desu**

ここにこれを見に来ただけです。 *Koko ni kore o mi ni ki**ta dake desu**.*
I just came here to see this.

少し眠かっただけです。どうもすみません。
*Sukoshi nemukat**ta dake desu**. Dōmo sumimasen.*
I was just a little sleepy. I'm sorry.

8. Used instead of **hodo** in the pattern "*...ba...hodo*"

努力すればするだけうまくなれます。
*Doryoku **sureba suru dake** umaku naremasu.*
The harder you try, the better you will be able to do it.

→ See *hodo* and *ba*.

9. Used in the pattern "*...dake de naku...mo*"

彼は日本語だけでなく中国語も韓国語も話せます。
*Kare wa Nihongo **dake de naku** Chūgokugo **mo** Kankokugo **mo** hanasemasu.*
He can speak not only Japanese but also Chinese and Korean.

→ See also *kagiri* and *shika*.

dakedo だけど [CONJUNCTION]

but, however, though, still, nevertheless

Dakedo, or its polite counterpart *desu kedo* or *desu keredo*, is placed at the beginning of a sentence or at the end of a clause and means 'but' or 'however.'

1. At the beginning of a sentence

   あの車がとても欲しい。だけど高すぎるよ。
   Ano kuruma ga totemo hoshii. **Dakedo** *takasugiru yo.*
   I want that car very much. But it's too expensive for me.

   だけどそんなことはしなければよかった。
   Dakedo *sonna koto wa shinakereba yokatta.*
   But I wish I hadn't done such a thing.

   彼は親切です。だけどあまり好きではありません。
   Kare wa shinsetsu desu. **Dakedo** *amari suki dewa arimasen.*
   He is kind. Still, I don't like him very much.

2. At the end of a clause, after (adjectival) nouns (+ **nano/nan**)

   今日は雨だけどやっぱり出かけますか。
   Kyō wa **ame dakedo** *yappari dekakemasu ka.*
   Will you go out as arranged, though it is rainy today?

   部長はあいにく留守ですけどどういたしましょうか。
   Buchyō wa ainiku **rusu desu kedo** *dō itashimashō ka.*
   I'm sorry the chief is away, but what shall I do for you?

   犬なんだけど人間の食べ物しか食べないんです。
   Inu nan dakedo *ningen no tabemono shika tabanai n desu.*
   It is a dog, but it eats only human foods.

3. After verbs and adjectives in the dictionary, **nai-**, or **ta-** form + **no/n**

   相撲を観たいんだけどどこでチケットを買ったらいいのか分かりません。
   Sumō o mitai **n dakeko** *doko de chiketto o kattara ii no ka wakarimasen.*
   I want to see sumo wrestling, but I don't know where I can buy a ticket.

   最新の携帯電話を買ったんだけど使うのがむずかしいです。
   *Saishin no keitai denwa o kat***ta n dakedo** *tsukau no ga muzukashii desu.*
   I bought the newest mobile phone, but it is difficult to use.

   高かったんだけどどうしても欲しかったんです。
   *Takakat***ta n dakedo** *dōshitemo hoshikatta n desu.*
   It was expensive, but I really wanted it.

→ See also *daga, dakedo, demo, ga, keredo(mo),* and *shikashi.*

dare だれ [INTERROGATIVE]

who

Dare is an interrogative pronoun that means 'who.' Its respectful form is *donata* or *dochira*. Depending on the particle that follows it, *dare* means not just 'who' but also 'whom' or 'whose.' It cannot be marked by the topic particle *wa*, because an interrogative word cannot become a topic. (→ See also *wa*.) It creates an indefinite pronoun if followed by the particle *ka* (*dare-ka* 'someone'), a negative pronoun if followed by the particle *mo* used with a negative predicate (*dare-mo . . . nai* 'no one . . .'), and a free-choice pronoun if followed by *demo* (*dare-demo* 'anyone').

1. Used with *ga*

   だれが勝つと思いますか。***Dare ga** katsu to omoimasu ka.*
   Who do you think will win?

   だれがこれを壊したのか知っていますか。
   ***Dare ga** kore o kowashita no ka shitte imasu ka.*
   Do you know who broke this?

2. Used with *o, ni, to*

   だれを探しているんですか。***Dare o** sagashite iru n desu ka.*
   Who are you looking for?

   だれに相談したいのですか。***Dare ni** sōdan shitai no desu ka.*
   Who do you want to consult with?

   だれといっしょに旅行に行くんですか。
   ***Dare to** isshoni ryokō ni iku n desu ka.*
   With whom are you going on a trip?

3. Used with *no*

   あれはだれの車ですか。じゃまです。
   *Are wa **dare no** kuruma desu ka. Jama desu.*
   Whose car is that? It's in my way.

   これはだれの鞄か分かりますか。 *Kore wa **dare no** kaban ka wakarimasu ka.*
   Do you know whose bag this is?

4. Followed by linking verbs

   あそこに立っている人はどなたですか。
   *Asoko ni tatte iru hito wa **donata desu** ka.*
   Who is the person standing over there?

5. Forming indefinite pronouns

   その部屋にだれか（が）いるみたいです。
   *Sono heya ni **dareka** (ga) iru mitai desu.*
   Somebody seems to be in the room.

昨日，だれか来ましたか。 *Kinō **dareka** kimashita ka?*
Did anyone come yesterday?

→ See *ka* and Interrogatives used in indefinite pronouns under Interrogatives.

6. Forming negative pronouns

何度かけてもだれも電話に出ません。
*Nando kaketemo **daremo** denwa ni **demasen**.*
No matter how many times I call, nobody answers the phone.

→ See *mo* and Interrogatives used in indefinite pronouns under Interrogatives.

7. Forming free-choice pronouns

だれでもすぐにこのロボットを操作できます。
***Daredemo** suguni kono robotto o sōsa dekimasu.*
Anyone can easily operate this robot.

→ See *demo* and Interrogatives used in indefinite pronouns under Interrogatives.

darō だろう [LINKING VERB OF CONJECTURE]

will (be), shall (be), would (be), probably

Darō or its polite counterpart, *deshō*, can be placed at the end of a sentence and shows that the statement expressed by the sentence is "probably" true. (→ See also *mitai da, kamoshirenai, rashii, sōda <conjecture>*, and *yō da <conjecture>*.)

1. After (adjectival) nouns

あの人が私たちの学校に新しく来た先生でしょう。
*Ano hito ga watashi tachi no gakkō ni atarashiku kita **sensei deshō**.*
That person is probably the new teacher who has come to our school.

東京はあす雨のち曇りでしょう。
*Tōkyō wa asu ame nochi **kumori deshō**.*
It will be rainy and then cloudy in Tokyo tomorrow.

彼女はとてもきれいでしょう。(with rising intonation)
*Kanojo wa totemo **kirei deshō**.*
She is very beautiful, isn't she?

2. After (adjectival) nouns + ***ja nai**, **datta**,* or ***ja nakatta***

あの人は日本人じゃないでしょう。 *Ano hito wa **Nihonjin ja nai deshō**.*
I guess that person is not Japanese.

あのレストランはあまり静かじゃないだろう。
*Ano resutoran wa amari **shizuka ja nai darō**.*
I guess that restaurant is not very quiet.

山田さんがいなかったなら、きっと静かだっただろう。
Yamada san ga inakatta nara, kitto shizuka datta darō.
If Ms. Yamada was not there, it would surely have been quiet.

彼は優秀な学生じゃなかっただろう。
Kare wa yūshū na gakusei ja nakatta darō.
I guess he was not an excellent student.

3. After verbs and adjectives in the dictionary form

副社長は三時までに戻るでしょう。
Fukushachō wa san ji made ni modoru deshō.
The vice president will probably be back by three.

あなたもいっしょに行くでしょう。(with rising intonation)
Anata mo isshoni iku deshō.
You will go together, won't you?

そんなことをしたら叱られるだろう。
Sonna koto o shitara shikarareru darō.
You'll be scolded if you do such a thing.

→ See Passive form under Verbs.

4. After verbs and adjectives in the *nai*-form

その仕事は締め切りまでにできないでしょう。
Sono shigoto wa shimekiri made ni dekinai deshō.
The work will probably not be completed by the deadline.

今日は残業しなければならないだろう。
Kyō wa zangyō shinakereba naranai darō.
I think I'll have to work after hours today.

→ See also *nakereba ikenai / nakeraba naranai.*

5. After verbs and adjectives in the *ta*-form

田中さんはもう東京に着いただろう。
Tanaka san wa mō Tōkyō ni tsuita darō.
Mr. Tanaka must have already arrived at Tokyo.

---

dasu 出す [AUXILIARY VERB]

abruptly begin (doing something), (do something) and take out, (do something) and go out

Dasu is attached at the end of a verb in the combining form, and means 'to abruptly start doing something, to do something to bring out some result or item, or to do something and move out from somewhere.'

1. To abrupty start doing something

   駅に行く途中みぞれが降り出した。
   *Eki ni iku tochū mizore ga **furidashita**.*
   Sleet began to fall on my way to the train station.

   夜になって風がひどく吹き出した。
   *Yoru ni natte kaze ga hidoku **fukidashita**.*
   When night came, it began to blow hard.

   彼は座ってたばこを吸い出した。 *Kare wa suwatte tabako o **suidashita**.*
   He sat down and began to smoke.

   彼女は何を言い出すか分からないから困る。
   *Kanojo wa nani o **iidasu** ka wakaranai kara komaru.*
   I'm in difficulties because I can't imagine what she will start to say.

   → See also *hajimeru* and *kakeru*.

2. To do something and bring out something or result

   彼はケースから何か取り出した。 *Kare wa kēsu kara nanika **toridashita**.*
   He took something out of his case.

   このカードでコンビニの端末機からお金を引き出すことができる。
   *Kono kādo de konbini no tanmatsu ki kare okane o **hikidasu** koto ga dekiru.*
   With this card you can withdraw money from a terminal in convenience stores.

   いい解決策を見つけ出した。 *Ii kaiketsusaku o **mitsukedashita**.*
   I found out a great solution.

3. To do something and move out from somewhere

   私は学生時代によく授業を抜け出した。
   *Watashi wa gakusei jidai ni yoku jugyō o **nukedashita**.*
   I would often skip out of classes when I was a student.

---

datte だって [CONJUNCTION]

because, but

Datte is a sentence-initial conjunction word that means 'because' or 'but.' It is used in an informal context, mostly in a response to someone's command or question, with emotion. (→ See also *demo*.)

「どうしてまた野球のバットを買ったんだ？」「だってお父さんが買ってもいいって言ったから。」
*"Dōshite mata yakyū no batto o katta n da?" "**Datte** otōsan ga katte mo ii tte itta kara."*
"Why did you buy a baseball bat again?" "Because you, Dad, said that it is okay to buy it."

「行きたくないの。」「だって疲れているんだもん。」
*"Ikitakunai no." "**Datte** tsukarete iru **n da mon**."*
"You don't want to go?" "Because I'm too tired."

「もう寝る時間ですよ。」「だって眠くないんだもの。」
*"Mō neru jikan desu yo." "**Datte** nemuku nai **n da mono**."*
"It's time for you to go to bed." "But I'm not sleepy."

Note that the ending *n da mon* or *n da mono* in the above sentence is used by a female or a child.

datte だって [PARTICLE]

also, even

The particle *datte* follows a noun to mean 'even' or 'also.' If it follows an interrogative pronoun, it creates a free-choice indefinite pronoun like 'anyone' and 'anything.' Its slightly formal counterpart is *demo*. (→ See *demo* and Interrogatives used in indefinite pronouns under Interrogatives.)

1. After nouns

   金持ちだって不幸なときもある。
   ***Kanemochi datte** fukō na toki mo aru.*
   Even rich people are unhappy sometimes.

   「あんなことはいやだ。」「私だっていやだ。」
   *"Anna koto wa iya da." "**Watashi datte** iya da."*
   "I hate such a thing." "Me, too."

2. After interrogative pronouns

   だれだってそれには怒りますよ。
   ***Dare datte** sore ni wa okorimasu yo.*
   Anyone naturally gets angry at that.

   彼はスポーツなら何だってできます。
   *Kare wa supōtsu nara **nan datte** dekimasu.*
   As for sports, he can play anything.

de で [PARTICLE]

at, in, on, by, with, from, because of, for

The particle *de* follows a noun and shows that the item denoted by the noun is some item (e.g. tools, ingredients, materials, location, methods, means, time, cost, condition, reasons, causes, and basis) that is used for or underlies the action or state denoted by the predicate. This sense of *de* should not be confused with *de,* the combining form of the linking verb *da.*

1. The location used for performing an action

私は毎日学校で日本語を勉強します。
*Watashi wa mainichi **gakkō de** Nihongo o benkyō shimasu.*
I study Japanese at school every day.

彼は部屋でサッカーを観ています。
*Kare wa **heya de** sakkā o mite imasu.*
He is watching football in his room.

父は部屋で寝ています。 *Chichi wa heya **de** nete imasu.*
My father is sleeping in the room.

→ See also *ni*.

2. The location where an event takes place

今晩彼女の家でパーティーがあります。
*Konban kanojo no **ie de** pātī ga arimasu.*
There will be a party at her house tonight.

屋根で何か音がする。 *Yane **de** nanika oto ga suru.*
I hear a sound on the roof.

会議は３号室であります。 *Kaigi wa **san gō shitsu de** arimasu.*
The meeting will be held in room 3.

祇園祭は七月に京都市内であります。
*Gion matsuri wa shichi gatsu ni **Kyōto shinai de** arimasu.*
The Gion festival is held in the city of Kyoto in July.

→ See also *ni*.

3. The basis used for comparison

富士山は日本でいちばん高い山です。
*Fuji san wa **Nihon de** ichiban takai yama desu.*
Mt. Fuji is the highest mountain in Japan.

日本食で寿司がいちばん好きです。
***Nihonshoku de** sushi ga ichiban suki desu.*
I like sushi the best in Japanese food.

4. Methods or means

私は電車で仕事に行きます。 *Watashi wa **densha de** shigoto ni ikimasu.*
I go to work by train.

そのニュースは昨日の新聞で読みました。
*Sono nyūsu wa kinō no **shinbun de** yomimashita.*
I read the news in yesterday's newspaper.

最近はよくインターネットで情報を調べます。
*Saikin wa yoku **inānetto de** jōhō o shirabemasu.*
Nowadays I often retrieve information on the Internet.

名前はインクで書いて下さい。鉛筆で書かないように。
*Namae wa **inku de** kaite kudasai. **Enpitsu de** kakanai yō ni.*
Please write your name in ink. You can't write in pencil.

5. Materials or ingredients

日本酒は米で作られる。 *Nihonshu wa **kome de** tsukurareru.*
Japanese sake is made from rice.

この建物はコンクリートでできている。
*Kono tatemono wa **konkurīto de** dekite iru.*
This building is made of concrete.

→ See also *kara*.

6. Reasons or causes

佐藤さんは風邪で休んでいます。 *Satō san wa **kaze de** yasunde imasu.*
Mr. Sato is absent with a cold.

彼女のお父さんは癌で亡くなりました。
*Kanojo no otōsan wa **gan de** nakunarimashita.*
Her father died of cancer.

おかげ様でうまくいきました。 ***Okage sama de** umaku ikimashita.*
It went smoothly thanks to you.

このレストランはおいしいパンで有名です。
*Kono resutoran wa **oishii pan de** yūmei desu.*
This restaurant is very famous for its delicious bread.

7. Conditions that accompany the action

新幹線は時速三百キロ以上のスピードで走る。
*Shinkansen wa **jisoku san byakkiro ijō no supīdo de** hashiru.*
The Shinkansen runs at a speed of more than 300 km per hour.

友達は心配な様子でお見舞いに来てくれました。
*Tomodachi wa **shinpai na yōsu de** omimai ni kite kuremashita.*
My friend called on me to inquire about my health with an anxious look.

あの子供は裸足で走ってるよ。
*Ano kodomo wa **hadashi de** hashitteru yo.*
That child is running around barefoot.

タコは生で食べますか。 *Tako wa **nama de** tabemasu ka.*
Do you eat octopi raw?

家族でレストランに行きました。 ***Kazoku de** resutoran ni ikimashita.*
I went to the restaurant with my family.

8. The length of time used for the action

一時間で戻ります。 ***Ichi jikan de** modorimasu.*
I'll be back in an hour.

9. The point in time at which a terminating action takes place

休みは明日で終わります。 *Yasumi wa **ashita de** owarimasu.*
The vacation will be over tomorrow.

10. The cost used for the action

このマウンテンバイクはネットオークションで五万円で買いました。
*Kono maunten baiku wa netto ōkushon de **goman en de** kaimashita.*
I bought this mountain bike for fifty thousand yen at an auction web site.

11. The age at which some change takes place

私は三十才で結婚したい。 *Watashi wa **san jussai de** kekkon shitai.*
I want to marry at the age of thirty.

兄は２５才で社長になった。 *Ani wa **ni jū go sai de** shachō ni natta.*
My big brother became a company president at the age of twenty-five.

12. Quantity/amount that serves as the basis for some state

このトマトは四個で二百円しました。
*Kono tomato wa **yon ko de** ni hyaku en shimashita.*
These tomatoes cost two hundred yen for four.

---

de aru である [(WRITTEN STYLE) LINKING VERB]

to be

De aru, or its polite counterpart, *de arimasu*, is used in lieu of the linking verbs, *da/desu*, in written forms or in formal speech when one wants to explicitly affirm the statement.

1. After (adjectival) nouns

金閣寺は14世紀に建てられた寺である。
*Kinkakuji wa jū yon seiki ni taterareta **tera de aru**.*
Kinkakuji is a temple built in the fourteenth century.

2. After verbs and adjectives in the dictionary form + *no*

When the speaker states a fact as an explanation for the previously mentioned matter, *no de aru* often follows the statement. (→ See *no da*.)

こうすれば問題は解決されるのである。
*Kō sueba mondai wa kaiketsu sareru **no de aru**.*
The problem will be solved in this way.

結局彼の言うことが正しいのである。
*Kekkyoku kare no iu koto ga tadashii **no de aru**.*
After all, what he says is correct.

→ See also *da* and *no da*.

dekiru できる [VERB]

can do, be completed, be made

Dekiru is an intransitive verb, and has multiple meanings. It can express potential, meaning 'to be able to do something.' In this case, the understood direct object noun is usually marked by the particle *ga* rather than the particle *o*, because *dekiru* is an intransitive verb. *Dekiru* also means 'to be completed,' 'to be made,' and 'to come to exist.'

1. 'To be able to perform'

   「車の運転ができますか。」「はい、できます。」
   "Kuruma no unten ga dekimasu ka." "Hai, dekimasu."
   "Can you drive a car?" "Yes, I can."

   フランクは日本語がよくできます。韓国語もよくできます。
   Furanku wa Nihongo ga yoku dekimasu. Kankokugo mo yoku dekimasu.
   Frank speaks good Japanese. He also speaks good Korean.

2. 'To be completed'

   やっと宿題ができました。 *Yatto shukudai ga dekimashita.*
   Now my homework is finished.

   出発の用意ができました。 *Shuppatsu no yōi ga dekimashita.*
   Preparation for departure is completed.

3. 'To be made'

   味噌と豆腐は大豆からできます。 *Miso to tōfu wa daizu kara dekimasu.*
   Miso and tofu are made from soybeans.

   夕ごはんができました。 *Yūgohan ga dekimashita.*
   Dinner is ready.

4. 'To come to existence'

   東京スカイツリーという新しいタワーができた。
   Tōkyō Sukai Tsurī to iu atarashii tawā ga dekita.
   A new tower called Tokyo Sky Tree has been built.

   彼女は３人目の子供ができました。
   Kanojo wa san nin me no kodomo ga dekimashita.
   She is going to have the third baby.

   急用ができたので失礼します。 *Kyūyō ga dekita node shitsurei shimasu.*
   Some urgent business has come up, so I have to leave.

   駅前に面白い店ができました。
   Ekimae ni omoshiroi mise ga dekimashita.
   An interesting shop has been opened in front of the train station.

→ See also *ga* and *koto ga dekiru.*

demo でも [CONJUNCTION]

but, however

The conjunction *demo* is placed at the beginning of a sentence and means 'but' or 'however.' Its formal or written-style counterpart is *shikashi*. (→ See also *daga, dakedo, demo, ga, keredo(mo)*, and *shikashi*.)

でも、もう遅すぎるよ。 ***Demo**, mō ososugiru yo.* **But it's too late now.**

demo でも [PARTICLE]

even, in spite of, any . . . , something, anything,

I. *DEMO* THAT FOLLOWS (ADJECTIVAL) NOUNS

The particle *demo* can follow a noun to show that the item denoted by the noun is some kind of example, meaning '. . . or something,' or the least expected item, meaning 'even. . . .' It may follow a particle associated with the noun except when the particle is *ga* or *o*.

1. After (adjectival) nouns

   コーヒーでも飲みたいです。 ***Kōhī demo** nomitai desu.*
   I'd like to drink coffee or something.

   大人でもその漢字を知らない人がいます。
   ***Otona demo** sono kanji o shiranai hita ga imasu.*
   There are even some grownups who don't know that kanji.

   彼は日曜日でもときどき働きます。
   *Kare wa **Nichiyōbi demo** tokidoki hatarakimasu.*
   He sometimes works even on Sundays.

   雨でも予定通り祭りを開催します。
   ***Ame demo** yotei dōri matsuri o kaisai shimasu.*
   They will hold the festival according to schedule even if it is rainy.

2. After some particles

   天気のいい日には東京からでも富士山が見えます。
   *Tenki no ii hi ni wa Tōkyō **kara demo** Fuji san ga miemasu.*
   Even from Tokyo, Mt. Fuji can be seen when the weather is fine.

II. *DEMO* THAT FOLLOWS INTERROGATIVE WORDS

The particle *demo* can follow an interrogative word to form a free-choice expression such as 'anyone,' 'anything,' and 'anywhere.' It may follow a particle associated to the noun except when the particle is *wa*, *ga*, or *o*.

1. Following *dare* 'who' (+ particles)

   だれでもそんなことは知っていますよ。
   Dare demo *sonna koto wa shitte imasu yo.*
   Anybody knows such things. (Anybody knows that.)

   だれとでもすぐに仲良くなれます。
   Dare to demo *sugu ni nakayoku naremasu.*
   I can become friendly with anybody soon.

2. Following *nan* 'what' (+ particles)

   食べ物はだいたい何でも食べられます。
   Tabemono wa daitai ***nan demo*** *taberaremasu.*
   I can eat almost any (kind of) food.

   何とでも言わせてあげます。 ***Nan to demo*** *iwasete agemasu.*
   I let you say whatever you like.

   飲み物は何でもいいです。 *Nomimono wa* ***nan demo*** *ii desu.*
   Any drink is fine.

3. Following *doko* 'where'

   彼はどこ(に)でも遊びに行きます。
   Kare wa ***doko (ni) demo*** *asobi ni ikimasu.*
   He goes anywhere to play.

   パソコンメーカーはどこでもいいです。
   Pasokon mēkā wa ***doko demo*** *ii desu.*
   Any manufacturer of personal computers is all right. (I don't care.)

   (The above sentence may be converted to the following.)

   どこのパソコンメーカーでもいいです。
   Doko no *pasokon mēkā* ***demo*** *ii desu.*

4. Following *itsu* 'when'

   返事はいつでもいいですか。 *Henji wa* ***itsu demo ii*** *desu ka.*
   Will anytime be all right to reply?

   お返事はいつでもけっこうです。 *Ohenji wa* ***itsu demo*** *kekkō desu.*
   You can take your own time for your reply.

5. Following *dō* 'how'

   もうどうでもいいです。 *Mō* ***dō demo*** *ii desu.*
   Now any way is all right. (I don't care.)

→ See aslo *datte, mo, ikura . . . temo/demo,* and *temo/demo.*

---

deshō でしょう → See ***darō***.

---

desu です → See ***da***.

dewa では [CONJUNCTION]

if so, well, then, so, well then, good-bye

Dewa can function as a sentence-initial conjunction that shows the following statement, suggestion, or question is something logically expected from the preceding context, roughly meaning 'if so.' *Dewa* can also be uttered in a conversational context, signaling the transition from one stage to another during the conversation, for example, signaling the timing for leaving or doing something else. *Dewa* changes to *jā* or *ja* in an informal context.

1. Meaning 'if so'

   ではもうあきらめます。***Dewa** mō akiramemasu.* **If so, I give up.**

   「ちょっとスーパーに行ってきます。」「じゃあ、卵を買ってきてくれない?」
   *"Chotto sūpā ni itte kimasu." "**Jā**, tamago o katte kite kurenai?"*
   "I'll go to the supermarket." "Okay, then, could you get me some eggs?"

   では, なぜそうしたんですか。 ***Dewa**, naze sō shita n desu ka.*
   Then, why did you do it?

2. Signaling the timing for leaving or doing something else

   ではこれで失礼します。 ***Dewa** kore de shitsurei shimasu.*
   Well, I must be leaving now.

   「じゃまた。」「あ、どうも。じゃ。」 *"**Ja**, mata." "A, dōmo. **Ja**."*
   "Then, see you again." "Oh, bye. See you."

   じゃあ, 次の問題をしましょう。 ***Jā**, tsugi no mondai o shimashō*
   Okay then. Let's work on the next exercise.

dewa では [DOUBLE PARTICLE]

in, at, as for, judging from, by

The combination of the particle *de* and the particle *wa* forms a sequence, *dewa*. When a noun is followed by *dewa*, the noun marked by *de* for whatever reason (e.g. location of activity, basis for comparison, and tools) is stressed or contrasted with another item understood in the context by the presence of *wa*. (→ See also *de, ja <contraction>, ni yoreba,* and *wa*.)

東京では駐車料金が高すぎます。
***Tōkyō dewa** chūsha ryōkin ga takasugimasu.*
In Tokyo, parking fees are too high.

数学では彼はほかのクラスメートよりも優秀です。
***Sūgaku dewa** kare wa hoka no kurasumēto yori mo yūshū desu.*
In mathematics he is superior to all his classmates.

私の意見ではこちらの方がいいと思います。
Watashi no iken dewa *kochira no hō ga ii to omoimasu.*
In my opinion, I think this is better.

あの様子では彼は受け入れそうもない。
Ano yōsu dewa *kare wa ukeiresō mo nai.*
Judging from his look, it doesn't seem he will accept it.

電波時計では1時15分40秒です。
Denpa dokei dewa *ichiji jū go fun yon jū byō desu.*
It is fifteen minutes forty seconds past one by my radio watch.

dō どう [INTERROGATIVE]

how, what, how about

Dō is an interrogative word that can function as an adverb or as an adjectival noun to ask about the state of people and things or the manner of actions. When used before a noun, use *donna* instead of *dō*.

1. Followed by a verb + ***no/n desu***

   (may be replaced by the phrase *dō yatte* or *dono yō ni shite*)

   それはどうするんですか。 *Sore wa* ***dō suru n desu*** *ka.* **How shall I do it?**

   それはどうやってするんですか。 *Sore wa* ***dō yatte suru n desu*** *ka.*
   How shall I do it?

   それはどのようにしてするんですか。
   Sore wa dōno yō ni ***shite suru n desu*** *ka.*
   How shall I do it?

   駅までどう行くんですか。 *Eki made* ***dō iku n desu*** *ka.*
   How can I go to the train station?

2. Followed by ***desu***

   (may be replaced by the more polite word *ikaga*)

   「今日は気分はいかがですか。」「おかげさまで。」
   "Kyō wa kibun wa ***ikaga desu*** *ka." "Okage sama de."*
   "How are you feeling today?" "Fine, thank you."

   「コーヒーでも一杯どうですか。」「いいですね。」
   "Kōhī demo ippai ***dō desu*** *ka." "Ii desu ne."*
   "How about a cup of coffee (or something)?" "Fine."

   京都旅行はどうでしたか。 *Kyōto ryokō wa* ***dō deshita*** *ka.*
   How did you like your trip to Kyoto?

   それをやってみたらどうですか。 *Sore o yatte mitara* ***dō desu*** *ka.*
   How would it be if you try it? (Why don't you try it?)

3. Used with the verb *omou*

この絵をどう思いますか。 *Kono e o **dō omoimasu** ka.*

What do you think of this picture?

→ See also *dōshite*.

dochira どちら [INTERROGATIVE]

which one, where

Dochira means 'which one' and is used in a question that compares two items. (→ See Comparisons.) It is sometimes contracted to *dotchi*. *Dochira* is also used as the polite version of *dare*, *doko*, and *dore*. (→ See *dare*, *doko*, and *dore*.)

りんごと，バナナと，どちらの方が好きですか。
*Ringo to banana to **dochira** no hō ga suki desu ka.*
Which one do you like, apples and bananas?

高橋さんはどちらからですか。 *Takahashi san wa **dochira** kara desu ka.*
Where are you from, Mr. Takahashi?

doko どこ [INTERROGATIVE]

where, what

Doko is used to ask for location, and its respectful form is *dochira*. (→ See *dochira*.) It is an interrogative word, so it should not be marked by the topic particle *wa*. (→ See also *wa*.)

1. Followed by *desu*

「郵便局はどこですか。」「あの銀行の向こうです。」
*"Yūbinkyoku wa **doko desu** ka." "Ano ginkō no mukō desu."*
"Where is the post office?" "It's on the other side of that bank."

「田中さんは今どこですか。」「出張で名古屋です。」
*"Tanaka san wa ima **doko desu** ka." "Shutchō de Nagoya desu."*
"Where is Mr. Tanaka now?" "He is in Nagoya on business."

2. Followed by a locational particle

彼女はどこに住んでいるんですか。
*Kanojo wa **doko ni** sunde iru n desu ka.*
Where does she live?

「休みに（は）どこへ行くんですか。」「どこにも行きません。」
*"Yasumi ni (wa) **doko e** iku n desu ka." "**Doko ni** mo ikimasen."*
"Where are you going for the vacation?" "I won't go anywhere."

どこで会うんですか。 ***Doko de** au n desu ka.* **Where shall we meet?**

「彼女はどこから来ましたか。」「アメリカからです。」
*"Kanojo wa **doko kara** kimashita ka." "Amerika kara desu."*
"Where did she come from?" (Where is she from?) "She's from the U.S."

3. Followed by the possessive particle **no**

どこのホテルに泊まるんですか。 **Doko no** *hoteru ni tomaru n desu ka.*
At what hotel will you stay?

4. Followed by subject marker **ga**

それのどこがわるいんですか。 *Sore no **doko ga** warui n desu ka.*
What's wrong with it?

dokoro de(wa) nai どころで (は) ない [PREDICATIVE PHRASE]

be out of the question, be more than . . . , this is not an occasion for

Dokoro dewa nai is used to emphasize the outrageous level of the degree of the given state, by denying the appropriateness of performing the action or accepting the state denoted by the preceding phrase.

1. After verbs

今旅行に行くどころではない。 *Ima ryokō ni iku **dokoro dewa nai**.*
Going on a trip now is out of the question.

冗談を言っているどころでない。 *Jōdan o itte iru **dokoro de nai**.*
This is not an occasion for joking.

2. After adjectives

運がいいどころではありません。奇跡です。
*Un ga **ii dokoro dewa arimasen**. Kiseki desu.*
It is more than good luck. It is a miracle.

dokoro ka どころか [PHRASE]

far from, to say nothing of, not to speak of, much more, (not) . . . much less, not only . . . but . . . , not . . . on the contrary

. . . Dokoro ka . . . (mo) is used for mentioning two cases and emphasizes the second case in comparison with the first case.

1. After (adjectival) noun

雨どころか雪になりそうです。 ***Ame dokoro ka** yuki ni nari sō desu.*
It looks more like snow than rain.

彼は日本語どころか中国語も話せます。
*Kare wa **Nihongo dokoro ka** Chūgokugo mo hanasemasu.*
He can speak not only Japanese but Chinese as well.

肉どころか魚も食べません。 ***Niku dokoro ka*** *sakana mo tabemasen.*
I don't even eat fish, much less meat.

ドイツ語どころか英語も私にはむずかしいです。
Doitsugo dokoro ka Eigo mo *watashi ni wa muzukashii desu.*
English is difficult for me, to say nothing of German.

2. After verbs/adjectives in the dictionary form

彼は笑うどころか怒ってしまった。
Kare wa waru ***dokoro ka*** *okotte shimatta.*
Far from laughing, he got totally angry.

彼は賢いどころか天才だ。 *Kare wa kashikoi* ***dokoro ka*** *tensai da.*
He is not only clever but a genius.

3. After verbs in the ***nai***-form

彼は手伝わないどころか文句を言っている。
*Kare wa tetsudawa**nai dokoro ka** monku o itte iru.*
Not only does he not help, but he complains.

dōmo どうも [ADVERB]

hello, good-bye, thank you, sorry, very (much), indeed, somehow, just

Dōmo is an adverb that applies to expressions of gratitude and apology to show one's sincere attitude, but can also be used by itself to show gratitude or apology. It is also used by itself as a brief greeting. When used with a negative predicate, it means 'somehow.'

1. Used to express gratitude

「お先にどうぞ。」「これはどうも。」 *"Osaki ni dōzo." "Kore wa* ***dōmo."***
"Please go ahead. (After you.)" "Oh, thanks."

ご親切どうもありがとうございます。
Goshinsetsu ***dōmo arigatō gozaimasu.***
Thank you very much for your kindness.

2. Used to express apology

「痛い。」「あ，どうも。大丈夫ですか。」 *"Itai." "A,* ***dōmo.*** *Daijōbu desu ka."*
"Ouch." "Oh, sorry. Are you all right?"

(*Sumimasen* [I'm sorry] is dropped after *dōmo*.)

遅れてどうもすみません。 *Okurete* ***dōmo sumimasen.***
I'm very sorry to be late.

3. Used in greetings

「やあ。」「やあ，どうも。」 *"Yā." "Yā,* ***dōmo."***
"Hi." "Hi, how are you?" (Glad to see you.)

「これで失礼します。」「どうも。」 *"Kore de shitsurei shimasu." "Dōmo."*
"I'm leaving now." "Good-bye. Thank you."

4. Used with negative predicates to mean 'somehow'

あなたの言うことがどうもわかりません。
*Anata no iu koto ga **dōmo wakarimasen**.*
I just can't understand what you say.

どうもあの人は気に入らない。 ***Dōmo** ano hito wa ki ni **iranai**.*
Somehow, I don't like that man.

→ See also *chotto* and *dōshitemo*.

donna どんな [INTERROGATIVE]

what kind of . . .

Donna is placed before a noun to mean 'what kind of. . . .' When used before the linking verb *desu*, use *dō* instead of *donna*. (→ See *dō* and *nan*.)

新しいマネージャーはどんな人ですか。
*Atarashii manējā wa **donna hito** desu ka.*
What kind of person is the new manager?

山田さんの部屋はどんな部屋ですか。
*Yamada san no heya wa **donna heya** desu ka.*
What kind of room is yours, Ms. Yamada?

山田さんの部屋はどうですか。 *Yamada san no heya wa **dō desu** ka.*
How is your room, Ms. Yamada?

dono どの → See *dore*.

dono kurai どのくらい [INTERROGATIVE]

how many, how much, how long, how far, how tall, how often

Dono kurai or *dono gurai* can be used to ask the amount/quantity/size of items, length of time, or distance. It may be used interchangeably with *dore kurai* or *dore gurai*. It functions as an adverb, but it can also be used right before *desu ka*. (→ See also *kurai*.)

どのくらいゲームソフトを集めましたか。
***Dono kurai** gēmu sofuto o atsumemashita ka.*
How many game software titles have you collected?

どのくらい砂糖を入れますか。 ***Dono kurai** satō o iremasu ka.*
How much sugar will you put in?

ここから駅までどのくらいかかりますか。
*Koko kara eki made **dono kurai** kakarimasu ka.*
How long does it take from here to the train station?

車は税金を入れてどのくらいかかりますか。
*Kuruma wa zeikin o irete **dono kurai** kakarimasu ka.*
How much does a car cost including tax?

身長と体重はどのくらいですか。
*Shinchō to taijū wa **dono kurai** desu ka.*
What is your height and weight?

１日にどのくらいイーメールをしますか。
*Ichi nichi ni **dono kurai** īmēru o shimasu ka.*
How many times a day do you send e-mail?

dore どれ [INTERROGATIVE]

which one

Dore is an interrogative pronoun that means 'which one' and is used to ask about items other than people and locations. Use *dare* and *doko* to ask about people and locations, respectively. (→ See *dare* and *doko*.) Its polite version, *dochira*, can be used to ask about any item including people and locations. It is an interrogative word, so should not be marked by the topic particle *wa*. (→ See *wa*.) *Dono* must be used instead of *dore* when functioning as an adjective placed before a noun. In this case, the noun can denote any item including people and locations, as in *dono hito* 'which person,' *dono inu* 'which dog,' and *dono heya* 'which room.' When *dore* or *dono* are combined with *mo*, *ka*, and *demo*, they mean 'no,' 'some,' or 'any.' (→ See *demo*, *ka*, *mo*, and *nani*.)

1. Used as an interrogative pronoun

   このデジカメのうちどれがいちばん安いですか。
   *Kono dejikame no uchi **dore** ga ichiban yasui desu ka.*
   Which is the cheapest of these digital cameras?

   どれがいちばん好きですか。　***Dore** ga ichiban suki desu ka.*
   Which do you like best?

   この３つの携帯のうちどれを選びますか。
   *Kono mittsu no keitai no uchi **dore** o erabimasu ka.*
   Which of these three mobile phones do you choose?

2. Used as an interrogative adjective in the form of ***dono***

   どの映画が面白いと思いますか。
   ***Dono eiga** ga omoshiroi to omoimasu ka.*
   Which movie do you think is interesting?

3. Used with *mo* to indicate a thing that is not specific or particular

この漢字の本はどれも外国人にはむずかしすぎる。
*Kono kanji no hon wa **dore mo** gaikokujin ni wa muzukashisugiru.*
Any of these kanji books is too difficult for a foreigner.

4. Used with *ka* to create an indefinite pronoun

このうちどれかいただけますか。 *Kono uchi **dore ka** itadakemasu ka.*
Can you spare me any of these?

5. Used with *demo* to express free choice

どれでもいいですからお好きなのをお選び下さい。
***Dore demo** ii desu kara osuki na no o oerabi kudasai.*
Any one of them is fine, so please pick the one you like.

dōshite どうして [INTERROGATIVE]

why, in what way, how

Dōshite means 'why' or 'how.' When it means 'why,' the question usually ends in *n desu ka*. To ask about the method, *dōyatte* tends to be used instead of *dōshite*, to avoid ambiguity.

1. Asking a reason

どうして仕事に遅れたんですか。 ***Dōshite** shigoto ni okureta n desu ka.*
Why were you late for work?

→ See also *naze*.

2. Asking a method

この漢字は どうして/どうやって 書くんですか。
*Kono Kanji wa **dōshite/dō yatte** kaku n desu ka.*
How do you write this Chinese character?

→ See also *dō*.

dōshitemo どうしても [ADVERB]

no matter what, (not) . . . by any means, at any cost, can't help (doing something), simply (not)

The adverb *dōshitemo* is used to emphasize unchangeable situations or decisions. (→ See also *ikura . . . temo/demo*.)

どうしてもそれが必要なんです。 ***Dōshitemo** sore ga hitsuyō na n desu.*
I need it at any cost.

どうしても彼女のことを考えてしまいます。
***Dōshitemo** kanojo no koto o kangaete shimaimasu.*
I can't help thinking of her.

どうしても複雑な漢字が覚えられません。
Dōshitemo fukuzatsu na kanji ga oboeraremasen.
I just can't memorize complicated kanji.

どうしても野球の試合では負けたくありません。
Dōshitemo yakyū no shiai de wa maketaku arimasen.
We simply don't want to lose the baseball game.

どうしても明日までにこの申込書を提出しなければなりません。
Dōshitemo ashita made ni kono mōshikomisho o teishutsu shinakereba narimasen.
I must submit this application by tomorrow no matter what.

dōzo どうぞ [ADVERB]

please, certainly, sure, here it is

Dōzo is an adverb used to encourage others to do some action. It can be used by itself if what action is expected is understood in the context.

こちらへどうぞ。 *Kochira e dōzo.* (Come) this way, please.

どうぞこちらにおすわり下さい。 ***Dōzo** kochira ni **osuwari kudasai.***
Please be seated here.

「ちょっと携帯電話を貸してくれませんか。」「はい, どうぞ。」
"Chotto keitai denwa o kashite kuremasen ka." "Hai, dōzo."
"Can I use your mobile phone for a while?" "Yes, certainly." (Here it is. Use it.)

「展示品の写真を撮ってもいいですか。」「どうぞ。」
"Tenjihin no shashin o tottemo ii desu ka." "Dōzo."
"Can I take a photo of the exhibit?" "Sure (, take it)."

e へ [PARTICLE]

toward . . .

The grammatical particle *e* is used to mark the noun that shows the direction of movement. *E* is often interchangeably used with *ni*, but they have slightly different nuances and *ni* has many other functions that *e* does not have.

ちょっとトイレへ行ってきます。 *Chotto **toire e** itte kimasu.*
I'm going to the restroom for a moment.

「奈良へ行ったことがありますか。」「残念ながらまだありません。」
*"**Nara e** itta koto ga arimasu ka." "Zannennagara mada arimasen."*
"Have you been to Nara?" "To my regret, I haven't yet."

あの角を右へ曲がるとバス停があります。
*Ano kado o **migi e** magaru to basutei ga arimasu.*
If you turn to the right at that corner, you'll find a bus stop.

→ See also *made* and *ni*.

fu 不 [PREFIX]

in-, un-, dis-

The prefix *fu* precedes (adjectival) nouns in Sino-Japanese vocabulary to add a negative meaning. (→ See also *han <prefix>*.)

私たちは不都合な事実を暴きます。
*Watashi tachi wa **futsugō na** jijitsu o abakimasu.*
We disclose an inconvenient fact.

改めて手続きは不必要です。 *Aratamete tetsuzuki wa **fuhitsuyō** desu.*
Another procedure is unnecessary.

結果には不満足です。 *Kekka ni wa **fumanzoku** desu.*
I'm dissatisfied with the result.

ga が [PARTICLE]

subject marker, nominative case marker, but, and

The particle *ga* can serve as a case particle or as a conjunctional particle.

I. *GA* [CASE PARTICLE]

subject marker, nominative case marker

The case particle *ga* can mark the subject of the sentence. However, when the subject noun is also treated as the topic of the sentence, being marked by *wa*, *ga* cannot be present. That is a part of the reason why the particle *wa* often wrongly gives the impression of being the subject marker.[1]

The case particle *ga* can also mark the understood object of some predicates. States such as desires, preferences, and needs are most commonly expressed by adjectives (e.g. *hoshii* 'to want') or adjectival nouns (e.g. *suki da* 'to like,' *kirai da* 'to hate,' *hitsuyō da* 'to need') rather than verbs in Japanese. Accordingly, these

---

1. Note that the topic particle (*wa*) is disallowed in relative clauses (and some adverbial clauses that are constructed as relative clauses). (→ See Clauses.) Thus, the particle *wa* that occurs in the relative clauses is considered to function as a contrastive marker. (→ See *wa*.) As a result, the perception of the item marked by *ga* often differs depending on whether it is in the main sentence or in a relative clause. When *ga* is used in the main sentence, the item marked by *ga* is in many cases perceived as a piece of new information (because it is not treated as the topic) and/or often gives an emphatic impression. By contrast, when *ga* is used in a relative clause, the item marked by *ga* does not give such an emphatic impression. Similarly when *ga* is used in noun complement clauses, it also does not give an emphatic impression.

adjectives and adjectival nouns employ *ga* to mark their understood objects because the particle *o* cannot be available if there is no verb. Interestingly, some verbs that express potential or necessity, for example, *dekiru* 'to be able to do' and *iru* 'to need' also employ *ga* to mark their objects even though they are verbs. When the desire for an action is expressed by a verb followed by the suffix *tai*, the direct object can be marked by either *ga* or *o*. (→ See also *tai*.)

1. After the subject noun that denotes the newly introduced item in the context

   Note that an item can be marked by *ga* when introduced for the first time, but is marked by *wa* afterward in the same context as more details about it are explained.

   紹介します。この人が鈴木さんです。彼は私の旧友です。
   Shōkai shimasu. **Kono hito ga** *Suzuki san desu.* **Kare wa** *watashi no kyūyū desu.*
   Let me introduce him. This is Mr. Suzuki. He is my old friend.

   Note that *wa* can also mark an introduced item as below if the speaker knows that the listener recognizes him but that he/she does not have its information (his name).

   この人は鈴木さんです。彼は私の旧友です。
   Kono hito wa *Suzuki san desu.* **Kare wa** *watashi no kyūyū desu.*
   This is Mr. Suzuki. He is my old friend.

   この寺が清水寺ですね。清水寺は高い舞台で有名ですよね。
   Kono tera ga *Kiyomizudera desu ne.* **Kiyomizudera wa** *takai butai de yūmei desu yo ne.*
   This temple is Kiyomizudera, isn't it? Kiyomizudera is famous for its high stage, isn't it?

   昔お爺さんがいました。お爺さんは毎日山へ狩りに行きました。
   Mukashi **ojīsan ga** *imashita.* **Ojīsan wa** *mainichi yama e kari ni ikimashita.*
   There once lived an old man. The old man went hunting in the mountain every day.

2. After the subject noun that denotes the item that underwent some (sudden) change

   お爺さんは毎日山へ狩りに行きました。しかしある日そのお爺さんがいきなり熊に殺されました。
   Ojīsan wa *mainichi yama e kari ni ikimashita. Shikashi aru hi sono* **ojīsan ga** *ikinari kuma ni korosaremashita.*
   The old man went hunting in the mountain every day. But one day the old man was abruptly killed by a bear.

   彼は私の旧友です。彼がいま自転車にぶつかったんです。
   Kare wa *watashi no kyūyū desu.* **Kare ga** *ima jitensha ni butsukatta n desu.*
   He is my old friend. He bumped into the bike just now.

3. After the subject noun that denotes the item that was just noticed by the speaker

Note that both the item marked by *ga* and the following predicate express new information because the speaker notices the whole event at a time. The item is later marked by *wa* if the speaker explains it in the same context.

あ，雨が降ってきました。この雨は雪になりますね。
*Ah, **ame ga** futte kimashita. Kono **ame wa** yuki ni narimasu ne.*
A rain has begun to fall. I guess this rain will turn to snow.

とてもおいしい匂いがします。これは焼き肉の匂いですね。
*Totemo oishii **nioi ga** shimasu. **Kore wa** yakiniku no nioi desu ne.*
It smells very delicious. I guess this is a smell of roast meat.

あ，403号の新幹線がきた。急ごう。新幹線はすぐに発車するよ。
*A, yon maru san gō no **shinkansen ga** kita. Isogō. **Shinkansen wa** suguni hassha suru yo.*
Oh, the Shinkansen 403 has come. Hurry up. The Shinkansen starts immediately.

4. After the subject noun that denotes the item considered to be the only item in the context

This *ga* may give an emphatic impression because the item marked by *ga* is picked out.

「誰が最優秀選手ですか。」「一郎が最優秀選手です。」
*"Dare ga saiyūshū senshu desu ka." "**Ichirō ga** saiyūshū senshu desu."*
"Who is the most valuable player?" "Ichiro is the MVP."

私がそれをします。私は得意なんです。
***Watashi ga** sore o shimasu. Watashi wa tokui na n desu.*
I'll do it. (Let me do it./I should do it.) I am good at it.

5. After the subject noun that is described temporarily in a neutral manner

今まだ外は雨が降っています。 *Ima mada soto wa **ame ga** futte imasu.*
It is still raining outside.

今日は空が青いですねぇ。 *Kyo wa **sora ga** aoi desu nee.*
The sky is blue today, isn't it?

だいぶ前からお客さんが来て待っています。
*Daibu mae kara **okyaku san ga** kite matte imasu.*
A guest came a long time ago and has been waiting for you.

交差点の向こうに地下鉄の入り口があります。入り口はわかりやすいです。
*Kōsaten no mukō ni chikatetsu no **iriguchi ga** arimasu. **Iriguchi wa** wakariyasui desu.*
There's an entrance to a subway across the crossing. The entrance is easy to find.

Note that if the item is not described temporarily but explanatorily, it is marked by *wa*:

地下鉄の入り口は交差点の向こうにあります。入り口はわかりやすいです。

*Chikatetsu no **iriguchi wa** kōsaten no mukō ni arimasu. **Iriguchi wa** wakariyasui desu.*

The entrance to the subway is across the intersection. The entrance is easy to find.

6. In the . . . *wa* . . . *ga* construction

The item marked by *ga* usually belongs to, or has something to do with, the item marked by *wa* and serves as the topic. Such sentences may appear to have multiple subjects.

「象はどんな動物ですか。」「象は鼻が長いです。」

*"**Zō wa** donna dōbutsu desu ka." "**Zō wa** hana **ga** nagai desu."*

"What kind of animal is an elephant?" "As for an elephant, its trunk is long."

私は肩がひどく凝っています。 ***Watashi wa** kata **ga** hidoku kotte imasu.*

I feel very stiff in the shoulders.

馬場さんは背が高いです。 ***Baba san wa** se **ga** takai desu.*

Mr. Baba is tall. (As for Mr. Baba, the back is high.)

(The phrase *se ga takai*, meaning 'to be tall,' is an idiom derived from this structure.)

私は兄が弁護士をしています。 ***Watashi wa** ani **ga** bengoshi o shite imasu.*

My brother practices law. (As for me, a brother practices law.)

日本は女性が寿命が長いです。 ***Nihon wa** josei **ga** jumyō **ga** nagai desu.*

As for Japan, women's life expectancy is long.

7. After the subject noun that is apprehended or perceived sensually

The subject noun that is apprehended or perceived sensually, that is, through the senses, often expressed by the verb *suru*, may become the understood object, but marked by the particle *ga*.

隣の部屋からガスの臭いがしますよ。

*Tonari no heya kara **gasu no nioi ga shimasu** yo.*

A smell of gas is coming from the next room, I tell you. (I smell gas from the next room.)

このパンはシナモンの味がします。

*Kono pan wa **shinamon no aji ga shimasu**.*

There is a taste of cinnamon in this bread. (This bread has a taste of cinnamon.)

別に何も音がしなかったです。 *Betsu ni nani mo **oto ga shinakatta** desu.*

No particular sound was heard. (I didn't hear any particular sound.)

→ See also *suru*.

8. After a subject or (understood) object noun that is (with) an interrogative

As interrogatives cannot serve as a referent, they are naturally marked by *ga* rather than *wa* if they serve as a grammatical subject or an understood object as discussed above.

何がそんなに面白いんですか。 ***Nani ga*** *sonna ni omoshiroi n desu ka.*
What is so funny?

何が言いたいんですか。 ***Nani ga*** *iitai n desu ka.*
What do you want to say?

この本を読んでどんな問題が分かりましたか。
*Kono hon o yonde **donna mondai ga** wakarimashita ka.*
What problem did you find after reading this book?

9. After the subject noun in a relative clause

The subject particle *ga* in a relative clause may be replaced by the particle *no.* (→ See also *no.*)

私が買ったカメラは日本製のデジタル一眼レフです。
Watashi ga katta kamera *wa Nihonsei no dejitaru ichigan refu desu.*
私の買ったカメラは日本製のデジタル一眼レフです。
Watashi no katta kamera *wa Nihonsei no dejitaru ichigan refu desu.*
The camera I bought is a Japanese-made digital single-lense reflex camera.

10. After the subject noun in adverbial clauses

洋子さんが来たら教えて下さい。 ***Yōko san ga kitara*** *oshiete kudasai.*
When Yoko comes, please tell me.

彼が東京に来るなら私が案内します。
Kare ga Tōkyō ni kuru nara *watashi ga annai shimasu.*
If he is coming to Tokyo, I'll give him a tour.

私はあなたがいっしょにいるととても楽しいです。
*Watashi wa **anata ga isshoni iru to** totemo tanoshii desu.*
If you stay with me, I feel very happy.

11. For the understood object of some emotional state

私はお金よりも自由時間がほしいです。
*Watashi wa okane yori mo **jiyū jikan ga hoshii** desu.*
I want free time more than money.

日本食の中では豆腐がいちばん好きです。
*Nihonshoku no naka dewa **tōfu ga** ichiban **suki** desu.*
Of Japanese foods I like tofu the best.

私は彼のイケメンがうらやましい。
*Watashi wa kare no **ikemen ga urayamashii**.*
I envy his good-looking face.

私はもっと資金が必要です。 *Watashi wa motto **shikin ga hitsuyō** desu.*
I need more funds.

留学するには奨学金が要ります。
*Ryūgaku suru ni wa **shōgakukin ga irimasu**.*
I need a scholarship in order to study abroad.

本当のことが知りたい。 *Hontō no **koto ga shiritai**.*
I want to know the truth.

→ See also *hoshii*.

12. For the understood object of potential verbs

   The understood object is marked by *ga* rather than by *o* when the verb is in the potential form (→ See Potential form under Verbs.) or has a potential meaning to start with. (→ See also Spontaneous-Potential verbs under Verbs.)

   私はワードとエクセルができます。
   *Watashi wa **Wādo to Ekuseru ga dekimasu**.*
   I can operate Word and Excel.

   窓から海が見えます。 *Mado kara **umi ga miemasu**.*
   We can see the ocean from the window.

   この大学の学生なら，映画が5ドルで見られます。
   *Kono daigaku no gakusei nara, **eiga ga** godoru de **miraremasu**.*
   If you are a student of this university, you can see the movie for five dollars.

   母は英語がわかりません。 *Haha wa **eigo ga wakarimasen**.*
   My mother does not understand English.

   足音が聞こえませんか？ ***Ashioto ga kikoemasen** ka?*
   Don't you hear footsteps?

13. For the understood object of having

   'To have' is often expressed by the verb *aru* or *iru* 'to exist' in Japanese. So, what one has is marked by the particle *ga* when the verb *aru* or *iru* is used.

   今お金がぜんぜんありません。 *Ima **okane ga** zenzen **arimasen**.*
   I have no money now.

   姉は友達がたくさんいます。 *Ane wa **tomodachi ga** takusan **imasu**.*
   My sister has many friends.

II. *GA* [CONJUNCTIONAL PARTICLE]

The conjunctional particle *ga* follows a clause showing that the preceding and following clauses are in contrast or conflict. (→ See *daga, keredo(mo)*, and *noni*.) However, it can also loosely connect two sentences that are not in conflict or contrast, and indicate the temporal or logical transition between the two statements. The clause before *ga* can have the character of an independent sentence in terms of formality, and can be in either polite or plain styles. However, the predicates in the main clause and in the clause followed by *ga* should have the same style, either plain or polite. The main sentence may end in a presumptive form with *darō*. If the main sentence is in the polite form, but the predicate in the clause marked by *ga* is in the plain form, it gives the impression that the speaker is slightly emotional. Also note that many speakers often stop talking after uttering a clause with *ga*, without completing the sentence. This is very common when one just states his/her desire, request, or a problem and wants to elicit suggestions or permission from the listener.

1. Expressing conflicts and contrasts

   私はお酒は飲みますがたばこは吸いません。
   *Watashi wa osake wa nomimasu **ga** tabako wa suimasen.*
   I drink alcohol but don't smoke cigarettes.

   彼は頑張りましたがだめでした。
   *Kare wa ganbarimashita **ga** dame deshita.*
   He tried hard, but he failed.

   お疲れでしょうがもう少しご辛抱願います。
   *Otsukare deshō **ga** mō sukoshi goshinbō negaimasu.*
   I guess you are tired, but I'd like you to be patient just a little longer.

   映画は面白くなかったのですが最後まで見ました。
   *Eiga wa omoshiroku nakatta no desu **ga** saigo made mimashita.*
   Although the movie wasn't interesting, I watched it to the end.

   日本語の勉強は必要なんですが漢字がむずかしいんです。
   *Nihongo no benkyō wa hitsuyō na n desu **ga** kanji ga muzukashii n desu.*
   Studying Japanese is necessary, but the problem is that kanji are difficult.

2. Indicating the transition

   田中と申しますが，社長にお会いできますか。
   *Tanaka to mōhimasu **ga**, shachō ni oai dekimasu ka.*
   My name is Tanaka. Would it be possible to see the boss?

   その映画を観ましたがとても面白かったですよ。
   *Sono eiga o mimashita **ga** totemo omoshirokatta desu yo.*
   I saw that movie, and it was very interesting.

   今日は何もすることがないんですがどうしようかな。
   *Kyō wa nani mo suru koto ga nai n desu **ga** dō shiyō kana.*
   I have nothing to do today. I wonder what to do.

3. At the end of a sentence-fragment clause

   The sentence-fragment clause can state a desire, a request, or a problem and elicit suggestions or permissions from the listener.

ちょっとお願いがあるんですが…。 *Chotto onegai ga aru n desu **ga** ...*
I have a favor to ask you . . . (so will you help me?)

これが分からないんですが…。 *Kore ga wakaranai n desu **ga** ...*
I don't understand this . . . (so will you teach me?)

今とても忙しいんですが…。 *Ima totemo isogashii n desu **ga** ...*
I'm very busy now . . . (so I can't help you)

ちょっとお腹が空いたんですが…。 *Chotto onaka ga suita n desu **ga** ...*
I'm a little hungry . . . (Shall we go somewhere to eat?)

これは私には高すぎるんですが…。
*Kore wa watashi ni wa takasugiru n desu **ga** ...*
This is too expensive for me . . . (Do you have another, cheaper one?)

4. Following clauses in the plain form

   Ga can follow clause predicates in the plain form if used in formal written forms. When an explanatory effect is needed, the clause that ends in *no da* or *n da* is used before *ga*.

   この商品は安い（のだ）が品質が良くない。
   *Kono shōhin wa yasui **(no da) ga** hinshitsu ga yokunai.*
   These goods are cheap, but the quality is not good.

   彼のうちを訪ねた（のだ）が会えなかった。
   *Kare no uchi o tazune**ta (no da) ga** aenakatta.*
   I dropped in at his house, but I could not see him.

   高い（のだ）がどうしても買わなければならない。
   *Takai **(no da) ga** dōshitemo kawanakereba naranai.*
   It's expensive, but I need to buy it at any cost.

   彼は学生（なの）だが会社を起こしている。
   *Kare was **gakusei (na no) da ga** kaisha o okoshite iru.*
   He is a student but started a company.

   彼は誠実（なの）だが能力が足りない。
   *Kare was **seijitsu (na no) da ga** nōryoky ga tarinai.*
   He is sincere but lacks the ability.

5. After concessive clauses, often with interrogatives and verbs in the volitional form

   The main sentence that follows the concessive clause generally states that the action expressed in the concessive clause does not have an influence on the resulting fact.

   どのパソコンを買おうが大差はない。
   *Dono pasokon o kaō **ga** taisa wa nai.*
   Whichever personal computer you may buy, it doesn't make much difference.

だれが何と言おうが気にしない。 **Dare ga nan to iō ga** ki ni shinai.
Whoever may say whatever, I don't care.

犯人がどこに逃げようが必ず捕まるだろう。
Hannin ga doko ni nigeyō ga kanarazu tsukamaru darō.
Wherever the criminal escapes, he/she will surely be caught.

太郎と花子が結婚しようが知ったことじゃない。
Tarō ga Hanako to kekkon shiyō ga shitta koto ja nai.
Even if Taro marries Hanako, I don't care.

雨が降ろうが風が吹こうが助けに行くよ。
Ame ga furō ga kaze ga fukō ga tasuke ni iku yo.
I will go to help you, although it may rain or it may blow.

garu がる [ADJECTIVE SUFFIX]

(someone) wants/feels (something)

The suffix *garu* can be attached to the root of adjectives that express psychological states such as desires, emotions, and sensations and create a verb that means 'to show the signs of. . . .' (→ See also *sō da* <conjecture>.) Because it creates a verb, the understood object is marked by the particle *o*, rather than the particle *ga*. Interestingly, *garu* is used only for describing the third person and also the second person's psychological state in a main clause. The underlying idea is that the speaker should have no direct way of knowing the third or the second person's psychological states but can only express the signs of them. *Garu* usually takes the *. . . te iru* form unless the state is one's nature. It is not usually used for adjectival nouns except in some cases (e.g. *iya-garu* 'to hate').

1. Used with adjectives that express desires
   彼はもっといい車を欲しがっています。
   *Kare wa motto ii kuruma **o hoshigatte imasu**.*
   He wants a better car.

→ See also *hoshii*.

2. Used with adjectives that express emotions
   子供はすぐお化けの話をこわがります。
   *Kodomo wa sugu obake no hanashi **o kowagarimasu**.*
   Children are easily scared by ghost stories.

   彼女は失恋して今悲しがっています。
   *Kanojo wa shitsuren shite ima **konashigatte imasu**.*
   She had a broken heart, and now she is grieving.

3. Used with adjectives that express sensations

あのけが人はひどく痛がっています。
*Ano keganin wa hidoku **itagatte imasu**.*
That injured person looks to be in terrible pain.

彼はとても寒がっています。 *Kare wa totemo **samugatte imasu**.*
He is very sensitive to cold.

4. After adjective phrases made of verbs and *-tai*

彼女はヨーロッパに行きたがっています。
*Kanojo wa Yōroppa ni **ikitagatte imasu**.*
She is eager to visit Europe.

太郎さんはあなたにとても会いたがっていました。
*Tarō san wa anata ni totemo **aitagatte imashita**.*
It looked like Taro longed to see you.

→ See also *tai*.

go ご(御) [PREFIX]

The prefix *go* is attached at the beginning of (adjectival) nouns that are Sino-Japanese vocabulary (words originated from Chinese or words read in *on*-reading, the Chinese way of reading kanji) and indicates politeness (respect, humility, refinement). For native Japanese vocabulary, the prefix *o* is used instead of *go*. However, there are a number of exceptions, where *o* is used for Sino-Japanese vocabulary. (→ See also *o <prefix>* and Honorifics.)

ご旅行のご出発はいつですか。
***Goryokō** no **goshuppatsu** wa itsu desu ka.* (respectful)
When is your departure for your trip?

ご無理をなさらないようにして下さい。
***Gomuri** o nasaranai yō ni shite kudasai.* (respectful)
Please don't overwork yourself.

ご立派な邸宅ですね。 ***Gorippa na** teitaku desu ne.* (respectful)
It's a magnificent mansion, isn't it?

こういうご時勢なんですね。 *Kōiu **gojisei** na n desu ne.* (courteous)
It's a sign of the times, isn't it?

2. Followed by verbal noun of kanji in the Chinese reading

ご協力します。 ***Gokyōryoku** shimasu.* (humble)   **I'll help you.**

ご参加下さいませんか。 ***Gosanka** kudasai masen ka.* (respectful)
Won't you join us?

goro 頃 [SUFFIX]

about, around

The suffix *goro* follows a noun that specifies a point in time, and means 'approximately,' 'about,' or 'around.' The particle *ni* may or may not be used after *goro*, but the presence of *ni* stresses the time phrase.

1. After specific time expressions

   私は今朝は七時頃(に)起きました。
   *Watashi wa kesa wa **shichi ji goro (ni)** okimashita.*
   I got up about seven o'clock this morning.

   十日頃 (に) もう一度会って話しましょう。
   ***Tōka goro (ni)** mō ichido atte hanashimashō.*
   Let us meet again around the 10th and talk about it.

2. After *itsu* or *nan ji*

   その橋はいつごろ出来上がりますか。
   *Sono hashi wa **itsu goro** dekiagarimasu ka.*
   About when will that bridge be completed?

   何時頃 (に) 伺いましょうか。 ***Nan ji goro (ni)** ukagaimashō ka.*
   At about what time shall I call on you?

gurai ぐらい → See *kurai*.

hajimeru 始める [AUXILIARY VERB]

begin, start (doing)

The verb *hajimeru* can serve as an auxiliary verb, following other verbs in the combining form, to mean 'to start ...ing.'

   私の友達も最近日本語を勉強し始めました。
   *Watashi no tomodachi mo saikin Nihongo o benkyō **shihajimemashita**.*
   My friend also began to study Japanese recently.

   来月からヨガと柔道を習い始めます。
   *Raigetsu kara yoga to jūdō o **naraihajimemasu**.*
   I will start learning yoga and judo beginning next month.

   → See also *dasu*, *kakeru*, and *owaru*.

hajimete はじめて [ADVERB]

for the first time

The adverb *hajimete* was derived from the *te*-form of the verb *hajimeru*, which means 'to begin.' It can be placed where an adverb is placed in a sentence, but it is often used right after a verb in the *te*-form, forming a phrase, or before *da/desu*, forming a predicate. The polite version of this form, *hajimemashite*, is commonly used when one introduces oneself, literally meaning 'we will start our relation' but actually similar to 'How do you do?' in English.

1. Modifying a verb

   私ははじめて海外に行きます。 *Watashi wa **hajimete** kaigai ni **ikimasu**.*
   I am going overseas for the first time.

2. Followed by *desu*

   日本に行くのはこれがはじめてです。
   *Nihon ni iku no wa kore ga **hajimete** desu.*
   This is my first time to go to Japan.

   彼が日本に来たのはこれがはじめてです。
   *Kare ga Nihon ni kita no wa korega **hajimete** desu.*
   This is the first time that he has come to Japan.

   こんなに暑いのは生まれてはじめてです。
   *Konnani atsui no wa umarete **hajimete** desu.*
   I've never experienced such heat in my life.

3. After verbs in the *te*-form

   失ってはじめて友情の大切さが分かりました。
   *Ushinatte hajimete yūjō no taisetsusa ga **wakarimashita**.*
   I realized the value of friendship when I lost it.
   (I lost friendship and for the first time I realized its value.)

han 半 [NOUN]

a half

Han means 'a half' and is often used for expressing quantity, amount, time, and distance, following counters.

東京から大阪まで新幹線で約2時間半です。
*Tōkyō kara Ōsaka made Shinkansen de yaku ni **jikan han** desu.*
It takes about two and a half hours by Shinkansen from Tokyo to Osaka.

打ち合わせは2時半から半時間の予定です。
*Uchiawase wa ni **ji han** kara **han jikan** no yotei desu.*
The preliminary meeting is scheduled for half an hour from half past two.

私のうちは空港から5マイル半です。
*Watashi no uchi wa kūkō kara go **mairu han** desu.*
My house is five and a half miles distant from the airport.

han 反 [PREFIX]

anti-

Han precedes nouns and adds the meaning 'anti-' or 'opposed.' (→ See also *fu*.)

反体制派グループがデモをあおっている。
Han taiseiha gurūpu ga demo o aotte iru.
The antiestablishment group is stirring up the demonstration march.

反首相グループが別の候補を立てた。
Han shushō gurūpu ga betsu no kōho o tateta.
The anti–prime minister group put up another candidate.

反政府ゲリラがこの地域を占拠している。
Han seifu gerira ga kono chiiki o senkyō shite iru.
Anti-government guerrillas occupy this area.

hazu da はずだ [PREDICATIVE PHRASE]

to be supposed/expected to (do), be sure to (do), ought to (do)

Hazu is an unsubstantial noun that roughly means 'the case that is supposedly true.' It can be placed at the end of a sentence followed by *da* or *desu* to mean 'it is supposed to be the case that. . . .' It is used when the speaker draws a conclusion based on the circumstantial evidence or preexisting understandings. (→ See *ni chigai nai, mitai da*, and *yō da <conjecture>*.) *Hazu* follows words, phrases, or clauses and creates a new *no*-type adjectival noun.

1. After adjectival nouns + **na/no**

   この界隈はにぎやかなはずです。
   Kono kaiwai wa **nigiyaka na hazu** desu.
   This neighborhood is supposed to be bustling.

   彼は病気のはずです。 Kare wa **byōki no hazu desu**.
   He is supposed to be sick.

2. After nouns + **no**

   彼女は今学生のはずです。
   Kanojo wa ima **gakusei no hazu** desu.
   I'm sure she is a student now.

3. After (adjectival) nouns + **ja nai, datta,** or **ja nakatta**

   彼は辛いものが好きじゃないはずです。
   Kare wa karai mono ga suki ja **nai hazu** desu.
   I suppose that he does not like hot spicy foods.

4. After verbs and adjectives in the dictionary form

彼はもうすぐここに着くはずです。
*Kare wa mō sugu koko ni tsuku **hazu desu**.*
He is supposed to arrive here soon.

このカメラは旧タイプだからもっと安いはずです。
*Kono kamera wa kyū taipu dakara motto yasui **hazu desu**.*
This camera ought to be much cheaper because it's an old type.

5. After verbs and adjectives in the *nai*-form

彼女はそんなことをしないはずだ。
*Kanojo wa sonna koto o shi**nai hazu desu**.*
I don't expect that she is going to do such a thing.

6. After verbs and adjectives in the *ta*-form

私はその時そう言ったはずです。
*Watashi wa sono toki sō it**ta hazu desu**.*
I'm sure I told you so at that time.

7. Before the particle *no* that precedes a noun

死んだはずの人がどうしてここにいるんですか。
***Shinda hazu no hito** ga dōshite koko ni iru n desu ka?*
Why is the person who was supposed to be dead here?

ここに置いたはずの鍵がないんです。
*Koko ni **oita hazu no kagi** ga nai n desu.*
The key that is supposed to have been placed here disappeared.

明日試験を受けるはずの人がどうしてこんなところでお酒を飲んでいるの？
*Ashita shiken o **ukeru hazu no hito** ga dōshite konna tokoro de osake o nonde iru no?*
Why is the person who is supposed to take an exam tomorrow drinking sake in such a place?

8. Before *ga nai*

彼がそんな単純なミスをしたはずがない。
*Kare ga sonna tanjun na misu o shita **hazu ga nai**.*
He cannot have made such a simple mistake.

長距離バスがまだ来ていないはずがない。
*Chōkyori basu ga mada kite inai **hazu ga nai**.*
It is impossible that the long-distance bus has not arrived yet.
(The long-distance bus should have already arrived.)

彼の話が本当のはずがない。
*Kare no hanashi ga hontō no **hazu ga nai**.*
His story cannot be true.

そんなにお金が儲かるはずがありますか。
*Sonna ni okane ga mōkaru **hazu ga arimasu ka**.*
Is it possible that one would make so much money?

In the above example, *hazu ga arimasu ka* is interpreted as *hazu ga nai.*

9. Before ***ni natte iru***

ここに来ているはずになっていますが。
*Koko ni kite iru **hazu ni natte** imasu ga.*
He is supposed to be here, but . . .

---

hazu ga nai はずがない [PREDICATIVE PHRASE] → See ***hazu da.***

---

hō 方 [NOUN]

---

side, one (of the two items)

Hō is a noun that literally means 'side,' but it makes sense only if there are two items being discussed in the context and it is preceded by a demonstrative, a word, or a phrase that clarifies which one is being referred to. It is typically used in comparative sentences and also expressions such as . . . *hō ga ii* and . . . *hō ga mashida.* (→ See also Comparisons, *yori*, and *hō ga ii*.)

1. After demonstrative adjectives

あれよりこの方が便利です。 *Are yori **kono hō** ga benri desu.*
This is more convenient than that.

2. After nouns + ***no***

金曜日の方が木曜日よりも忙しいです。
***Kin'yōbi no hō** ga Mokuyōbi yori mo isogashii desu.*
I am busier on Friday than Thursday.

パンよりご飯の方が好きです。 *Pan yori **gohan no hō** ga suki desu.*
I like rice better than bread.

山下さんは結婚と仕事とでは仕事の方をとりました。
*Yamashita san wa kekkon to shigoto to de wa **shigoto no hō** o torimashita.*
Between marriage and a job, Ms. Yamashita chose her job.

3. After verbs and adjectives in the dictionary form

バスで行く方が電車で行くより便利でしょう。
*Basu de iku **hō** ga densha de iku yori benri deshō.*
It will be more convenient to go by bus than by train.

今日は家で休む方がいい。 *Kyō wa ie de yasumu **hō** ga ii.*
I would rather take a rest at home today.

カメラは軽い方が便利ですよ。 *Kamera wa karui **hō** ga benri desu yo.*
A lighter camera is handier.

4. After verbs in the *nai*-form

そんな映画は観ない方がましです。
*Sonna eiga wa mi**nai hō** ga mashi desu.*
It is better for me not to see such a movie.

5. After verbs in the *ta*-form

歩いて行った方が早かったですね。
*Aruite it**ta hō** ga hayakatta desu ne.*
It would have been faster to go on foot.

hodo ほど [PARTICLE]

about, or so, (not) as . . . as . . . , to the extent of, enough to (do), the more . . . the more . . .

The particle *hodo* follows a variety of items, creating a phrase that expresses the approximate degree or extent of some state or action.

1. After nouns that express some quantity and amount

京都駅はここから1キロほどです。
*Kyōto eki wa koko kara **ichi kiro hodo** desu.*
Kyoto Station is about one kilometer from here.

十分ほどここで待って下さい。 ***Jippun hodo** koko de matte kudasai.*
Please wait here about ten minutes.

そのコーヒーを1キロほど下さい。 *Sono kōhī o **ichi kiro hodo** kudasai.*
I'll take about one kilogram of that coffee.

→ See also *bakari* and *kurai*.

2. After adjectival nouns with *na*

便利なら便利なほどいいです。 *Benri nara **benri na hodo** ii desu.*
The more convenient, the better.

→ See also *ba . . . hodo*.

3. After verbs and adjectives in the dictionary form

海外留学ができるほどお金がたまりました。
*Kaigai ryūgaku ga deki**ru hodo** okane ga tamarimashita.*
I saved enough money to study abroad.

この漢字の本は外国人でも読めるほどやさしいです。
*Kono kanji no hon wa gaikokujin demo yome**ru hodo** yasashii desu.*
This kanji book is so easy that even a non-native can read it.

彼とは話せば話すほど好きになる。
*Kare to wa hanaseba hanas**u hodo** suki ni naru.*
The more I talk with him, the better I like him.

鞄は軽ければ軽いほどいい。 *Kaban wa karukereba karui **hodo** ii.*
Bags are better when lighter.

→ See also *ba . . . hodo.*

4. After verbs in the ***nai**-form*

私はもう歩けないほど疲れました。
*Watashi wa mō aruke**nai hodo** tsukaremashita.*
I am so tired that I can't walk any more.

5. After verbs in the ***ta**-form*

この中古の車は思ったほど高くはなかった。
*Kono chūko no kuruma wa omot**ta hodo** takaku wa nakatta.*
This used car was not as expensive as I had expected.

6. After nouns, used with a negative predicate

For negating a sentence with a comparison of equivalents, *hodo* must be
used along with a negative predicate.

英語はたぶん日本語ほどむずかしくありません。
*Eigo wa tabun **Nihongo hodo** muzukashiku ari**masen**.*
Probably English is not as difficult as Japanese.

私は兄ほどよく勉強しません。
*Watashi wa **ani hodo** yoku benkyō shi**masen**.*
I do not study as hard as my big brother.

時間ほど貴重なものはない。 *Jikan **hodo** kichō na mono wa **nai**.*
There is nothing as precious as time.

→ See Comparisons.

---

hō ga ii 方がいい [PREDICATIVE PHRASE]

it would be better to (do), you had better (do)

Hō ga ii can follow verbs used for giving suggestions and advices. *To omoimasu,*
which means 'I think,' often follows this expression, making it sound less assertive. It follows verbs in the *ta*-form (plain affirmative past) and the *nai*-form
(plain negative past). It can also follow verbs in the dictionary form, but the
expression sounds more direct than when it is followed by verbs in the *ta*-form.

1. After verbs in the ***ta**-form*

彼女に謝った方がいい。 *Kanojo ni ayamat**ta hō ga ii**.*
It would be better to apologize to her.

タバコはもうやめた方がいいと思います。
*Tabako wa mō yame**ta hō ga ii** to omoimasu.*
I think it really would be better for you to give up smoking.

2. After verbs in the **nai**-form

安物は買わない方がいいですよ。 *Yasumono wa kawanai hō ga ii desu yo.*
It would be better for you not to buy cheap articles.

3. After verbs in the dictionary form

今日は傘を持っていく方がいい。 *Kyō wa kasa o motte iku hō ga ii.*
You had better take along an umbrella today.

→ See also *hō*.

---

hoka ほか [NOUN]

some/any other . . . apart from, besides, except (for), somewhere/anywhere else

Hoka can be followed by *no* and function as an attribute for the following noun, meaning 'some other. . . .' For example, *hoka no hon* means 'some other book.' The noun may be omitted if contextually understood, thus *hoka no* means 'some other item.' *Hoka* can be preceded by a noun plus *no*, and also followed by *ni* or *wa*, defining the set to which the statement or question applies, meaning 'other than. . . .' The preceding noun can be omitted if understood; thus *hoka ni wa* means 'other than that' or 'besides.' Finally, *hoka* can be used as a noun that means 'some other place' or 'somewhere.'

1. Used in the form '**Hoka no** (noun)'

イベントはほかの日がいいです。 *Ibeto wa **hoka no hi** ga ii desu.*
Some other day is better for the event.

ほかの人に頼みます。 ***Hoka no hito** ni tanomimasu.*
I'll ask somebody else for it.

ほかのを見せてください。 ***Hoka no** o misete kudasai.*
Please show me another.

2. Used in the form '(noun + **no**) **hoka ni/wa**'

彼女のほかにここに知り合いはいません。
***Kanojo no hoka ni** koko ni shiriai wa imasen.*
I have no acquaintances here besides her.

ビールのほかは何も要りません。 ***Bīru no hoka wa** nani mo irimasen.*
I don't need anything other than beer.

ほかにだれが行くんですか。 ***Hoka ni** dare ga iku n desu ka.*
Who else is going?

3. Meaning 'some other places'

ほかでもっと安いのが手に入ります。
***Hoka de** motto yasui no ga te ni hairimasu.*
You can get a cheaper one somewhere else.

ほかを探してください。 *Hoka o sagashite kudasai.*
Please look for it somewhere else.

→ See also *igai*.

hoka nai ほかない [PREDICATIVE PHRASE]

can do nothing but (do), cannot help (doing) something

Verbs in the dictionary forms can be followed by *hoka nai* to mean that the actions denoted by them are the only possible options that one can take. (→ See also *shika*.)

諦めるほかありません。 *Akiramer**u hoka arimasen.***
I can do nothing but give up.

ここで待つほかないですね。 *Koko de matsu **hoka nai** desu ne.*
There is nothing to be done but wait here, is there?

hoshii 欲しい [ADJECTIVE]

want

The adjective *hoshii* is used for expressing one's desire for items. The understood object (the item one wants) is marked by the particle *ga*. (→ See also *ga*.) This adjective is used for expressing the first person's desire or asking the second person's desire. For expressing the third person's desire, *hoshii* must be followed by *gatte iru* or *sō da* as in *hoshigatte iru* or *hoshisō da*. This is because *hoshii* expresses the inner desire. (→ See also *garu* and *sō da* <conjecture>.) To express one's desire for his/her own actions rather than items, do not use *hoshii*, but use the suffix *tai* right after the verb that expresses the action. (→ See also *hoshii* <auxiliary adjective> and *tai*.)

私はカメラが欲しいです。彼はパソコンを欲しがっています。
*Watashi wa **kamera ga hoshii** desu. Kare wa **pasokon o hoshigatte imasu.***
I want a camera. He wants a personal computer.

今何が欲しいんですか。 *Ima **nani ga hoshii** n desu ka.*
What do you want now?

hoshii 欲しい [AUXILIARY ADJECTIVE]

want (someone to do something)

The auxiliary adjective *hoshii* follows verbs in the *te*-form and expresses what one wants someone else to do. The person who performs the action is marked by the particle *ni*. (→ See also *tai*.) To express what one does not want the person to do, use the verb in the *nai*-form followed by the particle *de*. (→ See also *nai de*.)

私は兄にもう少しまじめに働いて欲しいんです。
*Watashi wa ani ni mō sukoshi majime ni **hataraite hoshii** n desu.*
I want my brother to work a bit more seriously.

ちょっと手伝って欲しいんですが。 *Chotto **tetsudatte hoshii** n desu ga.*
I want you to help me for a while.

行かないで欲しいです。彼も行かないで欲しそうです。
Ikanaide hoshii desu. Kare mo ikanaide hoshisō desu.
I don't want you to go. He also seems to want you not to go.

hotondo ほとんど [ADVERB]

almost, hardly, scarcely, little, few

Hotondo means 'mostly' and is used in either affirmative or negative sentences. It can also be followed by the particle *no* to become a noun modifier.

1. Used in an affirmative sentence

    仕事はほとんど終わりました。 *Shigoto wa **hotondo** owarimashita.*
    The work is almost finished.

2. Used in a negative sentence

    今週はほとんど日本語を勉強しませんでした。
    *Konshū wa **hotondo** Nihongo o benkyō shimasen deshita.*
    I have hardly studied Japanese this week.

    高くてほとんどだれもそれを買いません。
    *Takakute **hotondo** dare mo sore o kaimasen.*
    Hardly anybody buys it because it's expensive.

3. Followed by *no*

    ほとんどの日本人は勤勉だ。 ***Hotondo no** Nihonjin wa kinben da.*
    Most Japanese people are diligent.

→ See also *mettani* and *amari*.

ichiban いちばん [ADVERB]

the superlative degree of an adjective/adverb

Ichiban literally means 'the first,' 'number one,' or 'the first place,' but can also be used to express superlative comparison when used with adjectives, adverbs, and adjectival nouns to mean 'most,' 'the most,' or 'the best.' Its formal counterpart is *mottomo*. (→ See also *mottomo* and Comparisons.)

どの店がいちばん安いですか。 *Dono mise ga **ichiban yasui** desu ka.*
Which shop is the cheapest?

「だれがいちばん上手に日本語を話しますか。」「フランクです。」
*"Dare ga **ichiban jōzu ni** Nihongo o hanashimasu ka." "Furanku desu."*
"Who speaks Japanese the best?" "Frank does."

私はアルコールの中でビールがいちばん好きです。
*Watashi wa arukōru no naka de bīru ga **ichiban suki desu**.*
I like beer the best of alcoholic drinks.

私は今いちばんイギリスへ行きたい。
*Watashi wa ima **ichiban** Igirisu e ikitai.*
I want to go to England the most now.

igai 以外 [NOUN]

except (for), but, besides, in addition to, apart from, (those) other than

Igai is a Sino-Japanese noun that means '(things/actions/facts) other than (that).' It must follow a noun, a verb in the dictionary form or in the *nai*-form, or a clause in the plain form, occasionally followed by *to iu koto*. It is often followed by the particle *ni* or *wa*. (→ See also *hoka*.)

1. After nouns

   水曜日と日曜日以外は毎日働いています。
   ***Suiyōbi to Nichiyōbi igai wa** mainichi hataraite imasu.*
   I work every day except Wednesday and Sunday.

   雑誌以外はあまり何も読みません。
   ***Zasshi igai wa** amari nani mo yomimasen.*
   Other than magazines I read almost nothing.

   私はあなた以外に日本人の友人がいません。
   *Watashi wa **anata igai ni** Nihonjin no yūjin ga imasen.*
   I have no Japanese friends apart from you.

2. After a verb in the dictionary form or in the ***nai**-form

   逃げる以外に方法がない。 ***Nigeru igai ni** hōhō ga nai.*
   There is no other way except to run away.

   やせるには，食べない以外に方法がない。
   *Yaseru ni wa, **tabenai igai ni** hōhō ga nai.*
   There is no other solution except not to eat in order to lose weight.

3. After a clause (+ ***to iu koto***)

   昨日は郵便屋さんが来た以外はだれも来なかった。
   *Kinō wa **yūbinya san ga kita igai wa** dare mo konakatta.*
   No one came yesterday except that a mailman came.

私は彼が先生だということ以外はなにも知りません。
*Watashi wa **kare ga sensei da to iu koto igai wa** nani mo shirimasen.*
I know nothing except that he is a teacher.

igo 以後 [NOUN]

(in *or* on and) after, since, from (now) on

The noun *igo* can be used by itself to mean 'from now on,' or with a time expression to mean 'after' or 'since.' It is often followed by particles such as *wa*, *ni*, and *no*.

以後，気をつけて下さい。 ***Igo**, ki o tsukete kudasai.*
Please be more careful from now on.

午後7時以後に電話して下さい。 ***Gogo shichiji igo ni** denwa shite kudasai.*
Please call me after 7 p.m.

次の月曜日以後は大阪にいます。
***Tsugi no Getsuyōbi igo wa** Ōsaka ni imasu.*
I'll be in Osaka from next Monday on.

来月以後の予定を教えて下さい。 ***Raigetsu igo no** yotei o oshiete kudasai.*
Please let me know the schedule next month and after.

→ See also *ikō, irai,* and *kara.*

ijō 以上 [NOUN]

more than, over, mentioned above, (not) any longer, (no) more, once . . . , now that . . . , since, as long as

The noun *ijō* can follow quantity/amount/time expressions or demonstrative pronouns to mean 'more than. . . .' (→ See also *yori*.) It can also follow a clause to mean 'as long as.' It can be also used by itself to mean 'everything mentioned or done.'

1. After quantity/amount/number expressions

   そこまで行くのに1時間以上かかります。
   *Soko made iku no ni **ichi jikan ijō** kakarimasu.*
   It will take more than one hour to get there.

   このトンネルは2キロメートル以上あります。
   *Kono tonneru wa **ni kiro mētoru ijō** arimasu.*
   This tunnel is more than two kilometers long.

   ここは二十才以上の人しか入れません。
   *Koko wa **hatachi ijō** no hito shika hairemasen.*
   Only people who are twenty and over are allowed to enter here.

2. After the demonstrative pronouns

これ以上ここで待てません。 ***Kore ijō** koko de matemasen.*
I can't wait here any longer.

それ以上は無理です。 ***Sore ijō** wa muri desu.*
Any more than that is impossible.

3. At the end of a clause

それをやると決めた以上努力しなければなりません。
***Sore o yaru to kimeta ijō** doryoku shinakereba narimasen. (kara niwa can*
replace ijō)
Now that you've decided to do it, you must work hard.

ここまでやった以上完成しよう。 ***Koko made yatta ijō** kansei shiyō.*
As long as we've come this far, let's complete it.

4. Used by itself with particles

以上で，報告を終わります。 ***Ijō de**, hōkoku o owarimasu.*
That's all, for my report.

以上の理由でこれは中止になりました。
***Ijō no riyū** de kore wa chūshi ni narimashita.*
This was cancelled for the reasons mentioned above.

---

ikenai いけない [ADJECTIVE]

bad, not good

Ikenai literally means 'bad' but is often used for expressing prohibitions and
obligations by following a phrase or a clause that shows some condition. (→
See also *tewa ikenai / dewa ikenai, nakereba ikenai / nakereba naranai,* and *neba
naranai.*)

1. Used by itself with particles

それのどこがいけないのですか。 *Sore no doko ga **ikenai** no desu ka.*
What's wrong with it?

「いけませんよ！」 *"**Ikemasen** yo!"* **"That's bad!"**

雨が降るといけないから傘を持っていった方がいいですよ。
*Ame ga furu to **ikenai** kara kasa o motte itta hō ga ii desu yo.*
It's better to take along an umbrella, because it'll be bad if it rains.

2. To express prohibitions

ここでタバコを吸ってはいけません。 *Koko de tabako o sutte **wa ikemasen**.*
You must not smoke here.

あまりお酒を飲んではいけないよ。 *Amari osake o nonde **wa ikenai** yo.*
You mustn't drink too much.

3. To express obligations

もう行かなければいけません。 *Mō **ikanakereba ikemasen**.*
I have to go now.

行かなければいけませんでした。 ***Ikanakereba ikemasen** deshita.*
I had to go.

ikō 以降 [NOUN]

from . . . on, after

Ikō is a noun that denotes the time after the specified time.

来週以降はとても忙しいです。 ***Raishū ikō wa** totemo isogashii desu.*
I'll be very busy from next week on.

今晩九時以降に電話して下さい。
*Konban **ku ji ikō ni** denwa shite kudasai.*
Please call me after nine tonight.

→ See also *igo*, *irai*, and *kara*.

iku いく [AUXILIARY VERB]

to keep (doing) from now on, get/become (some state describing the subject) from
now on, (to do something) on the way

The auxiliary verb *iku* is used after verbs in the *te*-form and expresses the initia-
tion and the continuation of the action. For expressing the development of
some state, the verb *naru* 'to become' or *suru* 'to do/make' is used along with an
adverb or an adverbial phrase. (→ See also *naru* and *suru*.)

毎日漢字を3つずつ覚えていきたいと思います。
*Mainichi kanji o mittsu zutsu **oboete ikitai** to omoimasu.*
I plan to memorize three kanji every day from now on.

あそこでお茶を飲んでいきませんか。 *Asoko de ocha o **nonde ikimasen** ka.*
Shall we have tea over there before we go?

気温は徐々に高くなっていきます。 *Kion wa jojo ni **takaku natte ikimasu**.*
The temperature keeps on rising gradually.

テストの問題を少しずつ難しくしていきます。
*Tesuto no mondai o sukoshizutsu **muzukashiku shite ikimasu**.*
I shall make the questions in the test gradually more difficult.

一人で何でもできるようになっていかなければなりません。
*Hitori de nan demo dekiru **yō ni natte ikanakereba** narimasen.*
You must become able to do everything by yourself little by little.

→ See also *kuru*.

ikura ... temo/demo いくら...ても/でも [ADVERBIAL PHRASE]

no matter how (much/hard), at the . . . est, even . . .

The interrogative degree adverb *ikura* 'how much' can be used with verbs, adjectives, and the linking verb in the *te*-form along with the particle *mo* to create an adverbial phrase that means 'no matter how much. . . .'

1. With verbs in the ***te***-form

   いくら頑張ってもよくならない。 ***Ikura ganbattemo*** *yoku naranai.*
   No matter how hard I try, it doesn't go well.

2. With adjectives in the ***te***-form

   いくら遅くても五時までに着きたい。
   Ikura osokutemo *go ji made ni tsukitai.*
   I want to arrive there by five at the latest.

3. With ***de*** (the ***te***-form of ***da***)

   いくら天才でもその問題は解けない。
   Ikura tensai demo *sono mondai wa tokenai.*
   Even a genius cannot solve that problem.

→ See also *demo* and *temo/demo*.

inai 以内 [NOUN]

within, less than, not more than

Inai is a noun that denotes length, quantity, or amount within the specified limitations.

五分以内に戻ります。 ***Go fun inai*** *ni modorimasu.*
I'll be back within five minutes.

旅行の費用は五万円以内です。
Ryokō no hiyō wa ***go man en inai*** *desu.*
The expense for the trip will be less than fifty thousand yen.

駅はここから歩いて十五分以内の所です。
Eki wa koko kara aruite ***jū go fun inai*** *no tokoro desu.*
The train station is within fifteen minutes' walk from here.

3人以内なら，料金は同じです。
San nin inai *nara, ryōkin wa onaji desu.*
If there are three or fewer people, the fee should be the same.

→ See also *made*.

irai 以来 [CONJUNCTION]

since

Irai is a noun that denotes the time after the specified point in time in the past. It follows nouns or verbs in the *te*-form.

先月以来雨が降っていません。 **Sengetsu irai** *ame ga futte imasen.*
It has not rained since last month.

私は教師になって以来五年になります。
*Watashi wa kyōshi ni natte **irai** go nen ni narimasu.*
It is five years since I became a teacher.

→ See also *igo*, *ikō*, and *kara*.

irassharu いらっしゃる [AUXILIARY VERB]

be . . . ing, have (done), be (done), have been . . . ing

The auxiliary verb *irassharu* is the honorific version of the auxiliary verb *iru*. It is an *u*-verb, but its *masu*-form is *irasshaimasu* rather than *irassharimasu*. (→ See *iru <auxiliary verb>* and *oru*.)

何を書いていらっしゃるんですか。 *Nani o kaite **irassharu** n desu ka.*
What are you writing?

irassharu いらっしゃる [VERB]

to be, there be, exist, stay, have, go, come

The verb *irassharu* is the honorific version of the verb *iru*. It is an *u*-verb, but its *masu*-form is *irasshaimasu* rather than *irassharimasu*. (→ See *iru <verb>* and *oru*.)

あそこに田中先生がいらっしゃいますよ。
*Asoko ni Tanaka sensei ga **irasshaimasu** yo.*
Professor Tanaka is over there.

ご兄弟はいらっしゃいますか。 *Gokyōdai wa **irasshaimasu** ka.*
Do you have any siblings?

今日はどちらにいらっしゃるんですか。
*Kyō wa dochira ni **irassharu** n desu ka.*
Where are you going today?

たくさんのお客さんがいらっしゃり嬉しいです。
*Takusan no okyakusan ga **irasshari** ureshii desu.*
Many customers came, and I'm glad.

林さんがいらっしゃっています。 *Hayashi san ga **irasshatte** imasu.*
Mr. Hayashi has come here. (Mr. Hayashi is here.)

iru いる [AUXILIARY VERB]

be . . . ing, have (done), be (done), have been . . . ing

The auxiliary verb *iru* follows verbs in the *te*-form, as in *tabete iru* or *yonde iru*, and expresses a progressive state, a habitual state, or a resulting state (a state that results from a previous event). The initial syllable *i* tends to drop in informal speech, as in *tabeteru/yonderu* and *tabetemasu/yondemasu*. (→ See also *aru <auxiliary verb>*, *irassharu <auxiliary verb>*, and *oru*.)

1. Progressive state

   私は今，英字新聞を読んでいます。
   Watashi wa ima eiji shinbun o yonde imasu.
   I am reading an English-language newspaper.

   私は今友人を待っています。 *Watashi wa ima yūjin o matte imasu.*
   I am waiting for a friend of mine now.

   昨日からずっと雨が降っています。 *Kinō kara zutto ame ga futte imasu.*
   It has been raining since yesterday.

   「何をして(い)たんですか。」「メールをして(い)ました。」
   "Nani o shite(i)ta n desu ka." "Mēru o shite(i)mashita."
   "What were you doing?" "I was e-mailing."

   何をすべきか考えて(い)ます。 *Nani o subeki ka kangaete(i)masu.*
   I am thinking what to do.

   彼がどこで仕事をして(い)るのか知っていますか。
   Kare ga doko de shigoto o shite(i)ru no ka shitteimasu ka.
   Do you know where he is working?

2. Habitual State

   私は毎日英字新聞を読んでいます。
   Watashi wa mainichi eiji shinbun o yonde imasu.
   I read (subscribe to) an English-language newspaper.

3. Resulting State

   その店はもう閉まっています。 *Sono mise wa mō shimatte imasu.*
   That store is closed already.

   車の窓が開いていますよ。 *Kuruma no mado ga aite imasu yo.*
   Your car window is open.

   あなたはとても疲れてるみたいだ。
   Anata wa totemo tsukareteru mitai da.
   You look very tired.

   「この言葉を知ってますか。」「いいえ，知りません。」
   "Kono kotoba o shittemasu ka." "Iie, shirimasen."
   "Do you know this word?" "No, I don't know it."

(Many English verbs expressing a condition or state such as 'to know' must be in the *te iru* construction in Japanese. However, the negative of *shitte iru* (*shitteru*) is not *shitte imasen*, but *shirimasen*. → See *shiru*.)

iru いる [VERB]

to be, be present, there be, exist, stay, have

The verb *iru* expresses the existence of animate items or the existence of human relationships that one has. When the item that exists is marked by the particle *wa* rather than the particle *ga*, the location where it exists serves as the new piece of information. (→ See also *aru <verb>*, *irassharu <verb>*, and *oru*.)

この動物園には珍しい動物がいます。
Kono dōbutsuen ni wa mezurashii dōbutsu ga imasu.
There are unique animals in this zoo.

姉は今広島にいます。 *Ane wa ima Hiroshima ni imasu.*
My elder sister is now staying (or living) in Hiroshima.

私は兄弟が三人います。 *Watashi wa kyōdai ga san nin imasu.*
I have three brothers or sisters.

isshoni 一緒に [ADVERB]

with (someone), together, at the same time

Isshoni means 'together,' and is often used with a phrase that specifies the identity of the accompanying item marked with the particle *to*.

1. After nouns + **to**
   「だれといっしょにそこへ行ったのですか。」「友達とです。」
   ***Dare to isshoni** soko e itta no desu ka." "Tomodachi to desu."*
   "Who did you go there with?" "With my friend."

   豚肉はキャベツといっしょに炒めるとおいしいですよ。
   *Butaniku wa **kyabetsu to isshoni** itameru to oishii desu yo.*
   Pork tastes good if you stir-fry it with cabbage.

→ See also *to*.

2. Used as an adverb
   今から一緒に食事をしませんか。
   *Ima kara **isshoni** shokuji o shimasen ka.*
   Shall we have dinner together now?

   電車とバスがいっしょに着きました。
   *Densha to basu ga **isshoni** tsukimashita.*
   The train and the bus have arrived at the same time.

itadaku いただく [AUXILIARY VERB]

to get (somebody) to do something, to receive some benefit from someone else's action

The auxiliary verb *itadaku* is the humble counterpart of the auxiliary verb *morau*. (→ See *morau <auxiliary verb>*.) It follows verbs in the *te*-form, and is used when one receives some service from his/her superior.

そうしていただきます。 *Sō shite itadakimasu.*
I'll have you do so. (I hope you'll kindly do so.)

ちょっとこれを持っていただきたいのですが。
Chotto kore o motte itadakitai no desu ga.
I'd like you to hold this for a while.

この原稿を見ていただけますか。
Kono genkō o mite itadakemasu ka.
Would you look through this manuscript (for me)?

彼は先生にレポートを見ていただきました。
Kare wa sensei ni repōto o mite itadakimashita.
He had his teacher look through his report.

すみませんが，駅に行く道を教えていただけませんか。
Sumimasen ga, eki ni iku michi o oshiete itadakemasen ka.
Excuse me, but could you tell me the way to the train station?

→ See also Requests.

itadaku いただく [VERB]

to receive

The verb *itadaku* is the humble counterpart of the verb *morau*. (→ See *morau <verb>*.) *Itadaku* is used when the giver is someone to whom the speaker's respect is due. Note that *itadakimasu* is used as a set phrase that one must say before starting eating in Japan.

いただきます。 *Itadakimasu.* *Lit.,* I'll be given food.

「先生から手紙をいただきましたか。」「はい，いただきました。」
"Sensei kara tegami o itadakimashita ka." "Hai, itadakimashita."
"Did you get a letter from your teacher?" "Yes, I did."

「これをいただきたいのですが。」「はい，どうぞ。」
"Kore o itadakitai no desu ga." "Hai, dōzo."
"I'd like to have this." "Sure, please have it."

itsu いつ [INTERROGATIVE]

when, what time

Itsu is an interrogative word that means *when*. It may be followed by a particle such as *kara* and *made*.

1. Used in a main question

   いつここへ来たんですか。 ***Itsu** koko e kita n desu ka.*
   When did you come here?

   彼女はいつから病気なんですか。
   *Kanojo wa **itsu kara** byōki na n desu ka.*
   Since when has she been sick?

   いつまで日本にいるんですか。 ***Itsu made** Nihon ni iru n desu ka.*
   Until when are you in Japan?

   「次の会はいつにしましょうか。」「う～ん，いつにしましょう。」
   *"Tsugi no kai wa **itsu ni** shimashō ka." "Ūn, **itsu ni** shimashō."*
   "When shall we meet?" "Well, when shall we meet?"

2. Used in an embedded question

   いつできるのか尋ねましたか。 ***Itsu** dekiru no ka tazunemashita ka.*
   Did you ask when it will be finished?

   いつ始まるのか分かりません。 ***Itsu** hajimaru no ka wakarimasen.*
   I don't know when it begins.

3. Used with ***ka, mo,*** or ***demo***

   いつかいっしょに韓国に行きましょうよ。
   ***Itsuka** isshoni Kankoku ni ikimashō yo.*
   Let's go to South Korea together someday.

   あの人はいつも文句ばかり言っている。
   *Ano hito wa **itsumo** monku bakari itte iru.*
   That person is always complaining.

   「いつがよろしいですか。」「いつでもけっこうです。」
   *"Itsu ga yoroshii desu ka." "**Itsudemo** kekkō desu."*
   "When will be convenient for you?" "Any time will be all right."

   → See also Interrogatives, *ka, mo,* and *demo*.

ittan いったん [ADVERB]

once

Ittan is mostly used in a conditional clause with conjunctional particles such as *ba* and *to*, meaning 'once.' (→ See also *ba, to,* and Conditionals.)

いったん始めればこのようにスムーズにいきます。
Ittan hajimereba kono yō ni sumūzu ni ikimasu.
Once you begin, it goes smoothly like this.

一部の学生は大学にいったん入学すると勉強をやめる。
*Ichibu no gakusei wa daigaku ni **ittan** nyūgaku suru **to** benkyō o yameru.*
Some students quit studying once they enter college.

ja (jā) じゃ（じゃあ）[CONJUNCTION] → See *dewa* [CONJUNCTION].

ja じゃ [CONTRACTION]

contracted form of *de wa*

Ja in negative sentences is a euphonically changed form of *de wa*. It occurs in the negative form of *da/desu* and when the verb in the *te*-form ends in *de* and is followed by *wa*.

1. After (adjectival) nouns

   これは私の鞄じゃありません。あれが私のです。
   *Kore wa watashi no **kaban ja** arimasen. Are ga watashi no desu.*
   This is not my bag. That is mine.

   (indicates a condition when followed by the negative form of a potential verb)

   この天気じゃ出かけられない。 *Kono **tenki ja** dekakerarenai.*
   We can't go out in this weather.

   このコンピューターじゃそれはできません。
   *Kono **konpyūtā ja** sore wa dekimasen.*
   It can't be done with this computer.

2. When a verb in the **te**-form ends in **de** and followed by **wa**

   ここで遊んじゃいけません。 *Koko de asonja ikemasen.*
   You must not play here.

→ See also *cha, dewa,* and *ikenai.*

jū 中 [NOUN]

all over, throughout, within

Jū follows a noun that denotes a place or a period of time, to mean 'all over (the place)' or 'throughout (the period).' However, it can be the variant of *chū* in ... *chū ni*, which means 'during' or 'within.' (→ See also *aida* and *chū ni*.)

1. After a noun that denotes a place

日本中を電車で旅行したいと思います。
Nihon jū *o densha de ryokō shitai to omoimasu.*
I think I'd like to travel by train all over Japan.

2. After a noun that denotes a period of time

私は冬休み中スキーをしていました。
*Watashi wa **fuyu yasumi jū** sukī o shite imashita.*
I was skiing throughout my winter vacation.

昨日は一日中テレビを見ていました。
*Kinō wa **ichi nichi jū** terebi o mite imashita.*
I was watching TV all day long yesterday.

3. Used as a euphonically different version of ***chū ni***

今週中にそれを仕上げて下さい。
Konshū jū ni *sore o shiagete kudasai.*
Please complete it within this week.

ka か [PARTICLE]

(either) . . . or . . . , whether

The particle *ka* can be used as a case particle, a conjunctional particle, or a sentence-final particle. In addition, it follows an interrogative word, forming an indefinite pronoun such as *dareka* 'someone' or *nanika* 'something.'

I. *KA* [CASE PARTICLE]

The case particle *ka* follows words and phrases to list alternative items and concepts.

1. After each of multiple nouns (except for the last one)

大学へはバスか地下鉄で行けます。
*Daigaku e wa **basu ka chikatetsu** de ikemasu.*
You can go to the university by either bus or subway.

すしか，さしみか，てんぷらが食べられます。
Sushi ka, sashimi ka, tenpura *ga taberaremasu.*
We can eat sushi, sashimi, or tempura.

→ See *to* and *ya*.

2. After each of multiple verbs in the dictionary form

大学に行くか就職するか決めなければならない。
*Daigaku ni **iku ka** shūshoku **suru ka** kimenakereba naranai.*
I have to decide on either going to college or getting a job.

遊園地に行くか映画を見に行くかしましょう。
*Yūenchi ni iku **ka** eiga o mi ni iku **ka** shimashō.*
Let's either go to an amusement park or go to see a movie.

II. *KA* [CONJUNCTIONAL PARTICLE]

The clause that is used before *no da* can be followed by *no* and *ka*. (→ See *no da*.) However, *no* and additional elements might be optional, as indicated by the parentheses in the following examples.

1. For forming an embedded yes-no question with optional **dōka**

   高橋さんは来る(の)か(どうか)分かりません。
   Takahashi san wa kuru (no) ka (dōka) wakarimasen.
   I do not know if Ms. Takahashi will come.

   これが本物(なの)か(どうか)分かりません。
   Kore ga honmono (na no) ka (dōka) wakarimasen.
   I don't know whether or not this is the real thing.

   明日テストがあるか(どうか)知っていますか。
   Ashita tesuto ga aru ka (dō ka) shitte imasu ka.
   Do you know whether we have a test tomorrow?

2. For forming an embedded content question

   明日だれが来る(の)か分かりますか。
   Ashita dare ga kuru (no) ka wakarimasu ka.
   Do you know who will come tomorrow?

   何が起こった(の)か分かりません。
   Nani ga okotta (no) ka wakarimasen.
   I don't know what happened.

   この字はどうやって書く(の)か教えて下さい。
   Kono ji wa dō yatte kaku (no) ka oshiete kudasai.
   Please teach me how to write this character.

   彼女にどうする(の)か尋ねましたが答えませんでした。
   Kanojo ni dō suru (no) ka tazunemashita ga, kotaemasen deshita.
   I asked her what she would do, but she didn't answer.

   田中さんはいつテストがある(の)か知っていますか。
   *Tanaka san wa **itsu tesuto ga aru (no) ka** shitte imasu ka.*
   Mr. Tanaka, do you know when we'll have a test?

   何をすればいい(の)か教えてください。
   Nani o sure ba ii (no) ka oshiete kudasai.
   Please let me know what I should do.

KAGIRI 211

III. *KA* [SENTENCE-FINAL PARTICLE]

The sentence-final particle *ka* shows that the sentence is a question. Note that *ka* is replaced by *kai*, or simply dropped when the question is in the informal style. If *ka* follows a negative verb, it is perceived as an invitation or suggestion. (→ See Questions.)

1. For forming a yes-no question

   「これはあなたの鞄ですか。」「はい，そうです。」
   "Kore wa anata no kaban desu ka." " Hai, sō desu."
   "Is this your bag?" "Yes, it is. "

   「刺身は食べますか。」「はい，食べます。」
   "Sashimi wa tabemasu ka." "Hai, tabemasu."
   "Do you eat sashimi?" "Yes, I do."

2. For forming a content question

   彼のことをどう思いますか。 *Kare no koto o dō omoimasu ka.*
   What do you think of him?

3. Following a negative predicate for suggesting and requesting

   一緒にコンサートに行きませんか。 *Isshoni konsāto ni ikimasen ka.*
   Why don't we go to the concert together?

   自転車を貸してくれませんか。 *Jitensha o kashite kuremasen ka.*
   Would you please lend me your bicycle?

IV. *KA* [INDEFINITE PRONOUN FORMATIVE]

The suffix *ka* can follow interrogative words to create indefinite pronouns that show the existence of a kind of item without specifying which one. (→ See Interrogatives.)

先生は誰かとどこかへ行きました。
*Sensei wa **dare ka** to **doko ka** e ikimashita.*
The teacher went somewhere with somebody.

何か飲むものが欲しいですね。 ***Nani ka** nomu mono ga hoshii desu ne.*
We want something to drink, don't we?

いつかカラオケに行きませんか。 ***Itsu ka** karaoke ni ikimasen ka.*
Why don't we go to karaoke someday?

kagiri 限り [NOUN]

as long as . . . , as far as . . . is concerned, as . . . as possible, unless, not later than, just

Kagiri literally means 'limitation' but can be combined with verbs and some nouns to create an adverbial phrase that shows the limitation of the statement.

1. After verbs in the dictionary form

   私の知る限り彼は嘘をついたことがない。
   *Watashi no shiru **kagiri** kare wa uso o tsuita koto ga nai.*
   As far as I know, he has never told a lie.

   ここにいる限り静かにしなければならない。
   *Koko ni i**ru kagiri** shizuka ni shinakereba naranai.*
   We must keep quiet as long as we stay here.

2. After verbs in the **nai**-form

   雨が降らない限り予定通り行われます。
   *Ame ga fura**nai kagiri** yotei dōri okonawaremasu.*
   It will be held as scheduled unless it rains.

3. After nouns expressing deadline

   申し込みは明日限りです。 *Mōshikomi wa **asu kagiri** desu.*
   Applications must be made no later than tomorrow.

4. After specific nouns + **ni**

   今回に限り罰は与えません。 ***Konkai ni kagiri** batsu wa ataemasen.*
   This time only I won't punish you.

5. After **dekiru**

   できる限り早く出かけたいと思います。
   ***Dekiru kagiri** hayaku dekaketai to omoimasu.*
   I'd like to leave as soon as possible.

   できる限り頑張りたいと思います。 ***Dekiru kagiri** ganbaritai to omoimasu.*
   I am thinking of trying my best as much as I can.

→ See also *dake*.

kakeru かける [AUXILIARY VERB]

to be about to, be on the point of doing, be ready to do, be half done

The auxiliary verb *kakeru* follows a verb in the combining form, and expresses that the action is about to start. When a noun is created with a verb followed by *kake*, as in *tabe-kake*, it refers to an item in which the action in its initial phase is done or nearly halfway done. (→ See also *dasu, hajimeru*, and *sō ni natta*.)

1. After verbs in the combining form, in the **te iru** construction

   ホームに上がった時特急が発車しかけていました。
   *Hōmu ni agatta toki tokkyū ga hassha **shikakete imashita**.*
   The limited express train was about to leave when I went up to the platform.

あの会社は倒産しかけているらしいです。
*Ano kaisha wa tōsan **shikakete iru** rashii desu.*
I hear that company is on the verge of bankruptcy.

この犬は死にかけています。 *Kono inu wa **shinikakete imasu**.*
This dog is dying.

2. After verbs in the combining form, to form nouns

お皿の食べかけのご飯を全部食べられますか。
*Osara no **tabekake** no gohan o zenbu taberaremasu ka.*
Can you eat all the cooked rice on the plate that you half-finished (ate half-way)?

昨日読みかけの本でも読もう。 *Kinō **yokimake** no hon demo yomō.*
I'll read the book I began to read but stopped yesterday.

kamawanai かまわない [ADJECTIVE]

fine, not a problem

The adjective *kamawanai*, derived from the negative form of *kamau* (to mind), means 'fine' or 'not a problem' and is often used for politely giving permission. (→ See also *kekkō, temo ii / demo ii,* and *yoroshii*.)

この車を使ってもかまいませんよ。
*Kono kuruma o tsukattemo **kamaimasen** yo.*
It's okay to use this car.

kamoshirenai かもしれない [PREDICATIVE PHRASE]

may, might, possibly

Kamoshirenai or its polite form, *kamoshiremasen*, can be placed at the end of a clause and shows that the statement expressed by the clause is "possibly" true. (→ See also *darō*.) The particle *no* that is a part of *no da* is often inserted between the clause and *kamoshiremasen*, making the statement sound like an explanation as is typical in the *no da* construction. (→ See *no da*.)

1. After (adjectival) nouns (+ *na no*)

When the particle *no* is used, the noun must be followed by *na*.

日本語はあなたには簡単（なの）かもしれません。
*Nihongo wa anata ni wa **kantan (na no) kamoshiremasen**.*
The Japanese language might be easy for you.

田中さんは優しい人（なの）かもしれませんね。
*Tanaka san wa yasahii hito **(na no) kamoshiremasen** ne.*
Mr. Tanaka may be a kind person.

2. After (adjectival) nouns (+ *ja nai, datta,* or *ja nakatta* (+ *no*))

あれは猫じゃないかもしれない。トラの子供かもしれない。
*Are wa **neko ja nai kamoshirenai.** **Tora no kodomo kamoshirenai.***
That one may not be a cat. It may be a tiger's baby.

あれは夢だった（の）かもしれない。
*Are wa yume **datta (no) kamoshirenai.***
That might have been a dream.

3. After verbs and adjectives in the dictionary form (+ *no*)

明日は午後雪が降るかもしれないでしょう。
*Asu wa gogo yuki ga fu**ru kamoshirenai** deshō.*
It may snow tomorrow.

彼の言うことが正しい（の）かもしれません。
*Kare no iu koto ga tadashi**i (no) kamoshiremasen.***
Possibly what he says is right.

知らない間に個人情報を盗まれるかもしれません。
*Shiranai aida ni kojin jōhō o nusumare**ru kamoshiremasen.***
Our identity may be stolen without our knowing it.

→ See also Passive form under Verbs.

4. After verbs and adjectives in the *nai*-form (+ *no*)

彼は一緒に行かない（の）かもしれない。
*Kare wa isshoni ika**nai (no) kamoshirenai.***
He may not go together (with us).

入院しなければならないかもしれない。
*Nyūin shinakereba nara**nai kamoshirenai.***
I may have to be hospitalized.

→ See also *nakereba ikenai / nakereba naranai.*

5. After verbs and adjectives in the *ta*-form (+ *no*)

その方がよかった（の）かもしれません。
*Sono hō ga yoka**tta (no) kamoshiremasen.***
It might have been better.

彼女はもう帰った（の）かもしれない。
*Kanojo wa mō kae**tta (no) kamoshirenai.***
She may have already gone back home.

---

kana かな [PARTICLE]

I wonder if . . .

Kana is added at the end of a sentence in an informal style when the speaker is unsure about the status of the statement. It can be replaced by *kashira* in a female speech.

1. After verbs and adjectives in the dictionary, **nai-**, and **ta-** form

   電車に間に合うかな。*Densha ni maniau **kana**.*
   I wonder if I can catch the train.

   彼女はもう行ったかな。*Kanojo wa mō it**ta kana**.*
   I wonder if she has gone already.

   これでいいかな。*Kore de ii **kana**.*
   I wonder if this is all right.

   これでよかったかな。*Kore de yokat**ta kana**.*
   I wonder if this has been all right.

   窓を開けてもいいかな。*Mado o aketemo ii **kana**.*
   I wonder if it's okay to open the window?

2. After (adjectival) noun (+ **na no**)

   先生は元気(なの)かな。*Sensei wa **genki (na no) kana**.*
   I wonder if my teacher is fine.

   これは誰の鞄 (なの) かな。*Kore wa dare no **kaban (na no) kana**.*
   I wonder whose bag this is.

kanarazushimo 必ずしも [ADVERB]

(not) always, (not) necessarily, (not) all

Kanarazushimo is used with a predicate in the negative form, to mean 'not always . . .' or 'not necessarily. . . .' It is often used with *kagiranai* 'not limited.'

お金は必ずしも必要ではない。
*Okane wa **kanarazushimo** hitsuyō dewa **nai**.*
Money is not always necessary.

それが必ずしもうまくいくとは限らない。
*Sore ga **kanarazushimo** umaku iku to wa **kagiranai**.*
It will not necessarily go well.

先生が必ずしも正しいとは限りません。
*Sensei ga **kanarazushimo** tadashii to wa **kagirimasen**.*
The teacher is not always right.

kara から [PARTICLE]

from, after, because

The particle *kara* can function as a case particle, a conjunctional particle for verbs in the *te*-form, or for clauses.

I. *KARA* [CASE PARTICLE]

from, out of, at, through

The particle *kara* follows nouns that express the origin, the source, or the beginning point in terms of time, place, and other notions for the event or action expressed by the predicate of the sentence. (→ See also *yori*.)

1. Source

   豆腐や納豆は大豆から作られます。
   *Tōfu ya nattō wa **daizu kara** tsukuraremasu.*
   Tofu, natto, and things like them are made from soybeans.

   → See also *de*.

2. Origin

   私は日本からです。 *Watashi wa **Nihon kara** desu.* **I'm from Japan.**

   風邪から肺炎になりました。 ***Kaze kara** haien ni narimashita.*
   I developed pneumonia from a cold.

3. Beginning point in time, space, and other notions

   夏休みは7月20日からです。
   *Natsu yasumi wa **shichi gatsu hatsuka kara** desu.*
   The summer vacation is from July 20th.

   学校は八時半から始まります。
   *Gakkō wa **hachi ji han kara** hajimarimasu.* (*kara* may be replaced with *ni*)
   School begins at eight thirty.

   あの店は午前十時から午後六時まで開いています。
   *Ano mise wa **gozen jū ji kara** gogo rokuji made aite imasu.*
   That store is open from 10 a.m. to 6 p.m.

   昨日から風邪をひいています。 ***Kinō kara** kaze o hiite imasu.*
   I've had a cold since yesterday.

   東京から京都までバスで来ました。
   ***Tōkyō kara** Kyōto made basu de kimashita.*
   I came from Tokyo to Kyoto by bus.

   彼女は怒って部屋から出て行った。
   *Kanojo wa okotte **heya kara** dete itta.*
   She got angry and went out of the room.

   窓から花火を見ることができます。
   ***Mado kara** hanabi o miru koto ga dekimasu.*
   We can watch fireworks through the window.

今日は教科書の30頁から35頁を読みましょう。
*Kyō wa kyōkasho no **30 pēji kara** 35 pēji o yomimashō.*
Let's read from page 30 to page 35 in the textbook today.

あの店は食べ物から家具まで売っている。
*Ano mise wa **tabemono kara** kagu made utte iru.*
That store sells (all sorts of things) from foods to furniture.

→ See also *made.*

II. *KARA* [CONJUNCTIONAL PARTICLE]

after . . . , since . . . , because . . .

When *kara* follows a verb in the *te*-form, it means 'after doing something' or 'since doing something.' In fact, *kara* is optional after verbs in the *te*-form. However, *kara* emphasizes that the action denoted by the verb before *kara* must or should precede the action denoted by the verb after *kara*. Accordingly, *kara* should not be used when the order of actions is inherently fixed or unchangeable. (→ See also *ikō, igo,* and *irai.*)

When *kara* follows a clause in the plain form or in the polite form, it creates an adverbial clause that expresses the reason or the cause for the action or state expressed by the main clause. Unlike *node, kara* often gives the impression that the speaker's reasoning is subjective, insistent, or emotional when the predicate before *kara* is in the plain form while the predicate in the main clause is in the polite form. By contrast, if both predicates are in the polite form, the sentence sounds polite and thus does not create the same impression about the speaker's judgment, although it still gives a slightly subjective impression. (→ See also *node.*)

1. After verbs in the *te*-form

   説明を聞いて(から)質問して下さい。
   *Setsumei o kii**te kara** shitsumon shite kudasai.*
   Please listen to my explanation first. And then ask me a question.

   今日は外で食べて(から)帰りましょう。
   *Kyō wa soto de tabe**te kara** kaerimashō.*
   Let's eat out first and then go home today.

   今夜は飲んで(から)寝ます。 *Kon'ya wa non**de kara** nemasu.*
   I'll drink first and go to bed tonight.

   日本に来て(から)六ヶ月になります。
   *Nihon ni ki**te kara** rokkagetsu ni narimasu.*
   It is six months since I came to Japan.

   *彼はドアを開けてから出て行きました。
   Kare wa doa o akete kara** dete ikimashita.* (* = inappropriate)
   (Intended meaning: He went out after opening the door.)

彼はドアを開けて出て行きました。
Kare wa doa o akete dete ikimashita.
He went out after opening the door.

2. After verbs and adjectives in the dictionary form

雨が降るから傘を持って行った方がいい。
Ame ga furu kara kasa o motte itta hō ga ii.
It's better to take along an umbrella because it's going to rain.

高いからそれは買いません。 *Takai kara sore wa kaimasen.*
I'm not buying it because it is expensive.

3. After verbs and adjectives in the *nai*-form

誰にも言わないから教えて下さい。
Dare ni mo iwanai kara oshiete kudasai.
I won't tell anybody, so please tell me.

これは高くないから今ここで買った方がいい。
Kore wa takakunai kara ima koko de katta hō ga ii.
You should buy it here now because it is not expensive.

4. After verbs and adjectives in the *ta*-form

たくさん食べたからもう要らない。 *Takusan tabeta kara mō iranai.*
I don't need any more, because I ate a lot.

怖かったから一目散に逃げました。
Kowakatta kara ichimokusan ni nigemashita.
I ran away for my life because I was scared.

行きたくなかったから行きませんでした。
Ikitaku nakatta kara ikimasen deshita.
I didn't go, because I didn't want to.

5. After (adjectival) nouns + the linking verb

明日は休みだからどこかへ遊びに行こう。
Asu wa yasumi da kara dokoka e asobi ni ikō.
Tomorrow is a holiday. So let's go somewhere to have fun.

昨日は休みだったから一日中インターネットをしていました。
Kinō wa yasumi datta kara ichi nichi jū intānetto o shite imashita.
Yesterday was a holiday, so I was surfing on the Internet all day long.

午後は雨でしょうから傘を持っていきましょう。
Gogo wa ame deshō kara kasa o motte ikimashō.
Let us take along an umbrella, because it will be rainy this afternoon.

これは大変ですから私に任せて下さい。
Kore wa taihen desu kara watashi ni makasete kudasai. (polite)
Please leave it to me, because it is burdensome.

6. After verbs in the *masu*-form

私がしますから休んで下さい。
Watashi ga shimasu kara yasunde kudasai. (polite)
I'll do it, so please take a rest.

確認しますから少々お待ち下さい。
Kakunin shimasu kara shōshō omachi kudasai. (politely speaking to a customer)
I'll confirm it, so please wait a moment.

Note that sentences with an adverbial clause in the polite form with *node* sound more polite than sentences with an adverbial clause in the plain form with *node*. Such slight contrasts over the choice between plain and polite and between *kara* and *node* are summarized below:

Plain form + *kara*	subjective, insistent, or emotional
Plain form + *node*	neutral and objective
Polite form + *kara*	polite (slightly subjective)
Polite form + *node*	very polite (objective)

The clause that precedes *kara* can end in elements such as *darō* or *deshō*, while the clause that precedes *node* cannot, indicating a sentence-like status of the clause preceding *kara*.

雨が降るでしょうから，傘をもっていかれた方がよろしいですよ。
Ame ga furu deshō kara, kasa o motte ikareta hō ga yoroshii desu yo.
It will probably rain, so it is better to bring an umbrella.

Kara can also end a sentence, being followed by the linking verb, as in ...*kara da* or ...*kara desu*. The consecutive clause, if any, is usually placed at the beginning of the sentence, followed by *no wa*. Note that the sentence before *kara da/desu* must be in the plain form.

私が授業を休んだのは風邪をひいたからです。
Watashi ga jugyō o yasunda no wa kaze o hiita kara desu.
It is because I caught a cold that I was absent from lesson.

kashira かしら → See *kana.*

kata 方 [NOUN]

method/way, person

Kata is syntactically a noun but cannot be used by itself. It means either 'method' or 'person.'

1. Following a verb in the combining form to mean 'method' or 'way'

    Kata can follow a verb in the combining form to create a noun that means 'the way of . . . ing.' If the verb requires a direct object, the latter is marked by the particle *no* rather than the particle *o*. An alternative way of expressing the same idea is to use a noun, *hōhō* (方法). However, *hōhō* follows a verb in the dictionary form, and the understood direct object remains to be marked by *o*.

    ひらがなとカタカナの書き方を教えて下さい。
    *Hiragana to katakana **no kakikata** o oshiete kudasai.*
    Please teach me how to write hiragana and katakana.

    子供みたいなしゃべり方や食べ方をしないように。
    *Kodomo mitai na **shaberikata** ya tabekata o shinai yōni.*
    Don't talk or eat like a kid.

    日本語の勉強の仕方が分かりません。
    *Nihongo no benkyō **no shikata** ga wakarimasen.*
    I don't know how to study Japanese.

    ハイブリッドカーのエンジンをかける方法を教えて下さい。
    *Haiburiddo kā no enjin **o kakeru hōhō** o oshiete kudasai.*
    Please teach me how to start the engine of the hybrid car.

2. Preceded by a demonstrative adjective to mean 'person'

    Kata can be used for politely referring to a person. Unlike the noun *hito*, which means 'person,' *kata* cannot stand by itself and must be preceded by an adjective or an adjectival noun.

    この方はどなたですか。 *Kono **kata** wa donata desu ka.*
    Who is this person?

    あの方は伊藤さんですね。じゃあ，どの方が吉田さんですか。
    *Ano **kata** wa Itō san desu ne. Jā, dono **kata** ga Yoshida san desu ka.*
    That person is Mr. Ito, isn't he? Then who is Mr. Yoshida?

    あの方は本当にきれいな方ですね。
    *Ano **kata** wa hontō ni kirei na **kata** desu ne.*
    That person is a truly beautiful person.

    お急ぎの方はこちらへどうぞ。 *Oisogi no **kata** wa kochira e dōzo.*
    Those who are in a hurry, please come this way.

kawari ni 代わりに [ADVERBIAL PHRASE]

instead of, for, as, in exchange for, in return (for), to make up for

Kawari is a noun that means 'replacement.' It can form an adverbial phrase, being preceded by a variety of modifiers and followed by the particle *ni*, so the sentence can express how the given situation was made up or complemented.

1. After nouns + **no**

   彼が私の代わりにその会に出てくれました。
   *Kare ga **watashi no kawari ni** sono kai ni dete kuremashita.*
   He attended the meeting instead of me.

   デジカメはメモの代わりになる。
   *Dejikame wa **memo no kawari ni** naru.*
   A digital camera will do for (taking) notes.

2. After verbs in the dictionary form

   英語を教える代わりに日本語を教えて下さい。
   *Eigo o oshieru **kawari ni** Nihongo o oshiete kudasai.*
   Please teach me Japanese in exchange for teaching you English.

   手伝う代わりにお金を貸してくれませんか。
   *Tetsudau **kawari ni** okane o kashite kuremasen ka.*
   Will you lend me money in return for my helping you?

3. After verbs in the **nai**-form

   何も食べない代わりにたくさんジュースを飲んだ。
   *Nani mo tabe**nai kawari ni** takusan jūsu o nonda.*
   I didn't eat anything but instead drank a lot of juice.

4. After verbs in the **ta**-form

   彼はお金を無駄にした代わりに一生懸命働いている。
   *Kare wa okane o muda ni shi**ta kawari ni** isshōkenmei hataraite iru.*
   He is working hard to make up for having wasted money.

   誕生日に何ももらわなかった代わりに，高いクリスマスプレゼントを
   もらった。
   *Tanjōbi ni nani mo morawa**nakatta kawari ni**, takai kurisumasu purezento
   o moratta.*
   **I received a very expensive Christmas present, as I did not receive a birth-
   day present (from him).**

5. Used as an independent adverb

   代わりにこのペンダントをあげます。
   Kawari ni kono pendanto o agemasu.
   I will give you this pendant in return.

kekka 結果 [NOUN/ CONJUNCTION]

as a result/consequence (of), after (doing)

Kekka is a noun that literally means 'result' but can create an adverbial phrase
that shows the cause or the basis for the fact expressed by the main clause.

1. After a (verbal) noun + **no**

   検査の結果，手術が必要だと分かりました。
   Kensa no kakka, shujutsu ga hitsuyō da to wakarimashita.
   As a result of the checkup, I was shown to need a surgical operation.

   再考の結果，修正することにした。
   Saikō no kekka, shūsei suru koto ni shita.
   Upon reconsideration, I've decided to correct (it).

   無用な工事の結果，通りは交通渋滞が起こった。
   Muyō na kōji no kekka, tōri wa kōtsū jūtai ga okotta.
   As a result of the unnecessary construction, the street has become congested with traffic.

2. After verbs in the **ta**-form

   考えた結果，辞めることにしました。
   Kangae**ta kekka**, yameru koto ni shimashita.
   After consideration, I've decided to resign.

   インターネットが普及した結果，市場が増大した。
   Intānetto ga fukyū shi**ta kekka**, shijō ga zōdai shita.
   The market has grown as a result of the Internet's spread.

   いくつもの要因が絡み合った結果，奇妙な現象が見られた。
   Ikutsumo no yōin ga karamiatta kekka, kimyō na genshō ga mirareta.
   As a result of a mix of factors, a strange phenomenon was observed.

3. After a demonstrative adjective **kono**, **sono**, or **ano**

   その結果，数が減少している。   **Sono kekka**, kazu ga genshō shite iru.
   As a result, their numbers are decreasing.

kekkō 結構 [ADJECTIVAL NOUN]

fine, not necessary

The adjective *ii* can be replaced by *kekkō* in a polite context. For giving permission to one's superior, *kekkō* is preferred to *ii*. (→ See also *kamawanai*, *temo ii/ demo ii*, and *yoroshii*.)

   こちらの部屋をお使いになっても，結構ですよ。
   Kochira no heya o otsukai ni nattemo, **kekkō** desu yo.
   You may use this room.

   これは登録されなくても，結構ですよ。
   Kore wa tōroku sarenakute mo, **kekkō** desu yo.
   You do not have to register for this one.

   おつりは結構です。   Otsuri wa **kekkō** desu.
   No need to give me the change.

keredo(mo) けれど(も) [CONJUNCTION]

however, though, although, but

Keredomo is used either as a sentence-initial conjunction or as a clause-final conjunction and shows that the following sentence/clause expresses some state/event that is not expected by the preceding sentence/clause. Its meaning is 'although . . .' or 'but.' (→ See *ga, dakedo,* and *noni*.) *Re* and/or *mo* in it are often dropped in conversations, as in *kedomo, keredo,* or *kedo*.

1. At the beginning of a sentence

   The sentence-initial conjunction *keredomo* means 'however.' Its more commonly used counterpart is *demo*, and its more formal counterpart is *shikashi*. (→ See also *demo* and *shikashi*.)

   私は彼に来るように何度も頼んだ。けれども来なかった。
   Watashi wa kare ni kuru yō ni nando mo tanonda. **Keredomo** *konakatta.*
   I repeatedly asked him to come. But he didn't.

2. At the end of clauses, after (adjectival) nouns + **da/desu**

   彼はまじめだけれども面白くありません。
   Kare wa **majime da keredomo** *omoshiroku arimasen.*
   He is earnest, but not interesting.

   きれいですけれど、つまらない人です。
   Kirei desu keredo, *tsumaranai hito desu.*
   She is pretty, but a boring person.

3. At the end of a clause, after verbs and adjectives in the dictionary, **nai-,** or **ta**-form

   太郎とはよく話すけれどもとてもいい人です。
   Tarō to wa yoku hanasu **keredomo** *totemo ii hito desu.*
   I often talk with Taro, and I think he is a nice person.

   旅行に行きたいけれども暇がありません。
   Ryokō ni ikitai **keredomo** *hima ga arimasen.*
   Though I want to go on a trip, I have no time.

   彼はあまり勉強しないけれども成績がいい。
   Kare wa amari benkyō shinai **keredomo** *seiseki ga ii.*
   He doesn't study hard, but he gets good grades.

   高くないけど、よくない。 *Takaku* **nai kedo,** *yoku nai.*
   It is not expensive, but is not good.

   店に行ったけれども閉まっていました。
   Mise ni itta **keredomo** *shimatte imashita.*
   I went to the store, but it was closed.

そんなものは欲しくなかったけれども買ってしまいました。
*Sonna mono wa hoshiku nakatta **keredomo** katte shimaimashita.*
Though I didn't want such a thing, I bought it in spite of myself.

4. Without the main sentence

The main sentence is often omitted in conversations, with the speaker's wishes and expectations left to be inferred.

今ちょっと忙しいんですけれども。 *Ima chotto isogashii n desu **keredomo**.*
I'm a little too busy now. (so I can't help you)

kesshite 決して [ADVERB]

never, by no means, (not) at all, on no account

Kesshite is used with a negative predicate to mean 'by no means.' It is used especially when the speaker is emotionally involved in his/her statement.

あなたのことは決して忘れません。
*Anata no koto wa **kesshite** wasure**masen**.*
I shall never forget you.

この問題は決して難しくはありません。
*Kono mondai wa **kesshite** muzukashiku wa ari**masen**.*
This problem is by no means difficult.

彼は決してそんなことをする人ではない。
*Kare wa **kesshite** sonna koto o suru hito dewa **nai**.*
He is the last person to do such a thing.

→ See also *chittomo*, *mattaku*, and *zenzen*.

koko ここ → See **kore**.

komu 込む [AUXILIARY VERB]

to put in something with an action, (something) to come in with an action, to do something steadily or strongly or from the heart

The auxiliary verb *komu* follows a verb in the combining form and adds a meaning of physically inserting something or investing time and effort by the action denoted by the preceding verb.

列にこっそり入り込むのはよくない。
*Retsu ni kossori **hairikomu** no wa yoku nai.*
It's bad to cut in line.

どこにパソコンのコンセントを差し込めますか。
*Doko ni pasokon no konsento o **sashikomemasu** ka.*
Where can I plug in a personal computer?

つい眠り込んでしまいました。 *Tsui **nemurikonde** shimaimashita.*
I drifted off to sleep.

ラッシュアワーでは客は電車に詰め込まれます。
*Rasshu awā de wa kyaku wa densha ni **tsumekomaremasu**.*
Passengers are packed into cars during the rush hours.

人工心臓を埋め込む技術が開発された。
*Jinkō shinzō o **umekomu** gijutsu ga kaihatsu sareta.*
The technique to implant an artificial heart has been developed.

数百時間つぎ込んで作りました。
*Sū hyaku jikan **tsugikonde** tsukurimashita.*
I put in hundreds of hours and made it.

kore これ [DEMONSTRATIVE]

this, these, it

Kore is a demonstrative pronoun and can refer to (non-human) items that are visible for the speaker and the listener and are situated close to the speaker but may or may not be close to the listener. It can be directly followed by particles and linking verbs just as nouns can. For referring to locations, use *koko* 'here' instead of *kore*. For referring to a person, use the demonstrative adjective *kono* with a common noun such as *hito* 'person' and *gakusei* 'student.' The polite form of *kore* is *kochira*, which means not only 'this one' but also 'this person' or 'this way.'

1. *Kore/kochira/koko* (demonstrative pronoun)

これが昨日買ったカメラです。 ***Kore ga** kinō katta kamera desu.*
This is the camera that I bought yesterday.

これを見たことがありますか。 ***Kore o** mita koto ga arimasu ka.*
Have you ever seen this?

これからがんばります。 ***Kore kara** ganbarimasu.*
I'll work hard from now on.

こちらが私の旧友の石川さんです。
***Kochira ga** watashi no kyūyū no Ishikawa san desu.*
This is my old friend, Ms. Ishikawa.

ここが私の家です。 ***Koko ga** watashi no ie desu.* **This is my house.**

「今日の新聞はどこにありますか。」「ここにあります。」
*"Kyō no shinbun wa doko ni arimasu ka." **"Koko ni** arimasu."*
"Where is today's newspaper?" "Here it is."

前から欲しいレンズはこれです。 *Mae kara hoshii renzu wa **kore desu**.*
The lens I've wanted is this.

神戸行きのプラットホームはここですか。
*Kōbe yuki no purattohomu wa **koko desu** ka.*
Is the platform for the train to Kobe here?

2. ***Kono*** (demonstrative adjective)

この靴を下さい。 ***Kono kutsu** o kudasai.*
Give me these shoes. (I'll take these shoes.)

今度買ったのはこの車です。 *Kondo katta no wa **kono kuruma** desu.*
The one I bought this time is this car.

→ See also *are* and *sore*.

---

koso こそ [PARTICLE]

The focus particle *koso* stresses and highlights the item it is attached to. It follows a noun and its associated particle. It can also follow some clauses or phrases. *Koso* can be placed right after a particle, but *ga* and *o* must be preceded by *koso*.

1. After nouns (+ a particle)

これこそ私の知りたい情報です。
***Kore koso** watashi no shiritai jōhō desu.*
This is the very information that I want to know.

私こそお礼を言わなければなりません。
***Watashi koso** orei o iwanakereba narimasen.*
I (not you) should be expressing thanks.

この会社でこそ私の実力が発揮できる。
***Kono kaisha de koso** watashi no jitsuryoku ga hakki dekiru.*
I can use my ability in this company.

こういう時にこそ，貯金が役立ちます。
***Kō iu toki ni koso**, chokin ga yakudachimasu.*
My savings become useful in this kind of situation.

それでこそ，男だ。 ***Sore de koso**, otoko da.*
With that, you can be considered a man.

2. After clauses

あなたが好きだからこそ，言うのです。
***Anata ga suki da kara koso**, iu no desu.*
I say it because I like you.

あたたがいればこそ，私は生きられる。
***Atata ga ire ba koso**, watashi wa ikirareru.*
If you are there (near me), I can live.

koto こと [NOUN AND NOMINALIZER]

thing (in the abstract sense), . . . ing, to (do), (the fact) that

Koto is an abstract noun that means 'thing,' 'fact,' 'occasions,' or 'matter.' As an unsubstantial noun, it also functions as a nominalizer following clauses, so the latter can occur in a position where only nouns can occur in a sentence. Certain verbs that express mental activities such as *shiru* 'to know' and *nozomu* 'hope' need a clause followed by *koto* or *no* to complete their meanings. (→ See also Noun complement clauses under Clauses.)

1. Used by itself

   あいつはことの重大さが (or を) わかっていない。
   *Aitsu wa **koto** no jūdaisa ga (or o) wakatte inai.*
   He does not understand the gravity of the matter.

2. After nouns + ***no***

   彼女のことはよく知っています。 ***Kanojo no koto** wa yoku shitte imasu.*
   I know her circumstances well. (I know her well.)

   父のことを考えていました。父のことが心配です。
   ***Chichi no koto** o kangaete imashita. **Chichi no koto** ga shinpai desu.*
   I was thinking about my father. I am very worried about him.

3. After adjectival nouns + ***na/no***

   好きなことをするべきです。 ***Suki na koto** o suru beki desu.*
   You should do what you like.

   病気のことを心配しているのでしょう。
   ***Byōki no koto** o shinpai shite iru no deshō.*
   (He/She) must be worried about his/her illness.

4. After verbs and adjectives in the dictionary form

   今日はすることがたくさんあります。
   *Kyō wa suru **koto** ga takusan arimasu.*
   I have a lot of things to do today.

   見ることは信じることです。 *Miru **koto** wa shinjiru **koto** desu.*
   Seeing is believing.

   よく休むことが必要です。 *Yoku yasumu **koto** ga hitsuyō desu.*
   It is necessary (for you) to get enough rest.

   日本は地震が多いことはよく知られている。
   *Nihon wa jishin ga ōi **koto** wa yoku shirarete iru.*
   That earthquakes are frequent in Japan is well known.

   世の中が平和になることを期待します。
   *Yononaka ga heiwa ni naru **koto** o kitai shimasu.*
   I hope that the world will be peaceful.

5. After verbs and adjectives in the *nai*-form

分からないことが沢山ありますので，色々教えてください。
Wakaranai koto ga takusan arimasu node, iroiro oshiete kudasai.
There are so many things I do not know (around here), so please teach (or help) me.

6. After verbs and adjectives in the *ta*-form

花子さんがヨーロッパに行ったことを知っていますか。
Hanako san ga Yōroppa ni itta koto o shitte imasu ka.
Did you know that Hanako has gone to Europe?

私が言ったことを彼に伝えて下さい。
Watashi ga itta koto o kare ni tsutaete kudasai.
Please tell him what I've said.

(Note that the above *koto* is used differently, and it indicates the contents of statement.)

7. After declarative statement (used as a command form)

敷地内に入らないこと。 ***Shikichi nai ni hairanai koto.***
Don't enter the premises.

→ See also *koto ga aru, koto ga dekiru, koto ni naru, koto ni suru, mono, no, to,* and *to iu.*

koto ga aru ことがある [PREDICATIVE PHRASE]

there are occasions when . . . , have (done) . . . , had an experience that . . .

Koto ga aru consists of *koto* (nominalizer), *ga* (subject particle), and *aru* (verb), and means there are occasions in which one did/does such and such. (→ See *koto* and *aru.*) *Koto ga aru* directly follows verbs in the plain form. Depending on whether the verb is in the non-past form or in the past form, the sentence expresses habits or experiences, respectively.

1. After verbs in the dictionary form, expressing habits

あの人と話すことがほとんどありません。
Ano hito to hanasu koto ga hotondo arimasen.
I seldom have occasion to talk with that person.

2. After verbs in the *nai*-form, expressing habits

たまに朝食と昼食を取らないことがあります。
Tama ni chōshoku to chūshoku o toranai koto ga arimasu.
There are occasions when I don't have breakfast and lunch.

3. After verbs in the **ta**-form, expressing experiences

「北海道へ行ったことがありますか。」「いいえ，ありません。」
"Hokkaidō e itta koto ga arimasu ka." "Iie, arimasen."
"Have you ever been to Hokkaido?" "No, I haven't."

まだネットオークションで買い物をしたことがありません。
Mada netto ōkushon de kaimono o shita koto ga arimasen.
I haven't shopped on e-Bay yet.

4. After verbs that end in **nakatta**, expressing experiences

父の話しを聞かなかったことがあります。
Chichi no hanashi o kikanakatta koto ga arimasu.
There were some occasions that I did not listen to my father.

koto ga dekiru ことができる [PREDICATIVE PHRASE]

can (do), to be able to (do)

Koto ga dekiru consists of *koto* (nominalizer), *ga* (subject particle), and *dekiru* (verb) and expresses one's potential, meaning 'to be able to do such and such.' (→ See *koto* and *dekiru*.) *Koto ga dekiru* directly follows verbs in the dictionary form. A simpler way of expressing one's potential is to use verbs in the potential form. (→ See Potential form under Verbs.)

1. After verbs in the dictionary form

午後三時までに来ることができますか。
Gogo san ji made ni kuru koto ga dekimasu ka.
Are you able to come by 3 p.m.?

私はあまり漢字を書くことができません。
Watashi wa amari kanji o kaku koto ga dekimasen.
I cannot write many Chinese characters.

飛行機の予約を取ることができました。
Hikōki no yoyaku o toru koto ga dekimashita.
I was able to make a plane reservation.

2. After verbs in the **nai**-form

秘密を漏らさないことができますか。
Himitsu o morasanai koto ga dekimasu ka.
Can you keep (from letting out) a secret?

koto ni naru ことになる [PREDICATIVE PHRASE]

it is decided that, to be scheduled to (do), to be expected to (do)

Koto ni naru follows a verb in the dictionary form or in the *nai*-form to express the decision made by someone or some group, which is obscured in the statement. The speaker may have been involved in the decision making, but even so, it is implied that he/she cannot be the sole decision maker. *Naru* can be in the progressive form, as in ... *koto ni natte imasu*, if one wants to imply that the decision is being in effect for now, but might change later. (→ See also *koto ni suru*.)

1. After verbs in the dictionary form

    次はあなたが行くことになります。 *Tsugi wa anata ga iku koto ni narimasu.*
    You will have to go next.

    今度沖縄事務所に転勤することになりました。
    Kondo Okinawa jimusho ni tenkin suru koto ni narimashita.
    It was decided that I'll be transferred to the Okinawa office shortly.

    来月，結婚することになりました。
    Raigetsu kekkon suru koto ni narimahsita.
    It's been decided that I (we) get married next month.

    彼は九時の電車で着くことになっています。
    Kare wa kuji no densha de tsuku koto ni natte imasu.
    He is due to arrive by the nine o'clock train.

    私たちは昼休みに図書館で会うことになっています。
    Watashi tachi wa hiru yasumi ni toshokan de au koto ni natte imasu.
    We are to meet at the library at the noon recess.

2. After verbs in the *nai*-form

    この製品はもう生産しないことになりました。
    Kono seihin wa mō seisan shinai koto ni narimashita.
    It was decided that we will not make this product anymore.

koto ni suru ことにする [PREDICATIVE PHRASE]

to decide to (do), make up one's mind to (do)

Koto ni suru follows a verb in the dictionary form or in the *nai*-form to express one's decision. *Suru* can be in the progressive form if one wants to imply that the decision is holding for now, but might change later. (→ See also *koto ni naru*.)

1. After verbs in the dictionary form

    タバコをやめることにしました。 *Tabako o yameru koto ni shimashita.*
    I've made up my mind to give up smoking.

2. After verbs in the *nai*-form

    無駄遣いはしないことにしました。
    Muda dukai wa shinai koto ni shimashita.
    I've decided not to waste money.

寝る前に本を読むことにしています。
*Neru mae ni hon o yomu **koto ni shite imasu.***
I make it a rule to read a book before going to bed.

夜更かししないことにしています。
*Yofukashi shi**nai koto ni shite imasu.***
I make it a rule not to stay up late.

kudasai くださ い [AUXILIARY VERB]

please give . . . to me, please do something (for me)

Kudasai is a derived form of the verb *kureru* 'to give me/us.' (→ See *kureru*.)
Kudasai can also function as an auxiliary verb following verbs in the *te*-form to
request someone to do something. (→ See also *chōdai*.) Depending on the context and the content of what you are requesting, it might sound quite direct
and could be interpreted as a command. Thus, to your superior, use its polite
and indirect variations such as . . . *te kudasai masen ka*. (→ See Requests and
Honorifics.) If your superior asks you for permission, you can use . . . *te kudasai*
as a positive reply to him/her. Negative requests can be expressed by . . . *nai de*
plus *kudasai*. (→ See *nai de*.)

1. For requesting an item, following nouns + *o*

    明日朝八時に電話を下さい。*Asu asa hachiji ni **denwa o kudasai**.*
    Please give me a call at 8 a.m. tomorrow.

    このジャケットとズボンを下さい。 ***Kono jaketto to zubon o kudasai.***
    **Please give me this jacket and these slacks. (I'll take this jacket and these
    slacks.)**

2. For requesting someone to do something

    暑いので窓を開けてください。*Atsui node mado o ake**te kudasai**.*
    Please open the window, because it's hot.

    「入ってもいいですか。」「ええ，どうぞ，入ってください。」
    *"Haittemo ii desu ka." "Ē, dōzo haitte **kudasai**."*
    "Can I come in?" "Yes, please come in."

    すみません。この漢字の書き方を教えて下さい。
    *Sumimasen. Kono kanji no kakikata o oshiete **kudasai**.*
    Excuse me. Please teach me how to write this kanji.

3. For requesting someone not to do something

    まだ行かないでください。ここにいてください。
    *Mada ika**nai de kudasai**. Koko ni i**te kudasai**.*
    Please don't leave yet. Please stay here.

kudasaru くださる [AUXILIARY VERB]

to do (something) for (me), do (me) a favor by doing (something)

The auxiliary verb *kudasaru* is the honorific counterpart of the auxiliary verb *kureru*. (→ See *kureru <auxiliary verb>*.) The conjugated form, *kudasai*, can be used for requesting. (→ See also *kudasai* and Requests.)

先生が調べてくださいました。*Sensei ga shirabete kudasaimashita.*
The teacher checked it (for me).

見せてくださいませんか。*Misete kudasaimasen ka.*
Couldn't you show it (to me)?

kudasaru くださる [VERB]

to give

The verb *kudasaru* is the honorific counterpart of the verb *kureru*. (→ See *kureru <verb>*.) *Kudasaru* is used when the giver is someone to whom the speaker's respect is due. Note that *kudasaru* is slightly irregular. Its combining form is *kudasari*, but it becomes *kudasai* when followed by the polite suffix *masu* as in *kudasaimasu*.

先生が手紙を下さいました。*Sensei ga tegami o kudasaimashita.*
The teacher gave me a letter.

kurai くらい [PARTICLE]

about, approximately, as . . . as . . . , to the extent of, only, at least, enough . . . to (do)

The particle *kurai* or *gurai* follows quantity/amount phrases and means 'approximately.' It can also follow nouns, verbs, and adjectives to show the extent of some state/property understood in the context. (→ See also *dono kurai* and *hodo*.)

1. After number + counter
   十冊くらい日本語の本を買いました。
   Jissatsu kurai Nihongo no hon o kaimashita.
   I bought about ten Japanese-language books.

   彼女はオーストラリアに三ヶ月くらいいました。
   Kanojo wa Ōsutoraria ni san kagetsu kurai imashita.
   She was in Australia for about three months.

毎日一時間くらいは勉強しなければならない。
*Mainichi **ichi jikan kurai** wa benkyō shinakereba naranai.*
One must study at least one hour every day.

(*Kurai + wa* means "at least.")

2. After nouns

だれもあなたくらい上手にはテニスができません。
*Dare mo **anata kurai** jōzu ni wa tenisu ga dekimasen.*
Nobody can play tennis as well as you.

それができるのはあなたくらいです。
*Sore ga dekiru no wa **anata kurai** desu.*
You are the only one who can do it.

3. After demonstrative pronouns

それくらい私でも分かります。　*Sore kurai watashi demo wakarimasu.*
Even I can understand that much.

これくらいはいいパソコンを買った方がいい。
Kore kurai wa ii pasokon o katta hō ga ii.
It's better to buy a personal computer as good as this one.

→ See also *are, kore,* and *sore.*

4. After **dono** or **dore**

これはどのくらいしますか。　*Kore wa dono kurai shimasu ka.*
About how much does this cost?

駅まで歩いてどのくらいかかりますか。
Eki made aruite dono kurai kakarimasu ka.
How long does it take to walk to the train station?

一週間にどのくらい外食をしますか。
Isshūkan ni dono kurai gaishoku o shimasu ka.
How often do you eat out in a week?

大学までどれぐらいかかりますか。
Daigaku made dore gurai kakarimasu ka.
How long does it take to go to the university?

→ See also *dono* and *dore.*

5. After verbs and adjectives in the dictionary form

泣いている赤ん坊が泣きやむぐらい面白い。
Naite iru akambō ga nakiyamu gurai omoshiroi.
It is very funny to the extent that even a crying baby will stop crying.

この日本語の本は外国人が読めるくらいやさしいです。
Kono Nihongo no hon wa gaikokujin ga yomeru kurai yasashii desu.
This Japanese book is easy enough for a non-native to read.

肉眼で読めるくらい大きい字だった。
Nikugan de yomeru kurai ōkii ji datta.
The characters were big enough to be visible to the naked eye.

エアコンがききすぎて，寒いくらいだった。
Eakon ga kikisugite, samui kurai datta.
The air conditioning was working too well, and it was almost cold.

6. After verbs and adjectives in the *nai*-form

もう歩けないくらい疲れた。 *Mō arukenai kurai tsukareta.*
I am tired to the extent that I can't walk any more. (I am too tired to walk any more.)

もう二度と見たくないくらい嫌いになりました。
Mō nido to mitakunai kurai kirai ni narimashita.
I've come to dislike it to the extent that I don't want to see any more. (I dislike it so much that I don' t want to see it any more.)

今日は我慢できないくらい寒いです。
Kyō wa gaman dekinai kurai samui desu.
It is so cold today that I can't endure it. (It is colder than I can endure today.)

7. After *onaji*, used in equal degree comparison

カタカナはひらがなと同じくらい覚えるのがむずかしい。
*Katakana wa hiragana to **onaji kurai** oboeru no ga muzukashii.*
Katakana are as difficult as hiragana to learn.

kureru くれる [AUXILIARY VERB]

to do (something) for (me), do (me) a favor by doing (something), let (me) be satisfied with doing (something)

The auxiliary verb *kureru* is used after a verb in the *te*-form, and shows that the action is performed for the benefit of the speaker by someone else, or for the benefit of the speaker's insiders by some of the speaker's outsiders. Just like the verb *kureru*, the auxiliary verb *kureru* is replaced by *kudasaru*, depending on the relationship between the action performer and the person who receives the benefit of the action. (→ See *kudasaru* <auxiliary verb> and *kureru* <verb>.)

彼女がおいしい料理を作ってくれました。
*Kanojo ga oishii ryōri o tsukette **kuremashita**.*
She prepared a delicious dish for me.

だれが手伝ってくれましたか。 *Dare ga tetsudatte **kuremashita** ka.*
Who helped you?

ちょっとペンを貸してくれませんか。
*Chotto pen o kashite **kuremasen** ka.*
Won't you kindly lend me your pen for a while?

先生は丁寧に日本語を教えてくださいます。
Sensei wa teinei ni Nihongo o oshiete kudasaimasu.
The teacher teaches us Japanese thoroughly.

(*Kudasaru* shows respect to a giver.)

→ See also *ageru, kudasai, morau,* and Verbs of giving and receiving under Verbs.

kureru くれる [VERB]

to give (something to me)

The verb *kureru* means 'to give,' but the recipient must be the speaker or must be the speaker's insider when the giver is his/her outsider. If the giver is the speaker's insider, the recipient must be closer to the speaker than to the giver. (→ See *ageru* and *kudasaru* <verb>.) However, in a question sentence, the second person can be the recipient. *Kureru* is replaced by *kudasaru* when the giver is someone to whom the speaker wishes to show respect.

彼女は私の誕生日にすてきなプレゼントをくれました。
Kanojo wa watashi no tanjōbi ni suteki na purezento o kuremashita.
She gave me a nice present for my birthday.

よしこちゃんが妹におりがみをくれました。
Yoshiko chan ga imōto ni origami o kuremashita.
Yoshiko gave my little sister some origami paper.

山田さんのお母さんは母にクッキーをくださいました。
Yamada san no okāsan wa haha ni kukkī o kudasaimashita.
Ms. Yamada's mother gave my mother some cookies.

彼は電話をくれましたか。 *Kare wa denwa o kuremashita ka.*
Did he give you a call?

kuru くる [AUXILIARY VERB]

to come to (do), begin to (do), have done (to some extent), have been (doing), get/become (some state describing the subject), (to do something and then) come back

The auxiliary verb *kuru* follows verbs in the *te*-form and shows that the action/state started before the time of speech and is gradually progressing, or simply means to do some action and come back. (→ See also *iku*.)

1. Expressing gradually progressing actions and state

   日本語の話し方が分かってきました。
   Nihongo no hanashikata ga wakatte kimashita.
   I have come to understand how to speak Japanese.

風が吹いてきました。 *Kaze ga **fuite kimashita**.*
It began to blow. (and will continue to blow)

これまでたくさん漢字を覚えてきました。
*Kore made takusan kanji o **oboete kimashita**.*
I have learned a lot of kanji so far.

今の仕事に慣れてきましたか。 *Ima no shigoto ni **narete kimashita** ka.*
Have you become accustomed to your present job?

この頃だいぶ暖かくなってきましたね。
*Kono goro daibu atataka**ku natte kimashita** ne.*
It is getting much warmer recently, isn't it?

(*Natte*, *te*-form of *naru*, is always used between *ku*-form and *kuru*.)

2. Meaning to do something and come back

スーパーに買い物に行ってきます。 *Sūpā ni kaimono ni **itte kimasu**.*
I'll go shopping at a supermarket. (and then come back)

kuse ni くせに [ADVERBIAL PHRASE]

though, in spite of

Kuse ni creates an adverbial phrase that means 'in spite of . . .' or 'though . . .' for emotionally making a negative and critical statement. (→ See also *keredomo, ni mo kakawarazu*, and *noni*.)

1. After nouns + **no**

子供のくせに，大人の話にはいってくる。
*Kodomo **no kuse ni**, otona no hanashi ni haitte kuru.*
(He) is only a child but joins in adult conversations.

2. After adjectival nouns + **na/no/ja nai**

あいつはバカなくせに格好を付けている。
*Aitsu wa **baka na kuse ni** kakkō o tsukete iru.*
That guy tries to look good, though he is a fool.

彼は暇なくせに仕事が遅い。 *Kare wa **hima na kuse ni** shigoto ga osoi.*
He is slow to do his work, though he has nothing to do.

彼は彼女が嫌いじゃないくせに格好をつけている。
*Kare wa kanojo ga **kirai ja nai kuse ni** kakkō o tsukete iru*
He tries to look uninterested in her, though he doesn't dislike her.

3. After verbs and adjectives in the dictionary form

彼は収入が低いくせに見栄を張っている。
*Kare wa shūnyū ga hikui **kuse ni** mie o hatte iru.*
He is pretentious in spite of the small income.

知っているくせに惚けていますね。 *Shitte iru kuse ni tobokete imasu ne.*
You know the answer, but you are pretending not to know it, right?

4. After verbs and adjectives in the *nai*-form

彼はなにもしないくせに忙しそうにしている。
Kare wa nani mo shinai kuse ni isogashisō ni shite iru.
He pretends to be busy, though he doesn't do anything.

5. After verbs and adjectives in the *ta*-form

彼は私を騙したくせに平然としている。
Kare wa watashi o damashita kuse ni heizen to shite iru.
He remains calm, though he deceived me.

彼は前は気が弱かったくせに今は威張っている。
Kare wa mae wa ki ga yowakatta kuse ni ima wa ibatte iru.
He is domineering now, though he was chicken-hearted before.

mada まだ [ADVERB]

still, yet

Mada means 'still' or 'yet' depending on whether the sentence is affirmative or negative.

1. In affirmative statements (or questions)

彼は疲れてまだ寝ています。 *Kare wa tsukarete **mada** nete imasu.*
He is fatigued and still sleeping.

私の言ったことをまだ覚えていますか。
*Watashi no itta koto o **mada** oboete imasu ka.*
Do you still remember what I said?

お父さんはまだお元気ですね。 *Otōsan wa **mada** ogenki desu ne.*
Your father is still well, isn't he?

2. In negative sentences

九時の飛行機がまだ着いていません。
*Ku ji no hikōki ga **mada** tsuite imasen.*
The nine o'clock plane has not arrived yet.

「もうできましたか。」「まだできません。」
*"Mō dekimashita ka?" "**Mada** dekimasen."*
"Have you completed it yet?" "No, not yet."

→ See also *mō*.

made まで [PARTICLE]

until, to, (from . . .) through, up to, as far as, before

The case particle *made* expresses the ending point or limit in terms of time/ space/quantity/diversity to which some activity or state continues or applies. It can follow nouns or verbs in the dictionary form. It is often used with the particle *kara* 'from.' (→ See also *kara* and *made ni*.)

1. After nouns

   金曜日から日曜日まで旅行に出かけます。
   *Kin'yōbi kara **Nichiyōbi made** ryokō ni dekakemasu.*
   I'll be away on a trip from Friday through Sunday.

   事務所は工事で来週の水曜日まで閉まっています。
   *Jimusho wa kōji de raishū no **Suiyōbi made** shimatte imasu.*
   The office is closed for construction through next Wednesday.

   京都までの切符を二枚下さい。 ***Kyōto made** no kippu o ni mai kudasai.*
   Give me two tickets for Kyoto, please.

   神戸から上海まで客船で行きます。
   *Kōbe kara **Shanhai made** kyakusen de ikimasu.*
   I'm going as far as Shanghai from Kobe by passenger boat.

   20ページから25ページまで読んで下さい。
   *Ni juppēji kara **ni jū go pēji made** yonde kudasai.*
   Please read up to page twenty-five from page twenty.

   このスポーツワゴン車は9人まで乗れます。
   *Kono supōtsu wagonsha wa **kyū nin made** noremasu.*
   This sports wagon can hold up to nine persons.

   あの店ではトイレットペーパーから車まで，何でも売っています。
   *Ano mise de wa toirettopēpā kara **kuruma made**, nan demo utte imasu.*
   That store sells all sorts of things, ranging from toilet tissues to cars.

2. After verbs in the dictionary form

   雨が止むまで喫茶店で雨宿りしましょう。
   *Ame ga yamu **made** kissaten de amayadori shimashō.*
   Let's take shelter from the rain in a coffee shop till it stops.

   次の特急電車が来るまで15分あります。
   *Tsugi no tokkyū densha ga kuru **made** jū go fun arimasu.*
   There are fifteen minutes until the next limited express train comes.

3. After verbs in the dictionary form, followed by ***mo nai/arimasen***

   エネルギーを節約すべきことは言うまでもありません。
   *Enerugī o setsuyaku subeki koto wa iu **made mo arimasen**.*
   It goes without saying that we should save energy.

   真相を知っている。聞くまでもない。
   *Shinsō o shitte iru. Kiku **made mo nai**.*
   I know the truth. That answer should be obvious.

made ni までに [DOUBLE PARTICLE]

by (the time when . . .), before

The combination of the particles *made* and *ni* expresses the deadline or due date. (→ See also *made* and *ni*.)

1. After nouns

   今週の終わりまでにこの仕事を終えなければなりません。
   *Konshū no **owari made ni** kono shigoto o oenakereba narimasen.*
   I have to finish this work by the end of this week.

2. After verbs in the dictionary form

   彼女が来るまでに用意しておきましょう。
   *Kanojo ga **kuru made ni** yōi shite okimashō.*
   Let's be prepared by the time she comes.

mae 前 [NOUN]

before, ago, previous, prior, last, former, in front of, forward

Mae is a noun that can be used independently to mean 'before' or 'front,' but it can also be used to create a temporal/locational adverbial phrase by following nouns and verbs and often by being followed by a particle such as *ni* and *de*. When it follows a verb, the verb must be in the dictionary form. (→ See also *ato*.)

1. Used by itself with particles

   前を歩いて下さい。 ***Mae o** aruite kudasai.* **Walk in front, please.**

   そのことは前のページに書いてあります。
   *Sono koto wa **mae no** pēji ni kaite arimasu.*
   That matter is written about on the previous page.

   トイレは前の車両にあります。 *Toire wa **mae no** sharyō ni arimasu.*
   The lavatory is in the front car.

   前にどこかで会ったことがありませんか。
   ***Mae ni** dokoka de atta koto ga arimasen ka.*
   Haven't we met somewhere before?

   前の総理大臣はだれでしたか。 ***Mae no** sōri daijin wa dare deshita ka.*
   Who was the former prime minister?

   前の連休に日本アルプスへ登山に行ってきました。
   ***Mae no** renkyū ni Nihon Arupusu e tozan ni itte kimashita.*
   I went mountain climbing in the Japanese Alps during the last consecutive holidays.

2. After nouns followed by **no**

富士山の前の湖の前にすてきなホテルがあります。
***Fuji san no mae no mizuumi no mae** ni suteki na hoteru ga arimasu.*
There is a nice hotel in front of the lake before Mt. Fuji.

彼女の前でその話はやめよう。
***Kanojo no mae** de sono hanashi wa yameyō.*
Let's stop talking about it in front of her.

試験の前に勉強します。 ***Shiken no mae** ni benkyō shimasu.*
I'll study before the exam.

鈴木さんの前の先生はだれでしたか。
***Suzuki san no mae** no sensei wa dare deshita ka.*
Who was the teacher prior to Mr. Suzuki?

3. Directly after nouns that express (the length of) time

今三時五分前です。 *Ima san ji **go fun mae** desu.*
It is five minutes to three o'clock.

私は半年前に日本に来ました。
*Watashi wa **hantoshi mae** ni Nihon ni kimashita.*
I came to Japan half a year ago.

フランクはジョンが来る五分前に帰りました。
*Furanku wa Jon ga kuru **go fun mae** ni kaerimashita.*
Frank went home five minutes before John came.

一時前にここに戻ります。 ***Ichi ji mae** ni koko ni modorimasu.*
I'll be back here before one.

私は二ヶ月前からここで働いています。
*Watashi wa **ni kagetsu mae** kara koko de hataraite imasu.*
I've been working here since two months ago (for two months).

4. After verbs in the dictionary form

いつも寝る前にヨーグルトを飲みます。
*Itsumo ne**ru mae** ni yōguruto o nomimasu.*
I usually drink yogurt before I go to bed.

私たちが着く前に電車が出てしまった。
*Watashi tachi ga tsu**ku mae** ni densha ga dete shimatta.*
The train had left before we arrived.

大学に入る前から，勉強していました。
*Daigaku ni hai**ru mae** kara, benkyō shite imashita.*
I have been studying since before I entered the university.

maru まる [ADJECTIVE SUFFIX]

to change

Maru follows the root of certain adjectives and shows that some state or condition changes in a way expressed by the adjective. Its meaning is 'to become. . . .' The resulting form conjugates like a verb.

出発時刻が早まりました。急いでください。
*Shuppatsu jikoku ga **hayamarimashita**. Isoide kudasai.*
The time of departure has been brought forward. Please hurry up.

政権が変わる可能性が高まりました。
*Seiken ga kawaru kanōsei ga **takamarimashita**.*
It seems more likely that the regime will be changed. (The possibility that the regime will be changed has become high.)

彼女に対する愛情がすごく深まりました。
*Kanojo ni taisuru aijō ga sugoku **fukamarimashita**.*
My affection for her has become much deeper.

両国の関係は今後深まるでしょう。
*Ryōkoku no kankei wa kongo **fukamaru** deshō.*
The two countries will get deeply involved.

近年環境保護運動が強まっている。
*Kinnen kankyō hogo undō ga **tsuyomatte** iru.*
The environmental protection movement is gathering force these days.

台風が弱まってきました。 *Taifū ga **yowamatte** kimashita.*
The typhoon is becoming weak.

その店の評判が一気にひろまりました。
*Sono mise no hyōban ga ikki ni **hiromarimashita**.*
The shop has been much more widely talked about.

日本の諺で「雨降って地固まる」と言います。
*Nihon no kotowaza de "Ame futte zi **katamaru**." to iimasu.*
A Japanese proverb says, "The rain falls and the soil settles."

marude まるで [ADVERB]

entirely, (not) at all, as if, as though

Marude means 'entirely not . . .' or 'not at all' when used with a negative predicate. (→ See *mattaku* and *zenzen*.) However, *marude* means 'as if' or 'as though' when used together with *yō da* or *mitai da* to express a simile. (→ See *mitai da, ppoi*, and *yō da* <*resemblance*>.)

1. Used with a negative predicate to mean 'not at all'

ここに書いてあることはまるで話にならない。
*Koko ni kaite aru koto wa **marude** hanashi ni nara**nai**.*
What is written here is not at all worthy of discussion.

その意味がまるで分かりません。 *Sono imi ga **marude** wakari**masen**.*
I don't understand the meaning of it at all.

2. Used with *yō*

あの学生はまるで先生のようですね。
*Ano gakusei wa **marude** sensei no **yō** desu ne.*
That student is just like a teacher.

Note that *yō* is often preceded by a clause + *ka no* when used with *marude*.

彼はまるで何も知らないかのように話す。
*Kare wa **marude** nani no shiranai (**ka no**) **yō** ni hanasu.*
He talks as if he knows nothing at all.

彼はまるで何でも知っているかのような顔をしている。
*Kare wa **marude** nan demo shitte iru (**ka no**) **yō na** kao o shite iru.*
He looks as if he knew everything.

3. Used with *mitai*

まるであなたがそれをしたみたいだ。
***Marude** anata ga sore o shita **mitai** da.*
It sounds as though you had done it yourself.

---

masen ません → See ***masu***.

---

masen ka ませんか → See ***masu***.

---

mashō ましょう → See ***masu***.

---

masu ます [VERB SUFFIX]

expressing politeness

The polite verb suffix *masu* follows verbs in the combining form. Its variants include *masen* (non-past negative form), *mashita* (past/perfect affirmative form), *masen deshita* (past/perfect negative form), and *mashō* (volitional form). (→ See *Masu*-form under Verbs.)

1. Future actions

この夏休みはどこかへ行きますか。
*Kono natsu yasumi wa dokoka e iki**masu** ka.*
Are you going anywhere during this summer vacation?

後で電話します。 *Ato de denwa shi**masu**.* **I'll call you later.**

太郎さんはあとで図書館に行きます。
*Tarō san wa ato de toshokan ni iki**masu**.*
Taro will go to the library later.

2. Past/present habitual actions

すみませんが，私は生の食べ物はぜんぜん食べません。
*Sumimasen ga, watashi wa nama no tabemono wa zenzen tabe**masen**.*
I'm sorry, but I don't eat raw food at all.

子供の頃は毎朝たまごを食べました。
*Kodomo no koro wa maiasa tamago o tabe**mashita**.*
I used to eat eggs every morning when I was a child.

私は毎朝ご飯と味噌汁を食べます。
*Watashi wa mai asa gohan to miso shiru o tabe**masu**.*
I eat rice and miso soup every morning.

彼女は新聞を読みません。 *Kanojo wa shinbun o yomi**masen**.*
She doesn't read a newspaper.

私はあまり酒を飲みません。 *Watashi wa amari sake o nomi**masen**.*
I don't drink alcohol much.

彼はもうその会社では働いていません。
*Kare wa mō sono kaisha de wa hatarai**te imasen**.*
He is not working at that company any more.

3. Invitations and suggestions

私の新しいハイブリッドカーでドライブに行きましょう。
*Watashi no atarashii haiburiddo kā de doraibu ni iki**mashō**.*
Let's go for a drive in my new hybrid car.

あしたは映画を観に行きませんか。
*Ashita wa eiga o mi ni iki**masen** ka.*
Won't you go see a movie tomorrow?

お茶でも飲みましょうか。 *Ocha demo nomi**mashō** ka.*
Shall we have tea or something?

お茶でもいっしょに飲みませんか。 *Ocha demo isshoni nomi**masen** ka.*
Would you have some tea (or something) with me?

4. Volition

私が代わりにそれをしましょう。 *Watashi ga kawari ni sore o shi**mashō**.*
I will do it in place of you.

いっしょにおいしい料理を食べましょう。
*Isshoni oishii ryōri o tabe**mashō**.*
Let's have some good food together.

窓を閉めましょうか。 *Mado o shime**mashō** ka.*
Shall I shut the window?

5. Simple past

昨日は山田さんに会いました。 *Kinō wa Yamada san ni ai**mashita**.*
I met Ms. Yamada yesterday.

私はきのう市内でフランクに会いました。
*Watashi wa kinō shinai de Furanku ni ai**mashita**.*
I met Frank in the city yesterday.

昨日はクラスに行きませんでした。
*Kinō wa kurasu ni iki**masen deshita**.*
I did not go to class yesterday.

6. Present perfect actions

ちょうど今空港に着きました。 *Chōdo ima kūkō ni tsuki**mashita**.*
I've just arrived at the airport.

7. Experiences

何度か富士山に登りました。 *Nandoka Fuji san ni nobori**mashita**.*
I've climbed Mt. Fuji several times.

8. Finished action before the time of speech

その映画はもう観ました。 *Sono eiga wa mō mi**mashita**.*
I've already seen that movie.

もうその本は読みましたか。 *Mō sono hon wa yomi**mashita** ka.*
Have you read the book yet?

9. Past perfect actions

私が着いたときちょうど電車が出ました。
*Watashi ga tsuita toki chōdo densha ga de**mashita**.*
The train had just left when I arrived there.

Te-imashita can also be used to clearly express a past perfect action.

私が着いたとき電車がすでに出ていました。
*Watashi ga tsuita toki densha ga sude ni de**te imashita**.*
The train had already gone when I arrived there.

mattaku まったく [ADVERB]

quite, completely, really, indeed, (not) at all, (not) in the least

Mattaku can be used in either affirmative sentences or negative sentences, meaning 'completely' or 'not at all.' (→ See also *chittomo* and *zenzen*.)

1. In an affirmative sentence

まったく驚きました。 ***Mattaku** odorokimashita.* **I was really surprised.**

まったくその通りです。 ***Mattaku** sono tōri **desu**.* **You're quite right.**

2. In a negative sentence

彼はまったく信用できません。 *Kare wa **mattaku** shin'yō deki**masen**.*
He is not at all trustworthy.

それが何かまったく分かりません。
*Sore ga nani ka **mattaku** wakarimasen.*
I don't have the faintest idea what it is.

mawaru まわる [AUXILIARY VERB]

(to do something) around, here and there

The auxiliary verb *mawaru* follows verbs in the combining form to show that the action is performed frantically and extensively.

乗り換えで歩き回って疲れました。
*Norikae de **arukimawatte** tsukaremashita.*
I was tired after walking around to change trains.

ストーカーがあなたを探しまわっていますよ。
*Sutōkā ga anata o **sagashimawatte** imasu yo.*
A stalker is wandering around looking for you.

彼女はみんなに電話でふれまわるから注意しなきゃ。
*Kanojo wa minna ni denwa de **furemawaru** kara chūi shinakya.*
Be careful of her, because she rings everyone up to spread rumors.

me 目 [SUFFIX]

number . . .

The suffix *me* follows a numeral plus a counter to make a quantity phrase into an ordinal number phrase to express the position of something in a sequence.

二つ目の交差点を右に曲がってください。
*Futatsu **me** no kōsaten o migi ni magatte kudasai.*
Please make a right at the second intersection.

3人目の人はよかったね。 *San nin **me** no hito wa yokatta ne.*
The third person was good, wasn't he?

mettani めったに [ADVERB]

seldom, rarely, (not) very often

Mettani is used in a sentence with a negative verb, meaning 'rarely.' (→ See also *amari*, *chittomo*, and *hotondo*.)

私はめったに飲みに行きません。 *Watashi wa **mettani** nomi ni ikimasen.*
I rarely go out for a drink.

彼女とはめったに会いません。 *Kanojo to wa **mettani** aimasen.*
I don't see her very often.

miru みる [AUXILIARY VERB]

try (doing), do (something) and see (the result)

The auxiliary verb *miru* follows a verb in the *te*-form, jointly meaning 'to do something and see,' or 'to try doing something.' *Te mitai* is commonly used to express one's desire, meaning 'would like to try (to do). . . .'

> ネットでそれを調べてみます。 *Netto de sore o shirabete mimasu.*
> **I'll try investigating it on the Internet.**

> おかしいですね。もう一度メールを送信してみます。
> *Okashii desu ne. Mō ichido mēru o sōshin shite mimasu.*
> **It's strange. I'll try sending the e-mail again.**

> 今考えてみると計画は無茶でした。
> *Ima kangaete miru to keikaku wa mucha deshita.*
> **Now that I think about it, the plan was reckless.**

> 格好いい人がいます。会ってみますか。
> *Kakko ii hito ga imasu. Atte mimasu ka.*
> **I know a cute guy. Are you interested in meeting him?**

> 電子ブックを読んでみます。 *Denshi bukku o yonde mimasu.*
> **I'll try reading an electronic book.**

> この果物を一口食べてみよう。
> *Kono kudamono o hito kuchi tabete miyō.*
> **I'll try a bite of this fruit (and see how it tastes).**

> ではあの靴を履いてみますか。 *Dewa ano kutsu o haite mimasu ka.*
> **Then will you try those shoes on?**

> この冬は北海道へスノーボードをしに行ってみたい。
> *Kono fuyu wa Hokkaidō e sunō bōdo o shini itte mitai.*
> **I'd like to go snowboarding in Hokkaido this winter.**

> いつか外国に行ってみたいです。 *Itsuka gaikoku ni itte mitai desu.*
> **I'd like to travel abroad some day.**

> 海でひと泳ぎしてみたい。 *Umi de hito oyogi shite mitai.*
> **I feel like a swim in the sea.**

mitai da みたいだ [PREDICATIVE PHRASE]

like . . . , seem to, look like

Mitai da can be placed at the end of a sentence to express supposition based on what the speaker has seen or heard and also slightly based on what he/she has guessed. (→ See also *yō da <conjecture>*, *sō da <conjecture>*, and *rashii <conjecture>*.) It also expresses simile. (→ See also *yō da <resemblance>* and *marude*.)

1. After (adjectival) nouns (+ *ja nai, datta, ja nakatta*)

あの人は店員みたいですよ。ちょっと聞きましょうか。
*Ano hito wa **ten'in mitai desu** yo. Chotto kikimashō ka.*
That person seems to be a store clerk. Let's ask him.

あの人は結婚する前にフライトアテンダントだったみたいですよ。
*Ano hito wa kekkon suru mae ni **furaito atendanto datta mitai desu** yo.*
It appears that she was a flight attendant before getting married.

この電子辞書は便利みたいですから，買いましょう。
*Kono denshi jisho wa **benri mitai desu** kara, kaimashō.*
This electronic dictionary appears to be convenient, so let's buy it.

2. After verbs and adjectives in the dictionary form

彼女は疲れているみたいだ。 *Kanojo wa tsukarete i**ru mitai da.***
She seems to be tired.

あの先生は厳しいみたいですよ。 *Ano sensei wa kibish**ii mitai desu** yo.*
It appears that that professor is very strict.

3. After verbs and adjectives in the *nai*-form

彼女はすもうに興味がわかないみたいです。
*Kanojo wa sumō ni kyōmi ga waka**nai mitai desu**.*
It looks like she doesn't take interest in sumo wrestling.

4. After verbs and adjectives in the *ta*-form

彼は日本語の試験に合格したみたいです。
*Kare wa Nihongo no shiken ni gōkaku shi**ta mitai desu**.*
He seems to have passed the Japanese exam.

パーティーは楽しかったみたいです。 *Pātī wa tanoshika**tta mitai desu**.*
It seems that the party was fun.

5. To form adjectival nouns to express simile

彼は学者みたいです。 *Kare wa **gakusha mitai desu**.*
He looks like a scholar.

彼は芸術家みたいな格好をしている。
*Kare wa **geijutsuka mitai na** kakkō o shite iru.*
He is dressed just like an artist.

あなたみたいに日本語が話せません。
***Anata mitai ni** Nihongo ga hanasemasen.*
I can't speak Japanese like you.

mo も [PARTICLE]

too, also, (not) either, as many/much/long as, no less than, both . . . and . . . , as
well as, neither . . . nor . . . , (not) even, even if, any . . .

The most basic meaning of the particle *mo* is 'also.' However, depending on the sentence, it may be understood as 'even,' 'both,' 'all,' 'as well as,' or 'as much as.' If used in a negative sentence, it may be understood as 'neither,' 'no one,' 'nothing,' 'nowhere,' and so on. (→ See Interrogatives used in indefinite pronouns under Interrogatives.)

1. After nouns

   私は柔道が好きです。相撲も（また）好きです。
   *Watashi wa jūdō ga suki desu. **Sumō mo** (mata) suki desu.*
   I like judo. I like sumo, too.

   「とってもお腹が空きました。」「私もです。」
   *"Tottemo onaka ga sukimashita." "**Watashi mo** desu."*
   "I'm very hungry." "So am I."

   「納豆は好きではありません。」「私もです。」
   *"Nattō wa suki dewa arimasen." "**Watashi mo** desu."*
   "I don't like *nattō*." "Me neither."

2. After nouns, with negative verbs

   私もこの漢字は読めません。 ***Watashi mo** kono kanji wa yome**masen**.*
   I also can't read this kanji.

   私は簡単な漢字も分かりません。
   *Watashi wa kantan na **kanji mo** wakari**masen**.*
   I don't know even simple kanji.

→ See also *demo*.

3. After each of two nouns

   私はひらがなもカタカナも覚えました。
   *Watashi wa **hiragana mo katakana mo** oboemashita.*
   I learned both hiragana and katakana.

4. After quantity/amount phrases

   このジャケットは10万円もしました。
   *Kono jaketto wa **jū man en mo** shimashita.*
   This jacket cost me as much as one hundred thousand yen.

   きのうは３時間も漢字の勉強をしました。
   *Kinō wa **san jikan mo** kanji no benkyō o shimashita.*
   I studied kanji as long as three hours yesterday.

5. After an interrogative word (+ particle) with a negative predicate

   だれもその会に参加しませんでした。
   ***Dare mo** sono kai ni sanka shi**masen** deshita.*
   Nobody joined the meeting.

   明日はどこにも出かけません。 *Ashita wa **doko ni mo** dekakemasen.*
   I won't go out anywhere tomorrow.

6. After an interrogative word (+ a noun (+ a particle)) to mean 'all'

あのことは会社のだれもが知っている。
*Ano koto wa kaisha no **daremo** ga shitte iru.*
Everyone in this company knows that fact.

年末はどこも混んでいる。 *Nenmatsu wa **dokomo** konde iru.*
Everywhere is crowded at the end of the year.

ATMはどの町にもあります。 *ATM wa **dono machi ni mo** arimasu.*
ATMs can be found in every town.

---

mō もう [ADVERB]

already, yet, more

The adverb *mō* means 'already' or 'yet' depending on the context.

1. Used with verbs in the *ta*-form

もう諦めた。 ***Mō** akirameta.* **I've already given up.**
もう仕事を終えました。 ***Mō** shigoto o oemashita.*
I have already finished the work

「観光バスはもう来ましたか。」「いいえ，まだです。」
*"Kankō basu wa **mō** kimashita ka." "Iie, mada desu."*
"Has the sightseeing bus come yet?" "No, not yet."

→ See also *mada*.

2. Used with verbs in the negative form

冷蔵庫にはもう何も食べるものがありません。
*Reizōko ni wa **mō** nani mo taberu mono ga arimasen.*
There's nothing more to eat in the refrigerator.

3. Used with the progressive form

フランクはもう到着しています。 *Franku wa **mō** tōchaku shite imasu.*
**Frank has already arrived. (Frank arrived a short while ago and now he is
waiting.)**

4. Used with the progressive form + ***deshō***

本田さんはもう駅に着いているでしょう。
*Honda san wa **mō** eki ni tsuite iru **deshō**.*
Mr. Honda has probably arrived at the train station by now.

(guessing that Honda may have arrived a short while ago and that now
he may be waiting)

5. Expressing length of time, used with ***ni naru***

結婚してもう十年になります。 *Kekkon shite **mō** jū nen **ni narimasu**.*
It has already been ten years since I got married.

6. In future sentences

   彼女はもう結婚するでしょう。 *Kanojo wa **mō** kekkon suru **deshō**.*
   She will marry soon.

   もう夜中になります。寝ましょう。 ***Mō** yonaka ni narimasu. Nemashō.*
   It will soon be midnight. Go to bed.

7. Before number + counter

   社長はもう２，３日で帰ります。
   *Shachō wa **mō ni san nichi** de kaerimasu.*
   The president will be back in another two or three days.

   もう一度見に行きたいですね。 ***Mō ichi do** mi ni ikitai desu ne.*
   We want to go and see it again, don't we?

   もう一杯コーヒーを飲みたいです。 ***Mō ippai** kōhī o nomitai desu.*
   I'd like to have another cup of coffee.

mono もの(物, 者) [NOUN]

thing/one which. . . , person, (one's) belongings, what . . .

Mono is a noun that means 'thing,' 'person,' or 'fact.' Unlike *koto, mono* is used to refer to concrete objects. (→ See also *mono da*.)

1. After the particle *no*

   ここの物をもっと大切にして下さい。
   *Koko **no mono** o motto taisetsu ni shite kudasai.*
   Please handle the things here more carefully.

   「この傘はあなたのものですか。」「いえ，たぶん太郎のものです。」
   *"Kono kasa wa **anata no mono** desu ka." "Ie, tabun **Tarō no mono** desu."*
   "Is this umbrella yours?" "No, it's Taro's."

   → See *no*.

2. After names + *to iu*

   初めまして。私は豊田という者です。
   *Hajimemashite. Watashi wa **Toyota to iu mono** desu.*
   How do you do? I'm a person called Toyota. (My name is Toyota.)

3. After clauses

   彼女が買う物はブランドものばかりだ。
   ***Kanojo ga kau mono** wa burando mono bakari da.*
   The things she buys are all top-brand articles.

   私が今欲しい物は最新式の携帯電話です。
   ***Watashi ga ima hoshii mono** wa saishinshiki no keitai denwa desu.*
   What I want now is the newest-style mobile phone.

あなたのデジカメは私が買ったものより性能がいいですね。
*Anata no dejikame wa **watashi ga katta mono** yori seinō ga ii desu ne.*
Your digital camera has better functions than the one I bought.

→ See Relative clauses under Clauses.

mono da ものだ [PREDICATIVE PHRASE]

would often, it is common that. . . , generally tend to (do), indeed

Mono da is often added at the end of a clause when one makes a general state-ment about generic facts, personal desires, and past habitual actions.

1. Generic facts, following verbs/adjectives in the dictionary form

   だれでも新しくて便利な物に興味を持つものです。
   *Dare demo atarashikute benri na mono ni kyōmi o motsu **mono desu**.*
   Anybody tends to take an interest in new and convenient things.

   楽しい時間のたつのは早いものです。
   *Tanoshii jikan no tatsu no wa hayai **mono desu**.*
   Pleasant time passes fast indeed.

2. Personal desires, following *-tai*

   できれば休暇を一ヶ月取ってみたいものです。
   *Dekireba kyūka o ikkagetsu totte mi**tai mono desu**.*
   I'd like to take a one-month vacation if indeed possible.

3. Past habitual actions, following verbs in the *ta*-form

   私はよくうちでパーティーを開いたものです。
   *Watashi wa yoku uchi de pātī o hirai**ta mono desu**.*
   I used to have parties at my house very often.

morau もらう [AUXILIARY VERB]

to get (somebody) to do something, to receive some benefit from someone else's action

The auxiliary verb *morau* is used after a verb in the *te*-form and shows that the person denoted by the subject has/had someone else perform some action or receives/received some benefit from someone else's action. The receiver of the action must not be more distant from the speaker than the action performer is. The action performer is usually marked by the particle *ni*. *Morau* is replaced by *itadaku* when the action performer is someone to whom the speaker wishes to show respect. (→ See also *ageru*, *itadaku*, and *kureru*.)

先生に日本語の作文を見ていただきました。
***Sensei ni** Nihongo no sakubun o **mite itadakimashita**.*
I had my composition in Japanese looked through by my teacher.

みんなに教室を掃除してもらいます。
Minna ni *kyōshitsu o sōji shite* ***moraimasu.***
I will get you all to clean the classroom.

彼に手伝ってもらった。 ***Kare ni*** *tetsudatte moratta.*
I got him to help me.

However, the following *ni* can be replaced by *kara*, because knowledge is transferred from the agent to the receiver, although *kara* is not always compatible with the auxiliary verb *morau*, unlike with the verb *morau*.

彼に文法を教えてもらった。(彼から)
Kare ***ni*** *bunpō o oshiete* ***moratta.*** *(Kare* ***kara****)*
I got him to teach me grammar.

その新製品を見せてもらえますか。
Sono shinseihin o misete ***moraemasu*** *ka.*
Can I get you to show me the new article?

(Compare the above first-person subject with the following second-person subject.)

その新製品を見せてくれますか。
Sono shinseihin o misete ***kuremasu*** *ka.*
Will you show me the book?

太郎さんにそれをしてもらいたいと思います。
Tarō san ni sore o shite ***moraitai*** *to omoimasu.*
I think I want to get Taro to do that.

morau もらう [VERB]

to receive

The verb *morau* means 'to receive.' Thus, the subject noun denotes the receiver. The receiver must be closer to the speaker than to the giver. The giver is marked by the particle *kara* or *ni* when the verb is *morau*. *Morau* is replaced by *itadaku* when the giver is someone to whom the speaker wishes to show respect. Their potential forms (*moraeru* or *itadakeru*) are frequently used in a form of (negative) question when one wishes to receive something. (→ See also *ageru*, *itadaku*, and *kureru*.)

アメリカにいる友人から絵はがきをもらいました。
Amerika ni iru yūjin ***kara*** *ehagaki o* ***moraimashita.***
I received a picture postcard from a friend in the U.S.

陽子さんは彼氏にネックレスをもらいました。
Yōko san wa kareshi ni nekkuresu o ***moraimashita.***
Yoko received a necklace from her boyfriend.

先生に辞書をいただきました。 *Sensei ni jisho o itadakimashita.*
I received a dictionary from my teacher.

「このカタログをもらえますか／もらえませんか。」「どうぞ。無料です。」
"Kono katarogu o moraemasu ka / moraemasen ka." "Dōzo. Muryō desu."
"Could I get this catalog?" "Sure. It's free."

moshi もし [ADVERB]

an adverb for a conditional clause

Moshi is an adverb placed at the beginning of a conditional clause. (→ See *ba*, *nara*, *tara*, and Conditionals.) It is used to stress the subjunctive when the action or state in the conditional clause is hypothetical or counterfactual. *Moshi* + *mo* is even more emphatic.

もし雨なら中止です。 *Moshi ame nara chūshi desu.*
In case of rain, it will be called off.

もしもっとお金があればそれを買うのに。
Moshi motto okane ga areba sore o kau no ni.
If I had more money, I would buy it.

もしあなたの助けがなかったらうまく行かなかっただろう。
Moshi anata no tasuke ga nakattara umaku ikanakatta darō.
If I had not gotten your help, it probably would not have gone well.

もしも，私が外国に行くなら，あなたはどうしますか？
Moshimo, watashi ga gaikoku ni iku nara, anata wa dō shimasu ka?
If I would go to a foreign country, what would you do?

mottomo もっとも [ADVERB]

the most, the best, most, fair, in fact, however

The adverb *mottomo* can be used to express superlative comparison when used with adjectives, adverbs, and adjectival nouns, meaning 'most,' 'the most,' or 'the best.' Its informal counterpart is *ichiban*. (→ See also *ichiban* and Comparison.) However, it also means 'in fact,' functioning as a sentence adverb. Note that there is an adjectival noun *mottomo*, which means 'fair' or 'rational.'

1. To express superlatives

もっとも多い答えは「分からない」だった。
Mottomo ōi kotae wa "Wakaranai." datta.
The most common answer was "I don't know."

サッカー選手が男の子にもっとも人気のある職業だ。
Sakkā senshu ga otoko no ko ni mottomo ninki no aru shokugyō da.
Soccer player is the most popular occupation for boys.

ここはもっとも頻繁に地震が起こる。
*Koko wa **mottomo hinpan ni** jishin ga okoru.*
In this area earthquakes occur most often.

多くの人はその歌手がもっとも好きだ。
*Ōku no hito wa sono kashu ga **mottomo suki da.***
Many people like the singer best.

2. Used as a sentence adverb

それは正しいだろう。もっとも大したことではないが。
*Sore wa tadasii darō. **Mottomo** taishita koto dewa nai ga.*
It may be true. However, it does not count much.

彼はよく働く。もっとも能力もあるが。
*Kare wa yoku hataraku. **Mottomo** nōryoku mo aru ga.*
He works hard. And, in fact, he is competent.

3. Used as an adjectival noun

彼女がかんかんに怒るのももっともです。
*Kanojo ga kankan ni okoru no mo **mottomo desu.***
She has good reason to be furious.

「やってられないです。」「もっともです。」
*"Yatterarenai desu." "**Mottomo desu.**"*
"It's too much trouble." (I can't do it anymore.) "I entirely agree with you."

n ん [NEGATIVE VERB SUFFIX]

not

In informal conversation, some speakers use *n* instead of *nai* for verbs in the negative form. It is often thought to be part of a dialect or idiolect but was, in fact, derived from the old negative suffix *nu*. However, the *n* in the polite negative suffix *masen* is still used in modern standard Japanese.

次のバスがなかなか来んなぁ。 *Tsugi no basu ga nakanaka **kon** nā.*
The next bus is a long time coming.

「君も行くの。」「行かんよ。」 *"Kimo mo iku no." "**Ikan** yo."*
"Are you going too?" "I'm not going."

早くせんと間に合わんよ。 *Hayaku **sen** to **maniawan** yo.*
If you don't hurry, you'll be late for it.

(*Sen* in the above form was derived from *senu*, the old form of the negative of *suru*.)

na な [PARTICLE]

never (do), don't (do), how I wish

The particle *na* can be added at the end of a sentence in the informal plain form to seek agreement from the listener or to confirm the rightness of the statement. It is like the plain counterpart of the particle *ne*. (→ See *ne*.) Depending on the intonation and the choice of sentence adverbs (e.g. *yokumo* 'how dare'), *na* might be used emphatically. *Na* can express a plain negative command when used after a verb in the dictionary form and said with a firm intonation. It can also express a friendly informal command, if used after a verb in the combining form. It can also be placed at the end of a sentence or a clause (e.g. conditional clause) to show some emotion with a nuance of self-talk. In the latter case, *na* is prolonged.

1. At the end of sentences in the informal style

   あれはフランクの車だな。 *Are wa Furanku no kuruma **da na**.*
   That's Frank's car, isn't it?

   これは高いな。 *Kore wa takai **na**.* **How expensive this is!**

   よく食べるな。 *Yoku taberu **na**.* **You eat a lot!**

   よくもそんなことが言えたな。 *Yokumo sonna koto ga **ieta na**.*
   How dare you say such a thing?

   きれいな家に住みたいな。 *Kirei na ie ni sumitai **na**.*
   I want to live in a beautiful house!

2. After verbs in the dictionary form to express a plain negative command

   そんな馬鹿なことはするな。 *Sonna baka na koto wa suru **na**.*
   Don't do such a stupid thing.

   The negative command with *na* sounds blunt, but if we also add *yo* it sounds affectionate or friendly:

   そんな馬鹿なことはするなよ。 *Sonna baka na koto wa suru **na yo**.*

3. After verbs in the combining form to express a plain command

   やめな。 ***Yame na**.* **Stop it.**

   急いで早く来な。 *Isoide hayaku **kina**.*
   Hurry up and get over here!

   → See also *kudasai, nasai,* and *tewa ikenai/dewa ikenai*.

4. After a conditional clause to express envy or longing

   もっとお金と時間があればな。 ***Motto okane to jikan ga areba na**.*
   How I wish I had more money and time!

---

nado など [PARTICLE]

and so on, etc., and the like, or something like that, things such as . . . , the likes of, (not) . . . absolutely

The particle *nado* follows a single noun or multiple nouns conjoined by the particle *ya*; it means 'and so on,' and shows that the item is just one of the examples. (→ See also *to*, *toka*, and *ya*.) The resulting phrase constitutes a noun phrase, thus can be followed by any case particle and used in a sentence.

私はよく景色などを写真に撮ります。
*Watashi wa yoku **keshiki nado** o shashin ni torimasu.*
I often take photos of scenery and the like.

ゴルフなどはしますか。 ***Gorufu nado** wa shimasu ka.*
Do you play golf or any other sport like that?

私はよくコンビニで弁当やお茶などを買います。
*Watashi wa yoku konbini de **bentō ya ocha nado** o kaimasu.*
I often buy a boxed lunch, green tea, and so on at a convenience store.

寿司や刺身などの生ものは食べられますか。
***Sushi ya sashimi nado** no namamono wa taberaremasu ka.*
Can you eat raw foods such as sushi, sashimi, and the like?

テレビゲームなどはしません。 ***Terebi gēmu nado** wa shimasen.*
I don't play games like video games.

私などにはその仕事は無理です。
***Watashi nado** ni wa sono shigoto wa muri desu.*
It is impossible for the likes of me to do the work.

nagara ながら [PARTICLE]

while, as, although, in spite of

Nagara can follow a verb in the combining form and form an adverbial phrase showing the action that simultaneously takes place with the action expressed by the main sentence. (→ See also *aida*.) *Nagara* can also follow an adjective in the dictionary form or an adjectival noun, besides a verb in the combining form, to show the state that is in contrast with the state expressed by the main sentence. (→ See also *daga*, *ga*, *keredo(mo)*, and *noni*.)

1. After verbs in the combining form

    いつもラジオを聴きながら眠ります。
    *Itsumo rajio o **kikinagara** nemurimasu.*
    I usually fall asleep while listening to the radio.

    スタバでコーヒーを飲みながら話しましょう。
    *Sutaba de kōhī o **nominagara** hanashimashō.*
    Let's talk over a cup of coffee at Starbucks.

彼女は約束をしながらあまり守りません。
*Kanojo wa yakusoku o **shinagara** amari mamorimasen.*
Although she makes promises, she seldom keeps them.

2. After adjectives in the dictionary form

   この携帯電話は小さいながらたくさん機能を持っている。
   *Kono keiwai denwa wa **chīsai nagara** takusan kinō o motte iru.*
   Though it is small, this mobile phone has many functions.

3. After adjectival nouns

   彼は病気ながらやってきました。 *Kare wa **byōki nagara** yatte kimashita.*
   He came up in spite of illness.

---

nai ない [ADJECTIVE; VERB/ADJECTIVE SUFFIX]

not

Nai is syntactically an adjective and conjugates like an adjective. It can function as a substitute for the negative form of the verb *aru* 'to exist.' It also functions as a part of the negative counterpart of *da* (linking verb) in the form of *ja nai* or *dewa nai*. It also functions as a negative suffix for verbs and adjectives. Its *ta*-form is *nakatta* (plain) or *nakatta desu* (polite), and its *te*-form is *naide* (after verbs) or *nakute* (after adjectives or verbs to express a cause for some emotion or event).

1. Used as the substitute for the negative form of *aru*

   ここにおいてあった鞄がない。 *Koko ni oite atta kaban ga **nai**.*
   The bag I left here is missing.

   例外のない規則はない。 *Reigai no nai kisoku wa **nai**.*
   There are no rules that have no exceptions.

   → See also *aru*.

2. Used as a part of the negative counterpart of *da*

   これは日本製のカメラではない。
   *Kore wa Nihonsei no kamera **dewa nai**.*
   This is not a Japanese-made camera.

3. Used to form verbs in the *nai*-form

   遅れてもう電車に間に合わない。 *Okurete mō densha ni ma ni **awanai**.*
   It's already too late to make the train.

   今，現金を持っていない。 *Ima, genkin o motte **inai**.*
   I don't have cash now.

   僕はまだ帰らないよ。
   *Boku wa mada **kaeranai** yo.* (informal conversation)
   I will not go home yet.

「いっしょに食べない。」「もう食べられない。」(informal conversation)
*"Isshoni **tabenai**." (with rising intonation) "Mō **taberarenai**."*
"Don't you eat with me?" "I can't eat any more."

来月は仕事をしないんです。 *Raigetsu wa shigoto o **shinai** n desu.*
I'm not going to work next month.

使わないものはクローゼットにしまってあります。
***Tsukawanai** mono wa kurōzetto ni shimatte arimasu.*
I leave things that I do not use in my closet.

4. Used to form adjectives in the ***nai**-form*

この電気自動車は思ったほど高くなかった。
*Kono denki jidōsha wa omotta hodo **takaku nakatta**.*
This electric car was not as expensive as I had expected.

5. Used in the ***te**-form, **naide***

ここでタバコは吸わないで欲しい。 *Koko de tabako wa **suwanaide** hoshii.*
I want you not to smoke here. (I don't want you to smoke here.)

努力しないで成功はしません。 *Doryoku **shinaide** seikō wa shimasen.*
You won't succeed without making efforts.

彼はお礼も言わないで帰ってしまった。
*Kare wa orei mo **iwanaide** kaette shimatta.*
He went home without expressing thanks.

→ See also *nai de* and *zu ni*.

6. Used in the ***te**-form, **nakute***

遊ぶ時間がなくて不満です。 *Asobu jikan ga **nakute** fuman desu.*
I am discontented because I have no time to play.

彼女が来られなくて残念です。 *Kanojo ga **korarenakute** zannen desu.*
We are sorry that she is not able to come.

給料がよくなくて，仕事をやめました。
*Kyūryō ga **yokunakute**, shigoto o yamemashita.*
As my salary was not good, I quit my job.

雨が降らなくて，農家は困りました。
*Ame ga **furanakute**, nōka wa komarimashita.*
As it did not rain, farmers were in trouble.

---

nai de ないで [ADVERBIAL PHRASE]

without (doing), not (do) and then (do)

The verbs in the *nai*-form plus the particle *de* create a phrase that literally means 'not do . . . and,' and is often translated into English as 'without doing. . . .' The phrase . . . *nai de* can be followed by *kudasai* (to request someone not to do something), by the main sentence that expresses the action one actually does, or by certain auxiliary verbs including *oku* and *iru*. An alternative form for . . . *nai de* (e.g. *tabenai de*) is . . . *zu ni* (e.g. *tabezu ni*), but the latter cannot be used before *kudasai*. (→ See also *nakute* and *zu ni*.)

1. Followed by **kudasai**

   勝手に写真を撮らないで下さい。　*Katte ni shashin o **toranai de kudasai**.*
   Please don't take a photo of me without my permission.

→ See also *kudasai*.

2. Followed by a verb phrase, meaning 'without doing . . .'

   宿題をしないで何をしているの。
   ***Shukudai o shinai de** nani o shite iru no.*
   What are you doing not doing your homework?

   朝食を食べて出勤しますか。それとも食べないで出勤しますか。
   *Chōshoku o tabete shukkin shimasu ka. Soretomo **tabenai de shukkin shimasu** ka.*
   Do you go to work after eating breakfast? Or do you go to work without eating breakfast?

   しゃべりながら食べますか。しゃべらないで食べますか。
   *Shaberi nagara tabemasu ka. **Shaberanai de tabemasu** ka.*
   Do you eat while talking? Or do you eat without talking?

   今日はテレビを見ないで宿題をした方がいい。
   *Kyō wa **terebi o minai de** shukudai o **shita** hō ga ii.*
   It's better to do your homework without watching TV today.

   cf. 今日はテレビを見ながら宿題をしない方がいい。
   *Kyō wa **terebi o minagara** shukudai o **shinai** hō ga ii.*
   It's better not to do your homework watching TV today.

→ See also *zu ni*, *te*, and *nagara*

3. Followed by auxiliary verbs/adjectives

   これ以上お金を使わないでおきます。
   *Kore ijō okane o **tsukawanai de okimasu**.*
   I'll stop using more money. (I will keep money without using it.)

   言いたいことを言わないでおくのを「言わぬが花。」という。
   *Iitai koto o **iwanai de oku** no o "Iwanuga hana." to iu.*
   Leaving unsaid what one would rather say is expressed as "No word is a flower [beautiful]."

   まだ本当のことを知らせないでいるんですか。
   *Mada hontō no koto o **shirasenai de iru** n desu ka.*
   You still haven't let (him) know the truth?

→ See also *hoshii, oku,* and *iru*.

nai uchi ni ないうちに [ADVERBIAL PHRASE]

before (an undesirable thing occurs)

When *uchi ni* follows a verb in the *nai*-form, it means 'before. . . .' (→ See *uchi ni* and *mae*.)

暗くならないうちに帰りましょう。 *Kuraku naranai uchi ni kaerimashō.*
Let's go home before it gets dark.

忘れないうちに彼女に電話しておこう。
Wasurenai uchi ni kanojo ni denwa shite okō.
I'll call her before I forget.

nakereba ikenai /nakereba naranai なければいけない/なければならない [PREDICATIVE PHRASE]

must, have to

Obligations and necessity are typically expressed by a sentence that has two parts. One is the condition part and the other is the judgment part. The condition part has a verb, an adjective, or a linking verb in the *nai*-form, which ends in *nakereba*, *nakute wa*, *nai to*, or *nakya* (informal). The judgment part can be either *ikenai* or *naranai*, but the former sounds more subjective (the speaker's idea) than the latter. (→ See also *beki da*, *nakutewa ikenai*, *neba naranai*, *ro*, and *zaru o enai*.)

1. Used for verbs
   もっと勉強しなければいけない。 *Motto benkyō shinakereba ikenai.*
   You must study harder.

   「私も行かなければいけませんか。」「いえ, けっこうです。」
   "Watashi mo ikanakereba ikemasen ka." "Ie, kekkō desu."
   "Do I have to go, too?" "No, you don't need to."

   九時までに会社に行かなければなりません。
   Kuji made ni kaisha ni ikanakereba narimasen.
   I have to go to the company by nine o'clock.

   もっと単語を覚えなければなりません。
   Motto tango o oboenakereba narimasen.
   I have to learn more words.

2. Used for adjectives
   荷物はもっと軽くなければいけません。
   Nimotsu wa motto karuku nakereba ikemasen.
   The luggage needs to be lighter.

アパートは駅にもっと近くなければならない。
*Apāto wa eki ni motto chikaku **nakereba naranai**.*
The apartment house needs to be much closer to the train station.

3. Used for (adjectival) nouns + *de*

辞書は便利でなければいけない。
*Jisho wa **benri de nakereba ikenai**.*
Dictionaries must be convenient.

高齢者に親切でなければいけません。
*Kōreisha ni **shinsetsu de nakereba ikemasen**.*
You must be kind to old people.

話は論理的でなければならない。
*Hanashi wa **ronriteki de nakereba naranai**.*
The speech needs to be logical.

nakute なくて [ADVERBIAL PHRASE]

because not

Verbs and adjectives in the negative *te*-form end in *nakute* as in *tabenakute* and *takakute*. However, verbs have an alternative form, *nai de* as in *tabenai de*. (→ See also *nai de*.) When a verb expresses a cause or conditions, *nakute* is used. (→ See also *nakutemo ii* and *nakute wa ikenai*.) In other contexts, *nai de* is used.

この車は高くなくて、いいですよ。
*Kono kuruma wa taka**kunakute**, ii desu yo.*
This car is not expensive and is good.

英語が分からなくて、試験がよくできませんでした。
*Eigo ga wakara**nakute**, shiken ga yoku dekimasen deshita.*
As I did not understand English, I could not do well in the exam.

子供が朝ごはんを食べなくて、困っています。
*Kodomo ga asagohan o tabe**nakute**, komatte imasu.*
I'm having a problem because my child does not eat breakfast.

毎日朝ごはんを食べないで、学校に行きます。
*Maiasa asagohan o tabe**nai de**, gakkō ni ikimasu.*
I go to school without eating breakfast every day.

明日は7時に起きなくてはいけません。
*Ashita wa shichi ji ni oki**nakute wa ikemasen**.*
I have to wake up at 7 o'clock tomorrow.

この本は読まなくてもいいですよ。
*Kono hon wa yoma**nakute mo ii** desu yo.*
You don't have to read this book.

nakutemo ii なくてもいい [PREDICATIVE PHRASE]

need not, (not) have to

The lack of obligations and necessity is typically expressed by a sentence that has two parts. One is the condition part and the other is the judgment part. The condition part has a verb, an adjective, or a linking verb in the negative *te*-form plus the particle *mo*. The judgment part is usually *ii* or its variant, *yoi*. (→ See also *nakutewa ikenai*, *nakereba ikenai / nakereba naranai*, *neba naranai*, *temo/demo*, and *temo ii / demo ii*.)

1. For verbs

   そんなに急いでやらなくてもいいです。
   *Sonna ni isoide **yaranakutemo ii** desu.*
   You need not do it so hastily.

   電話をしてくれればわざわざ来なくてもよかったですよ。
   *Denwa o shite kurereba wazawaza **konakutemo yokatta** desu yo.*
   If you had given me a call, you need not have come all this way.

   これは書かなくてもいいですか。 *Kore wa **kakanakutemo ii** desu ka.*
   Is it all right if I don't write this?

2. For adjectives

   車は動けば新しくなくてもよいです。
   *Kuruma wa ugokeba atarashi**ku nakutemo yoi** desu.*
   As long as the car moves, it needn't be new.
   (The car needn't be new; it just has to run.)

3. After (adjectival) nouns + *ja/de*

   お気に入りの車なら新車じゃなくてもいいです。
   *Okiniiri no kuruma nara **shinsha ja nakute mo ii** desu.*
   It does not have to be a brand new car if it's my favorite car.

   返事は今日でなくてもいいです。 *Henji wa **kyō de nakutemo ii** desu.*
   A reply does not need to be made today.

   文法の説明は完全でなくてもよい。
   *Bunpō no setsumei wa **kanzen de nakutemo yoi**.*
   The explanation of grammar does not need to be perfect.

nakutewa ikenai なくてはいけない [PREDICATIVE PHRASE]

need to . . . , must . . . , have to . . .

Obligation and necessity can be expressed by a sentence that has two parts. One is the condition part, and the other is judgment part. The condition part has a verb, an adjective, or a linking verb in the negative *te*-form plus the particle *wa*.

The judgment part is usually *ikenai* or its variant, *naranai*. (→ See also *beki da, nakereba ikenai/nakereba naranai, nakutemo ii, neba naranai,* and *zaru o enai*.)

1. For verbs

この漢字は覚えなくてはいけませんよ。
*Kono kanji wa **oboenakutewa ikemasen** yo.*
You need to memorize this kanji.

明日ボストンに行かなくてはいけません。
*Ashita Bosuton ni **ikanakutewa ikemasen**.*
I need to go to Boston tomorrow.

2. For adjectives

ピザは熱くなくてはいけません。 *Piza wa **atsukunakutewa ikemasen**.*
Pizzas must be hot.

あの大学に入るには数学の成績がよくなくてはいけません。
*Ano daigaku ni hairu ni wa sūgaku no seiseki ga **yokunakute wa ikemasen**.*
In order to enter that college, you must have a good grade in math.

3. After (adjectival) nouns + *de*

寝室は静かでなくてはいけません。
*Shinshitsu wa **shizuka de nakutewa ikemasen**.*
Bedrooms have to be quiet.

朝ごはんは日本食でなくてはいけません。
*Asagohan wa **nihonshoku de nakutewa ikemasen**.*
My breakfast has to be Japanese-style.

nan 何 [INTERROGATIVE]

what, how many, several, a few, many

Nan is a euphonically changed form of *nani*. (→ See *donna* and *nani*.) *Nan* is often used before the particle *no*, and should be used before the linking verbs *da/desu*, counters, or numeric digits.

1. Before the particle *no*

何の音楽が好きですか。 ***Nan** (or **nani**) **no ongaku** ga suki desu ka.*
What (kind of) music do you like?

2. Before *da/desu*

これは何ですか。 *Kore wa **nan desu** ka.* What is this?

3. Before counters

「今何時ですか。」「二時十五分です。」
*"Ima **nan ji** desu ka." "Ni ji jū go fun desu."*
"What time is it now?" "It's two fifteen."

「終わるまで何分かかりますか。」「半時間です。」
*"Owaru made **nan pun** kakarimasu ka." "Han jikan desu."*
"How many minutes will it take to finish it?" "Half an hour."

外国に何回行ったことがありますか。
*Gaikoku ni **nan kai** itta koto ga arimasu ka.*
How many times have you been abroad?

4. Before counters, followed by **ka** or **mo**

やっと何人か来ました。 *Yatto **nan nin ka** kimashita.*
At least some people have finally come.

花子さんには何日か前に会いました。
*Hanako san ni wa **nan nichi ka** mae ni aimashita.*
I saw Hanako a few days ago.

日本人が何人も来ました。 *Nihonjin ga **nan nin mo** kimashita.*
Many Japanese came.

5. Before numeric digits

私は電子書籍を何十冊も買いました。
*Watashi wa denshi shoseki o **nan jissatsu mo** kaimashita.*
I bought dozens of books in e-book form.

外国語を覚えるのに何年もかかります。
*Gaikokugo o oboeru no ni **nan nen mo** kakarimasu.*
It takes many years to master a foreign language.

---

nani 何 [INTERROGATIVE]

what, which, why, that thing

Nani is an interrogative pronoun used for asking the identity of non-human items. If it is used for a human, the question is understood as a part of a criticism. It can be followed by a variety of particles such as *ga, o, ni, de*, and *kara*. Like other interrogative pronouns, it cannot be followed by the topic particle *wa*. It can be used right before nouns or within a Sino-Japanese compound. It is pronounced as *nan* when placed before the linking verbs *da/desu*, counters, or numeric digits, and it is often pronounced as *nan* when placed before the particle *no*. (→ See *nan*.)

1. Before a particle

あなたが買った福袋には何が入っていましたか。
*Anata ga katta fukubukuro ni wa **nani ga** haitte imashita ka.*
What was in the lucky grab bag you bought?

デパートで何を買うんですか。 *Depāto de **nani o** kau n desu ka.*
What are you going to buy in the department store?

今何がいちばん欲しいですか。 *Ima **nani ga** ichiban hoshii desu ka.*
What do you want most now?

何を話しているんですか。 ***Nani o** hanashite iru n desu ka.*
What are you talking about?

将来何になりたいのですか。 *Shōrai **nani ni** naritai no desu ka.*
What do you want to be in the future?

お酒は何でできていますか。 *Osake wa **nani de** dekite imasu ka.*
What is sake made of?

「何をなくした。」「何って何ですか。」「さいふだ。」
*"**Nani o** nakushita." "**Nanitte** nan desu ka." "Saifu da."*
"I lost that." "What is it you mean by 'that'?" "My wallet."

(*Nani* may indicate what the speaker cannot clearly recall immediately.
→ See also *are*.)

何，ここでさぼってるんですか。 ***Nani**, koko de sabotteru n desu ka.*
Why are you loafing here?

2. Before a noun

何色が好きですか。 ***Nani iro** ga suki desu ka.*
What color do you like?

3. Within a Sino-Japanese compound

うちでは何語を話すのですか。*Uchi de wa **nani go** o hanasu no desu ka.*
What language do you speak at home?

何州の何市の出身ですか。 ***Nani shū** no **nani shi** no shusshin desu ka.*
Which city in which state are you from?

---

naosu 直す [AUXILIARY VERB]

to redo, do . . . over again

The auxiliary verb *naosu* follows a verb in the combining form and shows that
the action is repeated.

彼女のメールを何度も読み直しました。
*Kanojo no mēru o nando mo **yominaoshimashita**.*
I read her e-mail over and over again.

この字が読めないので書き直して下さい。
*Kono ji ga yomenai node **kakinaoshite** kudasai.*
Please rewrite this character because I can't read it.

考え直して行くことにしました。
***Kangaenaoshite** iku koto ni shimashita.*
I changed my mind and decided to go.

失敗しました。写真を撮り直しましょう。
*Shippai shimashita. Shashin o **torinaoshimashō**.*
I failed. Let me retake your picture.

nara なら [PARTICLE]

if, supposing . . . , on condition that . . . , as for

Nara derives from the conditional form of the linking verb *da*. It may be followed by the conditional particle *ba*, as in *naraba*. *Nara* can directly follow (adjectival) nouns (with particles), but it can also follow a clause that ends in a verb or an adjective in the dictionary form, in the *ta*-form, or in the *nai*-form. In the latter case, *no* or *n* can be optionally placed before *nara*. *Nara* can occasionally follow verbs in the *masu*-form (with *no*). (→ See *no da* and Conditionals.)

1. After (adjectival) nouns and pronouns

明日雨ならば延期します。 *Ashita **ame naraba** enki shimasu.*
If it is rainy tomorrow, we will postpone it.

彼が病気ならば仕方がありません。
*Kare ga **byōki naraba** shikata ga arimasen.*
If he is ill, there is nothing we can do about it.

それならなぜやめないんですか。 ***Sore nara** naze yamenai n desu ka.*
If that's the case, why don't you stop?

私ならそんなものは買いません。
*Watashi **nara** sonna mono wa kaimasen.*
If it were me, I would not buy such a thing.

彼女なら喜んでしてくれるでしょう。
*Kanojo **nara** yorokonde shite kureru deshō.*
Certainly, she'd be happy to do it for you.

お金なら要りません。 ***Okane nara** irimasen.*
If it's money (you're offering), I don't need it.

英語なら話せます。 ***Eigo nara** hanasemasu.*
If it's English (you need), I can speak it.

歴史的な街なら京都がいい。 ***Rekishiteki na machi nara** Kyōto ga ii.*
As for historical cities, Kyoto is nice.

結婚ならまだ相手がいません。 ***Kekkon nara** mada aite ga imasen.*
If you're talking about my marriage, I have no partner yet.

「先生はどこですか。」「先生なら図書館にいらっしゃいますよ。」
*"Sensei wa doko desu ka." "**Sensei nara** toshokan ni irasshaimasu yo."*
"Where is the teacher?" "If you're looking for your teacher, he/she is in the library."

「トイレに行きたいんですが。」「トイレなら二階にありますよ。」
*"Toire ni ikitai n desu ga." "**Toire nara** ni kai ni arimasu yo."*
"I want to go to a restroom." "If you're looking for a restroom, it's on the second floor."

2. After nouns + particle

来週までなら出来上がります。 ***Raishū made nara** dekiagarimasu.*
I will be able to complete it by next week (if you can wait till then).

3. After verbs and adjectives in the dictionary, **nai-**, or **ta**-form optionally followed by **no/n**

ちゃんと返してくれる（の）なら貸してあげましょう。
*Chanto **kaeshite kureru (no) nara** kashite agemashō.*
On condition that you return it to me without fail, I will lend it to you.

そんなに安い（ん）なら買います。 *Sonna ni **yasui (n) nara** kaimasu.*
If it is so cheap, I'll buy it.

あなたができない（の）なら私がしましょう。
*Anata ga **dekinai (no) nara** watashi ga shimashō.*
If you cannot do it, I will do it for you.

欲しかった（の）なら言ってくれればよかったのに。
*Hoshikatta **(no) nara** itte kurereba yokatta no ni.*
If you wanted it, you should have told me so.

4. After verbs in the **masu**-form (with **no**)

東京にいらっしゃいます（の）なら，是非うちにお寄りください。
*Tōkyō ni **irasshaimasu (no) nara**, zehi uchi ni oyori kudasai.*
If you are coming to Tokyo, please come to visit our house.

naru なる [VERB]

to become, get, turn, come (grow) to, learn to

Naru means 'to become' and expresses some change. The word/phrase that denotes the outcome of the change is marked by the particle *ni* (or *to*) or takes some adverbial form.

1. After (adjectival) nouns + **ni**

兄は研究者になりました。 *Ani wa **kenkyūsha ni narimashita**.*
My big brother became a scholar (or a researcher).

私はデザイナーになりたいです。 *Watashi wa **dezainā ni naritai** desu.*
I want to be a designer.

よく休みなさい，そうしないと病気になりますよ。
*Yoku yasumi nasai, sō shinai to **byōki ni narimasu** yo.*
Sleep well—if you don't, you'll become sick.

実際に見れば相撲が好きになりますよ。
*Jissai ni mireba sumō ga **suki ni narimasu** yo.*
If you actually watch sumo, you'll grow to like it.

2. After adjectives or adjective-like suffixes in the *ku*-form

外はもう暗くなりました。 *Soto wa mō kura**ku narimashita**.*
It has already grown dark outside.

彼女はそれを見て青くなった。 *Kanojo wa sore o mite ao**ku natta**.*
She saw it and turned pale.

いつから彼女と会わなくなったのですか。
*Itsu kara kanojo to awana**ku natta** no desu ka.*
Since when did you stop meeting her?

彼女の声を聞くと会いたくなります。
*Kanojo no koe o kiku to aita**ku narimasu**.*
If I hear her voice, I'll grow to want to see her.

3. After *yō ni*, following verbs

私は日本語が分かるようになりました。
*Watashi wa Nihongo ga **wakaru yō ni narimashita**.*
I have come to understand Japanese.

あの学生は最近遅刻しないようになりました。
*Ano gakusei wa saikin chikoku **shinai yō ni narimashita**.*
That student stopped being late.

最近よく酒を飲むようになった。 *Saikin yoku sake o **nomu yō ni natta**.*
I've come to drink a lot recently.

ギターが弾けるようになりました。 *Gitā ga **hikeru yō ni narimashita**.*
I've come to be able to play the guitar. (I've learned to play the guitar.)

→ See also *yō da <resemblance>*.

4. After *koto ni*, following verbs

ここで働くことになりました。 *Koko de hataraku koto ni narimashita.*
It's been decided that I work here.

→ See *koto ni naru*.

nasai なさい [AUXILIARY VERB]

Do . . .

Nasai follows a verb in the combining form to create a command form, which can be appropriately used in instructions in exams and manuals and commands by parents to their children. As it is a command form, it should not be used to one's superiors at all, and is better not to use it to one's colleagues unless with a friendly intonation and sentence-final particles. There is a more informal and rude command form, which is called a plain command form: e.g. *tabero* or *nome*.

> 答えを紙に書きなさい。 *Kotae o kami ni **kakinasai**.*
> **Write your answers on the paper.**

> 早くしなさい。 *Hayaku **shinasai**.*   **Hurry up.**

→ See also *kudasai*, *na*, and *ro*.

naze なぜ [INTERROGATIVE]

why

Naze means 'why' and can be used for asking reasons. Questions with *naze* usually end in *n desu ka* or *no (desu) ka*.

> 「なぜ休んだのですか。」「風邪をひいたんです。」
> *"**Naze** yasunda **no desu ka**." "Kaze o hiita n desu."*
> **"Why were you absent?" "I caught a cold."**

> 彼になぜ約束を破ったのか尋ねましたか。
> *Kare ni **naze** yakusoku o yabutta **no ka** tazunemashita ka.*
> **Did you ask him why he broke his promise?**

> なぜそうしないの。 ***Naze** sō shinai **no**.*
> **Why don't you do so? (You should do so.)**

→ See also *dōshite* and *ka*.

nazenaraba なぜならば [CONJUNCTION]

because

Nazenaraba, or simply *nazenara*, is used at the beginning of a sentence that states the reason for the fact previously introduced in the discourse. The sentence with this word often ends in *kara desu*. (→ See *kara*.) This word is used in written or in a formal speech. In conversation, *naze ka to iu to*, *naze ka to ieba*, *nande ka to iu to*, or *nande ka to ieba* (Lit., *to tell why it is*) is commonly used.

> 彼は来ないでしょう。なぜならば行きたくないと言っていたからです。
> *Kare wa konai deshō. **Nazenaraba** ikitaku nai to itte ita **kara desu**.*
> **He may not come. Because he said he didn't want to come.**

> 私は行けないです。なぜかと言うと急に用事が入ったからです。
> *Watashi wa ikenai desu. **Nazeka to iu to** kyū ni yōji ga haitta **kara desu**.*
> **I can't go. Because some business has suddenly turned up.**

n da んだ → See *no da.*

n desu んです → See *no da.*

ne ね [PARTICLE]

isn't it?, right?, okay?

The particle *ne* can be placed at the end of the sentence to seek agreement from the conversational partner, to confirm the rightness of the statement, or to soften the tone of the statement. The sentence can be in the polite style or in the informal plain style. The particle *ne* can also follow any phonologically stable phrases, as filler or a short confirmation marker.

1. At the end of a sentence to elicit agreement

   「今日は天気がとてもいいですね。」「そうですね。」
   *"Kyō wa tenki ga totemo ii desu **ne**." "Sō desu **ne**."*
   "The weather is very nice today, isn't it?" "Yes, it is."

   「今日は寒くないですね。」「ええ，そうですね。」
   *"Kyō wa samuku nai desu **ne**." "Ē, sō desu **ne**."*
   "Today isn't cold, is it?" "Right (, it's not)."

2. At the end of a sentence to confirm the fact

   本田さんも行きますね。 *Honda san mo ikimasu **ne**.*
   You're going, too, Mr. Honda, aren't you?

   これいらないね。 *Kore iranai **ne**.* **This one, you don't need it, right?**

3. After commands and requests (*nasai/kudasai*) to soften the tone of the voice

   ぜひパーティーに来て下さいね。 *Zehi pātī ni kite **kudasai ne**.*
   By all means, please come to our party, OK?

4. After phrases used as a friendly filler

   だからね，もっとね，頑張ってね，欲しいんですよね。
   *Dakara **ne**, motto**ne**, ganbatte **ne**, hoshii n desu yo **ne**.*
   That's why, you know, I want you, listen to me, to work/study harder, are you OK?

→ See also *yo.*

neba naranai ねばならない [PREDICATIVE PHRASE]

have to, must

Neba naranai can replace *nakereba naranai* to express obligation. (→ See *nakereba ikenai / nakereba naranai* and *zaru o enai*.) *Neba* is the conditional form of the old negative verb suffix *zu* or *nu*.

もう行かねばなりません。 *Mō **ikaneba narimasen**.* I have to leave now.

若いうちはもっと仕事せねばなりません。
*Wakai uchi wa motto shigoto **seneba narimasen**.*
You must work harder while you are young.

(This uses the antiquated form *se[neba]* instead of the more common *shi[nakereba]*.)

---

ni に [PARTICLE]

---

at, in, on, for, from, to, toward, per, in order to (do), and

The particle *ni* is one of the most frequently used particles in Japanese. It follows (adjectival) nouns and verbs, often indicating the target/purpose of actions and states.

I. NOUNS + *NI*

Ni follows a noun that expresses the target of an action/state, the criterial target for evaluation, location of existence, time/frequency of actions, the agent of an action in specific grammatical constructions, and many additional concepts.

1. The destination or direction

   彼らは今朝飛行機でバンコクに向かいました。
   *Karera wa kesa hikōki de **Bankoku ni** mukaimashita.*
   They left for Bangkok by plane this morning.

   今朝ボストンに着きました。 *Kesa **Boston ni** tsukimashita.*
   I arrived in Boston this morning.

   私の別荘は海に面しています。
   *Watashi no bessō wa **umi ni** menshite imasu.*
   My cottage faces the sea.

   荷物は棚に置いて下さい。 *Nimotsu wa **tana ni** oite kudasai.*
   Please put your baggage on the shelf.

   東京に家を建てました。 ***Tōkyō ni** ie o tatemashita.*
   I built a house in Tokyo.

   → See *e*.

2. The recipient of items or services

   田中さんに書類を送りました。 ***Tanaka san ni** shorui o okurimashita.*
   I sent the documents to Mr. Tanaka.

   私は彼に中古車をあげました。
   *Watashi wa **kare ni** chūkosha o agemashita.*
   I gave him my used car.

毎週金曜日にフランクに日本語を教えています。
*Maishū Kinyōbi ni **Furanku ni** Nihongo o oshiete imasu.*
I teach Frank Japanese every Friday.

子供に本を読んであげました。 ***Kodomo ni** hon o yonde agemashita.*
I read a book to my child.

祖父が私にお金をくれました。 *Sofu ga **watashi ni** okane o kuremashita.*
My grandfather gave me money.

3. The target of mental state

部長に従って行動します。 ***Buchō ni** shitagatte kōdō shimasu.*
I act at the direction of the division manager.

高校生のとき，両親に反抗しました。
*Kōkōsei no toki, **ryōshin ni** hankō shimashita.*
I rebelled against my parents when I was a high school student.

彼の武勇伝には飽きてしまいました。
*Kare no **buyūden ni** wa akite shimaimashita.*
I completely tired of the tale of his heroic exploits.

日本の社会に慣れるのに3年かかった。
*Nihon no **shakai ni** nareru no ni san nen kakatta.*
It took three years for me to get used to Japanese society.

4. The purpose of actions

彼女はデパートへ買い物に行きました。
*Kanojo wa depāto e **kaimono ni** ikimashita.*
She went to the department store to shop.

彼は香港へ旅行に行った。 *Kare wa Honkon e **ryoko ni** itta.*
He has gone on a trip to Hong Kong.

あなたはテレビゲームにお金を使いすぎます。
*Anata wa **terebi gēmu ni** okane o tsukaisugimasu.*
You spend too much money on video games.

5. The occasion for the action

子供の誕生日に昆虫の図鑑を買ってやった。
*Kodomo no **tanjōbi ni** konchū no zukan o katte yatta.*
I bought my child an illustrated reference book on insects for his birthday.

高校入学のお祝いに3万円あげた。
*Kōkō nyūgaku no **oiwai ni** sanman en ageta.*
I gave (him) 30,000 yen for celebrating his entering high school.

6. The outcome of a change

私は将来建築家になりたいです。
*Watashi wa shōrai **kenchikuka ni** naritai desu.*
I want to be an architect in the future.

山田さんは息子を医者にした。 *Yamada san wa musuko o **isha ni** shita.*
Mrs. Yamada made her son a doctor.

この小麦粉はクッキーにします。 *Kono komugiko wa **kukkī ni** shimasu.*
I'll make this flour into cookies.

この1万円札をドルに換えてください。
*Kono ichi man en satsu o **doru ni** kaete kudasai.*
Please change this 10,000 yen bill into dollars.

狐は女の人に化けました。 *Kitsune wa **onna no hito ni** bakemashita.*
The fox disguised itself as a beautiful woman.

→ See *naru*.

7. The criterial target for evaluation and comparison

   ビタミンB2とB6は目にいいです。
   *Bitamin bī tsū to bī roku wa **me ni** ii desu.*
   Vitamin B2 and B6 are good for the eyes.

   お酒は肝臓に悪いですよ。 *Osake wa **kanzō ni** warui desu yo.*
   Alcohol is bad for your liver.

   この日本語の本は一年生にはむずかしすぎる。
   *Kono Nihongo no hon wa **ichi nensei ni** wa muzukashisugiru.*
   This Japanese book is too difficult for first-year students.

   かつて外国に比べると日本人はよく働くと言われた。
   *Katsute **gaikoku ni** kuraberu to Nihonjin wa yoku hataraku to iwareta.*
   It used to be said that the Japanese work hard compared with (people of) foreign countries.

8. Decisions and choices

   「何にしますか。」「私はてんぷらにします。」
   *"**Nani ni** shimasu ka?" "Watashi wa **tenpura ni** shimasu."*
   "What would you like to have?" "I will have tempura."

   専攻は人類学に決めました。 *Senkō wa **jinruigaku ni** kimemashita.*
   I decided to take anthropology as my academic major.

   カナダに行くことになりました。 ***Kanada ni** iku koto ni narimashita.*
   It's been decided that we go to Canada.

→ See *koto*, *koto ni naru*, and *koto ni suru*.

9. The location of existence especially when the verb is *iru* or *aru*

   壁に変な虫がいる。 ***Kabe ni** hen na mushi ga iru.*
   A strange insect is on the wall.

   「彼女は今どこにいますか。」「あそこにいます。」
   *"Kanojo wa ima **doko ni imasu** ka." "**Asoko ni imasu**."*
   "Where is she now?" "She is over there."

郵便局は図書館の左側にあります。
*Yūbinkyoku wa toshokan no **hidari gawa ni arimasu**.*
The post office is on the left of the library.

(Do not use *ni*, but use *de* for the location where an event takes place.)

→   See *de*.

10. Affiliations, interests, etc., especially when the verb is ***iru*** or ***aru***

今, 営業部にいます。 *Ima **eigyōbu ni imasu**.*
I currently belong to the sales department.

どのグループに所属した方がいいですか。
***Dono gurūpu ni** shozoku shita hō ga ii desu ka.*
Which group is it better for me to belong to?

私には異性の友達がいません。
***Watashi ni** wa isei no tomodachi ga **imasen**.*
I do not have any friends of the opposite gender.

私はクラシック音楽に興味があります。
*Watashi wa **kurashikku ongaku ni** kyōmi ga **arimasu**.*
I have an interest in classical music.

私には音楽の才能がぜんぜんありません。
***Watashi ni** wa ongaku no sainō ga zenzen **arimasen**.*
 I do not have talent in music at all.

11. The location of living when the verb is ***sumu***

加藤さんは広島に住んでいます。
*Katō san wa **Hiroshima ni sunde** imasu.*
Mr. Kato lives in Hiroshima.

(However, the verb *seikatsu suru* 'to live' takes the particle *de* instead of *ni* because its focus is activities associated with living.)

加藤さんは広島で生活しています。
*Katō san wa **Hiroshima de** seikatsu shite imasu.*
Mr. Kato lives in Hiroshima.

12. The time of the action

The particle *ni* is needed after a noun that expresses the time of the action if it is an absolute time such as a specific date or year. By contrast, *ni* is not needed if it expresses a relative time such as 'yesterday' or 'next year.'

「何時に電話をくれましたか。」「六時にしました。」
*"**Nan ji ni** denwa o kuremashita ka." "**Roku ji ni** shimashita."*
"(At) what time did you give me a call?" "I called at six."

来週の日曜日に京都へ行きます。
*Raishū no **Nichiyōbi ni** Kyōto e ikimasu.*
I'll go to Kyoto (on) next Sunday

夏休みに外国へ行こうかと考えています。
***Natsu yasumi ni** gaikoku e ikō ka to kangaete imasu.*
I'm thinking of going abroad for summer vacation.

13. The criterial target for frequency

このクラブのミーティングは年に三回開かれる。
*Kono kurabu no mītingu wa **nen ni** san kai hirakareru.*
The meeting of this club is held three times per year.

その試験には1.5人に1人が合格した。
*Sono shiken ni wa **itten go nin ni** hitori ga gōkaku shita.*
One person out of one point five passed the examination.

14. The source of receiving when the (auxiliary) verb is *morau*

このお土産は本田さんにもらいました。
*Kono omiyage wa **Honda san ni** moraimashita.*
I received this souvenir from Mr. Honda.

引っ越しは友達に手伝ってもらった。
*Hikkoshi wa **tomodachi ni** tetsudatte **moratta**.*
I got my friends to help me with my house-moving.

→ See *morau <(auxiliary) verb>*.

15. The agent of the action in specific grammatical constructions

犬が車にはねられた。(direct passive sentence)
*Inu ga **kuruma ni** hanerareta.*
A dog was hit by a car.

弟に部屋をそうじさせました。(make-causative sentence)
***Otōto ni** heya o sōji sasemashita.*
I made my little brother clean his room.

私にそれを説明させて下さい。(let-causative sentence)
***Watashi ni** sore o setsumei sasete kudasai.*
Please let me explain it.

弟に先に卒業されました。(indirect passive sentence)
***Otōto ni** saki ni sotsugyō saremashita.*
My little brother graduated before I did (and I was not happy with it).

あなたに行ってほしいんです。(a sentence with *hoshii*)
***Anata ni** itte hoshii n desu.*
I want you to go (there.)

→ See also *hoshii*, *rareru*, and *(s)aseru*.

16. Conjoining multiple nouns

私の好きな食べ物は魚に野菜です。
*Watashi no suki na tabemono wa **sakana ni yasai** desu.*
My favorite foods are fish and vegetables.

バニラに，チョコレートに，ストロベリーに。どれにしようかな。
***Banira ni, chokorēto ni, sutoroberī ni**. Dore ni shiyō kana.*
Vanilla, chocolate, strawberry . . . which one should I have?

→ See *to* and *toka*.

17. The understood direct object of verbs in English

さっき本屋でフランクに会いましたよ。
*Sakki hon'ya de **Furanku ni** aimashita yo.*
I met Frank at a bookstore a while ago.

この質問に簡潔に答えて下さい。
*Kono **shitsumon ni** kanketsu ni kotaete kudasai.*
Please answer this question briefly.

彼女にもう電話しましたか。 ***Kanojo ni** mō denwa shimashita ka.*
Have you called her yet?

この作品は独創力に欠けるがデザインのセンスに富む。
*Kono sakuhin wa **dokusōryoku ni** kakeru ga **dezain no sensu ni** tomu.*
This work lacks originality but has a rich sense of design.

いつでも私に連絡してください。
*Itsu demo **watashi ni** renraku shite kudasai.*
Please feel free to contact me at any time.

私は自転車に乗れません。 *Watashi wa **jitensha ni** noremasen.*
I cannot ride a bicycle.

毎日バスに乗ります。 *Mainichi **basu ni** norimasu.*
I take a bus every day.

II. ADJECTIVAL NOUN + *NI*

The particle *ni* can follow an adjectival noun to form an adverb. → See also Adjectival nouns.

彼は働きすぎて病気になった。
*Kare wa hatarakisugite **byōki ni** natta.*
He overworked and became ill.

静かにしてください。 ***Shizuka ni** shite kudasai.* **Please be quiet.**

彼ならそれは楽にできます。 *Kare nara sore wa **raku ni** dekimasu.*
He can do it easily. (I assure you.)

彼女なら積極的に手伝ってくれます。
*Kanojo nara **sekkyokuteki ni** tetsudatte kuremasu.*
She will enthusiastically help us. (I assure you.)

III. VERB (COMBINING FORM) + *NI*

The purpose of coming and going can be expressed by creating a phrase that consists of a verb in the combining form followed by the particle *ni*.

「初日の出を見に行きませんか。」「いいですね。」
*"Hatsuhinode o **mi ni iki**masen ka." "Ii desu ne."*
"Wouldn't you (like to) go and see the sunrise on New Year's Day?" "That would be nice."

カメラを買いに来たんですが。 *Kamera o **kai ni kita** n desu ga.*
I came to buy a camera, but . . . (will you help me?)

→ See also *tame ni*.

IV. *DARŌ/DESHŌ* + *NI*

The particle *ni* can follow a sentence that ends in *darō* or its polite counterpart, *deshō*, to indicate some situation that would probably prevail but is being prevented in the current circumstance.

あきらめなければうまく行くでしょうに。
*Akiramenakereba umaku iku **deshō ni**.*
If you don't give up, it will go well. (but you're about to give up)

もう少し勉強すれば，大学にも入れるだろうに。
*Mō sukoshi benkyō sure ba, daigaku ni mo haireru **darō ni**.*
If he studied a little more, he would be able to go to college. (but he is not studying)

V. *YŌ* + *NI*

The particle *ni* can follow *yō* to create an adverbial phrase that expresses the manner of an action while specifying the desired outcome. Its meaning is 'like . . . ,' 'so as to . . . ,' or 'so that. . . .' (→ See *yō da* <*resemblance*>.)

太郎はまるで犬のように走りまわった。
*Tarō wa marude inu no **yō ni** hashirimawatta.*
Taro ran around just like a dog.

風邪をひかないように気をつけてください。
*Kaze o hikanai **yō ni** ki o tsukete kudasai.*
Please be careful so you won't catch a cold.

ni chigai nai に違いない [PREDICATIVE PHRASE]

must

Ni chigai nai, which literally means that there is no error, can be placed at the end of a clause and show that the statement expressed by the clause is one's definite deduction, not necessarily based on some evidence. As it ends in *nai*, the conjugate pattern follows the one for adjectives. (→ See also *hazu da*.)

1. After (adjectival) nouns (+ *ja nai, datta, ja nakatta*)

   この鞄はフランクの鞄に違いない。
   *Kono kaban wa **Furanku no kaban ni chigai nai**.*
   This bag must be Frank's.

   あの歌手は日本では有名に違いない。
   *Ano kashu wa Nihon de wa **yūmei ni chigai nai**.*
   That singer must be famous in Japan.

   その死刑囚は殺人犯じゃなかったに違いない。
   *Sono shikeishū wa **satsujinhan ja nakatta ni chigainai**.*
   It must be the case that that death-row convict was not the murderer.

2. After verbs and adjectives in the dictionary form

   彼女はこの辺にすんでいるに違いない。
   *Kanojo wa kono hen ni sunde **iru ni chigai nai**.*
   She surely must be living around here.

   鈴木さんはもう来て待っているに違いありません。
   *Suzuki san wa mō kite matte **iru ni chigai arimasen**.*
   Mr. Suzuki must have already arrived and be waiting.

   お母さんは悲しいに違いありません。
   *Okāsan wa **kanashii ni chigai arimasen**.*
   Your mother must be sad.

3. After verbs and adjectives in the *nai*-form

   彼女は二度と手伝ってくれないに違いない。
   *Kanojo wa ni do to tetsudatte kure**nai ni chigai nai**.*
   It is certain that she will not help us again.

4. After verbs and adjectives in the *ta*-form

   彼は大学への進学をあきらめたに違いありません。
   *Kare wa daigaku e no shingaku o akirame**ta ni chigai arimasen**.*
   He must have given up hope of going on to university.

   あの車は高かったに違いない。
   *Ano kuruma wa takakat**ta ni chigai nai**.*
   That car must have been expensive.

ni kakete にかけて [ADVERBIAL PHRASE]

(extending) to, over

Ni kakete follows a noun and creates an adverbial phrase. It is actually part of
...*kara*...*ni kakete*, which shows the locational or temporal extent of the state
or the action expressed by the sentence. (→ See also *o tōshite*.)

夏から秋にかけて台風がよく来ます。
Natsu kara aki ni kakete taifū ga yoku kimasu.
Typhoons often come (in the period) from summer to autumn.

週末にかけて天気がよくなるでしょう。
Shūmatsu ni kakete tenki ga yoku naru deshō.
The weather will probably be good over the weekend.

九州から関西にかけて雨が降るでしょう。
Kyūshū kara Kansai ni kakete ame ga furu deshō.
It will be rainy (in the area) from Kyushu to Kansai.

ni kanshite に関して [ADVERBIAL PHRASE]

about, concerning, regarding, pertaining to

The verb phrase ...*ni kansuru* means 'to be related to....' Its derived form, ...*ni
kanshite*, follows nouns and pronouns and creates an adverbial phrase that shows
what the sentence is about. (→ See also *ni tsuite*.) The verb phrase ...*ni kansuru*
can be used in a relative clause, being placed before a noun to modify it.

そのことに関して何か言うことがありますか。
Sono koto ni kanshite nanika iu koto ga arimasu ka.
Regarding that matter, do you have anything to say?

この点に関して意見を述べて下さい。
Kono ten ni kanshite iken o nobete kudasai.
Please express your opinion on this point.

この契約書に関する質問はありませんか。
Kono keiyakusho ni kansuru shitsumon wa arimasen ka.
Do you have any questions concerning this agreement?

脳科学に関する本を探しています。
Nōkagaku ni kansuru hon o sagashite imasu.
I'm looking for a book on brain science.

nikui にくい [AUXILIARY ADJECTIVE]

to be hard/difficult (to do), can not (do) easily

The auxiliary adjective *nikui* follows a verb in the combining form to mean 'to be difficult to do. . . .' The resulting form patterns like adjectives.

1. Used as a sentence predicate

   箸は使いにくいですね。 *Hashi wa **tsukainikui** desu ne.*
   Chopsticks are hard to use, aren't they?

   彼女とは話しにくいです。 *Kanojo to wa **hanashinikui** desu.*
   She is difficult to talk with.

   (follows the subject it describes)

2. Used as a noun modifier

   覚えにくい漢字がまだたくさんあります。
   ***Oboenikui** kanji ga mada takusan arimasu.*
   There are still a lot of Chinese characters that are difficult to memorize.

3. Used as an adverb

   このテレビは古くて見にくくなってきました。
   *Kono terebi wa furukute **minikuku** natte kimashita.*
   This TV set is old and getting harder to watch.

→ See also *yasui*.

nimo kakawarazu にもかかわらず [ADVERBIAL PHRASE]

in spite of, although, for all . . . , after all . . . , in defiance of, nevertheless

Nimo kakawarazu follows nouns and clauses to form an adverbial clause that means 'in spite of . . .' or 'despite the fact that. . . .' It is used in a formal context. (→ See also *daga, keredo(mo),* and *noni*.)

1. After nouns

   ひどい雨にもかかわらず彼らは外で野球をした。
   *Hidoi **ame nimo kakawarazu** karera wa soto de yakyū o shita.*
   They played baseball outside in spite of heavy rain.

2. After verbs and adjectives in the dictionary form

   疲れているにもかかわらず彼は手伝ってくれました。
   *Tsukarete **iru nimo kakawarazu** kare wa tetsudatte kuremashita.*
   Although he was tired, he kindly helped me.

   彼女はお金があるにもかかわらず質素に暮らしている。
   *Kanojo wa okane ga **aru nimo kakawarazu** shisso ni kurashite iru.*
   Although she has a lot of money, she lives simply.

   とても安いにもかかわらず彼はそれを買わなかった。
   *Totemo **yasui nimo kakawarazu** kare wa sore o kawanakatta.*
   Although it was very cheap, he didn't buy it.

3. After verbs and adjectives in the **nai**-form

   だれも行かないにもかかわらず彼は一人で行った。
   *Dare mo ika**nai nimo kakawarazu** kare wa hitori de itta.*
   Nobody would go, but he went alone nevertheless.

4. After verbs and adjectives in the **ta**-form

   忠告したにもかかわらず彼はまた同じミスをした。
   *Chūkoku shi**ta nimo kakawarazu** kare wa mata onaji misu o shita.*
   Although I advised him, he made the same mistake again.

   天気がよかったにもかかわらず黒い雨が降った。
   *Tenki ga yokat**ta nimo kakawarazu** kuroi ame ga futta.*
   Though the weather was good, black rain fell.

5. At the beginning of a sentence

   それはほとんど不可能です。にもかかわらず太郎はあきらめません。
   *Sore wa hotondo fukanō desu. **Nimo kakawarazu** Tarō wa akiramemasen.*
   It is almost impossible. Nevertheless, Taro doesn't give up.

---

ni oite において [ADVERBIAL PHRASE]

in, at, on, as for

Ni oite is the combination of the particle *ni* and the verb *oku* in the *te*-form. It follows a noun and creates an adverbial phrase that specifies the location or the relevance of the action/state. It is slightly wordy and used only in formal contexts. Its prenominal form is . . . *ni okeru*.

1. Location

   ７階の広間において歓迎会が行われます。
   *Nana kai no **hiroma ni oite** kangeikai ga okonawaremasu.*
   The welcoming reception will be held in the hall on the seventh floor.

   日本における技術革新はめまぐるしかった。
   ***Nihon ni okeru** gijutsu kakushin wa memagurushikatta.*
   The technological revolution in Japan has happened very rapidly.

→ See also *de* and *ni*.

2. Relevance 'as to . . .'

   環境保護の点においては，この製品が他にまさります。
   ***Kankyō hogo no ten ni oite** wa, kono seihin ga ta ni masarimasu.*
   From the standpoint of environmental conservation, this product surpasses the other ones.

   その品物は品質において問題がある。
   *Sono shinamono wa **hinshitsu ni oite** mondai ga aru.*
   As for quality, there are problems with these articles.

ni sotte に沿って [ADVERBIAL PHRASE]

along, parallel to, in accordance with

Ni sotte is the combination of the particle *ni* and the *te*-form of the verb *sou* 'to be parallel to . . .' or 'to accord with. . . .' It follows a noun and creates an adverbial phrase that shows that the given action/state is done or exists in parallel to or in accordance with the item.

> 通りに沿ってたくさんブティックがあります。
> ***Tōri ni sotte** takusan butikku ga arimasu.*
> **There are a lot of boutiques along the street.**

> この線路は国道に沿って走っている。
> *Kono senro wa **kokudō ni sotte** hashitte iru.*
> **This railroad runs parallel to the national highway.**

> 彼は上司の方針に沿ってそれを実行した。
> *Kare wa jōshi no **hōshin ni sotte** sore o jikkō shita.*
> **He carried it out in accordance with his boss's policy.**

> (*Ni shitagatte* may replace *ni sotte* here.)

ni taishite に対して [ADVERBIAL PHRASE]

toward, against, whereas, in contrast to

Ni taishite is the combination of the particle *ni* and the *te*-form of the verb *taisuru* 'to be against' or 'to be in contrast with. . . .' It follows a noun or a clause plus *no*, and shows that the given action or state is toward, against, or in contrast to the item. (→ See also *ni*, *ni kansuru*, and *ni tsuite*.)

1. After nouns

> この提案に対してほかに何か異論がありますか。
> ***Kono teian ni taishite** hoka ni nanika iron ga arimasu ka.*
> **Do you have any other objections against this proposal?**

> 生徒たちは先生に対して素直な態度を取ります。
> *Seito tachi wa **sensei ni taishite** sunao na taido o torimasu.*
> **The students take an obedient attitude toward the teacher.**

> 私は彼女に対して好意を持っています。
> *Watashi wa **kanojo ni taishite** kōi o motte imasu.*
> **I feel affection toward her.**

> 私は他人のうわさに対して関心がない。
> *Watashi wa tanin no **uwasa ni taishite** kanshin ga nai.*
> **I have no interest in rumors about other people.**

彼は私に対して恨みを持っているようです。
*Kare wa **watashi ni taishite** urami o motte iru yō desu.*
He seems to have a grudge against me.

五人に対して一台コンピューターがあります。
***Go nin ni taishite** ichi dai konpyūtā ga arimasu.*
There is one computer to every five persons.

2. After verbs and adjectives in the dictionary form or the **ta**-form

空が青いのに対して山は赤かった。
*Sora ga aoi **no ni taishite** yama wa akakatta.*
In contrast to the blue sky was the red mountain.

与党がそれに賛成したのに対して野党は反対した。
*Yotō ga sore ni sansei shi**ta no ni taishite** yatō wa hantai shita.*
The ruling party supported it, whereas the opposition parties were against it.

3. After (adjectival) nouns + **na** + **no**

彼は弱い者には親切なのに対して強い者には冷たい。
*Kare wa yowai mono ni wa **shinsetsu na no ni taishite** tsuyoi mono ni wa tsumetai.*
He is kind toward the weak, whereas he is cool toward the strong.

ni totte にとって [ADVERBIAL PHRASE]

to, as far as . . . concerned, for

Ni totte follows nouns and creates an adverbial phrase that shows the item to which the statement applies. Typical predicates that follow this phrase are:

不 (必) 要だ	*fu(hitsu)yō da*	'to be unnecessary'
不可欠だ	*fukaketsu da*	'to be indispensable'
必要だ	*hitsuyō da*	'to be necessary'
意外だ	*igai da*	'to be a surprise'
簡単だ	*kantan da*	'to be easy'
困難だ	*konnan da*	'to be difficult'
深刻だ	*shinkoku da*	'to be serious'
易しい	*yasashii*	'to be easy'

日本にとって，自動車産業は重要だ。
***Nihon ni totte**, jidōsha sangyō wa jūyō da.*
The automobile industry is very important for Japan.

それは私にとって問題ではありません。
*Sore wa **watashi ni totte** mondai de wa arimasen.*
As far as I'm concerned that is not a problem.

あなたにとって日本語を覚えることはむずかしいですか。
Anata ni totte Nihongo o oboeru koto wa muzukashii desu ka.
Is it difficult for you to learn Japanese?

それはあなたにとって不都合なんですか。
Sore wa **anata ni totte** *futsugō na n desu ka.*
Is it inconvenient for you?

ni tsuite について [ADVERBIAL PHRASE]

about, concerning, in regard to, as to/for, of

Ni tsuite follows nouns to show what the statement is about. This adverbial phrase can be followed by the particle *no* and placed before another noun as its modifier.

何のことについて話しているんですか。
Nan no **koto ni tsuite** *hanashite iru n desu ka.*
What are you talking about?

その件についてあなたにまったく賛成です。
Sono ken ni tsuite anata ni mattaku sansei desu.
I quite agree with you concerning that matter.

日本語の文法についてまだたくさん問題がある。
Nihongo no bunpō ni tsuite mada takusan mondai ga aru.
There are still many problems with Japanese grammar.

日本の政治についてどう思いますか。
Nihon no seiji ni tsuite dō omoimasu ka.
What do you think of Japanese politics?

その神社についての資料はありませんでした。
Sono jinja ni tsuite no shiryō wa arimasen deshita.
There was no data concerning the Shinto shrine.

→ See also *ni kanshite* and *ni taishite*.

ni tsurete につれて [ADVERBIAL PHRASE]

as . . .

Ni tsurete follows a clause with a verb in the dictionary form to create an adverbial phrase that shows how some change takes place as a consequence of another change.

人は歳を取るにつれて温厚になる。
Hito wa toshi o toru ni tsurete onkō ni naru.
As a man grows older, he becomes gentler.

年が経つにつれて生活は楽になってきました。
Toshi ga tatsu ni tsurete seikatsu wa raku ni natte kimashita.
As the years go by, my life has become (more and more) comfortable.

ni yoreba によれば [ADVERBIAL PHRASE]

according to, from

Ni yoreba or *ni yoruto* can follow nouns to mean 'according to. . . .'

テレビのニュースによれば伊豆半島で大きな噴火があったらしい。
Terebi no nyūsu ni yoreba Izu Hantō de ōkina funka ga atta rashii.
According to the television news, it seems there was a big eruption on the Izu Peninsula.

聞くところによれば彼女は結婚するそうです。
Kiku tokoro ni yoreba kanojo wa kekkon suru sō desu.
From what I've heard, she is going to get married.

天気予報によればあしたは雨です。
Tenki yohō ni yoreba ashita wa ame desu.
According to the weather forecast, it will be rainy tomorrow.

ni yotte によって [ADVERBIAL PHRASE]

by (an agent), because of, due to, by means of, according to

The action performer (agent) in a passive sentence is expressed by *ni, ni yotte,* or *ni yori.* (→ See also *ni* and Passive form under Verbs.)

その小説は夏目漱石によって書かれた。
*Sono shōsetsu wa **Natsume Sōseki ni yotte** kakareta.*
The novel was written by Soseki Natsume.

公共施設での喫煙は規則によって禁止されています。
*Kōkyō shisetsu de no kitsuen wa **kisoku ni yotte** kinshi sarete imasu.*
Smoking in public facilities is prohibited by regulation.

試合は大雨によって中止された。 *Shiai wa **ōame ni yotte** chūshi sareta.*
The game was called off due to a heavy rain.

市民デモは武力によって鎮圧された。
*Shimin demo wa **buryoku ni yotte** chin'atsu sareta.*
The citizen demonstration was quelled by means of force.

ni wa には [DOUBLE PARTICLE]

for (in regard to), in order to

Ni wa is the combination of the two particles *ni* and *wa*, but is typically used when the sentence expresses judgmental facts. (→ See *ni* and *wa*.)

1. After nouns

   この服は子供には大きすぎます。
   *Kono fuku wa **kodomo ni wa** ōkisugimasu.*
   This dress is too big for children.

   このプラスチックは分解するので環境には優しい。
   *Kono purasuchikku wa bunkai suru node **kankyō ni wa** yasashii.*
   These plastics are environmentally friendly because they decompose.

2. After verbs in the dictionary form

   出かけるにはまだ早すぎます。 *Dekakeru ni wa mada hayasugimasu.*
   It is still too early to go out.

   世界中を旅行するにはたくさんお金がかかる。
   Sekai jū o ryokō suru ni wa takusan okane ga kakaru.
   To travel all over the world takes a great deal of money

   このパソコンは持ち運ぶには大変便利です。
   Kono pasokon wa mochihakobu ni wa taihen benri desu.
   This personal computer is very handy to carry.

   → See also *noni*, *tame ni*, and *wa*.

---

no の [PARTICLE]

. . . 's, of, at, in, on, to, from, by, for, one's

The particle *no* creates noun modifiers by following not only nouns but also certain kinds of particles and verbs in the *te*-form. It also functions as an indefinite pronoun that means '(the) one' or 'ones' and as a nominalizer that makes phrases and clauses noun-like. The particle *no* also replaces the particle *ga* in a relative clause. Lastly, it also functions as a sentence-final particle.

I. MODIFIER

The particle *no* can create a noun modifier by following another noun, a *no*-type adjectival noun, a certain kind of particle, or some verb in the *te*-form.

1. After (interrogative) nouns

   東京は日本の首都です。京都は昔の都です。
   *Tōkyō wa **Nihon no shuto** desu. Kyōto wa **mukashi no** miyako desu.*
   Tokyo is the capital of Japan. Kyoto is the ancient capital.

   「あれは何の木ですか。」「桜の木です。」
   *"Are wa **nan no ki** desu ka." "Sakura no ki desu."*
   "What (kind of) trees are they?" "They are cherry trees."

これは先生の本です。 *Kore wa **sensei no hon** desu.*
This is the teacher's book.

両替するのにどこの銀行がいいですか。
*Ryōgae suru no ni **doko no ginkō** ga ii desu ka.*
Which bank is good to exchange money?

ミネラルウォーターは売店の自動販売機で売っています。
*Mineraru uōtā wa **baiten no jidō hanbaiki** de utte imasu.*
Mineral water is sold at a vending machine at the stand.

体調が悪く午後の授業は休みます。
*Taichō ga waruku **gogo no jugyō** wa yasumimasu.*
I feel out of sorts, so I'll miss my afternoon classes.

日曜日のイベントは延期されました。
Nichiyōbi no ibento wa enki saremashita.
The event on Sunday was postponed.

芥川龍之介の小説を読んだことがありますか。
Akutagawa Ryūnosuke no shōsetsu o yonda koto ga arimasu ka.
Have you ever read a novel by Ryunosuke Akutagawa?

事故で10才の少年が死にました。
*Jiko de **jissai no shōnen** ga shinimashita.*
A ten-year-old boy was killed in the accident.

こちらが友人の田中です。(apposition)
*Kochira ga **yūjin no Tanaka** desu.*
This is my friend, (Mr.) Tanaka.

バスでポケットの中の財布を盗まれました。
*Basu de **poketto no naka no saifu** o nusumaremashita.*
I had the wallet in my pocket stolen on a bus.

机の上の携帯電話はだれのですか。
Tsukue no ue no keitai denwa wa dare no desu ka.
Whose is the mobile phone on the desk?

食事の後のデザートはアイスクリームにします。
Shokuji no ato no dezāto wa aisukurīmu ni shimasu.
I'll have ice cream for dessert after the meal.

2. After adjectival nouns

これもいいんですが，別の靴も見せて下さい。
*Kore mo ii n desu ga **betsu no kutsu** mo misete kudasai.*
This is nice, but please show me another pair of shoes.

本当の理由は何ですか。 *Hontō no riyū wa nan desu ka.*
What is the true reason?

3. After some particles

成田空港までの往復切符と片道切符を一枚下さい。
*Narita kūkō **made no ōfuku kippu to katamichi kippu** o ichi mai kudasai.*
Please give me a round-trip and a one-way ticket to Narita Airport.

先生へのお中元は何がいいですか。
*Sensei **e no ochūgen** wa nani ga ii desu ka.*
What is good as a midyear gift for the teacher?

被害者との交渉はなかなか難しい。
*Higaisha **to no kōshō** wa nakanaka muzukashii.*
The negotiation with the victim is quite difficult.

4. After some verbs in the **te**-form

その件についてのあなたの意見は極端です。
*Sono ken ni tsui**te no anata no iken** wa kyokutan desu.*
Your opinion concerning that matter is extreme.

命をかけての戦いだ。 *Inochi o kake**te no tatakai** da.*
It is a fight at the risk of my life.

子供を二人かかえての生活は簡単ではない。
*Kodomo o futari kakae**te no seikatsu** wa kantan dewa nai.*
Life with two children is not easy.

5. After some dependent nouns

彼らのための援助はまったく不要です。
*Karera no **tame no enjo** wa mattaku fuyō desu.*
The aid for them is quite unnecessary.

死んだはずの人があそこに立っていた。
*Shinda **hazu no hito** ga asoko ni tatte ita.*
The person who was supposed to be dead was standing over there.

II. PRONOUN

1. After nouns

あれは私のです。 *Are wa **watashi no** desu.* **That one is mine.**

このコインは日本のです。 *Kono koin wa **Nihon no** desu.*
This coin is a Japanese one.

2. After adjectival nouns + **na**

私が好きなのはこの魚です。 *Watashi ga **suki na no** wa kono sakana desu.*
The one I like is this fish.

3. After (adjectival) nouns + **ja nai, datta,** or **ja nakatta**

私が嫌だったのはこのクラスです。
*Watashi ga **iya datta no** wa kono kurasu desu.*
The one I did not like was this class.

クラスでアメリカ人じゃなかったのは私だけでした。
*Kurasu de **Amerikajin ja nakatta no** wa watashi dake deshita.*
The one who was not American in that class was just me.

4. After verbs and adjectives in the dictionary form, ***nai*-form**, or ***ta*-form**

これがDVDで，私が持っているのがブルーレイです。
*Kore ga dībuidī de, watashi ga mo**tte iru no** ga burūrei desu.*
This is a DVD, and the one I have is a Blu-ray Disc.

このカメラは高すぎます。もっと安いのはありませんか。
*Kono kamera wa takasugimasu. Motto yasui **no** wa arimasen ka.*
This camera is too expensive. Do you have any cheaper ones?

この方が私が買ったのよりいい。 *Kono hō ga watashi ga ka**tta no** yori ii.*
This is better than the one I bought.

マイクさんがまだ読めないのはどの漢字ですか。
*Maiku san ga mada yome**nai no** wa dono kanji desu ka.*
Which kanji is the one that Mike still cannot read?

→ See also *mono.*

III. NOMINALIZER

1. After (adjectival) nouns + ***na, ja nai, datta,*** or ***ja nakatta***

父が金持ちなのはいい投資をしたからだ。
*Chichi ga **kanemochi na no** wa ii tōshi o shita kara da.*
The reason my father is rich is because he made good investments.

会長がお酒が好きなのはよく知られている。
*Kaichō ga osake ga **suki na no** wa yoku shirarete iru.*
The fact that our C.E.O likes sake a lot is well-known.

完璧主義者だったのがよくなかった。
***Kanpekishugisha datta no** ga yoku nakatta.*
Being a perfectionist was not good.

2. After verbs and adjectives in the dictionary form, ***nai*-form**, or ***ta*-form**

漢字を覚えるのにいい方法があります。
*Kanji o oboe**ru no** ni ii hōhō ga arimasu.*
There is a good way to memorize Chinese characters.

たばこを吸うのをやめたいと思います。
*Tabako o **suu no** o yametai to omoimasu.*
I'd like to stop smoking.

書類を持って来るのを忘れました。
*Shorui o motte ku**ru no** o wasuremashita.*
I forgot to bring the papers.

蒸し暑いのはいやですね。 *Mushiatsu**i no** wa iya desu ne.*
Hot and humid weather is unpleasant, isn't it?

彼が宝くじに当たったのは事実です。
Kare ga takarakuji ni atatta no wa jijitsu desu.
It is true that he won the lottery.

彼にそれができないのはおかしい。
Kare ni sore ga dekinai no wa okashii.
It is strange that he can't do that.

→ See also *koto.*

IV. *GA/NO* ALTERNATION

The particle *ga* can be optionally replaced by *no* in a relative clause.

彼女の使ったシチューはとてもおいしいです。
***Kanojo no** tsukutta shichū wa totemo oishii desu.*
The stew she cooks is very delicious.

コーヒーの欲しい人は言って下さい。
***Kōhī no** hoshii hito wa itte kudasai.*
Those who want coffee, speak up, please.

→ See also *ga.*

V. SENTENCE-FINAL PARTICLE

Women or children often add the particle *no* at the end of a sentence. If the sentence takes a rising intonation, it is perceived as a question. If it takes a falling intonation, it is perceived as a statement.

一緒に行きたくないの。 *Isshoni ikitaku nai **no**.*
Don't you want to go with me? (rising intonation)
I don't want to go with you. (falling intonation)

→ See also *ka* and *no da.*

---

no da のだ [EXTENDED PREDICATIVE PHRASE]

It is the case that . . .

No da or its polite counterpart *no desu* follows a clause. It is often referred to as an "extended predicate" and is frequently used in conversations. It does not add any concrete meaning, but makes the conversational interaction smooth and effective. This ending is often used when the speaker wants to give some explanation or additional comment on some state or fact observable in the conversational context. It is also often used for eliciting a reply from one's conversational partner or softening the tone of his/her expressions when requesting, suggesting, or demanding. The particle *no* often contracts to a nasal sound *n*, as in . . . *n da* or . . . *n desu* in colloquial speech. (→ See also *kara* and *wake.*)

1. After verbs and adjectives in the dictionary form

   ちょっと尋ねたいことがあるんですが。

   *Chotto tazunetai koto ga aru **n desu** ga.*

   I have a small question that I want to ask you, but . . . (Is it all right? That's why I'm here . . .)

   今とても忙しいんですが。 *Ima totemo isogashii **n desu** ga.*

   I am very busy now. (so I can't help you; you should notice that I'm busy now)

2. After verbs and adjectives in the **ta**-form

   さっき彼女に電話したのですが，出ませんでした。

   *Sakki kanojo ni denwa shi**ta no desu** ga, demasen deshita.*

   I telephoned her a little while ago, but she didn't answer. (It's strange.)

   (If preceded by a past-tense sentence, a contrary statement often follows.)

   あの液晶テレビは安かったのですが，お金が足りませんでした。

   *Ano ekishō terebi wa yasukat**ta no desu** ga, okane ga tarimasen deshita.*

   That liquid crystal television was cheap, but I didn't have enough money (to buy it). (It was really cheap, but I unfortunately did not have enough money.)

3. After verbs and adjectives in the **nai**-form

   次の休暇はどこにも行かないのですか。

   *Tsugi no kyūka wa doko ni mo ika**nai no desu** ka.*

   Won't you go anywhere during the next vacation? (because you seem not to be planning)

4. After (adjectival) nouns + **na/datta**

   今日はとても暇なんです。 *Kyō wa totemo **hima na n desu**.*

   I am very free today. (That's why I'm doing nothing.)

   昨日は暇だったんですが，何もせずに過ごしました。

   *Kinō wa **hima datta n desu** ga, nani mo sezu ni sugoshimashita.*

   I was free yesterday, but I spent the day without doing anything.

5. Used in questions

   (A question with this phrase is usually asking for some explanation, while a question without it may indicate a request or invitation. When interrogative words are used in questions, *no desu ka* usually comes at the end to clearly indicate that some additional information is being asked for.)

   どうしてここへ来たんですか。 *Dōshite koko e kita **n desu ka**.*

   Why (or how) did you come here? (I ask because it is surprising that you came here.)

   テニスはするんですか。 *Tenisu wa suru **n desu ka**.*

   Do you play tennis? (I ask because you seem to play tennis or some sport.)

(Compare with *Tenisu o shimasu ka*, meaning 'Will you play tennis (with me)?')

お酒は飲まないんですか。 *Osake wa nomanai **n desu ka**.*
Don't you drink sake? (I ask because you don't seem to start drinking.)

(Compare with *Osake o nomimasen ka*, meaning 'Won't you drink some sake (with me)?')

node ので [PARTICLE]

because (of), on account of, as, since

The particle *node* follows a clause and creates an adverbial clause that expresses the reason or the cause for the action or state expressed by the main clause. *Node* and *kara* are sometimes used interchangeably, but the cause-result relationship expressed by *node* must be based on the speaker's objective judgment, whereas the one expressed by *kara* does not have to be. (→ *See kara.*)

1. After (adjectival) nouns + *na*

   今日は雨なので映画を見よう。 *Kyō wa **ame na node** eiga o miyō.*
   I'll see a movie today since it is rainy.

   彼女は多忙なので来られません。 *Kanojo wa **tabō na node** koraremasen.*
   She is unable to come because she is busy.

   明子はまだ幼児なので，このキャンプには参加できません。
   *Akiko wa mada **yōji na node**, kono kyampu ni wa sanka dekimasen.*
   Since Akiko is still a toddler, she cannot participate in this camp.

2. After (adjectival) nouns + *ja nai, datta,* or *ja nakatta*

   昨日は雨だったので，遠足は中止になった。
   *Kinō wa **ame datta node**, ensoku wa chūshi ni natta.*
   It rained yesterday, so the field trip was canceled.

3. After verbs and adjectives in the dictionary form

   用事があるのでもう失礼します。 *Yōji ga a**ru node** mō shitsurei shimasu.*
   Since I have an errand to do, I'll be leaving now.

   この本は面白いので薦めます。
   *Kono hon wa omoshiro**i node** susumemasu.*
   I recommend this book to you because it is interesting.

   (If *kara* replaced *node*, the reason would be "because I *think* the book is interesting.")

4. After verbs and adjectives in the *nai*-form

   彼女が行かないので私も行きません。
   *Kanojo ga ika**nai node** watashi mo ikimasen.*
   Since she's not going, I won't go either.

本は厚くないので読むのにあまり時間がかかりません。
Hon wa atsukunai node yomu no ni amari jikan ga kakarimasen.
The book is not thick, so it won't take very long to read it.

5. After verbs and adjectives in the **ta**-form

雷が鳴っていたのでゴルフはやめました。
Kaminari ga natte ita node gorufu wa yamemashita.
We stopped playing golf because it was thundering.

あのカメラは高すぎたので買いませんでした。
Ano kamera wa takasugita node kaimasen deshita.
I didn't buy that camera because it was too expensive.

6. After clauses with **desu/masu**

お嬢さんはまだ幼児ですので、このキャンプには参加できません。
Ojōsan wa mada yōji desu node, kono kyampu ni wa sanka dekimasen.
Since your daughter is still a toddler, she cannot participate in this camp.

送料が要りますので、全部で3,350円になります。
Sōryō ga irimasu node, zenbu de 3,350 en ni narimasu.
As shipping and handling need to be included, the total would be 3,350 yen.

こちらのパッケージは量が多いですので、お得ですよ。
Kochira no pakkēji wa ryō ga ōi desu node, otoku desu yo.
This package contains more, so it is more value.

今日は嵐ですので、ピクニックは中止いたします。
Kyō wa arashi desu node, pikunikku wa chūshi itashimasu.
It is stormy today, so we will cancel our picnic.

→ See also *kara, kuse ni, okage de, sei de*, and *tame ni*.

---

no desu のです → See **no da.**

---

nogasu 逃す [AUXILIARY VERB]

to miss a good chance to do

The verb *nogasu* means 'to miss something' and can also function as an auxiliary verb placed after a verb in the combining form, meaning 'to miss doing something.' The auxiliary verb *sokonau* has a similar meaning.

限定1万枚のDVDを買い逃しました。
Gentei ichi man mai no DVD o kainogashimashita.
I missed a good chance to buy a DVD of the limited 10,000 copies.

そのコンサートは見逃したくない。
Sono konsāto wa minogashitaku nai.
I don't want to miss the (good) chance to see the concert.

彼のミスを見逃すつもりですか。
*Kare no misu o **minogasu** tsumori desu ka.*
Are you going to overlook his mistake?

ノーベル賞学者の話を聞き逃しました。
*Nōberushō gakusha no hanashi o **kikinogashimashita**.*
I failed to listen to the lecture by the Nobel Prize–winning scholar.

→ See also *sokonau*.

noni のに [PARTICLE]

although, though, in spite of, while, to (do), for (doing), in (doing), I wish . . . , you should

Noni creates an adverbial phrase based on which the speaker judges the fact stated in the main sentence to be unexpected surprise, dissatisfaction, disappointment, regret, etc.

1. After verbs and adjectives in the dictionary form

   ハリケーンが近づいているのに出かけるんですか。
   *Harikēn ga chikazuite **iru noni** dekakeru n desu ka.*
   Are you going out even though a hurricane is coming?

   みんな休んでいるのに彼は一生懸命働いています。
   *Minna yasunde **iru noni** kare wa isshōkenmei hataraite imasu.*
   Though the others are taking a rest, he is working hard.

   同じものがあの店では高いのにこの店ではけっこう安い。
   *Onaji mono ga ano mise dewa takai **noni** kono mise dewa kekkō yasui.*
   While the same article in that store is expensive, it's rather cheap in this store.

   渋滞のために空港に着くのに二時間もかかりました。
   *Jūtai no tame ni kūkō ni tsuku **noni** ni jikan mo kakarimashita.*
   It took no less than two hours to get to the airport due to the traffic jam.

   この魚を料理するのに油が要ります。
   *Kono sakana o ryōri suru **noni** abura ga irimasu.*
   Oil is needed to cook this fish.

   あの店はいろいろなものを買うのにとても便利です。
   *Ano mise wa iroiro na mono o kau **noni** totemo benri desu.*
   That store is very convenient for buying various things.

   彼の家は歩いていくのに遠すぎます。
   *Kare no ie wa aruite iku **noni** tōsugimasu.*
   His house is too far to walk to.

2. After verbs and adjectives in the *nai*-form

彼はそのことを何も知らないのに偉そうにしている。
Kare wa sono koto o nani mo shiranai noni erasō ni shite iru.
Though he doesn't know anything about that, he acts like a know-it-all.

暑くないのにエアコンをつけるのはもったいない。
Atsukunai noni eakon o tsukeru no wa mottainai.
It's a waste (of money) to turn on the air conditioner when it isn't hot (out).

3. After verbs and adjectives in the *ta*-form

あれほど注意したのに彼女はやめなかった。
Are hodo chūi shita noni kanojo wa yamenakatta.
Even though I cautioned her to that extent, she would not stop it.

天気がよかったのにどこにも出かけませんでした。
Tenki ga yokatta noni doko ni mo dekakemasen deshita.
Even though the weather was good, I didn't go out anywhere.

電話してくれるようにたのんだのに。
Denwa shite kureru yō ni tanonda noni.
Even though I asked you to call me . . . (you didn't).

4. After (adjectival) nouns + *na/datta/de nai/de nakatta*

彼は元気なのによく仕事をさぼります。
Kare wa genki na noni yoku shigoto o saborimasu.
Though he is healthy, he often skips out of work.

今日は台風なのに釣りに行くんですか。
Kyō wa taifū na noni tsuri ni iku n desu ka.
Are you going fishing today in spite of the typhoon?

彼女は病気でないのによく学校を休みます。
Kanojo wa byōki de nai noni yoku gakkō o yasumimasu.
Though she is not sick, she is often absent from school.

あの人は金持ちだったのに今は貧乏です。
Ano hito wa kanemochi datta noni ima wa binbō desu.
Even though that person was rich, he is poor now.

5. After verbs and adjectives in the *ba/tara*-form + *ii/yokatta*

あなたも一緒に来ればいいのに。
Anata mo isshoni kureba ii noni.
I wish you would come with me . . . (but you won't)

往復切符を買えばよかったのに。
Ōfuku kippu o kaeba yokatta noni.
You should have bought a round-trip ticket. (but you didn't)

→ See also *ga*, *keredo(mo)*, *ni mo kakawarazu*, and *tame ni*.

o を [PARTICLE]

the direct object of a verb, the starting point of an action, a point of separation (from), a place where something or somebody is passing (through, along, in, across, over)

The most basic function of the particle *o* is to mark the direct object of the verb. The additional function of *o* is to mark the location that is covered by some movement such as walking, flying, swimming, turning, crossing, and passing as well as the location from which one is parting. Note that the particle *o* must be deleted when followed by some focus particles such as *wa*, *mo*, *bakari*, *dake*, and *shika*. However, *bakari* and *dake* can be followed by *o*. (→ See also *mo*, *bakari*, *dake*, *shika*, and *wa*.)

1. Marking the direct object of a verb

   「何を買ったんですか。」「珍しい掛軸を買いました。」
   *"**Nani o** katta n desu ka." "Mezurashii **kakejiku o** kaimashita."*
   "What did you buy?" "I bought a unique hanging scroll."

   私は毎週一回トムに日本語を教えています。
   *Watashi wa maishū ikkai Tomu ni **Nihongo o** oshiete imasu.*
   I teach Japanese to Tom once a week.

   彼女は私を「太郎君」と呼びます。
   *Kanojo wa **watashi o** "Tarō kun" to yobimasu.*
   She calls me "Taro kun."

   どこかで財布を取られました。 *Dokoka de **saifu o** toraremashita.*
   I had my wallet stolen somewhere.

   みんなをあっと驚かせよう。 ***Minna o** atto odorokaseyō.*
   I'll knock the breath out of everybody.

   夏休みを旅行して過ごしました。
   ***Natsu yasumi o** ryokō shite sugoshimashita.*
   I spent my summer vacation traveling.

2. Marking the place covered by some movement

   この通りをまっすぐに行って下さい。
   ***Kono tōri o** massugu ni itte kudasai.*
   Please go straight along this street.

   二つ目の角を右に曲がって下さい。
   ***Futatsume no kado o** migi ni magatte kudasai.*
   Please turn right at the second corner.

   日曜日は公園を歩きます。 *Nichiyōbi wa **kōen o** arukimasu.*
   I walk around inside the park on Sundays.

   鳥になって空を飛びたい。 *Tori ni natte **sora o** tobitai.*
   I want to become a bird and fly over the sky.

あの橋を渡って下さい。 **Ano hashi o** *watatte kudasai.*
Please cross that bridge.

新幹線はもう名古屋を通過しました。
*Shinkansen wa mō **Nagoya o** tsūka shimashita.*
The Shinkansen already passed through Nagoya.

3. Marking the place from where one is parting

彼女はさっき部屋を出て行きました。
*Kanojo wa sakki **heya o** dete ikimashita.*
She went out of the room a short while ago.

日本を離れて１０年になる。 **Nihon o** *hanarete jū nen ni naru.*
It's been 10 years since I left Japan.

有楽町で電車を降りてください。 *Yūrakuchō de **densha o** orite kudasai.*
Please get off the train at Yurakucho.

去年の三月に大学を卒業しました。
*Kyonen no san gatsu ni **daigaku o** sotsugyō shimashita.*
I graduated from college in March last year.

→ See also *kara.*

---

o お(御) [PREFIX]

an honorific prefix

The prefix *o* is attached at the beginning of (adjectival) nouns, verbs, and adjectives in Japanese native vocabulary to indicate politeness (respect, humility, refinement). For Sino-Japanese vocabulary (words of Chinese origin or words read in *on*-reading—the Chinese reading of kanji—regardless of whether they are written in kanji), *go* should be used instead of *o*, and no polite prefix should be used for non-Chinese foreign loans. However, there are exceptional cases where *o* is used for Sino-Japanese vocabulary or English loans. (→ See also *go* and Honorifics.)

1. Before verbs in the combining form

お帰りはいつですか。 **Okaeri** *wa itsu desu ka.* (respectful)
When is you return? (When will you return?)

お疲れですね。お手伝いしましょうか。
Otsukare *desu ne.* (respect) **Otetsudai** *shimashō ka.* (humble)
You're tired, aren't you? Shall I help you?

2. Before (adjectival) nouns

お体を大切にして下さい。
Okarada *o taisetsu ni shite kudasai.* (respectful)
Please take care of yourself.

忘れずにお花にお水をやってください。
*Wasurezu ni **ohana** ni **omizu** o yatte kudasai.* (courteous)
Please don't forget to water the flowers.

ひどい事故にあったそうでお気の毒です。
*Hidoi jiko ni atta sōde **okinodoku** desu.* (humble)
I feel sorry to hear that you were involved in a serious accident.

3. Before adjectives

この商品はいつもよりお安くなっております。
*Kono shōhin wa itsumo yori **oyasuku** natte orimasu.* (humble)
The price of this item is lower than usual. (the speaker humbly advertises)

だれもいないとお寂しいでしょう。
*Dare mo inai to **osabishii** deshō.* (respectful)
I guess you're lonely because nobody is with you.

4. Used for Sino-Japanese vocabulary (exceptional cases)

お弁当	*obentō*	a box lunch	お留守	*orusu*	being away
お茶	*ocha*	green tea	お料理	*oryōri*	cooking, a dish
お電話	*odenwa*	a telephone	お食事	*oshokuji*	a meal
お元気	*ogenki*	vigor, vitality	お掃除	*osōji*	sweeping, dusting
お返事	*ohenji*	a reply	お葬式	*osōshiki*	a funeral
お勘定	*okanjō*	counting money	お醤油	*oshōyu*	soy sauce
お荷物	*onimotsu*	a piece of luggage	お野菜	*oyasai*	vegetables

5. Used for English loanwords (exceptional cases)

おビール	*obīru*	beer	おトイレ	*otoire*	a toilet
おソース	*osōsu*	sauce	おズボン	*ozubon*	(Fr. *jupon*) pants, slacks

okage de おかげで [ADVERBIAL PHRASE]

thanks to, because of, due to, owing to

Okage de creates an adverbial phrase that shows the cause of a favorable result, but it may also be sarcastically used for showing the cause of an unfavorable result. Do not confuse it with *sei de*, which is always used when an unfavorable situation is caused. (→ See also *sei de* and *tame ni*.)

1. After nouns + *no*

みんなのおかげでうまくいきました。
***Minna no okage de** umaku ikimashita.*
It went smoothly thanks to you all.

あいつのおかげで嫌な目にあった。
Aitsu no okage de *iya na me ni atta.* (sarcastic)
I had a *great* time thanks to that guy.

台風のおかげで電車が不通になった。
Taifū no okage de *densha ga futsū ni natta.* (sarcastic)
The train service was interrupted because of a typhoon.

2. After verbs and adjectives in the dictionary form

みんなが手伝ってくれるおかげで助かります。
*Minna ga tetsudatte kureru **okage de** tasukarimasu.*
I am saved because everybody helps me.

息子が賢いおかげで彼女は鼻が高いです。
*Musuko ga kashikoi **okage de** kanojo wa hana ga takai desu.*
She is proud because her son is smart.

3. After verbs and adjectives in the ***ta***-form

就職できたおかげで安心しました。
*Shūshoku deki**ta okage de** anshin shimashita.*
I feel relieved because I have found a job.

教えてくれたおかげでよく分かりました。
*Oshiete kure**ta okage de** yoku wakarimashita.*
I've understood well, thanks to your lesson.

バーゲンで安かったおかげですぐに手に入りました。
*Bāgen de yasukat**ta okage de** sugu ni te ni hairimashita.*
It was cheap at a sale, so I could get it at once.

結婚できたおかげで地獄のような生活をしています。
*Kekkon deki**ta okage de** jigoku no yōna seikatsu o shite imasu.* (sarcastic)
Thanks to the fact I could get married, I'm leading a life like hell.

4. Used in a set-phrase ***okagesama de***

おかげ様でうまくいきました。 ***Okage sama de*** *umaku ikimashita.*
It went smoothly, thanks to you.

---

oki ni おきに [ADVERBIAL PHRASE]

at intervals of

Oki ni follows quantity phrases, meaning 'every,' indicating the intervals of some action.

私はうちで一日おきにお酒を飲みます。
*Watashi wa uchi de **ichi nichi oki ni** osake o nomimasu.*
I drink (alcohol) at home every other day.

この駅では普通電車は15分おきに来ます。
*Kono eki de wa futsū densha wa **jū go fun oki ni** kimasu.*
Local trains arrive every fifteen minutes at this train station.

この用紙には一行おきに書いて下さい。
*Kono yōshi ni wa **ichi gyō oki ni** kaite kudasai.*
Please write on every other line of this paper.

あの道路には五メートルおきに木が植えてあります。
*Ano dōro ni wa **go mētoru oki ni** ki ga uete arimasu.*
Trees are planted along that road at intervals of five meters.

oku おく [AUXILIARY VERB]

to do (something) for the next occasion, leave/keep (something) in some state

The verb *oku* 'to place' can be used as an auxiliary verb, being placed at the end of a verb in the *te*-form, meaning to do something for the future convenience or to keep someone or something in some state. (→ See also *aru* and Auxiliary verbs and adjectives.)

よく考えておきます。 *Yoku kangae**te okimasu**.*
I will think it over (by then).

部屋が暑いのでエアコンを付けておきます。
*Heya ga atsui node mado o ake**te okimasu**.*
The room is hot so I'll leave it air-conditioned.

そのことは秘密にしておきましょう。
*Sono koto wa himitsu ni shi**te okimashō**.*
Let's keep that matter a secret.

長い間待たせておいてごめんなさい。
*Nagai aida matase**te oite** gomen nasai.*
I'm sorry to have kept you waiting for so long.

そのことは知らないことにしておきます。
*Sono koto wa shiranai koto ni shi**te okimasu**.*
I'll keep pretending that I don't know about that.

o motte をもって [ADVERBIAL PHRASE]

by (means of), with

O motte is used to mean 'with' in a formal context.

1. After nouns

    結果は書面をもって通知いたします。
    *Kekka wa **shomen o motte** tsūchi itashimasu.*
    I'll inform you of the result by letter.

彼の能力をもってしても不可能でしょう。
*Kare no **nōryoku o motte** shitemo fukanō deshō.*
Even with his ability, it will be impossible to do.

2. After **kore**

これをもって閉会とします。 ***Kore o motte** heikai to shimasu.*
With this I would close the meeting.

→ See also *de* and *ni yotte*.

---

oru おる [(AUXILIARY) VERB]

to be (courteous verb)

Oru is the courteous version of the (auxiliary) verb *iru* 'be present.' (→ See *iru* and *irassharu*.)

「山田さんはうちにいらっしゃいますか。」「いいえ，今おりませんが。」
*"Yamada san wa uchi ni **irasshaimasu** ka." "Iie, ima **orimasen** ga."*
"Is Mr. Yamada at home?" "No, he is out now."

(The question shows respect, and the response shows courtesy.)

社長は今出かけております。 *Shachō wa ima dekake**te orimasu**.*
The company president is out now.

(courteously speaking to an outsider about one's own boss)

二時に入り口でお待ちしております。
*Ni ji ni iriguchi de omachi shi**te orimasu**.*
I'll be waiting for you at two o'clock at the entrance.

---

o tōshite を通して [ADVERBIAL PHRASE]

through (some method)

O tōshite is used to mean 'through (some method),' and used in a formal context.

私たちの調査を通していろいろなことが分かってきた。
***Watashi tachi no chōsa o tōshite** iroiro na koto ga wakatte kita.*
Through our investigation, various facts have come to be known.

→ See also *ni yotte*.

---

o tsūjite を通じて [ADVERBIAL PHRASE]

through, via, throughout, through the medium of

O tsūjite is placed after a noun, and means 'through.'

今日ではネットを通じて情報を集めることが多い。
*Kon'nichi dewa **netto o tsūjite** jōhō o atsumeru koto ga ōi.*
Today we often get information via the Internet.

デカルトは生涯を通じて独身を通した。
*Dekaruto wa **shōgai o tsūjite** dokushin o tōshita.*
Descartes stayed single all his life.

豊田氏を通じて返事します。 ***Toyota shi o tsūjite** henji shimasu.*
I'll reply (to you) through Mr. Toyota.

→ See also *o tōshite*.

owaru 終わる [AUXILIARY VERB]

to finish doing something

The auxiliary verb *owaru* follows verbs in the combining form to mean 'to finish . . . ing.' (→ See *hajimeru* and *shimau*.)

原稿は来週書き終わります。
*Genkō wa raishū **kakiowarimasu**. (= **kakioemasu**)*
I'll finish writing the manuscript next week.

この本は面白かったのですぐに読み終わりました。
*Kono hon wa omoshirokatta node sugu ni **yomiowarimashita**. (= **yomioemashita**)*
I read this book fast because it was interesting.

owaru 終わる [VERB]

to finish something

The verb *owaru* was originally an intransitive verb, meaning 'to come to an end.' However, *owaru* recently started to be able to be used either as a transitive verb or as a substitute for the transitive verb *owaru* 'to finish.' *Oeru* is preferred to *owaru* in formal speech contexts.

仕事が終わりました。／ *仕事が終えました
*Shigoto **ga owari**mashita. *Shigoto **ga oe**mashita. (* = ungrammatical)*
The work is finished.

仕事を終わりました。／ 仕事を終えました
*Shigoto **o owari**mashita. / Shigoto **o oe**mashita.*
I finished my work.

ppoi っぽい [NOUN/VERB/ADJECTIVE SUFFIX]

to have a tendency to, tend to (do something), -like

-Ppoi follows (adjectival) nouns and creates a modifier that patterns like an adjective, meaning 'to have a character, appearance, resemblance, or tendency' of the item denoted by the original (adjectival) noun. (→ See also *mitai da*, *rashii<conjecture/typicality>*, and *yō da <conjecture/resemblance>*.)

太郎さんはちょっと女っぽいけど花子さんはほんとに女っぽい。
*Tarō san wa chotto **onnappoi** kedo Hanako san wa hontoni **onnappoi**.*
Taro has an effeminate tendency, but Hanako is really ladylike.

私は風邪っぽいです。咳が出ます。それに熱っぽいです。
*Watashi wa **kazeppoi** desu. Seki ga demasu. Soreni **netsuppoi** desu.*
I have a touch of cold. I have a cough. And I have a slight fever.

今日は雨が降るっぽいね。でもまだ暑いっぽいよ。
*Kyō wa ame ga **furuppoi** ne. Demo mada **atsuippoi** yo.* (slang)
It looks like it's going to rain today. But it still feels hot.

rareru [VERB SUFFIX]

potential, passive, respect

Rareru can be found at the end of the verbs in the potential form, the passive form, or the respect form. *Ru*-verbs that end in *rareru* are ambiguous in three ways. For example, the *ru*-verb *akerareru* means 'can open,' 'will be opened,' or 'will open (honorific).'

I. POTENTIAL SUFFIX *(RAR)ERU*

The potential form of a verb can be created by replacing the final *ru* of a *ru*-verb and the final *u* of an *u*-verb with *rareru* and *eru*, respectively. The potential form of *suru* 'to do' is *dekiru*, and the potential form of *kuru* 'to come' is *korareru* or *koreru*. (→ See Potential form under Verbs.) Verbs in the potential form express one's potential and ability, meaning 'be able to do. . . .' The potential form can also express what one is permitted to do. The direct object of potential verbs is marked by *ga* or *o*. (→ See also *ga*.) Some verbs lexically have the meaning of 'potential' and are rarely used with *(rar)eru*. (→ See also Spontaneous-potential verbs under Verbs.)

山田さんは泳げますか。 *Yamada san wa **oyogemasu** ka.*
Mr. Yamada, can you swim?

この大学の学生だと、映画がただで見られます。
*Kono daigaku no gakusei da to, eiga ga tada de **miraremasu**.*
If you are a student in this college, you can watch the movie for free.

ホテルの部屋でインターネットができますか。
*Hoteru no heya de Intānetto ga **dekimasu** ka.*
Can I access the Internet in the room of the hotel?

ここで講義を受けられますか。 *Koko de kōgi o **ukeraremasu** ka.*
Can we take the lecture course here?

「ここで写真が撮れますか。」「いいえ, 撮れません。」
*"Koko de shashin ga **toremasu** ka." "Iie, **toremasen**."*
"Can I take a photo here?" "No, you cannot."

このカメラは写真がきれいに撮れます。いい写真が撮れます。
*Kono kamera wa shashin ga kirei ni **toremasu**. Ii shashin ga **toremasu**.*
This camera lets photos come out well. I can take nice photos.

II. PASSIVE SUFFIX *(R)ARERU*

The passive form of verbs is created by replacing the final *ru* of a *ru*-verb and the final *u* of an *u*-verb with *rareru* and *areru*, respectively. (→ See Passive form under Verbs for more details about how to create passive forms.) Not only transitive verbs but also intransitive verbs such as *kuru* 'to come' can be in the passive form (*korareru*), because the Japanese language allows not only "direct passive" sentences, where the direct object is treated as the subject of the sentence, but also so-called "adversative passive" sentences, where the direct object of a sentence does not have to be converted to the subject and even does not have to exist. Mostly the latter kind of passive sentence simply implies that the person denoted by the subject was annoyed, disturbed, or negatively influenced by the fact expressed by the sentence. The agent of the action is marked by the particle *ni* in both types of passive sentences. The agent of the action can also be marked by the phrase *ni yotte* in the direct passive.

1. Direct passive

   電車の中で財布が盗まれました。
   *Densha no naka de saifu ga **nusumaremashita**.*
   My wallet was stolen in the train.

   弟は父に叱られました。 *Otōto wa chichi ni **shikararemashita**.*
   My younger brother was scolded by my father.

   その小説は夏目漱石によって書かれた。
   *Sono shōsetsu wa Natsume Sōseki ni yotte **kakareta**.*
   The novel was written by Soseki Natsume.

2. Adversative passive

   電車の中で財布を 盗まれました。
   *Densha no naka de saifu o **nusumaremashita**.*
   I had my wallet stolen in the train.

   忙しい時にお客さんに来られて大変です。
   *Isogashii toki ni okyaku san ni **korarete** taihen desu.*
   I'm in trouble because I have guests when I'm busy.

私は帰る途中で雨に降られてずぶぬれになりました。
*Watashi wa kaeru tochū de ame ni **furarete** zubunure ni narimashita.*
I was caught in the rain on my way home, and I got soaking wet.

父に早く死なれてずいぶん苦労をしました。
*Chichi ni hayaku **shinarete** zuibun kurō shimashita.*
I had a hard time because my father died young.

鯉のぼりが風に吹かれて空高く泳いでいます。
*Koinobori ga kaze ni **fukarete** sora takaku oyoide imasu.*
Carp streamers are blowing high in the sky and waving.

III. RESPECTFUL SUFFIX *(R)ARERU*

The respectful form of a verb can be created by replacing the final *ru* of a *ru*-verb and the final *u* of an *u*-verb with *rareru* and *areru*, respectively. (→ See Respectful form under Verbs and Honorifics for more details about how to make respectful forms.)

この本は山田先生が書かれたのですか。
*Kono hon wa Yamada sensei ga **kakareta** no desu ka.*
Did Professor Yamada write this book?

---

rashii らしい [PREDICATIVE PHRASE (CONJECTURE)]

I hear, seem to, be likely to, like...,

Rashii or *rashii desu* can follow a clause and express hearsay or the speaker's objective conjecture. By contrast, *mitai da* or *yō da* represents objective conjectures and intuitive conjectures and gives the impression that the speaker is quite confident of his/her conjecture. There is a past form *rashikatta*, which means 'to have seemed,' but it is rarely used. Instead, the *ta*-form + *rashii* is commonly used, meaning 'to seem to have (done)' or expressing hearsay of a past event. (→ See also *mitai da, ppoi, sō da,* and *yō da <conjecture>*.)

1. After (adjectival) nouns
   彼女はインフルエンザらしい。 *Kanojo wa **infuruenza rashii**.*
   I hear she has influenza.

2. After (adjectival) nouns + *ja nai, datta,* or *ja nakatta*
   彼女は先週インフルエンザだったらしいです。
   *Kanojo wa senshū **infuruenza datta rashii** desu.*
   I hear she had influenza last week.

3. After verbs and adjectives in the dictionary form
   天気予報によると明日は晴れるらしい。
   *Tenki yohō ni yoru to ashita wa **hareru rashii**.*
   According to the weather forecast, it is likely to be clear tomorrow.

4. After verbs and adjectives in the **nai**-form

彼は肉は食べないらしい。 *Kare wa niku wa tabe**nai rashii**.*
It seems that he doesn't eat meat.

彼はあまりよくないらしい。 *Kare wa amari yoku**nai rashii**.*
It seems that he is not very well.

5. After verbs and adjectives in the **ta**-form

彼は先月ヨーロッパを旅行したらしい。
*Kare wa sengetsu Yōroppa o ryokō shi**ta rashii**.*
I hear he traveled in Europe last month.

彼が買ったバイクは軽自動車ほど高かったらしい。
*Kare ga katta baiku wa keijidōsha hodo takakat**ta rashii**.*
I hear that the motorcycle he bought was as expensive as a small car.

rashii らしい [PREDICATIVE PHRASE (TYPICALITY)]

typical ideal model of . . .

Rashii can follow a noun to make an adjective phrase that means 'typical of . . .'
or 'an ideal model of. . . .' The output is an adjective, so it conjugates like other
adjectives. (→ See also *ppoi*.)

私の彼氏は男らしい人なんです。
*Watashi no kareshi wa **otoko rashii** hito na n desu.*
My boyfriend is a very manly man.

学生なら学生らしくしなさい。
*Gakusei nara **gakusei rashiku** shinasai.*
If you are a student, act like a student.

そんなことをするのは彼女らしい。
*Sonna koto o suru no wa **kanojo rashii**.*
It is like her to do such a thing.

この町には図書館らしい図書館はありません。
*Kono machi ni wa **toshokan rashii** toshokan wa arimasen.*
There is no library-like library in this town.

今日の山田さんはいつもの山田さんらしくありませんね。
*Kyō no Yamada san wa itsumo no **Yamada san rashiku** arimasen ne.*
Ms. Yamada is not her usual self today.

ro ろ [VERB SUFFIX]

the verb suffix for the command form for *ru*-verbs and the irregular verb *suru*

Ro is a verb suffix used to create a command form for *ru*-verbs and the irregular verb *suru*. The command form of a verb can be created by replacing the final *ru* of a *ru*-verb and the final *u* of an *u*-verb with *ro* and *e*, respectively. The command forms of the irregular verbs *suru* 'to do' and *kuru* 'to come' are *shiro* and *koi*, respectively. (→ See Command form under Verbs for more details about command forms, including negative command forms.) The command form expresses a strong and emphatic command if used at the end of the sentence, and thus its use in conversation is not advised unless the speaker wants to sound rough. However, it is appropriately used in embedded sentences or in indirect speech. It is also used appropriately in athletic contexts such as cheering or instructing athletes in practices and competitions, or for affectionately advising family and friends when uttered in a friendly intonation and/or with the particle *yo*. The polite command can be expressed by *nasai*. (→ See also *kudasai* and *nasai*.)

> 上を見ろと書いてあります。 *Ue o miro to kaite arimasu.*
> **It says to look up.**

> 頑張れ！入れろ！あきらめるな！行け！
> *Ganbare! Irero! Akirameru na! Ike!*
> **Hold out! Shoot! Never give up! Keep going!**

> ちゃんとしろよ。 *Chanto shiro yo.* **Do it right, okay?**

ru る [VERB SUFFIX]

the verb suffix for plain non-past affirmative

I. VERB SUFFIX

The verb suffix *ru* is found at the end of a verb in the plain non-past affirmative form, which is also called the dictionary form (e.g. *tabe-ru* 'eat'). This suffix becomes *u* when the verb root ends in a consonant (e.g. *kak-u* 'write'). (→ See Dictionary form under Verbs.) The dictionary form can end sentences in informal conversations, followed by some sentence-ending particle or uttered with a certain contextually appropriate intonation. However, this form is also needed before certain predicative phrases, nouns, or particles even in polite/formal conversational contexts.

1. Future/habitual actions expressed in an informal conversation

> 僕はもう帰るよ。 *Boku wa mō kaeru yo.* **I will go home now.**

> 「よくカラオケに行く。」「うん，行く。」
> *"Yoku karaoke ni iku." (with rising intonation) "Un, iku."*
> **"Do you often go to karaoke?" "Yes, I do."**

2. Future/habitual actions expressed in a polite speech context

来月，日本に行くんです。 *Raigetsu, Nihon ni iku n desu.*
I'm going to Japan next month.

3. Before a noun

母が買うものは安いものばかりです。
Haha ga kau mono wa yasui mono bakari desu.
The things that my mother buys are all cheap things.

→ See also Relative clauses under Clauses and *n da.*

II. AFTER NOUNS

The suffix *ru* can be attached at the end of a noun to make a noun into a verb. This use of the suffix *ru* is not totally productive and mainly used by young people. The preceding nouns are often borrowed from English and abbreviated. Verbs from English can be occasionally used with this suffix. The outcome of this process is an *u*-verb.

Original Noun	The Form with *Ru*
ダブル *daburu* 'double'	ダブる *daburu* 'to double, overlap'
デコ *deko* 'decoration'	デコる *dekoru* 'to decorate'
ハーモニー *hāmoni* 'harmony'	ハモる *hamoru* 'to harmonize'
事故 *jiko* 'an accident'	事故る *jikoru* 'to have an accident, be in an accident'
マック *Makku* 'McDonald's'	マクる *makuru* to eat at McDonald's
メモ *memo* 'memo'	メモる *memoru* 'to take a memo'
ミス *misu* 'mistake'	ミスる *misuru* 'to make a mistake'
サボタージュ *sabotāju* 'sabotage'	サボる *saboru* 'to play truant, go slow'
トラブル *toraburu* 'trouble'	トラブる *toraburu* 'to get into trouble'

自転車で事故ってトラブった。 *Jitensha de **jikotte torabutta**.*
I had an accident on my bike and got into trouble.

授業をサボってマクろうよ。 *Jugyō o **sabotte makurō** yo.*
Let's cut class and go to eat at the Golden Arches.

アポがダブらないように日程をメモっとかなくちゃ。
*Apo ga **daburanai** yō ni nittei o **memottoka** nakucha.*
I have to make a note of my schedule so that I won't have an appointment conflict.

(s)aseru させる [VERB SUFFIX]

make (someone) do . . . , let (someone) do . . .

The causative form of verbs is created by replacing the final *ru* of a *ru*-verb and the final *u* of an *u*-verb with *saseru* and *aseru*, respectively. (→ See Causative form under Verbs for more details as well as *saseru's* simplified form *(s)asu*.) Causative verbs express situations where someone makes or let someone else do something. The causer is marked by the subject marker *ga*, and it is usually an animate item in Japanese causative sentences. The action performer is marked by the particle *ni* if the verb is originally a transitive verb, whereas it is marked by *o* if the verb is originally an intransitive verb. (Note that some intransitive verbs in the causative form allow the action performer to be marked by *ni* or *o* depending on the situation.) When a causative verb expresses permission, it is often used with the auxiliary verbs that express giving and receiving (*ageru*, *kureru*, *morau* and their honorific versions.)

1. Causative forms of transitive verbs

   子供にもっと野菜を食べさせた方がいい。
   Kodomo ni *motto yasai o* ***tabesaseta*** *hō ga ii.*
   It is better to make children eat more vegetables.

   猫にさしみを食べさせた。 ***Neko ni*** *sashimi o* ***tabesaseta.***
   I let my cat eat sashimi.

   私の部下にその書類を書かせよう。
   Watashi no ***buka ni*** *sono shorui o* ***kakaseyō.***
   I'll let my assistant write the papers.

   私に説明させてください。 ***Watashi ni*** *setsumei* ***sasete*** *kudasai.*
   Please let me explain.

2. Causative forms of intransitive verbs

   早く子供を寝かせた方がいい。 *Hayaku* ***kodomo o nekaseta*** *hō ga ii.*
   It's better to make the child go to bed early.

   女性を泣かせてはいけない。 ***Josei o nakasete*** *wa ikenai.*
   You should not make a lady cry.

   子供たちを好きなように遊ばせた。
   Kodomo tachi o *suki na yō ni* ***asobaseta.***
   I let the children play as they pleased.

3. Causative forms of intransitive verbs that allow the particle *ni* or *o*

   Some intransitive verbs (e.g. *iku*) in the causative form allow their action performer to be marked by either *ni* or *o*. Note that intransitive verbs that express emotion or emotional actions (e.g. *kanashimu* 'to be saddened' and *naku* 'cry') cannot allow their action performers to be marked by *ni*.

私の部下をそこに行かせよう。 *Watashi no **buka o** soko ni **ikaseyō**.*
I'll make/force my assistant go there.

私の部下にそこに行かせよう。 *Watashi no **buka ni** soko ni **ikaseyō**.*
I'll have my assistant go there. (The assistant will be asked to go there.)

4. Causative verbs used with auxiliary verbs of giving and receiving

ただ今より始めさせていただきます。
*Tadaima yori **hajimesasete itadakimasu**.*
Let me begin. (I'll humbly receive your permission to let me begin.)

あなたに私の好きな歌を聞かせてあげます。
*Anata ni watashi no suki na uta o **kikasete agemasu**.*
I will let you listen to my favorite songs.

ちょっとコピー機を使わせてくれませんか。
*Chotto kopīki o **tsukawasete kuremasen** ka.*
Will you let me use the copy machine for a while?

sashiageru さしあげる [AUXILIARY VERB]

to do something for the benefit of someone else

The auxiliary verb *sashiageru* is the honorific counterpart of the auxiliary verb *ageru*. (→ See *ageru <auxiliary verb>*.)

山田さんのお祖母さんを駅まで送って差し上げました。
*Yamada san no obāsan o eki made **okutte sashiagemashita**.*
I sent Ms. Yamada's grandmother to the train station.

sashiageru さしあげる [VERB]

to give

The verb *sashiageru* is the honorific counterpart of the verb *ageru*. (→ See *ageru <verb>*.) *Sashiageru* is used when the receiver is someone to whom the speaker's respect is due.

山田さん夫婦に結婚祝いを差し上げました。
*Yamada san fūfu ni kekkon iwai o **sashiagemashita**.*
I gave a wedding gift to Mr. Yamada and his wife.

よしこさんのお母さんにクッキーを差し上げました。
*Yoshiko san no okāsan ni kukkī o **sashiagemashita**.*
I gave cookies to Yoshiko's mother.

(s)asu さす → See (s)aseru.

sei de せいで [ADVERBIAL PHRASE]

due to, because of

Sei de creates an adverbial phrase that shows the reason for or the cause of an unfavorable result. Do not confuse it with *okage de*, which is usually used when a favorable situation is caused. (→ See also *okage de* and *tame ni*.)

1. After verbs and adjectives in the dictionary form

   収入が低いせいで生活が苦しいです。
   *Shūnyū ga hiku**i sei de** seikatsu ga kurushii desu.*
   My life is difficult due to a low income.

   変な噂を立てるせいで彼女は怒っています。
   *Hen na uwasa o tate**ru sei de** kanojo wa okotte imasu.*
   She is angry because somebody started an ugly rumor about her.

2. After verbs and adjectives in the **ta**-form

   道路が渋滞したせいでバスが予定通り来なかった。
   *Dōro ga jūtai shi**ta sei de** basu ga yotei dōri konakatta.*
   The bus did not arrive on schedule, because the road was jammed.

   忙しかったせいでそのことをすっかり忘れていました。
   *Isogashika**tta sei de** sono koto o sukkari wasurete imashita.*
   I'd completely forgotten it because I was so busy.

   私がばかだったせいで迷惑をかけました。
   *Watashi ga baka da**tta sei de** meiwaku o kakemashita.*
   I troubled you because I was a fool.

3. After verbs and adjectives in the **nai**-form

   お金が足りないせいで予約できなかった。
   *Okane ga tari**nai sei de** yoyaku dekinakatta.*
   I couldn't book it, because I did not have enough money.

   品質が良くないせいで売り上げが悪い。
   *Hinshitsu ga yoku**nai sei de** uriage ga warui.*
   Because the quality is not good, sales are weak.

4. After (adjectival) nouns + **na/no,** or nouns + **no**

   多忙なせいで仕事で小さなミスをしました。
   *Tabō **na sei de** shigoto de chīsana misu o shimashita.*
   I made a small mistake in my work because I was busy.

   彼の誤解のせいで私が弁解せざるを得なかった。
   *Kare **no gokai no sei de** watashi ga benkai sezaru o enakatta.*
   Due to his misunderstanding, I had to provide an explanation.

5. After demonstrative adjectives

そのせいで残業しています。 **Sono sei de** zangyō shite imasu.
Due to that, I'm working overtime.

shi し [PARTICLE]

emphatic listing of states and events (as reasons)

The particle *shi* can be used for emphatically listing the arguments for making a point in a relatively informal context. *Shi* follows verbs, adjectives, and *da* in the dictionary form, in the *nai*-form, or in the *ta*-form. The statement about the resultant events or states often follows.

田中さんは, 頭がいいし, きれいだし, 人の悪口を言わないし, 好きだ。
Tanaka san wa, atama ga ii **shi**, *kirei* **da shi**, *hito no warukuchi o iwa***nai shi**, *suki da.*
Ms. Tanaka is smart, pretty, and doesn't speak ill of others, so I like her.

山田さんは, 意地悪だし, 文句ばかり言うし, 嫌いだ。
Yamada san wa, ijiwaru da **shi**, *monku bakari iu* **shi**, *kirai da.*
Ms. Yamada is mean and complains all the time, so I dislike her.

あのテストは難しかったし, 問題も多かったし, 参った。
*Ano tesuto wa muzukashikat***ta shi**, *mondai mo ookat***ta shi**, *maitta.*
That exam was hard and had numerous questions, so I was beaten.

shika しか [PARTICLE]

nothing/nobody/nowhere but. . ., no more than . . ., no other . . . than . . ., only

The particle *shika* can follow nouns (and particles), quantity phrases, and verbs in the dictionary form. It must be used with a negative predicate. *Shika* indicates that the given state or action applies only to the item that it marks, and it emphasizes the lack of other items in the context. It is very similar to 'only' in English, although the latter does not require a negative predicate. (→ See also *dake* and *hoka*.)

1. After the subject or object noun

太郎しか約束の時間に来なかった。
Tarō shika *yakusoku no jikan ni konakatta.*
Nobody but Taro came at the time of our appointment.

私は野菜と魚しか食べません。
Watashi wa **yasai to sakana shika** *tabemasen.*
I eat nothing but vegetables and fish.

(used in place of the particle that indicates subject or object)

2. After number + counter

東京には一回しか行ったことがありません。
*Tōkyō ni wa **ikkai shika** itta koto ga ari**masen**.*
I've only been to Tokyo once.

私は三人しか日本の友人がいません。
*Watashi wa **san nin shika** Nihon no yūjin ga i**masen**.*
I have no more than three Japanese friends.

今，二千円しかお金をもっていません。
*Ima, **ni sen en shika** okane o motte i**masen**.*
I only have two thousand yen now.

3. After particle

今日は六時にしか会えません。 *Kyō wa rokuji **ni shika** ae**masen**.*
Today I can meet you at no other time except six.

閉店後はここからしか出られません。
*Heiten go wa koko **kara shika** derare**masen**.*
After closing time, you can only go out from here.

このタイプの電子機器はあの店でしか売っていません。
*Kono taipu no denshi kiki wa ano mise **de shika** utte i**masen**.*
Electronic devices of this type are sold nowhere but at that store.

4. After verbs in the dictionary form

ここで待つしかありません。 *Koko de matsu **shika** ari**masen**.*
There is nothing to do but wait here.

---

shikashi しかし → See **demo**.

---

shimau しまう [AUXILIARY VERB]

---

to finish (something), do by mistake/absent-mindedly/carelessly, do (something) completely

The verb *shimau* means 'to put away' or 'to store' and can also function as an auxiliary verb, following verbs in the *te*-form in order to emphasize the completion of the action, often expressing the speaker's satisfaction or regret depending on the nature of the action completed. (→ See also Auxiliary verbs under Auxiliary Verbs & Adjectives and *chau (jau)*.)

私はこの本を一晩で読んでしまった。
*Watashi wa kono hon o hitoban de yon**de shimatta**.*
I finished reading this book in a night.

私は彼女の作った料理を全部 食べてしまいました。
*Watashi wa kanojo no tsukutta ryōri o zenbu tabe**te shimaimashita**.*
I ate up all the dishes she prepared.

彼は東京駅で違う電車に乗ってしまった。
*Kare wa Tōkyō eki de chigau densha ni notte **shimatta.***
He took the wrong train at Tokyo Station by mistake.

トイレに傘を忘れてしまった。 *Toire ni kasa o wasurete **shimatta.***
I absent-mindedly left my umbrella in a restroom.

あの人が好きになってしまいそうです。
*Ano hito ga suki ni natte **shimaisō** desu.*
I feel I will really grow to like that person. (I have a feeling I'm going to fall for that person.)

→ See also *owaru.*

shiru 知る [VERB]

to know

To say you know something, use the verb *shiru* in the *te iru* construction as in *shitte iru* or *shitte imasu.* To say you do not know something, say *shiranai* or *shirimasen.* However, the latter simply means that you do not have the knowledge, and might sound a little blunt. If you want to show your cooperative attitude, it is better to say *wakaranai* or *wakarimasen.* The verb *wakaru* means either 'to know' or 'to understand.'

「彼のメールアドレスを知っていますか」「いえ，知りません。」
*"Kare no mēru adoresu o **shitte imasu** ka." "Ie, **shirimasen.**"*
"Do you know his e-mail address?" "No, I don't."

彼のメールアドレスは分かりません。
*Kare no mēru adoresu wa **wakarimasen.***
I don't know his e-mail address.

sō da そうだ [PREDICATIVE PHRASE (CONJECTURE)]

to look, seem, about to

For expressing immediate conjectures based on observations and to show the likeliness of the occurrence of some event or state, we can end a sentence with *sō da* or *sō desu. Sō* is in fact an adjectival noun formative. It follows another adjectival noun, a verb in the combining form, or an adjective's root and creates a new *na*-type adjectival noun, which means 'look like . . . ,' 'about to . . . ,' or 'likely to . . . .' It also follows the *nai*-forms, but the ending *i* must be replaced by *sa* as in *takaku nasasō* or *kowarenasasō.* The adjective *ii* and *yoi* both become *yosasō.* (→ See also *garu, mitai da, ppoi, rashii <conjecture>, sō da <hearsay>,* and *yō da <conjecture>.*)

1. After adjectival nouns

退屈そうでしたね。 **Taikutsu sō deshita** ne. You looked bored.

このケースは丈夫そうではありません。
*Kono kēsu wa **jōbu sō dewa arimasen**.*
This case doesn't look durable.

田中さんは嫌そうな顔をしていた。
*Tanaka san wa **iya sō na** kao o shiteita.*
Mr. Tanaka looked like he hated it.

2. After verbs in the combining form

この車は壊れそうです。 *Kono kuruma wa **koware sō desu**.*
This car is about to break.

壊れそうな車は買わない方がいいですよ。
***Kowaresō na** kuruma wa kawanai hō ga ii desu yo.*
It's better not to buy a car that appears likely to break down soon.

この車は壊れていそうです。 *Kono kuruma wa **kowarete isō desu**.*
This car looks broken.

雨が降りそうですね。 *Ame ga **furisō desu** ne.*
It looks like it's going to rain, doesn't it?

お腹が空いて死にそうです。 *Onaka ga suite **shini sō desu**.*
I'm dying of hunger. (I'm terribly hungry.)

寝坊して飛行機に遅れそうです。 *Nebō shite hikōki ni **okure sō desu**.*
I overslept and am close to missing my plane.

3. After the roots of (auxiliary) adjectives

あの人はとても優しそうな人ですね。
*Ano hito wa totemo **yasashisō na** hito desu ne.*
That person looks like a very kind person.

面白そうに見ていましたよ。 ***Omoshirosō ni** mite imashita yo.*
He was looking (at you) like he was enjoying it.

あのけが人はひどく痛そうです。 *Ano keganin wa hidoku **itasō desu**.*
That injured person looks to be in terrible pain.

電気自動車の調子は良さそうです。
*Denki jidōsha no choshi wa **yosasō desu**.*
The electric car seems to be in good condition.

彼はあなたに会えてとても嬉しそうでした。
*Kare wa anata ni aete totemo **ureshisō deshita**.*
He looked very glad to see you.

彼はもっといい車を欲しそうです。
*Kare wa motto ii kuruma o **hoshisō desu**.*
He seems to want a better car.

彼女はヨーロッパに行きたそうです。
*Kanojo wa Yōroppa ni iki**tasō desu.***
She appears to want to visit Europe.

太郎さんはあなたにとても会いたそうでした。
*Tarō san wa anata ni totemo ai**tasō deshita.***
It looked like Taro longed to see you.

→ See also *tai.*

4. After verbs, adjectives, and adjectival nouns in the **nai**-form

雨が降らなさそうですね。*Ame ga furana**sa sō desu** ne.*
It doesn't look like it's going to rain, does it?

彼女は元気がなさそうです。*Kanojo wa genki ga **nasasō desu.***
She seems to be low in spirit. (She does not seem well.)

この料理はあまりおいしくなさそうです。
*Kono ryōri wa amari **oishiku nasasō desu.***
This dish doesn't look very delicious.

林さんはこの仕事が嫌じゃなさそうですよ。
*Hayashi san wa kono shigoto ga **iya ja nasasō desu** yo.*
Mr. Hayashi does not look like he hates this job.

sō da そうだ [PREDICATIVE PHRASE (HEARSAY)]

they say that . . . , I heard that . . .

For expressing reported speech or hearsay, we can add *sō da* or *sō desu* at the end of a clause in the dictionary form, in the *ta*-form, or in the *nai*-form. (→ See also *rashii <conjecture>.*)

1. After (adjectival) nouns followed by a linking verb
   彼女は先週熱だったそうです。*Kanojo wa senshū **netsu datta sō desu.***
   I heard she had a fever last week.

2. After verbs and adjectives in the dictionary form
   明日は晴れるそうです。*Asu wa hare**ru sō desu.***
   I heard it will be sunny tomorrow.

   このビルが日本でいちばん高いそうです。
   *Kono biru ga Nihon de ichiban taka**i sō desu.***
   They say that this building is the tallest in Japan.

3. After verbs and adjectives in the **nai**-form
   田中さんは今日は来ないそうです。
   *Tanaka san wa kyō wa ko**nai sō desu.***
   I heard Mr. Tanaka won't come today.

パソコンは今高くないそうです。 *Pasokon wa ima takakunai sō desu.*
I heard (or hear) that personal computers are not expensive now.

4. After verbs and adjectives in the **ta-form**

彼女は怒っていたそうです。 *Kanojo wa okotte ita sō desu.*
I heard she was angry.

それはうまくいかなかったそうです。
Sore wa umaku ikanakatta sō desu.
They said it didn't go well.

sōiu そういう [ADJECTIVAL PHRASE]

that kind of, that type of, such (a)

Sōiu or *sonna* can function as a general noun modifier that means 'such' or
'that kind of. . . .'

そういう本は私には向いていません。
Sōiu hon wa watashi ni wa muite imasen.
That type of book is not suitable for me.

そういうわけで予約をキャンセルしました。
Sōiu wake de yoyaku o kyanseru shimashita.
Such being the case, I canceled the reservation.

そういうふうに言われても困ります。
Sōiu fū ni iwaretemo komarimasu.
I'll be in trouble if you speak like that.

soko そこ → See **sore**.

sokonau 損なう [AUXILIARY VERB]

to miss doing, make a mistake in doing, come near doing

The verb *sokonau* means to 'to lose' or 'to hurt.' It can also be used as an auxiliary verb following a verb in the combining form, in which case it means 'to
miss the opportunity to do . . .' or 'to make a mistake in doing. . . .' It is similar
to *nogasu*. (→ See also Auxiliary verb and *nogasu*.)

予約した新幹線に乗り損なったけど自由席には乗れる。
*Yoyaku shita Shinkansen ni **norisokonatta** kedo jiyū seki ni wa noreru.*
I missed the Shinkansen I booked, but I can take an unreserved seat.

その津波から逃げ損なって大勢の人が亡くなりました。
*Sono tsunami kara **nigesokonatte** ōzei no hito ga nakunarimashita.*
Many people were killed because they failed to escape from the tsunami.

書類に書き損ないました。もう一枚下さい。
*Shorui ni **kakisokonaimashita**. Mō ichi mai kudasai.*
I made a slip of the pen. Please give me another sheet (of the form).

彼を見損ないました。 *Kare o **misokonaimashita**.*
I was wrong in my estimation of him.

sō ni natta そうになった [PREDICATIVE PHRASE]

almost (did), nearly (did)

Sō ni natta follows verbs in the combining form and is used to mean that one almost or nearly did something. It may be replaced by *tokoro datta/deshita*, which follows a verb in the dictionary form. (→ See also *kakeru* and *tokoro*.)

寝坊して飛行機に遅れそうになった。
*Nebō shite hikōki ni **okureso ni natta**.*
I overslept and nearly missed the airplane.

電車を間違えそうになった。 *Densha o **machigaeso ni natta**.*
I almost took a wrong train.

煙で息が詰まりそうになりました。(＝煙で息が詰まるところでした。)
*Kemuri de iki ga **tsumariso ni narimashita**. (= Kemuri de iki ga tsumaru tokoro deshita.)*
I was almost suffocated by smoke.

sono その → See *sore*.

sore それ [DEMONSTRATIVE]

that, those, it

Sore is a demonstrative pronoun and can refer to (non-human) items that are visible to the speaker and the listener but are placed close to the listener and far from the speaker. It can be directly followed by a particle or the linking verb *da/ desu*, just like nouns. For referring to locations, use *soko* 'over there near you' instead of *sore*. For referring to a person, use the demonstrative adjective *sono* with a common noun such as *hito* 'person,' as in *sono hito*. The polite form of *sore* is *sochira*, which means not only 'that one near you' but also 'that person near you,' 'you,' or 'the direction toward you.' *Sore* can also be used anaphorically to refer to some item that is not visible to the speaker and the listener at the time of speech but is known to one of them. If both of them knows the item, *are* is used instead of *sore*.

→ See also *are* and *kore*.

1. **Sore/sochira/soko** (demonstrative pronoun), often followed by particles

「それは何ですか。」「携帯用カーナビです。」
*"**Sore wa** nan desu ka." "Keitaiyō kānabi desu."*
"What's that?" "It's a portable car navigation system."

それを貸して下さい。 **Sore o** kashite kudasai. Please lend it to me.

それでいいです。 **Sore de** ii desu. That will do.

そこへ電車で行けますか。 **Soko e** densha de ikemasu ka.
Can I get there by train?

そこで何をしていたんですか。 **Soko de** nani o shite ita n desu ka.
What were you doing there?

すぐそちらに行きます。 Sugu **sochira ni** ikimasu. I'll be there soon.

「ついに電子ブックリーダーを買いました。」「それは便利ですか。」
*"Tsui ni denshi bukku rīdā o kaimashita." "**Sore wa** benri desu ka."*
"Finally, I bought a digital book reader." "Is it convenient?"

「探しているのはこれですね。」「あ，それです。」
*"Sagashite iru no wa kore desu ne." "Ah, **sore** desu."*
"This is what you're looking for, isn't it?" "Oh, that's it."

2. **Sono** (demonstrative adjective), followed by nouns

その携帯はだれのですか。 **Sono keiwai** wa dare no desu ka.
Whose is that mobile phone?

3. **Sore/sochira/soko/sono** used anaphorically

その時ちょうどテレビを見ていました。
***Sono toki** chōdo terebi o mite imashita.*
Just at that time I was watching television.

「おもしろいニュースを聞きました。」「（それを）教えてください。」
*"Omoshiroi nyūsu o kikimashita." "(**Sore** o) oshiete kudasai."*
"I heard interesting news." "Tell me (it)."

「さっきだれかがあなたに会いに来ました。」「その人の名前を聞きましたか。」
*"Sakki dareka ga anata ni aini kimashita." "**Sono hito** no namae o kikimashita ka."*
"Somebody came a short while ago to see you." "Did you hear the person's name?"

sorede それで [CONJUNCTION]

as a result, therefore, and

Sorede can be used as a sentence initial conjunction to mean 'as a result' or 'consequently.' (→ See also *dakara*.)

寝坊しました。それで，会社に遅刻しました。
*Nebō shimashita. **Sorede**, kaisha ni chikoku shimashita.*
I overslept. As a result, I was late for work.

休みをもらいました。それで、北海道に行くことにしました。
*Yasumi o moraimashita. **Sorede**, Hokkaidō ni iku koto ni shimashita.*
I got a vacation. So, I decided to go to Hokkaido.

父が病気になったんです。それで，僕が働くことになったんです。
*Chichi ga byōki ni natta n desu. **Sorede**, boku ga hataraku koto ni natta n desu.*
My father became ill. That's why it was decided that I work.

sorehodo それほど [ADVERB]

(not) so, (not) very, (not) so many, (not) so much

Sorehodo is used with a negative predicate and means 'not so much.' It is often interchangeably used with a slightly more informal counterpart, *sonnani*. (→ See also *amari*.)

今日はそれほど暑くないですね。
*Kyō wa **sorehodo atsuku nai** desu ne.*
It isn't very hot today, is it?

これはそれほど高い電波時計ではありません。
*Kore wa **sorehodo takai** denpa dokei dewa **arimasen**.*
This is a not-so-expensive radio watch.

日本語はそれほど上手に話せません。
*Nihongo wa **sorehodo jōzu ni hanasemasen**.*
I cannot speak Japanese that well.

今それほどお金は持っていません。
*Ima **sorehodo okane** wa motte **imasen**.*
I don't have so much money now.

sorekara それから [CONJUNCTION]

and, then, after that, since then

Sorekara can be used as a sentence-initial conjunction to mean 'and then' with respect to the chronological order of actions or 'in addition' with respect to the list of actions. It can also be used in the middle of a sentence at certain positions, when actions or items are listed. (→ See also *soshite* and *sōsuruto*.)

1. Sentence-initially, clarifying the chronological order of the event

   昨日久しぶりに加藤さんと会った。それから一緒にビリヤードをした。
   *Kinō hisashiburi ni Katō san to atta. **Sorekara** isshoni biriyādo o shita.*
   I met with Mr. Kato after a long time yesterday. And then we played billiards together.

2. Sentence-initially, listing additional actions

   週末は新聞を読んだり，友達に電話をしたりします。それから，買い物にも行きます。
   *Shūmatsu wa shinbun o yondari, tomodachi ni denwa shitari shimasu. **Sorekara**, kaimono ni mo ikimasu.*
   On weekends, I do things like read newspapers and call my friends. In addition, I go shopping, too.

3. Sentence-internally, following a noun with **to**, listing additional items

   リンゴとミカンとそれからバナナを下さい。
   ***Ringo to mikan to sorekara banana** o kudasai.*
   Please give me apples, oranges, and bananas.

4. Sentence-internally, following verbs in the **te**-form, listing additional actions

   夜遅くまでインターネットをしてそれから寝ます。
   *Yoru osoku made Intānetto o shi**te sorekara nemasu.***
   I surf on the Internet till late at night, and then I go to bed.

   疲れたし，この喫茶店で休んで，それから帰ろう。
   *Tsukareta shi, kono kissaten de yasunde, **sorekara kaerō**.*
   I'm tired, so let's have a rest at this coffee shop and then go home.

5. Sentence-internally, following nouns with **de**, listing additional items or presenting additional statements

   これが有名な大仏殿で，それからあれが五重塔です。
   *Kore ga yūmei na **Daibutsuden de, sorekara** are ga Gojū no Tō desu.*
   This is the famous Hall of the Great Buddha, and that is the Five-Storied Pagoda.

   (stresses the contrast of two things)

6. Used as an adverb, meaning 'since then'

   それからずっとそこで働いています。
   ***Sorekara** zutto soko de hataraite imasu.*
   I've been working there since then.

   それから全然見かけません。
   ***Sorekara** zenzen mikakemasen.*
   I haven't seen (him) since then.

soreni それに [CONJUNCTION]

moreover, what is more, and also, besides

Soreni can be used as a sentence-initial conjunction to mean 'furthermore.' It can also be used in the middle of a sentence at certain positions. (→ See also *sorekara* and *soshite*.)

1. At the beginning of a sentence

   これは高すぎる。それにデザインがあまり好きではない。
   *Kore wa takasugiru. **Soreni** dezain ga amari suki de wa nai.*
   This is too expensive. Besides, I don't like the design very much.

2. After adjectives in the **te**-form

   彼女は優しくて、それにきれいです。
   *Kanojo wa yasashiku**te**, **soreni** kirei desu.*
   She is kind and, what is more, she is pretty.

   (stresses the addition of another quality of a person/thing)

3. After adjectival nouns + **de**

   彼は誠実で、それに勤勉です。
   *Kare wa **seijitsu de**, **soreni** kinben desu.*
   He is sincere and, moreover, he is diligent.

   (stresses the addition of another quality of a person/thing)

4. After adjectives in the dictionary form + **shi**

   今日は寒いし、それに疲れています。家にいます。
   *Kyō wa samui **shi**, **soreni** tsukarete imasu. Ie ni imasu.*
   Today is cold and, moreover, I am tired. I'll stay home.

   (stresses the addition of another state)

5. After nouns + **to**

   私はスイスとフランスとそれにスペインを旅行しました。
   *Watashi wa **Suisu to Furansu to soreni** Supein o ryokō shimashita.*
   I traveled in Switzerland, France, and also Spain.

sorezore それぞれ [ADVERB]

each, respectively, separately, one's own

Sorezore is used when a sentence includes a plural noun, and the given state or action applies to each one of the members in the group separately. *Sorezore* can be placed right after the plural noun and its associated particle, or can be followed by the particle *no* as in *sorezore no* and placed right before the noun that shows the item to be different.

1. After a subject (or topic) noun

私たちはそれぞれ好きなようにします。
***Watashi tachi wa sorezore** suki na yō ni shimasu.*
Each of us will do as each of us likes.

田中先生と山田先生はそれぞれ数学と歴史を教えています。
***Tanaka sensei to Yamada sensei wa sorezore** sūgaku to rekishi o oshiete imasu.*
Mr. Tanaka and Mr. Yamada teach math and history respectively.

2. After an indirect object noun

先生は生徒にそれぞれ問題を一問ずつ与えた。
*Sensei wa **seito ni sorezore** mondai o ichi mon zutsu ataeta.*
The teacher gave each of the students one question.

3. Followed by *no* + a noun (to modify the noun)

彼らはそれぞれの仕事を一生懸命している。
*Karera wa **sorezore no shigoto** o isshōkenmei shite iru.*
They work hard at their respective jobs.

---

soshite そして [CONJUNCTION]

and, and then, and after that

Soshite can be used as a sentence initial conjunction to mean 'and then,' just like *sorekara*. However, the order of actions is more strongly emphasized by *sorekara* than *soshite*. Furthermore, unlike *sorekara*, *soshite* cannot be used to mean 'in addition.' (→ See also *sorekara*, *soreni*, and *sōsuruto*.)

1. Sentence-initially

これからがんばって勉強します。そして大学に入ろうと思います。
*Kore kara ganbatte benkyō shimasu. **Soshite** daigaku ni hairō to omoi-masu.*
I will study hard from now on. And I think I'll try to get into a university.

2. Sentence-internally, following a verb in the *te*-form

これから本屋に行って，そしてデパートに行きます。
*Kore kara hon'ya ni itte, **soshite** depāto ni ikimasu.*
I will go to the bookstore, and then I will go to the department store.

---

sōsuruto そうすると [CONJUNCTION]

then

Sōsuruto can be used as a sentence-initial conjunction that means 'and then.' Unlike *sorekara*, which can also mean 'then,' *sōsuruto* introduces a sentence that denotes what happens or happened after the event expressed in the previous sentence. Thus, *sōsuruto* cannot be used for a sentence that denotes an event over which the speaker has control. For the latter situation, use *sorekara* or *soshite*. (→ See *sorekara*, *soshite*, and *to*.)

> このボタンを押してください。そうすると、エンジンがかかります。
> *Kono botan o oshite kudasai. **Sōsuruto**, enjin ga kakarimasu.*
> **Please press this button. Then, the engine will start.**

> ドアを開けた。そうすると、女の人が立っていた。
> *Doa o aketa. **Sōsuruto**, onna no hito ga tatte ita.*
> **I opened the door. Then, there was a woman standing there.**

sugiru 過ぎる [AUXILIARY VERB]

too much, too many, too. . . , excessively

Sugiru means 'to pass' when used as a verb. It means 'excessively' when used as an auxiliary verb, following a verb in the combining form, an adjective in the root form, or an adjectival noun.

1. After verbs in the combining form

   夕べは飲み過ぎました。 *Yūbe wa **nomisugimashita**.*
   I drank too much last night.

   たくさん古本を買い過ぎました。 *Takusan furuhon o **kaisugimashita**.*
   I bought too many secondhand books.

   あなたは働き過ぎます。 *Anata wa **hatarakisugimasu**.*
   You are working too hard.

2. After the roots of adjectives

   この服は私には大きすぎます。
   *Kono fuku wa watashi ni wa **ōkisugimasu**.*
   These clothes are too big for me.

   あのワゴン車は高すぎて買えません。
   *Ano wagonsha wa **takasugite** kaemasen.*
   That station wagon is so expensive that I can't buy it.

3. After adjectival nouns

   あなたは消極的すぎます。積極的にした方がいい。
   *Anata wa **shōkyokuteki sugimasu**. Sekkyokuteki ni shita hō ga ii.*
   You are too passive. You should be more assertive.

   その手続きは複雑すぎて一人ではできません。
   *Sono tetsuduki wa **fukuzatsu sugite** hitori de wa dekimasen.*
   The procedure is too complicated to do by myself.

sukoshi 少し [ADVERB]

a few, some, a little, a bit, a moment, (not) at all

Sukoshi means that the amount, quantity, or degree is small. It is placed where you usually place quantity phrases in a sentence. (→ See also *amari*, *chittomo*, and *chotto*.)

1. In affirmative sentences

   私はワインとビールを少し飲みます。
   *Watashi wa wain to bīru o **sukoshi** nomimasu.*
   I drink wine and beer a bit.

   少し日本語が話せますね。 ***Sukoshi** Nihongo ga hanasemasu ne.*
   You can speak a little Japanese, can't you?

   少しここで待って下さい。 ***Sukoshi** koko de matte **kudasai**.*
   Wait here a moment, please.

2. Followed by *mo* in negative sentences

   そんなことは少しも気にしません。
   *Sonna koto wa **sukoshi mo** ki ni shimasen.*
   I don't care a bit about that.

suru する [VERB]

do, play, work as . . . , perform (an action), cost, wear (an accessory), have (a meal, feeling), make (a sound), make (something into something else), treat (in some manner), decide on (something), possess (a figure, smell, etc.)

Suru is an irregular verb, conjugating as *suru*, *shinai*, *shimasu*, etc. Its courteous version is *itasu*; its honorific version is *nasaru*; and its potential substitute is *dekiru*. The main meaning of *suru* is 'to do,' but it is used for expressing a variety of actions and states (e.g. to play, to make, to decide, to cost, to smell, to have, and to be). Furthermore, it is used for creating so-called *suru*-verbs following Sino-Japanese compounds, Sino-Japanese morphemes, foreign loans, mimetic expressions, adverbs, etc. (→ See *Suru*-verbs under Verbs and Appendix 5.)

I. VARIOUS ACTIONS AND STATES

1. Actions (. . . *o suru*)

   兄はサッカーをします。 *Ani wa **sakkā o shimasu**.*
   My big brother plays soccer.

   妹はチェスと将棋をするのが好きです。
   *Imōto wa **chesu to shōgi o suru** no ga suki desu*
   My younger sister likes to play chess and shogi (Japanese chess).

レストランで軽い食事をしませんか。
*Resutoran de karui **shokuji o shimasen** ka.*
Why don't we have a light meal at the restaurant?

あなたはふだんどこで買い物をしますか。
*Anata wa fudan doko de **kaimono o shimasu** ka.*
Where do you usually go shopping?

私は毎週土曜日の夜にドライブをします。
*Watashi wa maishū Dōyōbi no yoru ni **doraibu o shimasu**.*
I drive around every Saturday night.

毎日インターネットをします。 *Mainichi **intānetto o shimasu**.*
I surf the Internet every day.

今晩イーメールをします。 *Komban **īmēru o shimasu**.*
I'll email you tonight.

本屋をしています。 ***Honya o shite** imasu.* **I run a bookstore.**

2. States (... *o suru*)

いい時計をしていますね。 ***Ii tokei o shite imasu** ne.*
You are wearing a very nice watch.

去年，病気をしたんです。 *Kyonen **byōki o shita** n desu.*
I was sick last year.

あの車は変わった形をしていますね。
*Ano kuruma wa kawatta **katachi o shite imasu** ne.*
That car has a unique shape, doesn't it?

多くの日本人は黒い髪の毛をしています。
*Ōku no Nihonjin wa kuroi **kaminoke o shite imasu**.*
Many Japanese have black hair.

私は出版社の社員をしています。
*Watashi wa shuppansha no **shain o shite imasu**.*
I am a publishing company employee.

II. SENSUAL QUALITY (... *GA SURU*)

このお茶はとてもいい匂いがします。
*Kono ocha wa totemo **ii nioi ga shimasu**.*
This tea has a very good smell. (This tea smells very good.)

このナイロンの鞄は柔らかい感じがします。
*Kono nairon no kaban wa **yawarakai kanji ga shimasu**.*
This nylon bag has a soft feeling. (This nylon bag feels soft.)

変な音がしませんでしたか。 ***Hen na oto ga shimasen** deshita ka.*
Didn't you hear a strange noise?

この花は甘い香りがする。 *Kono hana wa **amai kaori ga suru***.
This flower smells sweet.

たばこの煙の臭いがする。 ***Tabako no kemuri no nioi ga suru***.
I smell cigarette smoke.

III. CHANGES AND EFFORTS TO MAKE CHANGES

1. Change (*. . . o . . . ni suru*)

   彼は彼女を幸せにするでしょう。
   *Kare wa **kanojo o shiawase ni suru** deshō.*
   He will make her happy.

   あなたのお父さんはあなたを弁護士にするつもりですか。
   *Anata no otōsan wa **anata o bengoshi ni suru** tsumori desu ka.*
   Does your father intend to make you enter the law?

   私は父からもらった形見を大切にしています。
   *Watashi wa chichi kara moratta **katami o taisetsu ni shite imasu**.*
   I treasure the memento I received from my father.

2. Change (*. . . o . . . ku suru*)

   もっとスープを甘くした方がいいです。
   *Motto **sūpu o amaku shita** hō ga ii desu.*
   It's better to make the soup sweeter.

3. Change (*. . . ni suru, . . . ku suru*)

   If there is no direct object, the item that undergoes the change is understood as the subject of the sentence.

   静かにしてください。 ***Shizuka ni shite** kuradai.* Please be quiet.

   もう少しまじめにします。 *Mō sukoshi **majime ni shimasu**.*
   I'll be more serious.

   もう少し彼女に優しくしてあげなさい。
   *Mō sukoshi kanojo ni **yasashiku shite** agenasai.*
   Please treat her a little more kindly.

4. Effort to make changes (*. . . yō ni suru*)

   早く起きるようにします。 *Hayaku okiru **yō ni shimasu**.*
   I'll try to wake up earlier.

   宿題を忘れないようにします。 *Shukudai o wasurenai **yō ni shimasu**.*
   I'll try not to forget my homework.

   → See *yō ni suru*.

5. Attempt (*. . . (y)ō to suru*)

   あの男は人を殺そうとしたんだ。
   *Ano otoko wa hito o **korosō to shita** n desu.*
   That guy tried to kill a person.

ダイエットをして体重を減らそうとしたけれどだめでした。
*Daietto o shite taijū o **herasō to shita** keredo dame deshita.*
I tried to diet and to lose weight but I couldn't.

→ See Volitional form under Verbs.

IV. DECISION

1. Choice (. . . ***ni suru***)

ガソリン車じゃなくて電気自動車にします。
*Gasorinsha ja nakute **denki jidōsha ni shimasu**.*
I'll take an electric automobile, not a gas-powered one.

2. Decision (. . . ***koto ni suru***)

(*Koto ni* adds the meaning "decide" or "pretend" [to do].)

転職することにしました。 *Tenshoku suru **koto ni shimashita**.*
I decided to change my occupation.

大学院に行かないことにしました。 *Daigakuin ni ikanai **koto ni shimashita**.*
I decided not to go to graduate school.

3. Pretending (. . . ***ta koto ni suru***)

そのことは聞かなかったことにします。
*Sono koto wa kikanakatta **koto ni shimasu**.*
I'll pretend that I didn't hear that.

V. COST/PERIOD OF TIME

1. Cost (. . . ***suru***)

この電子辞書は３万円しました。
*Kono denshi jisho wa **san man en shimashita**.*
This electronic dictionary cost thirty thousand yen.

2. Period of time (. . . ***sureba/shitara***)

二、三日すれば梅雨が明けます。 ***Ni san nichi sureba** tsuyu ga akemasu.*
The rainy season will be over in two or three days.

あと十分したら終わります。 *Ato **jippun shitara** owarimasu.*
It will be over in ten more minutes.

→ See *ba* and *tara*.

VI. *SURU*-VERBS

1. Sino-Japanese compounds + ***suru***
街を案内します。 *Machi o **annai shimasu**.*   I'll show you around the city.

ここに名前と住所を記入して下さい。
*Koko ni namae to jūsho o **kinyū shite** kudasai.*
Please fill in your name and address here.

階段からころげて膝を怪我しました。
*Kaidan kara korogete hiza o **kega shimashita**.*
I fell down the stairs and hurt my knee.

今晩電話して下さい。 *Konban **denwa shite** kudasai.*
Please call me this evening.

バンを運転できますか。 *Ban o **unten dekimasu** ka.* **Can you drive a van?**

→ See *dekiru*.

2. Sino-Japanese morphemes + *suru*

自然を愛しています。 *Shizen o **ai-shite imasu**.* **I love nature.**

3. Foreign loans + *suru*

やっとエンジンがスタートしましたが，またストップしました。
*Yatto enjin ga **sutāto shimashita** ga, mata **sutoppu shimashita**.*
At last the engine started, but it stopped again.

4. After mimetic expressions + *suru*

緊張してどきどきします。 *Kinchō shite **dokidoki shimasu**.*
I get nervous and my heart pounds.

5. After certain adverbs + *suru*

ホテルでゆっくりしました。 *Hoteru de **yukkuri shimashita**.*
I relaxed at the hotel.

---

ta た [VERB/ADJECTIVE SUFFIX]

past action or state, completion of action or movement, lasting state as the result of an action or movement, experience at some undefined time

The verb suffix *ta* is used for verbs, adjectives, and *da* (linking verb) to express past/completed actions and states. The *ta*-form of a verb can be created by changing the vowel *e* at the end of its *te*-form to the vowel *a*. (→ See Verbs.) The *ta*-form of an adjective can be created by changing the vowel *i* at the end of its dictionary form to *katta*. (→ See Adjectives.) The *ta*-form of *da* is *datta*. (→ See Linking verbs *da/desu*.) *Ta* can also be used with negative forms and polite forms, as in *nakatta*, *mashita*, and *deshita*. (→ See Verbs, Adjectives, Linking verbs *da/desu*.)

I. USED FOR VERBS

The *ta*-form of verbs expresses past actions or events, completion of an action or movement, a lasting state as the result of an action, or movement and experiences at some undefined time.

1. Past actions

   「君も行った。」「うん，行った。」
   "Kimi mo itta." (with rising intonation) *"Un, itta."*
   "Did you go, too?" "Yes, I did."

   (*"Kimi mo itta ka."* would be rude.)

   先月はボストンに行ったんです。 *Sengetsu wa Bosuton ni itta n desu.*
   Last month I went to Boston.

   最近私はタバコをやめた。 *Saikin watashi wa tabako o yameta.*
   I stopped smoking recently.

   ドアの鍵が壊れた。 *Doa no kagi ga kowareta.*
   The lock on the door broke.

   夕べ遅くまで宿題をしました。食事はしませんでした。
   Yūbe osoku made shukudai o shimashita. Shokuji wa shimasen deshita.
   I did my homework till late last night. I did not eat.

2. Completed actions (not necessarily in the past)

   彼はもう帰ったよ。 *Kare wa mō kaetta yo.*
   He has gone home, I tell you.

   仕事はもう終わった。 *Shigoto wa mō owatta.* (completed action)
   The work is finished.

   この本は三回読んだ。 *Kono hon wa san kai yonda.*
   I've read this book three times. (experience at some undefined time)

   使ったものはすぐ片付けた方がいいですよ。
   Tsukatta mono wa sugu katazuketa hō ga ii desu yo.
   It is better to put away the things you have used right away.

   今晩仕事が終わった時に電話します。
   Konban shigoto ga owatta toki ni denwa shimasu. (a future event)
   When I have finished my work, I'll call you tonight.

   花子さんが作った料理はおいしいですよ。今作っています。
   Hanako san ga tsukatta ryōri wa oishii desu yo. Ima tsukutte imasu.
   The dishes Hanako is preparing are delicious. She is cooking now.

3. Noun modifer

   The verbs in the *ta*-form can be used as a noun modifier, expressing some continuing state.

   太郎さんは変わった人ですね。 *Tarō san wa kawatta hito desu ne.*
   Taro is a strange person, isn't he?

   困った事になりました。 *Komatta koto ni narimashita.*
   We now have a problem.

   間違った回答は直して下さい。 *Machigatta kaitō wa naoshite kudasai.*
   Please correct the wrong answers.

尖ったものは学校に持って来ないでください。
Togatta mono wa gakkō ni motte konai de kudasai.
Please do not bring sharp and pointed items to school.

誤ったことはしないように。 *Ayamatta koto wa shinai yō ni.*
Make sure not to do a wrong thing.

II. USED FOR ADJECTIVES

1. Past state

   このバッグは高くなかった。 *Kono baggu wa takaku nakatta.*
   This bag was not expensive.

   私はもっとゆっくりしたかったです。
   Watashi wa motto yukkuri shitakatta desu.
   I wanted to stay longer.

   彼女はコンサートは良くなかったと言っていました。
   Kanojo wa konsāto wa yoku nakatta to itte imashita.
   She said the concert was not good.

   彼にそれの何が良かったのか聞かなかった。
   Kare ni sore no nani ga yokatta no ka kikanakatta.
   I didn't ask him what was good about it.

   「自動車免許の試験はやさしかったですか。」「やさしくなかったです。」
   "Jidōsha menkyo no shiken wa yasashikatta desu ka." "Yasashiku nakatta desu."
   "Was the test for (your) driver's license easy?" "It wasn't."

   昨日見た3D映画はとてもすごかった。
   Kinō mita surī dī eiga wa totemo sugokatta.
   The 3D movie that I saw yesterday was really amazing. (past state)

2. A state just noticed

   締め切りに間に合ってよかった。 *Shimekiri ni maniatte yokatta.*
   I'm relieved to have met the deadline.

   ああ、おもしろかった。 *Ahh, omoshirokatta.* **Oh, that was funny.**

3. A continuing state

   日本語は私にはとても覚えにくかったです。
   Nihongo wa watashi ni wa totemo oboenikukatta desu.
   Japanese has been very difficult for me to learn.

4. Noun modifier

   楽しかった思い出は決して忘れません。
   Tanoshikatta omoide wa kesshite wasuremasen.
   I will never forget the pleasant memories.

5. Followed by *deshō/kamoshirenai*

この問題は彼らにはむずかしかったかもしれません。
Kono mondai wa karera ni wa muzukashikatta kamoshiremasen.
This problem might have been difficult for them.

III. USED FOR *DA* (LINKING VERB)

店員は中国人だった。日本人じゃなかった。
Ten'in wa chūgokujin datta. Nihonjin ja nakatta.
The store clerk was Chinese. He was not Japanese.

日本人じゃありませんでした。(日本人じゃなかったです。)
Nihonjin ja arimasen deshita. (Nihonjin ja nakatta desu.)
He was not Japanese.

---

tabi ni 度に [ADVERBIAL PHRASE]

every time, each time, whenever

Tabi is a noun that means 'time' or 'occasion,' but it cannot be used by itself. It follows a verb in the dictionary form and is used as a time expression along with the particle *ni*.

彼は会う度に仕事の不満を言う。
Kare wa au tabi ni shigoto no fuman o iu.
Every time he meets me, he complains about his job.

テレビショッピング番組を見る度に新しい物を買ってしまします。
Terebi shoppingu bangumi o miru tabi ni atarashii mono o katte shimaimasu.
Each time I see a television-shopping program, I end up buying another new thing.

---

tai たい [VERB SUFFIX]

want to, would like to, feel like (doing), wish to, hope to

Tai follows verbs in the combining form and creates an adjectival phrase that means 'to want to do. . . .' Like other adjectives that show psychological states, the adjectival phrase with *tai* is used only when the subject of the statement is the first person. It can be used when the subject is the second person if it is a question. However, it may not be used when the subject is the third person. The idea is that one should not be able to know someone else's mental state. For expressing the desire of the third person, use the suffix *garu* after *tai*, as in *tabetagaru* or *tabetagatte iru*, or use *sō da* as in *tabetasō da*. (→ See *garu* and *sō da* <conjecture>.) As the addition of *tai* makes a verb into an adjectival phrase, the understood object can be marked either by *ga* or by *o*. (→ See *ga* and *o*.) For expressing the speaker's wanting someone to do something, use *hoshii*. (→ See *hoshii*.)

少し休みたいです。 *Sukoshi **yasumitai** desu.* I'd like to rest for a while.

冷たい水 が／を 飲みたい。 *Tsumetai mizu ga/o **nomitai**.*
I feel like drinking cold water.

日曜日は働きたくありません。
*Nichiyōbi wa **hatarakitaku arimasen**. (ku-form + arimasen)*
I don't want to work on Sundays.

またいつかいっしょにお話をしたいですね。
*Mata itsuka isshoni ohanashi o **shitai** desu ne.*
I hope to talk with you again some day.

いつか日本語をマスターしたい。 *Itsuka Nihongo o masutā **shitai**.*
I hope to master Japanese some day.

歌舞伎を見たくありませんか。 *Kabuki o **mitaku arimasen** ka.*
Wouldn't you like to see a Kabuki performance?

ポールはイギリスに帰りたいと言ってます。
*Pōru wa Igirisu ni **kaeritai** to ittemasu.*
Paul says that he wants to go back to England.

花子さんは実は参加したくなかったらしい。
*Hanako san wa jitsu wa sanka **shitaku nakatta** rashii.*
I heard that Hanako didn't want to attend it in reality.

tame ni ために [ADVERBIAL PHRASE]

for, for . . .'s sake, because of, on account of, owing to, as a result of, in order to,
so as to, for the purpose of

Tame ni follows nouns and clauses and creates an adverbial phrase that shows
the purpose, the cause, the reason, or the benefit of the action or state. (→ See
also *kara* and *node*.) The predicate in the clause must be in the form used when
following a noun. (→ See also *ni*.)

1. After nouns followed by **no**

    それはあなたのためになるでしょう。 *Sore wa **anata no tame ni** naru deshō.*
    It will be good for you.

    何のためにそれをするんですか。 ***Nan no tame ni** sore o suru n desu ka.*
    For what purpose do you do that? (Why do you do that?)

    飛行機は台風のために欠航しています。
    *Hikōki wa **taifū no tame ni** kekkō shite imasu.*
    The air service is being canceled because of a typhoon.

    戦争のためにたくさん難民が出た。
    ***Sensō no tame ni** takusan nanmin ga deta.*
    There were many refugees as a result of the war.

祖父は癌のために亡くなりました。
*Sofu wa **gan no tame ni** nakunarimashita.*
My grandfather died of cancer.

(*De* may replace *tame ni* when expressing a cause.)

大学進学のために貯金をしなければなりません。
***Daigaku shingaku no tame ni** chokin o shinakereba narimasen.*
I have to save money for going on to college.

将来のためにもっと勉強したいと思います。
***Shōrai no tame ni** motto benkyō shitai to omoimasu.*
For the sake of my future, I think I'll study more.

2. After the demonstrative adjectives **kono, sono**, or **ano**

私たちはそのために協力しているんです。
*Watashi tachi wa **sono tame ni** kyōryoku shite iru n desu.*
That is why we are cooperating.

3. After adjectival nouns followed by **na, datta, ja nai,** or **ja nakatta**

母は身体が不自由なために苦労している。
*Haha wa **shintai ga fujiyū na tame ni** kurō shite iru.*
My mother is suffering because she is handicapped.

彼は不真面目なために嫌われている。
*Kare wa **fumajime na tame ni** kirawarete iru.*
He is disliked because he is insincere.

彼女は不注意だったために事故を起こしたんです。
*Kanojo wa **fuchūi datta tame ni** jiko o okoshita n desu.*
She caused the accident because she was careless.

4. After verbs and adjectives in the dictionary form

私はお金を貯めるために副業をしています。
*Watashi wa okane o tame**ru tame ni** fukugyō o shite imasu.*
I work for a second job in order to save money.

給料が低いために，家が買えない。
*Kyūryō ga hiku**i tame ni**, ie ga kaenai.*
Because my salary is low, I cannot buy a house.

5. After verbs and adjectives in the **nai**-form

給料が高くないために，家が買えない。
*Kyūryō ga takaku**nai tame ni**, ie ga kaenai.*
Because my salary is not high, I cannot buy a house.

環境を破壊しないために何ができるだろうか。
*Kankyō o hakai shi**nai tame ni** nani ga dekiru darō ka.*
What can we do so as not to disrupt the environment?

失敗しないためには注意が必要です。
Shippai shinai tame ni wa chūi ga hitsuyō desu.
Caution is necessary so as not to make a mistake.

6. After verbs and adjectives in the *ta*-form (to express reason or cause)

彼が休んだために何もできません。
Kare ga yasunda tame ni nani mo dekimasen.
We can't do anything because he is absent.

彼は忙しかったために体調を崩しました。
Kare wa isogashikatta tame ni taichō o kuzushimashita.
He spoiled his health, because he was (too) busy.

tara たら [PARTICLE]

if, when, after (doing), if only, if you're talking about/looking for . . . , why don't you (do)?

The *tara*-form of verbs, adjectives, and the linking verb can be created just by adding *ra* at the end of their *ta*-form, as in *tabetara*, *takakattara*, and *shizuka dattara*. (→ See *ta*.) The *tara*-form is used to create a conditional clause that can provide generic, temporal, hypothetical, or counterfactual conditions. It is important to remember that the event/state expressed by the main clause must be assumed to "follow" the event/state expressed by the *tara*-clause. The adverb *moshi* 'if' can be used at the beginning of the *tara*-clause if it expresses hypothetical or counterfactual conditions. (→ See *moshi*.)

1. *Tara*-clauses with verbs

このボタンを押したら，切符がでます。
***Kono botan o oshitara**, kippu ga demasu.* (generic condition)
If you press this button, a ticket will come out.

駅に着いたら電話して下さい。
***Eki ni tsuitara** denwa shite kudasai.* (temporal condition)
When you have arrived at the (train) station, please call me.

もし大雨が降ったら山登りに行くのはやめます。
*Moshi **ōame ga futtara** yamanobori ni iku no wa yamemasu.* (hypothetical condition)
If it rains heavily, I'll give up going mountain-climbing.

もし鳥になれたら，あなたのところに飛んで行けるのにな。
*Moshi **tori ni naretara**, anata no tokoro ni tonde ikeru no ni na.* (counterfactual condition)
If I could be a bird, I would be able to fly to you.

その本を読んだら私に貸して下さい。
***Sono hon o yondara** watashi ni kashite kudasai.* (temporal condition)
After you have read the book, please lend it to me.

新宿で買い物をしたら帰ります。
Shinjuku de kaimono o shitara kaerimasu. (temporal condition)
After shopping in Shinjuku, I'll go back home.

2. *Tara*-clauses with adjectives

難しかったら，私に聞いてください。
Muzukashikattara, watashi ni kiite kudasai. (hypothetical condition)
If it is difficult, ask me.

おいしくなかったら，食べなくてもいいですよ。
Oishiku nakattara, tabenakutemo ii desu yo.
If not delicious (for you), you don't need to eat it.

よろしかったらうちに遊びに来て下さい。
Yoroshikattara uchi ni asobi ni kite kudasai.
If it is okay with you, please come to visit us at home.

バーゲンで安くなったらそれを買うつもりです。
Bāgen de yasuku nattara sore o kau tsumori desu.
If it becomes cheap at a sale, I'll buy it.

3. *Tara*-clauses with (adjectival) nouns

もし私があなただったらそんなことはしません。
Moshi *watashi ga anata dattara* sonna koto wa shimasen.
If I were you, I wouldn't do such a thing.

あしたいい天気だったらテニスをしませんか。
Ashita ii tenki dattara tenisu o shimasen ka.
If the weather is good tomorrow, would you like to play tennis (with me)?

山田さんだったら今入院しています。
Yamada san dattara ima nyūin shite imasu.
If you're looking for Mr. Yamada, he is hospitalized now.

4. Expressing wishes and suggestions using the *tara*-form

日本語がもっと簡単だったらなあ。
*Nihongo ga motto **kantan dattara** nā.*
If only Japanese were much simpler.

ちゃんと調べてもらったら。(with rising intonation)
*Chanto shirabete **morattara**.*
What about having it properly checked out?

5. *Tara*-clause used for expressing what happened in the past

駅に着いたらみんなが待ってくれていました。
Eki ni tsuitara minna ga matte kurete imashita.
When I arrived at the train station, all had been waiting for me.

(The speaker should not have control over the past action expressed in the main clause.)

朝起きたら床で寝ていました。 ***Asa okitara** yuka de nete imashita.*
When I woke up in the morning, I found myself lying on the floor.

(Past actions performed by the speaker unconsciously are naturally expressed after *tara*.)

→ See also *ba*, *nara*, *to*, and *to sureba*.

tari たり [PARTICLE]

(some kind of) action/state like . . . , actions performed in turn, sometimes . . . and . . .

The *tari*-form of verbs, adjectives, and the linking verb can be created just by adding *ri* at the end of their *ta*-form, as in *tabetari*, *takakattari*, and *shizuka dattari*. (→ See *ta*.) The *tari*-form is used to list actions and properties as partial examples. (→ See *ya* and *toka* for a similar way of listing nouns.) The list of predicates in the *tari*-form are followed by the verb *suru* 'to do' with an appropriate sentence ending or some particle. The items listed in the *tari*-form often contrast with each other.

1. Verbs in the ***tari***-form

   私は趣味で絵を描いたり俳句を作ったりします。
   *Watashi wa shumi de e o **kaitari** haiku o **tsukuttari** shimasu.*
   I paint, write haiku poems and do other things as pastime activities.

   今日は映画を見たり買い物をしたりで楽しかった。
   *Kyō wa eiga o **mitari** kaimono o **shitari** de tanoshikatta.*
   I had a good time seeing a movie and going shopping today.

   (*De* expresses reason.)

   → See *de*.

2. Verbs in the ***tari***-form with contrasting actions

   彼女は酔うとよく泣いたり笑ったりします。
   *Kanojo wa you to yoku **naitari warattari** shimasu.*
   She often cries and laughs in turn when drunk.

   今日は雨が降ったり止んだりするでしょう。
   *Kyō wa ame ga **futtari yandari** suru deshō.*
   It will rain on and off today.

   彼は手伝ってくれたりくれなかったりする。
   *Kare wa **tetsudatte kuretari kurenakattari** suru.*
   He sometimes helps me and sometimes not.

   (often contrasted by affirmative and negative forms of a verb)

3. Adjectives in the **tari**-form

その劇は楽しかったり悲しかったりします。
*Sono geki wa **tanoshikattari kanashikattari shimasu**.*
The play is sometimes happy and sometimes sad.

4. (Adjectival) nouns with linking verbs in the **tari**-form

彼は親切だったり薄情だったりする。
*Kare wa **shinsetsu dattari hakujō dattari suru**.*
He is sometimes kind and sometimes cold-hearted.

---

te て [PARTICLE]

. . . and . . .

Te is a particle added at the end of a verb or an adjective to create a *te*-form, used for conjoining multiple verbs and adjectives. It is realized as *de* depending on the ending sound of the verbs and adjectives. We can use the *te*-form of verbs and adjectives to list actions and properties in one sentence while non-emphatically showing their relationships, which can be sequential, procedural, causal, parallel, contrasting, or conditional. The *te*-form or the combining form of the linking verb *da* is equivalent to *de*. (→ See *Te*-form under Adjectives, Linking Verb *(Da/Desu)*, and Verbs.)

I. VERBS IN THE *TE*-FORM

The verbs in the *te*-form can be used to list verbs in a sentence in order to specify actions in succession, a procedure, a reason or cause, an action simultaneous with main action, and a contrastive action. They can also be followed by auxiliary verbs (e.g. *oku*), auxiliary adjectives (e.g. *hoshii*), and particles (e.g. *wa* and *bakari*).

1. Actions in succession

ここで食べて帰ります。 *Koko de **tabete kaerimasu**.*
I'll eat here and go home.

2. Procedure

私は毎日自転車に乗って駅まで行きます。
*Watashi wa mainichi **jitensha ni notte** eki made ikimasu.*
I ride a bicycle and go to the train station every day. (go by bicycle)

3. Cause/reason

試験が終わってほっとした。 *Shiken ga **owatte** hotto shita.*
The examination is over and I'm relieved.

会えてうれしいです。 ***Aete** ureshii desu.* **I'm glad to meet you.**

遅くまで起きていて疲れました。 ***Osoku made okite ite*** *tsukaremashita.*
I sat up till late and got tired.

4. Simultaneous

私はいつも音楽を聴いて日本語を勉強します。
*Watashi wa itsumo **ongaku o kiite** Nihongo o benkyō shimasu.*
I always study Japanese while listening to music.

海外にはスーツケースを持って行きません。
*Kaigai ni wa **sūtsu kēsu o motte** ikimasen.*
I go abroad without a suitcase. (I don't go abroad with a suitcase.)

5. Conditional

外国と比べて日本は地震と台風が多い。
***Gaikoku to kurabete** Nihon wa jishin to taifū ga ōi.*
Compared with foreign countries, earthquakes and typhoons are frequent in Japan.

6. Contrast

その人は私を助けてくれて名前も言わなかった。
*Sono hito wa watashi o **tasukete kurete** namae mo iwanakatta.*
That person helped me but didn't even tell me his name.

妻はご飯を作って私は片付けます。
*Tsuma wa gohan o **tsukutte** watashi wa katazukemasu.*
My wife prepares the meal, and I clean up.

7. Followed by auxiliary verbs/adjectives

明日はお客さんが来るので、ビールを買っておきます。
*Ashita wa okyakusan ga kuru node, bīru o **katte okimasu.***
We will have some guests tomorrow, so I will buy beer in advance.

私は兄に泳げるようになってほしいです。
*Watashi wa ani ni oyogeru yō ni **natte hoshii** desu.*
I want my brother to become able to swim.

今晩うちに来てください。 *Konban uchi ni **kite kudasai.***
Please come to our house tonight.

→ See *oku*, *hoshii*, and *kudasai*.

8. Followed by particles

なまけものは枝にぶら下がって寝てばかりいます。
*Namakemono wa eda ni burasagatte **nete bakari** imasu.*
A sloth hangs from a branch and does nothing but sleep.

ここでタバコをすってはいけません。
*Koko de tabako o **sutte wa** ikemasen.*
You are not allowed to smoke here.

→ See *bakari*, *wa*, and *tewa ikenai /dewa ikenai*.

II. ADJECTIVES IN THE *TE*-FORM

彼女はとても優しくてきれいです。(list of properties)
*Kanojo wa totemo **yasashikute** kirei desu.*
She is very kind and pretty.

寒くてたまりません。(cause)
***Samukute** tamarimasen.*
It is so cold that I can't stand it.

今日は暑くなくてよかったですね。(cause)
*Kyō wa **atsuku nakute** yokatta desu ne.*
Fortunately, today was not hot, was it?

新幹線ののぞみは速くてこだまは遅いです。(contrasting)
*Shinkansen no Nozomi wa **hayakute** Kodama wa osoi desu.*
The *Nozomi* Shinkansen is fast and the *Kodama* is slow.

III. *DA* (LINKING VERB) IN THE *TE*-FORM

彼女は日本人で，まだ独身です。(parallel)
*Kanojo wa Nihonjin **de**, mada dokushin desu.*
She is Japanese and is still single.

彼女は病気で動けません。(causal)
*Kanojo wa byōki **de** ugokemasen.*
She is sick and cannot move.

---

te ageru てあげる → See ***ageru*** [AUXILIARY VERB].

---

te aru てある → See ***aru*** [AUXILIARY VERB].

---

te hoshii てほしい → See ***hoshii*** [AUXILIARY ADJECTIVE].

---

te iku ていく → See ***iku***.

---

te iru ている → See ***iru*** [AUXILIARY VERB].

---

te kara てから → See ***kara***.

---

teki 的 [NOUN SUFFIX]

-tic, -tical. -cal, etc.

Teki is a suffix that follows a variety of nouns and makes them into adjectival nouns.

1. Followed by ***da/desu***, forming a sentence predicate
   会の雰囲気は家庭的です。 *Kai no fun'iki wa **kateiteki** desu.*
   The atmosphere of the meeting is homey.

彼の態度はいつも「関係ないよ」的だ。
*Kare no taido wa itsumo "**Kankei nai yo**" teki da.*
His attitude is always such that he appears to be saying, "It has nothing to do with me."

(As of recently, *teki* has started to be placed at the end of a sentence to express a typical property of the given item referred to.)

2. Optionally followed by *na*, modifying nouns

それはとても現実的な計画です。
*Sore wa totemo **genjitsuteki na keikaku** desu.*
That is a very realistic plan.

それはアメリカ人的な考えですね。
*Sore wa **Amerikajinteki na kangae** desu ne.*
It's an idea that Americans may hold, isn't it?

そこまでやるのは自殺的行為だ。
*So ko made yaru no wa **jisatsuteki kōi** da.*
It's a suicidal act to go that far.

彼は芸術家的な人ですね。 *Kare wa **geijutsukateki na hito** desu ne.*
He is an artist-like person, isn't he?

3. Followed by *ni*, modifying verbs and adjectives

経済的に国が豊かでも一人一人は苦しい。
***Keizaiteki ni** kuni ga **yutaka** demo hitori hitori wa kurushii.*
Even though the country is economically rich, each individual is badly off.

---

te kuru てくる → See **kuru**.

---

te masu てます → See **iru** [AUXILIARY VERB].

---

te miru てみる → See **miru**.

---

temo/demo ても/でも [PARTICLE]

even if, though, no matter

Verbs, adjectives, and *da* (a linking verb) in the *te*-form can be followed by *mo* to create a concessive clause, meaning 'even if . . .' or 'even though. . . .' If the clause contains an interrogative word such as *dare*, it means something like 'no matter. . . .' (→ See also *demo* <particle> and *to shitemo*.)

1. With verbs in the *te*-form

うまくいっても油断しないようにして下さい。
*Umaku **ittemo** yudan shinai yō ni shite kudasai.*
Even if it goes well, please try not to be inattentive.

そのことについて聞いても彼女は答えませんでした。
*Sono koto ni tsuite **kiitemo** kanojo wa kotaemasen deshita.*
Though I asked her about that matter, she didn't answer.

雨が降っても嵐が吹いてもあなたに会いに行きます。
*Ame ga **futtemo** arashi ga **fuitemo** anata ni aini ikimasu.*
Even if it rains and the storm rages, I'm going out to see you.

何をしても面白くありません。 *Nani o **shitemo** omoshiroku arimasen.*
No matter what I do, I don't find it interesting.

いつ行っても彼は留守です。 *Itsu **ittemo** kare wa rusu desu.*
No matter when I visit him, he is always away.

どんなに速く走ってもバスに間に合いません。
***Donna ni** hayaku **hashittemo** basu ni maniaimasen.*
No matter how fast we may run, we won't be able to catch the bus.

いくら言っても子供は言うことを聞きません。
*Ikura **ittemo** kodomo wa iu koto o kikimasen.*
No matter how often I say it, the child doesn't listen (to what I say).

2. With adjectives in the *te*-form

どんなに高くてもあれが欲しい。
***Donna ni takakutemo** are ga hoshii.*
No matter how expensive that is, I want it.

たとえそこへ行きたくなくても行かなければなりません。
*Tatoe soko e ikitaku **nakutemo** ikanakereba narimasen.*
Even if you don't want to go there, you have to.

3. With adjectival nouns

いくら嫌でもそれを実行しなければならない。
*Ikura **iya demo** sore o jikkō shinakereba naranai.*
No matter how much you dislike it, you have to carry it out.

---

temo ii / demo ii てもいい ／ でもいい [PREDICATIVE PHRASE]

may, can, it is all right (even) if . . . , (not) have to (do), do without. . . , (not) feel like (doing)

Verbs, adjectives, and *da* (a linking verb) in the *te*-form can be followed by *mo ii*, as in . . . *temo ii* or . . . *demo ii*, expressing permission to conduct some action or adequacy of some state or condition. *Mo* is sometimes dropped. *Ii desu* may be replaced by *yoroshii desu*, *kekkō desu* or *kamaimasen*. (→ See *yoroshii*, *kekkō*, and *kamawanai*.) *Demo ii* often follows interrogative words, as in *Nan demo ii* 'Anything is fine.' (→ See *demo*.) When such *te*-forms are negative, as in . . . *nakute mo ii*, it expresses discretion. (→ See also *nakutemo ii*.)

1. With verbs in the **te**-form

このコピー機は自由に使ってもいいです。（使ってもけっこうです）
*Kono kopī ki wa jiyū ni **tsukattemo ii** desu. (**tsukattemo kekkō** desu)*
You can use this copying machine freely.

「入っていいですか。」「ええ，もちろん。」
*"**Haitte ii** desu ka." "Ē, mochiron."*
"May I come in?" "Yes, of course."

「もう帰ってもよろしいですか。」「いえ，いけません。」
*"Mō **kaettemo yoroshii** desu ka." "Ie, ikemasen."*
"May I leave now?" "No, you may not."

2. With (auxiliary) adjectives in the **te**-form

車は動けばいくら古くてもいいです。
*Kuruma wa ugokeba ikura furuku**temo ii** desu.*
If the car moves, it is all right no matter how old it is.

顔はよくなくてもいいです。心が大事です。
*Kao wa yokunaku**temo ii** desu. Kokoro ga daiji desu.*
It's all right even if one's face is not pretty. One's heart is important.

この本は来週までに返さなくてもいいですか。
*Kono hon wa raishū made ni kaesanaku**temo ii** desu ka.*
Is it okay not to return this book by next week?

そんなに急がなくてもいいですよ。待ちます。
*Sonna ni isoganaku**temo ii** desu yo. Machimasu.*
You don't have to hurry so much. I'll wait.

私は泳がなくてもいいです。見てます。
*Watashi wa oyoganaku**temo ii** desu. Mitemasu.*
I don't feel like swimming. I'll just watch.

マニュアルはなくてもいいです。 *Manyuaru wa naku**temo ii** desu.*
It's all right even if there isn't a manual. (I can do without a manual.)

3. With (adjectival) nouns + **da** in the **te**-form

アパートは安ければ不便でもいいです。
*Apāto wa yasukereba **fuben demo ii** desu.*
If the apartment rent is cheap, I don't mind even if it's inconvenient.

簡単でもいいですから書いて下さい。
***Kantan demo ii** desu kara kaite kudasai.*
Even something simple will be fine, so please write it.

新しい本じゃなくてもいいです。 *Atarashii hon ja naku**te mo ii** desu.*
It is fine even if it is not a new book.

---

te oku ておく → See **oku**.

te shimau てしまう → See **shimau**.

---

tewa ikenai /dewa ikenai てはいけない/ではいけない [PREDICATIVE PHRASE]

may, can, it is all right (even) if . . . , (not) have to (do), do without. . . , (not) feel like (doing)

Verbs, adjectives, and *da* (a linking verb) in the *te*-form can be followed by *wa ikenai*, as in . . . *tewa ikenai* or . . . *dewa ikenai*, expressing prohibition to conduct some action or unacceptability of some state or condition. (→ See *ikenai*.) When such *te*-forms are negative, as in . . . *nakute wa ikenai*, it expresses obligation. In the latter case, *ikenai* is often replaced by *naranai* to give the impression that the obligation is something inevitable rather than something imposed by the speaker. (→ See also *na* and *nakereba ikenai / nakereba naranai*.)

1. With verbs in the *te*-form

   公共施設内ではタバコをすってはいけません。
   Kōkyō shisetsu nai de wa tabako o sutte wa ikemasen.
   You are not allowed to smoke in public facilities.

   野菜をたくさん食べなくてはいけません。
   Yasai o takusan tabenakute wa ikemasen.
   You need to eat a lot of vegetables.

2. With adjectives in the *te*-form

   コレステロールは高くてはいけません。
   Koresuterōru wa takakute wa ikemasen.
   Cholesterol should not be high.

   鞄は持ちやすくなくてはいけません。
   Kaban wa mochiyasukunakute wa ikemasen.
   Bags should be easy to hold.

   面白いものじゃなくてはいけません。
   Omoshiroi mono ja nakute wa ikemasen.
   It has to be something interesting.

3. With (adjectival) nouns + *da* in the *te*-form

   妻には安いプレゼントではいけません。
   Tsuma ni wa yasui purezento de wa ikemasen.
   Cheap presents would not be acceptable to my wife.

---

to と [PARTICLE]

and, or, with (accompanied by), when(ever), once . . . , if, no matter, that

The particle *to* is used after nouns and after clauses.

1. After nouns to list items

   The particle *to* follows every noun listed within the same sentence, but *to* is often omitted, right after the last noun.

→ See also *ya*.

ついでに充電池と充電器を下さい。
*Tsuide ni **jūdenchi to jūdenki** o kudasai.*
While I'm here, I'll take rechargeable batteries and a battery charger.

水曜日と土曜日と日曜日（と）が私の休みです。
***Suiyōbi to Doyōbi to Nichiyōbi (to)** ga watashi no yasumi desu.*
Wednesday, Saturday, and Sunday are my holidays.

ジュースとアイスクリームのどっちにしますか。
***Jūsu to aisu kurīmu** no dotchi ni shimasu ka.*
Which would you like, juice or ice cream?

(For listing the choices for a comparative question, *to* follows every noun.)

うどんと，そばと，どちらが好きですか。
*Udon **to**, soba **to**, dochira ga suki desu ka.*
Between udon noodles and soba noodles, which one do you like better?

2. After nouns to specify accompaniments and collaborators

私は彼女と映画を見てきました。
*Watashi wa **kanojo to** eiga o mite kimashita.*
I went to see a movie with my girlfriend. (*Kanojo* also means a girlfriend.)

妹は犬と公園へ行きました。 *Imōto wa **inu to** kōen e ikimashita.*
My little sister went to the park with our dog.

「今だれと話していたんですか。」「彼氏のマイクとです。」
*"Ima **dare to** hanashite ita n desu ka." "Kareshi no **Maiku to** desu."*
"Who were you talking with just now?" "With my boyfriend, Mike."

彼女はだれと結婚するんですか。
*Kanojo wa **dare to** kekkon suru n desu ka.*
Who is she going to marry?

If the action is done unidirectionally, use *to* instead of *ni*. (→ See *ni*.)

駅で太郎さんと会います。 *Eki de **Tarō san to** aimasu.*
I'll see Taro at the station (by appointment). (Taro also comes to the station.)

太郎さんに会いに行きます。 ***Tarō san ni** ai ni ikimasu.*
I'll go to see Taro. (Taro is waiting for me somewhere.)

私の車が，山田さんの車とぶつかりました。
*Watashi no kuruma ga, Yamada san no kuruma **to** butsukarimashita.*
My car collided with Ms. Yamda's car.

私の車が山田さんの車にぶつかりました。
*Watashi no kuruma ga Yamada san no kuruma **ni** butsukarimashita.*
My car crashed into Ms. Yamada's car.

In the following sentence, *to* cannot be used.

歩いていてガラスの戸にぶつかりました。
*Aruite ite garasu no to **ni** butsukarimashita.*
I walked into a glass door.

3. After nouns, for evaluating similarities and differences

あなたの電波時計は私が持っているのと同じです。
*Anata no denpa dokei wa **watashi ga motte iru no to** onaji desu.*
Your radio watch is the same as the one that I have.

この本はあの本と似ているね。 *Kono hon wa ano hon **to** nite iru ne.*
This book is similar to that book, isn't it?

この品物は私が注文したのと違います。
*Kono shinamono wa watashi ga chūmon shita no **to** chigaimasu.*
This item is not the one I ordered.

(*No* right before the particle *to* in the above sentence serves as a pronoun.)

4. After adverbs

The particle *to* optionally follow some adverbs.

富士山をゆっくり（と）登りました。
*Fujisan o **Yukkuri (to)** noborimashita.*
I walked up the trail of Mt. Fuji slowly.

変な人がきょろきょろ（と）こっちを見ている。
*Hen na hito ga **kyorokyhoro (to)** kotchi o mite iru.*
A suspicious stranger is staring in our direction.

→ See Adverbs.

5. After clauses, marking a quotation clause

The particle *to* marks the quotation clause of verbs such as *omou* 'think,' *iu* 'say,' and *kaku* 'write.' The predicate in these clauses is usually in the dictionary form, *nai*-form, or *ta*-form but can also be in the plain command form. *Da* may occasionally be dropped right before the particle *to*. (→ See also *to omou*.)

夜行バスはもうすぐ着くと思います。
Yakō basu wa mō sugu tsuku to omoimasu.
I think the night bus will arrive soon.

これはいったい何だと思いますか。
Kore wa ittai nan da to omoimasu ka.
What do you think this actually is?

みんな禁煙をいいと思っています。 *Minna **kin'en o ii to** omotte imasu.*
Everybody thinks no smoking is good.

彼は手術をしたくないと言っていました。
*Kare wa **shujutsu o shitaku nai to** itte imashita.*
He said that he didn't want to have surgery.

彼は来月日本に行くと書いてきました。
*Kare wa **raigetsu Nihon ni iku to** kaite kimashita.*
He wrote to me that he is coming to Japan next month.

彼女は「いつでも遊びに来て下さい。」と言っていましたよ。
*Kanojo wa **"Itsu demo asobi ni kite kudasai." to** itte imashita yo.*
She said, "Please come and see me any time."

父はいつも勉強しろと言います。
*Chichi wa itsumo **benkyō shiro to** iimasu.*
My father always tells me to study.

店は10時から19時までと書いてあります。
*Mise wa jū ji kara jū ku ji **made to** kaite arimasu.*
It is written that the shop is open from ten to nineteen o'clock.

6. After clauses, forming conditional clauses

To can follow verbs, adjectives, and the linking verb in the dictionary form, in the *nai*-form, or in the polite non-past form (-*masu*, -*masen*, and *desu*) and create a conditional clause to express some situation where one event is always followed by another event (generic condition). In this case, the main clause must express something that always happens, and may not express the speaker's volitional action, requests, suggestions, permissions, commands, or desires.

彼はカラオケを歌い出すとなかなかやめない。
*Kare wa **karaoke o utaidasu to** nakanaka yamenai.*
Once he starts singing karaoke, he doesn't readily stop.

あの角を右に曲がるとバス停があります。
*Ano kado **o migi ni magaru to** basu tei ga arimasu.*
If you turn to the right at that corner, there's a bus stop.

勉強しないと，成績がおちるよ。 ***Benkyō shinai to**, seiseki ga ochiru yo.*
If you don't study, your grades will go down.

私は本屋に行くとよく立ち読みをしていた。
*Watashi wa **hon'ya ni iku to** yoku tachiyomi o shite ita.* (generic condition in the past)
I would often browse through books when I went to a bookstore.

それは高いとだれも買わないよ。もっと安くないとだめだよ。
*Sore wa **takai to** dare mo kawanai yo. **Motto yasuku nai to** dame da yo.*
No one buys it if it's expensive. It has to be cheaper.

昼になると，必ずお腹がすく。
Hiru ni naru to, kanarazu onaka ga suku.
I always get hungry at noon.

もし雨だと遠足は中止ですね。
*Moshi **ame da to** ensoku wa chūshi desu ne.*
If it rains, the field trip will be canceled, right?

そんなにほめられますと，恥ずかしい気がします。
***Sonnani homeraremasu to**, hazukashii ki ga shimasu.*
If I get praised that much, I feel bashful.

→ See also *sōsuruto*, *ba*, *tara*, *nara*, and Conditionals.

7. After clauses, creating a time adverbial clause

The time adverbial clause created by the particle *to* expresses some situation where one event was followed by another event. Importantly, the speaker should not have control over the second event, which is denoted by the main clause. The predicates before *to* must be in the dictionary form or *nai*-form, even if the event took place in the past.

夕べ飲み過ぎて今朝起きると頭痛がしました。
*Yūbe nomisugite **kesa okiru to** zutsū ga shimashita.*
When I got up this morning, I had a headache because I drank too much last night.

出かけるとすぐに雨が降り出した。
***Dekakeru to** sugu ni ame ga furidashita.*
As soon as I left home, it began to rain.

→ See also *sōsuruto*

8. After verbs in the volitional form

To follows a verb in the volitional form and creates a concessive clause with an interrogative word.

他人が何を言おうと私には関係ありません。
*Tanin ga **nani o iō to** watashi ni wa kankei arimasen.*
No matter what others may say, I have nothing to do with it.

→ See also *temo/demo*.

9. After adverbs

To can optionally follow certain adverbs including mimetic expressions.

もっとゆっくり（と）話してくれませんか。
*Motto **yukkuri (to)** hanashite kuremasen ka.*
Won't you speak more slowly?

酔っ払いがふらふら（と）歩いていますよ。
*Yopparai ga **furafura (to)** aruite imasu yo.*
A drunk is staggering around.

ガチャンと音がしました。 **Gachan to** oto ga shimashita.
It made a sound like "ga-chan." (= sound of "clunk")

10. After proper names

私は犬をポチと呼んでいます。 Watashi wa inu o **pochi to** yonde imasu.
I call my dog Pochi.

カーナビと呼ばれる機器が流行っています。
Kānabi to yobareru kiki ga hayatte imasu.
Equipment called car navigation systems are popular.

山田という人を知っていますか。 **Yamada to** iu hito o shitte imasu ka.
Do you know a person named Yamada?

→ See to iu.

11. Expressing judgments

裁判所は彼の行為を無罪とみなした。
Saibansho wa kare no kōi o **muzai to** minashita.
The court regarded his behavior as innocent.

私は町で最高だとされるホテルに泊まった。
Watashi wa **machi de saikō da to** sareru hoteru ni tomatta.
I stayed at a hotel reputed to be the best in town.

12. After a noun complement clause

ピアニストになりたいという（彼女の）希望がかなった。
Pianisuto ni naritai to iu (kanojo no) kibō ga kanatta.
Her wish to be a pianist was granted.

→ See to iu.

---

to iu という [ADJECTIVAL PHRASE]

called . . . , that (appositive), whether (appositive)

To iu consists of the quotation particle *to* and the verb *iu* 'to say.' (→ See *to* and *to ka*.) *To iu* is placed before a noun, and follows another noun or a clause, creating a noun complement clause that describes the identity or the content of the item denoted by the following noun. (→ See Noun complement clauses under Clauses.)

1. Providing the name of the given item

ザッパというギタリストが好きです。 **Zappa to iu gitarisuto** ga suki desu.
I like a guitarist called Zappa.

世界遺産の城は姫路という町にあります。
Sekai isan no shiro wa **Himeji to iu machi** ni arimasu.
A World Heritage Site castle is in the city of Himeji.

本田という人が会いに来ています。 ***Honda to iu hito*** *ga ai ni kite imasu.*
A Mr. Honda is here to see you.

2. Following a clause, identifying the content of a concept

彼女は彼が無事だという知らせを聞いて喜んだ。
*Kanojo wa **kare ga buji da to iu shirase** o kiite yorokonda.*
She was happy to hear the news that he was all right.

私たちが協力すべきかどうかという問題が検討された。
Watashi tachi ga kyōryoku subeki ka dōka to iu mondai *ga kentō sareta.*
The question whether we should cooperate was discussed.

首相になるという彼の野望は失敗に終わった。
Shushō ni naru to iu kare no yabō *wa shippai ni owatta.*
His ambition to become a prime minister ended in vain.

3. Following a clause, being placed before **koto** or **no**.

(*To iu* in the following sentences is optional.)

彼が離婚した（という）のは本当です。
Kare ga rikon shita (to iu) no *wa hontō desu.*
It is true that he has divorced.

彼女が入院している（という）ことを知っていますか。
Kanojo ga nyūin shite iru (to iu) koto *o shitte imasu ka.*
Do you know that she is in the hospital?

→ See also *koto* and *no*.

to ka とか [PARTICLE]

. . . and so on, etc.

The combination of two particles, *to* and *ka*, can be used after nouns or verbs in the dictionary form to list items and actions as examples. It is also used for quotation when the content is uncertain.

1. After nouns

私はトムとかマイクとよく親しい話をします。
*Watashi wa **Tomu to ka Maiku** to yoku shitashii hanashi o **shi**masu.*
I usually have intimate talks mainly with (people like) Tom and Mike.

私はロックとかジャズとか演歌をよく聴きます。
*Watashi wa **rokku to ka jazu to ka enka** o yoku kikimasu.*
I usually listen to (such music as) rock, jazz and *Enka*.

居酒屋とかよく行きますか。 *Izakaya **to ka** yoku ikimasu ka.*
Do you often go to places like *izakaya*?

→ See also *to* and *ya*.

2. After verbs in the dictionary form, followed by **suru**

一人の時はネットをするとかカメラをいじくるとかします。
*Hitori no toki wa netto o su**ru to ka** kamera o ijikuru **to ka shimasu.***
I am on the Net or tinker with my camera, etc., when I'm alone.

→ See *tari.*

3. After quoted uncertain statements and names

彼女は仕事を辞めるとか言っていました。
*Kanojo wa **shigoto o yameru to ka** itte imashita.*
She said something like she would quit her job.

花子とか言う女の人から電話ですよ。
***Hanako to ka** iu onna no hito kara denwa desu yo.*
There's a telephone call for you from a woman named something like Hanako.

→ See also *to* and *to iu.*

toki 時 [NOUN]

(at the time) when . . . , as . . . , while, whenever, in case of

Toki is a noun that means 'time' and can be used by itself. *Toki* can also be used to create a temporal adverbial clause that is structurally a noun, preceded by a relative clause that modifies it, optionally followed by the particle *ni*. (→ See Relative clauses under Clauses as well as *aida, ato, mae, tara, to, tsuide ni,* and *uchi ni.*)

1. Used by itself

父はよく「時は金なり」と言います。
*Chichi wa yoku '**Toki** wa kane nari' to iimasu.*
My father often says "Time is money."

2. After nouns followed by **no**

私は大学生の時に哲学を専攻していました。
*Watashi wa **daigakusei no toki ni** tetsugaku o senkō shite imashita.*
When I was a university student, I was majoring in philosophy.

火事の時にはこの赤いボタンを押して下さい。
***Kaji no toki ni** wa kono akai botan o oshite kudasai.*
Push this red button in case of fire.

緊急の時には電話を下さい。
***Kinkyū no toki ni** wa denwa o kudasai.*
Please call me in case of emergency.

3. After adjectival nouns followed by *na*

これは必要な時に自由に使って下さい。
*Kore wa **hitsuyō na toki ni** jiyū ni tsukatte kudasai.*
Please use this freely whenever you need it.

4. After (adjectival) nouns followed by ***datta, ja nai,*** or ***ja nakatta***

私が学生だった時には授業料は安かった。
***Watashi ga gakusei datta toki ni** wa jugyōryō wa yasukatta.*
When I was a student, the tuition was cheap.

5. After verbs and adjectives in the dictionary form

どこに行く時にも必ず携帯電話を持って行きます。
***Doko ni iku toki ni** mo kanarazu keitai denwa o motte ikimasu.*
When I go anywhere, I always carry my mobile phone.

家を出る時に小雨が降ってきました。
*Ie o deru **toki ni** kosame ga futte kimashita.*
It began to drizzle as I was leaving the house.

私は入浴している時によく読書をします。
*Watashi wa **nyūyoku shite iru toki ni** yoku dokusho o shimasu.*
I often read a book while taking a bath.

出かける時には戸締まりをしなさい。
***Dekakeru toki ni** wa tojimari o shinasai.*
When you go out, make sure to lock the doors.

今度そこへ行く時にはビデオカメラを持って行きましょう。
***Kondo soko e iku toki ni** wa bideo kamera o motte ikimashō.*
Let's take along a video camera the next time we go there.

暑い時はビールがうまい。
***Atsui toki** wa bīru ga umai.*
When it is hot, beer is tasty.

彼は私が悲しい時はいつも励ましてくれます。
*Kare wa **watashi ga kanashii toki** wa itsumo hagemashite kuremasu.*
He always cheers me up when I am sad.

6. After verbs and adjectives in the ***nai***-form

分からない時には，いつでも私に聞いてください。
***Wakaranai toki ni** wa, itsudemo watashi ni kiite kudasai.*
Whenever you don't understand something, please ask me.

7. After verbs and adjectives in the ***ta***-form

私が来た時には彼女はまだ来ていませんでした。
***Watashi ga kita toki ni** wa kanojo wa mada kite imasen deshita.*
When I came, she had not yet arrived.

困った時はいつでもお手伝いします。
Komatta toki wa itsu demo otetsudai shimasu.
I'll help you whenever you're in a bind.

食事をする時は「いただきます」,した時には「ごちそうさま」と言います。
Shokuji o suru toki wa "Itadakimasu," *shita toki ni* wa "Gochisō sama"to iimasu.
Before having a meal we say, "*Itadakimasu*," (and) after having it we say, "*Gochisō sama*."

tokoro ところ (所) [NOUN]

a place, a point in time

The noun *tokoro* literally means 'place,' but it can also be used to mean 'moment' when followed by a linking verb and preceded by phrases and clauses. (→ See also *bakari* and *chōdo*.)

1. After a noun + **no**, specifying whose place

    私のところに来て下さい。 **Watashi no tokoro** ni kite kudasai.
    Please come to the place where I am. (Please come to me.)

    東京に行った時は兄の所に泊まります。
    *Tōkyō ni itta toki wa **ani no tokoro** ni tomarimasu.*
    When I visit Tokyo, I'll stay at my older brother's.

2. After a quantity/amount phrase + **no**, specifying the location

    大学は駅から歩いて15分のところにあります。
    *Daigaku wa eki kara aruite **jū go fun no tokoro** ni arimasu.*
    The university is at a place that is fifteen minutes from the train station on foot. (The university is a fifteen-minute walk from the train station.)

    乗り換えの駅はここから約百メートルの所です。
    *Norikae no eiki wa koko kara yaku **hyaku mētoru no tokoro** desu.*
    The transfer station is about one hundred meters from here.

3. After verbs in the dictionary form, specifying the beginning moment of the action

    ちょうど仕事を終わるところです。
    *Chōdo shigoto o owaru **tokoro** desu.*
    I am just about to finish work.

    「どこへ行くんですか。」「温泉に泊まりに行くところです。」
    *"Doko e iku n desu ka." "Onsen ni tomari ni iku **tokoro** desu."*
    "Where are you going?" "I'm about to go stay at a hot spring."

    電話した時彼女は家を出るところでした。
    *Denwa shita toki kanojo wa ie o deru **tokoro** deshita.*
    She was about to leave home when I called her.

4. After verbs in the progressive form, specifying the moment in the middle of the action

新幹線に乗り遅れるところでした。
*Shinkansen ni noriokureru **tokoro** deshita.*
We were on the verge of missing the Shinkansen.

今そのことについて彼女と話しているところです。
*Ima sono koto ni tsuite kanojo to hanashite iru **tokoro** desu.*
I am in the middle of talking to her about that now.

5. After verbs in the ***ta*-form**, specifying the moment right after the action

ちょうど食事の準備ができたところです。
*Chōdo shokuji no junbi ga dekita **tokoro** desu.*
Dinner preparations have just been completed.

さきほど品川駅に着いたところです。
*Saki hodo Shinagawa eki ni tsuita **tokoro** desu.*
I arrived at Shinagawa station just now.

銀行を出たところで彼女に会いました。
*Ginkō o deta **tokoro** de kanojo ni aimashita.*
I met her just as I went out of the bank.

寝ようとしていたところへ電話がかかってきました。
*Neyō to shite ita **tokoro** e denwa ga kakatte kimashita.*
The telephone rang just as I was going to bed.

6. After adjectives in the dictionary form

お忙しいところどうもすいません。
*Oisogashii **tokoro**, dōmo suimasen.*
I'm sorry to trouble you when you are busy.

(usually to express the speaker's consideration toward the other person)

tokoro ga ところが [CONJUNCTION]

but, however, and

Tokoro ga usually functions as a sentence-initial conjunction that means 'but' or 'however.' It can also be used clause-finally, following a predicate in the past tense, to show the transition between the two actions/events. The sentence/clause immediately preceded by *tokoro ga* must express an unexpected event.

1. At the beginning of a sentence

彼にお金を貸してあげた。ところが，まだ返してくれない。
*Kare ni okane o kashite ageta. **Tokoro ga**, mada kaeshite kurenai.*
I lent him some money. However, he has not returned it to me yet.

東京はいい街です。ところが狭すぎます。
*Tōkyō wa ii machi desu. **Tokoro ga** semasugimasu.*
Tokyo is a nice city. But it's too cramped.

2. At the end of a clause, following a verb in the *ta*-form

買い物をしに来たところが店が閉まっていました。
*Kaimono o shi ni ki**ta tokoro ga** mise ga shimatte imashita.*
I came to do my shopping but the store was closed.

とにかくやってみたところがうまくいきました。
*Tonikaku yatte mi**ta tokoro ga** umaku ikimashita.*
At any rate, I tried it and it worked well.

→ See also *daga*, *dakedo*, *ga*, and *keredo(mo)*.

to omou と思う [PREDICATIVE PHRASE]

I think that

The verb *omou* takes a sentence marked by the particle *to* to complete its meaning. Note that when the subject is the third person, the verb must be in the progressive form. Even when the subject is the first person, the verb can be in the progressive form if the speaker thinks that his thinking could last only for a short time. The verb in the volitional form within the embedded clause plus *to omou* expresses one's intentions and willingness. The verb followed by *tai to omou* sounds refined rather than *tai* or *tai desu* when expressing one's future plan or desire. (→ See also *tai*, *to*, and *tsumori*.)

私は行こうと思います。 *Watashi wa ikō **to omoimasu**.*
I think I will go. (volitional form preceded)

行こうと思いますか。 *Ikō **to omoimasu** ka.*
Do you think you will go? (Do you want to go?)

彼は行くと思います。 *Kare wa iku **to omoimasu**.*
I think he will go. (not meaning 'He thinks he will go.')

彼が行くと思います。 *Kare ga iku **to omoimasu**.*
I think he will go. (emphasizing that the person who will go is him)

彼は行こうと思っています。 *Kare wa ikō **to omotte imasu**.*
He thinks he will go. (volitional form preceded)

私は大学院に行きたいと思います。
*Watashi wa daigakuin ni ikitai **to omoimasu**.*
I want to go to a graduate school. (a future plan)

私は行こうと思ってます。 *Watashi wa ikō **to omotte imasu**.*
I'm thinking of going.

彼は賢いと思います。 *Kare wa kashikoi **to omoimasu**.*
I think he is clever. (not meaning 'He thinks he is clever.')

彼は賢いと思いますか。 *Kare wa kashikoi **to omoimasu ka**.*
Do you think he is clever? (not meaning 'Does he think he is clever?')

彼は賢いと思っています。 *Kare wa kashikoi **to omotte imasu**.*
He thinks he is clever./I'm thinking he is clever.

to shitemo としても [ADVERBIAL PHRASE]

even though/if, supposing, no matter . . .

A concessive clause with a hypothetical condition can be expressed by a clause followed by *to shitemo*, to mean 'even if . . . is the case.' To emphasize that it is the hypothetical case, the adverb *tatoe* is often used with this construction. The particle *to* may be replaced by *ni*. (→ See also *temo/demo*.)

1. After verbs and adjectives in the dictionary form

   お金を持っているとしてもそんな高い物を買ってはいけない。
   *Okane o motte **iru to shitemo** sonna takai mono o katte wa ikenai.*
   Even though you have the money, you should not buy such an expensive thing.

   たとえ日本語がむずかしいとしてもあきらめずに勉強して下さい。
   *Tatoe Nihongo ga muzukash**ii to shitemo** akiramezu ni benkyō shite kudasai.*
   Even if Japanese is difficult, continue studying and don't give it up.

2. After verbs and adjectives in the *nai*-form

   たとえもう要らないとしても払わなければいけません。
   *Tatoe mō ira**nai to shitemo** harawanakereba ikemasen.*
   Even if you don't need it any more, you must pay for it.

3. After verbs and adjectives in the *ta*-form

   たとえ何が起こったとしてもあきらめません。
   *Tatoe nani ga okot**ta to shitemo** akiramemasen.*
   No matter what happens, I won't give up.

   彼がそれを知らなかったとしてもその過ちは許されない。
   *Kare ga sore o shiranakat**ta to shitemo** sono ayamachi wa yurusarenai.*
   Even if he didn't know about it, that is an unforgivable mistake.

4. After (adjectival) nouns + *da/datta*

   それが当然だとしても納得できません。
   *Sore ga tōzen **da to shitemo** nattoku dekimasen.*
   Even if it is natural, I just can't understand it.

たとえそれが本当だったとしても彼を軽蔑しません。
*Tatoe sore ga **hontō datta to shitemo** kare o keibetsu shimasen.*
Supposing that it were true, I wouldn't despise him.

to sureba とすれば [ADVERBIAL PHRASE]

if . . . (ever), assuming that . . . , if that is the case

A conditional clause with a hypothetical situation can be expressed by a clause followed by *to sureba*, to mean 'if . . . is the case.' *Sureba* (*ba*-form of *suru*) may be replaced with *shitara* or *suru to*. (→ See also *ba*, *nara*, *tara*, and *to*.)

1. After verbs and adjectives in the dictionary form

   車を買うとすれば小さいのがいい。
   *Kuruma o **kau to sureba** chīsai no ga ii.*
   If I ever buy a car, a small one would be better.

   彼が賢いとすれば何かいい計画をしているに違いない。
   *Kare ga **kashikoi to sureba** nanika ii keikaku o shite iru ni chigai nai.*
   Assuming that he is clever, he is no doubt making some good plan.

2. After verbs in the *nai*-form

   彼ができないとすればだれにしてもらおう。
   *Kare ga deki**nai to sureba** dare ni shite moraō.*
   Assuming that he can't, who shall we have do it?

3. After verbs and adjectives in the *ta*-form

   彼が嘘をついたとすれば彼女にも尋ねるべきだ。
   *Kare ga uso o tsui**ta to sureba** kanojo ni mo tazuneru beki da.*
   Assuming that he told a lie, you should also ask her about it.

4. After (adjectival) nouns + *da*

   彼が先生だとすれば何を教えているんだろう。
   *Kare ga **sensei da to sureba** nani o oshiete iru n darō.*
   Assuming that he is a teacher, I wonder what he is teaching.

   これがだめだとすればどんなものがよいのだろう。
   *Kore ga **dame da to sureba** donna mono ga yoi no darō.*
   Assuming that this is no good, what kind of things will be good?

5. At the beginning of a sentence

   彼は風邪をひいたと言っています。とすればあなたに頼まなければなりません。
   *Kare wa kaze o hiita to itte imasu. **To sureba**, anata ni tanomanakereba narimasen.*
   He says he has a cold. If that is the case, I have to ask a favor of you.

totemo とても [ADVERB]

very, terribly, (not) . . . at all, (not) . . . to

The adverb *totemo* means 'very' if used as a degree adverb that applies to some property expressed in an affirmative sentence. It is replaced by *amari* if used in a negative sentence that expresses some property. (→ See *amari*.) However, *totemo* can also mean '(not) at all' if used in a negative sentence that expresses potentials and probabilities. (→ See *mattaku* and *zenzen*.)

1. Before adjectives/adjectival nouns

   今日はとても暑いですね。 *Kyō wa **totemo atsui** desu ne.*
   Today is very hot, isn't it?

   そこはとても危険なので入ってはいけません。
   *Soko wa **totemo kiken na** node haitte wa ikemasen.*
   That place is very dangerous, so you must not go in.

2. Used with negative potential verbs

   あのばかな発言にはとても我慢できません。
   *Ano baka na hatsugen ni wa **totemo** gaman **dekimasen**.*
   I can't possibly put up with that loopy statement.

3. Used in statements expressing improbability

   とても間に合う見込みはありません。
   ***Totemo** maniau mikomi wa **arimasen**.*
   There is no hope at all that we'll make it in time.

tsu つ [VERB SUFFIX]

two opposite actions repeated

The suffix *tsu* follows verbs in the combining form and is used to express the situation where two opposite actions are repeated randomly.

   両国は持ちつ持たれつの関係だ。
   *Ryōkoku wa **mochitsu motaretsu** no kankei da.*
   The two countries have a give-and-take relationship.

   行きつもどりつそれを何度も考えました。
   Ikitsu modoritsu sore o nandomo kangaemashita.
   I thought of it over and over again while going back and forth.

tsui つい [ADVERB]

by mistake, in spite of oneself, just (a short time ago)

The adverb *tsui* modifies one's careless action or time expressions. (→ See also *shimau*.)

1. To modify one's action

   すみません。つい忘れていました。 *Sumimasen. **Tsui wasurete** imashita.*
   I am sorry I forgot it carelessly.

   つい大きな声で笑ってしまいました。
   ***Tsui** ōkina koe de **waratte** shimaimashita.*
   I could not help laughing loudly.

   つい口がすべりました。 ***Tsui** kuchi ga **suberimashita**.*
   I blurted it out thoughtlessly. (It was a slip of the tongue.)

2. To modify time expressions

   先生ならついさっき見かけました。 *Sensei nara **tsui sakki** mikakemashita.*
   I happened to see the teacher just a moment ago.

   つい先日こちらに参りました。 ***Tsui senjitsu** kochira ni mairimashita.*
   I came here only a few days ago.

   それを聞いたのはついきのうです。 *Sore o kiita no wa **tsui kinō** desu.*
   It is just yesterday that I heard it.

---

tsuide ni ついでに [ADVERBIAL PHRASE]

on the way, while . . . , incidentally

Tsuide ni follows verbs and nouns followed by *no* and creates an adverbial phrase that shows the situation where some opportunity is taken advantage of in order to do something else.

1. After verbs in the dictionary form

   銀行に行くついでにこの手紙をポストに入れてください。
   *Ginkō ni ik**u tsuide ni** kono tegami o posuto ni irete kudasai.*
   Please mail this letter on your way to the bank.

   コーヒーを頼むついでにケーキも注文しましょう。
   *Kōhī o tanom**u tsuide ni** kēki mo chūmon shimashō.*
   When we call for coffee, let's order some cake, too.

2. After verbs in the **ta**-form

   彼に会ったついでにそれを頼みました。
   *Kare ni at**ta tsuide ni** sore o tanomimashita.*
   I asked him to do it since I met him.

   温泉に行ったついでにマッサージもしてもらいました。
   *Onsen ni it**ta tsuide ni** massāji mo shite moraimashita.*
   When I visited a hot-spring, I had myself massaged.

3. After nouns + *no*

旅行のついでに昔の友人に会って来ました。
Ryokō no tsuide ni mukashi no yūjin ni atte kimashita.
I met my old friend while traveling.

4. At the beginning of a sentence

ついでに一つ大事なことを言っておきます。
Tsuide ni hitotsu daiji na koto o itte okimasu.
While I am at it, let me tell you one important thing.

---

tsumori da つもりだ [PREDICATIVE PHRASE]

to plan to . . . , to intend to . . . , to assume to . . .

Tsumori is a noun that literally means 'intention,' 'assumption,' 'expectation,' or 'plan.' *Tsumori* and *da* or *desu* (a linking verb) can be placed at the end of the sentence following clauses to mean 'plan to do . . . ,' 'assume to be . . . ,' etc. (→ See also *to omou*.)

1. After nouns + *no*

彼は芸術家のつもりでいます。 *Kare wa **geijutsuka no tsumori de** imasu.*
He fancies himself an artist.

何のつもりでそんなことをしたんですか。
***Nan no tsumori de** sonna koto o shita n desu ka.*
With what intention did you do such a thing?

2. After adjectival nouns + *na/no*

彼は勤勉なつもりでいる。 *Kare wa **kinben na tsumori de** iru.*
He considers himself diligent.

彼は病気のつもりでいる。 *Kare wa **byōki no tsumori de** iru.*
He assumes that he is sick.

3. After adjectival nouns + *datta*, *ja nai*, or *ja nakatta*

彼はそうするのが賢明だったつもりでいます。
*Kare wa sō suru no ga **kenmei datta tsumori de** imasu.*
He thinks it was wise of him to do so.

4. After verbs and adjectives in the dictionary form

どんな仕事を探すつもりですか。
*Donna shigoto o sagasu **tsumori desu** ka.*
What kind of job do you intend to look for?

彼女は自分では可愛いつもりでいる。
*Kanojo wa jibun de wa kawaii **tsumori de** iru.*
She fancies herself to be cute.

謝るつもりがあるなら，すぐ謝りなさい。
Ayamaru tsumori ga aru nara, sugu ayamarinasai.
If you have an intention to apologize, apologize immediately.

夏にアルバイトをしてお金を貯めるつもりです。
Natsu ni arubaito o shite okane o tameru tsumori desu.
I plan to work part-time and save money in summer.

この漆の重箱は彼女にあげるつもりでした。
Kono urushi no jūbako wa kanojo ni ageru tsumori deshita.
I intended to give this nest of lacquered boxes to her.

傷つけるつもりはありませんでした。
Kizutsukeru tsumori wa arimasen deshita.
I didn't mean to hurt you.

デーブは日本に住むつもりで日本語を勉強した。
Dēbu wa Nihon ni sumu tsumori de Nihongo o benkyō shita.
Dave studied Japanese with the intention of living in Japan.

5. After verbs and adjectives in the *nai*-form

私は今年の夏はどこにも行かないつもりです。
Watashi wa kotoshi no natsu wa doko ni mo ikanai tsumori desu.
I have no intention of going anywhere this summer.

彼は頭がよくないつもりです。
Kare wa atama ga yokunai tsumori desu.
He assumes that he is not smart.

6. After verbs and adjectives in the *ta*-form

ちゃんと書いたつもりですが。 *Chanto kaita tsumori desu ga.*
I thought that I wrote it properly, but . . . (didn't I?)

それで十分よかったつもりですが。
Sorede jūbun yokatta tsumori desu ga.
I thought it was good enough, but . . . (wasn't it?)

tsuzukeru 続ける [AUXILIARY VERB]

to continue doing, to keep on doing, to proceed to do, on end

Tsuzukeru can be a verb that means 'to continue,' but it can function as an auxiliary verb, following verbs in the combining form, to mean 'to continue doing (it).'

面白いから本を朝まで読み続けました。
Omoshiroi kara hon o asa made yomitsuzukemashita.
I continued reading a book till morning because it was interesting.

彼は３年間チャンスを待ち続けました。
*Kare wa san nen kan chansu o **machitsuzukemashita**.*
For three years he has waited for the chance.

私は当時そんなことばかり考え続けました。
*Watashi wa tōji sonna koto bakari **kangaetsuzukemashita**.*
I kept on thinking such thoughts those days.

物価は下がり続けています。 *Bukka wa **sagaritsuzukete imasu**.*
Prices continue to go down.

「とにかく。」と彼は話し続けた。 *"Tonikaku." to kare wa **hanashitsuzuketa**.*
"Anyway," he proceeded.

Note that *tsuzukete*, the *te*-form of the verb *tsuzukeru*, is often used as an adverb that means continuously.

続けてしゃべらないで, 少し聞きなさい。
***Tsuzukete** shaberanaide, sukoshi kikinasai.*
Don't talk continuously, but listen (to others) a little bit.

講演者は３時間続けて講義した。
*Kōensha wa san jikan **tsuzukete** kōgi shita.*
The speaker lectured for three hours at a stretch.

---

tte って [INFORMAL PARTICLE]

talking about . . . , speaking of . . .

In informal contexts, a topic noun is followed by *tte* instead of *wa* for emphasis. A quoted statement or a concessive clause can also be followed by *tte*. It is more commonly used in female speech than male speech.

1. After nouns and particles

    あのクラスって, 宿題が多いでしょう。
    ***Ano kurasu tte**, shukudai ga **ooi** deshō.*
    In that class, we get a lot of homework, right?

    デーブってとてもおもしろい人ですね。
    ***Dēbu tte** totemo omoshiroi hito desu ne.*
    Dave is a very interesting man, isn't he?

    あのゴールって彼が決めたんですよ。
    ***Ano gōru tte** kare ga kimeta n desu yo.*
    That goal—he scored it, you know.

    今週の金曜日までって, ちょっと無理じゃないの。
    ***Konshū no Kinyōbi made tte**, chotto muri ja nai no.*
    (Completing it) by this Friday is impossible, isn't it?

→ See also *wa*.

2. After verbs in the dictionary form (making the verb into noun equivalent)

漢字を覚えるってむずかしいですね。
*Kanji o oboe**ru tte** muzukashii desu ne.*
Memorizing kanji is difficult, isn't it?

3. After verbs in the **ta**-form (expressing concessive clauses)

今頃気づいたってもう遅いよ。 *Ima goro kizui**ta tte** mō osoi yo.*
Having noticed just now is really too late.

宝くじを何回買ったって当たりっこないよ。
*Takara kuji o nankai kat**ta tte** atarikko nai yo.*
Even if you play the lottery many times, you'll never hit it.

4. After quoted statement

(The main verb after the clause with -*tte* is often omitted when understood in the context.)

「彼女は行かないって言ってますよ。」「行かないって。」
*"Kanojo wa ikanai **tte** ittemasu yo." "Ikanai **tte**."*
"She says she won't go." "She won't? (Really?)"

絶対によくなるって。 *Zettai ni yoku naru **tte**.*
No doubt it will get better.

→ See also *to*.

5. Followed by *iu ka* as a filler to say "how should I say"

彼は優しい，っていうか，何にでも気がつくんですね。
*Kare wa yasashii, **tte iu ka**, nan ni demo ki ga tsuku n desu ne.*
He is kind, or how should I say, he is considerate in everything, isn't he?

uchi de / uchi kara うちで／うちから [ADVERBIAL PHRASE]

among, of

Uchi is a noun that means 'inside,' and creates an adverbial phrase following a noun and the particle *no*, meaning 'among' or 'out of,' and followed by a particle such as *de* and *kara*. However, such particles are not needed when ... *no uchi* follows a quantity/amount phrase. (→ See also Comparisons.)

彼らのうちでだれが日本語を話せますか。
***Karera no uchi de** dare ga Nihongo o hanasemasu ka.*
Which of them can speak Japanese?

三つのうちから好きなものを一つ選んで下さい。
***Mittsu no uchi kara** suki na mono o hitotsu erande kudasai.*
Please choose your favorite one among the three.

三人のうちでだれが一番好きですか。
Sannin no uchi de *dare ga ichiban suki desu ka.*
Who do you like the best among the three?

彼は一年のうち三ヶ月は仕事で日本にいません。
*Kare wa **ichi nen no uchi** san kagetsu wa shigoto de Nihon ni imasen.*
He is away from Japan on business for three months a year.

(*De* is dropped when a definite number is stated.)

十五人のうち十人が女性でした。　***Jū go nin no uchi*** *jū nin ga josei deshita.*
Ten out of fifteen persons were female.

uchi ni うちに [ADVERBIAL PHRASE]

within, during, in (some state), while, before (with a negative)

Uchi is a noun that means 'inside,' but when combined with the particle *ni*, it creates a time adverbial phrase/clause that in many cases shows the time period within which the action expressed by the main verb should be performed in order to prevent some problems understood in the context. (→ See also *aida* and *chū ni*.)

1. After nouns + ***no***

   数ヶ月のうちに日本語が話せるようになるでしょう。
   Sūkagetsu no uchi ni *Nihongo ga hanaseru yō ni naru deshō.*
   You'll be able to speak Japanese within a few months.

   夜のうちに出発の準備をしておきます。
   Yoru no uchi ni *shuppatsu no junbi o shite okimasu.*
   I'll finish my preparations for departure during the night.

   国会は混乱のうちに閉会した。
   *Kokkai wa **konran no uchi ni** heikai shita.*
   The National Diet closed amid confusion.

2. After verbs and adjectives in the dictionary form

   何でもできるうちにやっておくのがいいと思います。
   *Nan demo dekiru **uchi ni** yatte oku no ga ii to omoimasu.*
   I think it is good to get whatever possible done while you can.

   時間があるうちにその仕事を片付けてしまいたい。
   *Jikan ga aru **uchi ni** sono shigoto o katazukete shimaitai.*
   I want to get through with the task while I have time.

   明るいうちに家へ帰ってきなさい。　*Akarui **uchi ni** ie e kaette kinasai.*
   Come back home while it is still light (before dark).

   鉄は熱いうちに打て。　*Tetsu wa atsui **uchi ni** ute.*
   Strike while the iron is hot.

3. After verbs in the **nai**-form

暗くならないうちに家へ帰ってきなさい。
Kuraku naranai uchi ni ie e kaette kinasai.
Come back home before (it gets) dark.

雨が降らないうちにタクシーに乗りましょう。
Ame ga furanai uchi ni takushī ni norimashō.
Let's get on a taxi before it starts to rain.

忘れないうちにメモしておいた方がいい。
Wasurenai uchi ni memo shite oita hō ga ii.
It is better to jot it down before you forget.

冷めないうちにスープをどうぞ。 *Samenai uchi ni sūpu o dōzo.*
Please have your soup before it gets cold.

→ See also *nai*.

4. After adjectival nouns + **na**

まだここが安全なうちに去った方がいい。
Mada koko ga anzen na uchi ni satta hō ga ii.
You had better leave here while it is safe.

親が元気なうちに孝行したい。 *Oya ga genki na uchi ni kōkō shitai.*
I want to be a good son/daughter while my parents are well.

---

wa は [PARTICLE]

topic marker, contrast marker

The particle *wa* is represented by the hiragana は rather than わ, and is usually placed after a noun phrase or a noun phrase plus some particle other than *ga* or *o*. The particle *wa* marks the topic of a sentence or some item that is being contrasted. It is also used to mark the scope of negation. (→ See also *ga* and *tte*.)

I. TOPIC

Japanese sentences are usually preceded by a short phrase that serves as the topic of the sentence. The topic must be something that the speaker and the listener are already aware of as the referent, something that the listener knows that the speaker is referring to, or something that the speaker wants to explain or ask about to the listener. It may be a familiar item for them such as their mutual friend, an item that they can see in the conversational context, an item that was already introduced in the discourse, or an item that people generally know such as dogs and mountains. It can also be a person whom the speaker has never met or seen. For example, the speaker can ask about the listener's mother even if the speaker has never seen her before and she is not present in the conversational context, by saying *Anata no okāsan wa doko de umareta n desu ka* 'Where was your mother born?' Interrogative words cannot usually serve as topics. For example, a sentence like *Doko wa ikimashita ka*, which is intended to mean 'Where did you go?' is ungrammatical, whereas *Doko ni iki-mashita ka* is grammatical. Similarly, a specific item that the speaker wants to talk about but the listener would be ignorant of as a referent may not serve as the topic of the sentence unless introduced in advance in the discourse.

When the subject or the object also serves as the topic, it is marked only by *wa*. A sentence can usually have only one topic, and if there are two instances of *wa* in a sentence, one of them is usually understood as a contrastive marker. *Wa* is not allowed inside a relative clause except when it functions as a contrastive marker rather than as a topic marker. (→ See Relative clauses under Claus-es.) However, *wa* can function as a topic marker in a noun complement clause. (→ See also Noun complement clauses under Clauses.)

1. The subject noun phrase serving as the topic

   この人は鈴木さんです。彼は私の親友です。
   Kono hito wa Suzuki san desu. **Kare wa** watashi no shin'yū desu.
   This is Mr. Suzuki. He is my good friend.

   花子さんは髪がきれいですね。 **Hanako san wa** kami ga kirei desu ne.
   As for Hanako, her hair is beautiful, isn't it? (Hanako has beautiful hair, doesn't she?)

   花子は大学生です。経済を専攻しています。
   Hanako wa daigakusei desu. Keizai o senkō shite imasu.
   Hanako is a university student. She is majoring in economics.

   (The topic of the first sentence, Hanako, may remain as the topic of the subsequent sentence although it is covert.)

   今度買った車は日本製です。とても経済的な車です。
   Kondo katta kuruma wa Nihonsei desu. Totemo keizaiteki na kuruma desu.
   The car I bought recently is Japanese-made. It's a very economical one.

   日本語をマスターするのは難しいです。でも楽しいです。
   Nihongo o masutā suru no wa muzukashii desu. Demo tanoshii desu.
   It is difficult to master Japanese. But it's fun.

   → See also *no*.

   猫は好きですか。 **Neko wa** suki desu ka? **Do you like cats?**

   (If the speaker emphatically or emotionally asks if the listener likes cats, *ga* may be used instead.)

   → See also *ga*.

   え，猫が好きですか。私も猫が大好きなんです。
   E, **neko ga** suki desu ka? Watashi mo neko ga daisuki na n desu.
   Oh, do you like cats? I like cats very much too.

あの人がマイクです。彼はアメリカから来ました。
*Ano hito **ga** Maiku desu. **Kare wa** Amerika kara kimashita.*
That man is Mike. He came from the U.S.

あの人はマイクです。彼はアメリカから来ました。
*Ano hito **wa** Maiku desu. **Kare wa** Amerika kara kimashita.*
That man is Mike. He came from the U.S.

(The speaker knows the listener sees a man there, but the listener does not know his name.)

太郎は花子と付き合っているという噂はでたらめです。
*Taro **wa** Hanako to tsukiatte iru to iu **uwasa wa** detarame desu.*
The rumor that Taro has been seeing Hanako is nonsense.

(The first topic can be marked by *wa* even in the noun complement clause.)

→ See Noun complement clause under Clauses.

2. The object noun phrase serving as the topic

この本は花子が昨日貸してくれたんですが，もう読みました。
*Kono hon **wa** Hanako ga kinō kashite kureta n desu ga, mō yomimashita.*
Hanako lent this book to me yesterday, and I've already read it.

漢字は外国人が覚えるには難しすぎるかもしれません。
*Kanji **wa** gaikokujin ga oboeru ni wa muzukashisugiru kamo shiremasen.*
It may be too difficult for non-natives to learn kanji.

3. Other noun phrases just by themselves

車はワゴンがいい。 *Kuruma **wa** wagon ga ii.*
Speaking of cars, a station wagon is good.

スポーツは何が好きですか。 *Supōsu **wa** nani ga suki desu ka.*
Speaking of sports, what do you like? (What sport do you like?)

秋は紅葉が楽しみだ。 *Aki **wa** kōyō ga tanoshimi da.*
In autumn, we look forward to seeing the change of leaf colors.

4. Adverbial phrases (with a particle)

そんなにゆっくりは困ります。もっと早くお願いします。
*Sonna ni **yukkuri wa** komarimasu. Motto hayaku onegai shimasu.*
Doing it so slowly is a bad job. Do it faster. I ask it as a favor.

クラスではだれが一番背が高いですか。
*Kurasu **de wa** dare ga ichiban se ga takai desu ka.*
Who is the tallest in the class?

居酒屋にはよく行きますか。 *Izakaya **ni wa** yoku ikimasu ka.*
Do you often go to *izakaya* bars?

田中さんとはいつからつきあっているんですか。
Tanaka san to wa *itsu kara tsukiatte iru n desu ka.*
Since when have you been seeing Mr. Tanaka?

II. CONTRAST

The two or more items that are in contrast can be highlighted by the particle *wa*. They may appear in the same sentence or in separate sentences, but if understood, only one of them can appear in the sentence. The items being contrasted can be (adjectival) nouns, verbs, or adjectives. The particle *wa* can highlight the existence of some action/state while implying the lack of another action/state understood in the context. Depending on the context, *wa* provides the limitation of some discussion or evaluation, meaning 'as far as . . . is concerned' or 'among. . . .'

1. After noun phrases (with a case particle)

   今日は仕事を休みますが，明日は必ず働きます。
   Kyō wa *shigoto o yasumimasu ga,* ***asu wa*** *kanarazu hatarakimasu.*
   Today I'll take off from my job, but tomorrow I'll be sure to work.

   彼は行くそうですが，私はまだ分かりません。
   Kare wa *iku sō desu ga,* ***watashi wa*** *mada wakarimasen.*
   He says he will go, but I've not decided yet. (whether I will go or not)

   太郎は音楽を作って，花子は絵を描きます。
   Tarō wa *ongaku o tsukutte,* ***Hanako wa*** *e o kakimasu.*
   While Taro composes music, Hanako draws pictures.

   太郎は帰ったけど花子は残った。
   Tarō wa *kaetta kedo* ***Hanako wa*** *nokotta.*
   Taro went home but Hanako stayed.

   彼は日本酒は飲みません。 *Kare wa* ***Nihonshu wa*** *nomimasen.*
   He doesn't drink Japanese sake. (but he may drink beer)

   私は毎日三時間は勉強します。
   Watashi wa mainichi ***san jikan wa*** *benkyō shimasu.*
   I study at least three hours every day. (and sometimes longer)

   ここでは静かにして下さい。 ***Koko de wa*** *shizuka ni shite kudasai.*
   Please keep quiet here. (You can talk somewhere else.)

   あの服よりはこの方がいい。 ***Ano fuku yori wa*** *kono hō ga ii.*
   These clothes are better than those. (but possibly there are better ones than these)

   十時まではネットをしてもよろしいです。
   Jū ji made wa *netto o shitemo yoroshii desu.*
   You may have Net access until ten o'clock. (but not later)

これからは頑張ります。 **Kore kara wa** ganbarimasu.
From now on I'll do my best. (since I've been lazy)

東京では地価が高すぎますね。
Tōyō de wa chika ga takasugimasu ne.
In Tokyo land prices are too high, aren't they? (though they are cheap outside of Tokyo)

2. After verbs in the combining form

私は行きはしますが見るだけです。
Watashi wa **iki wa** shimasu ga miru dake desu.
I actually will go, but I will just see it.

3. After adjectives in the **ku**-form

安くはできますが分割払いは無理です。
Yasuku wa dekimasu ga bunkatsu barai wa muri desu.
I can give you a discount, but paying in installments is not allowed.

4. After adjectival nouns with **ni** or **de**

貧乏ではありますが幸せです。
Binbo de wa arimasu ga shiawase desu.
I am poor, but I am happy.

まじめにはなりましたが，まだやる気はありません。
Majime ni wa narimashita ga, mada yaru ki wa arimasen.
He became serious but still has not been motivated yet.

III. SCOPE OF NEGATION

Wa is conventionally used with the negative linking verb (. . . *de wa nai*). (→ See *dewa*.) *Wa* also marks the scope of negation, specifying exactly for what some situation does not apply, but implying that the same situation could apply in other contexts.

1. After noun phrases (with a case particle)

これは私のUSBではありません。たぶん太郎のでしょう。
Kore wa **watashi no yūesubī de wa** arimasen. Tabun Taro no deshō.
This is not my USB thumb drive. But I can guess it's Taro's.

この店（で）は買いません。 **Kono mise (de) wa** kaimasen.
I don't buy in this shop. (I may buy in another shop.)

私は夜中（に）は勉強しません。
Watashi wa **yonaka (ni) wa benkyō** shimasen.
I don't study at midnight. (I may study during the daytime.)

彼とはお酒を飲みません。 **Kare to wa** osake o nomimasen.
I don't drink sake with him. (I drink with another friend.)

2. After a verb in the combining form, followed by **shinai**

   彼は仕事を一生懸命にやりはしないが正確にする。
   *Kare wa shigoto o isshōkenmei ni **yari wa shinai** ga seikaku ni suru.*
   He does not do his job with all his might, but he does it accurately.

3. After adjectives in the **ku**-form

   ワゴン車は安くはありません。でも便利です。
   *Wagonsha wa **yasuku wa** arimasen. Demo benri desu.*
   A station wagon is not cheap. But it's convenient.

4. After adjectival nouns with **de** or **ni**

   彼女は病気ではありません。たぶん疲れているのでしょう。
   *Kanojo wa **byōki de wa** arimasen. Tabun tsukarete iru no deshō.*
   She is not sick. But maybe she is tired.

   それは簡単にはできません。でもなんとかできるでしょう。
   *Sore wa **kantan ni wa** dekimasen. Demo nantoka dekiru deshō.*
   You can't do it easily. But you'll complete it somehow or other.

---

wake わけ [NOUN]

---

the reason (why/for)

Wake can be used as a noun that means 'reason,' which can be used interchangeably with the noun *riyū*. However, it can also be used idiomatically to show the status of the statement.

I. REASON

1. After demonstrative adjectives

   そのわけを聞かせてください。 ***Sono wake** o kikasete kudasai.*
   Please let me hear the reason for that.

2. After adjectival nouns + **na**

   彼がずっと健康なわけは早寝早起きをしているからです。
   *Kare ga zutto **kenkō na wake** wa hayane hayaoki o shite iru kara desu.*
   The reason he remains healthy is that he always goes to bed early and gets up early (keeps early hours).

   別にそれが嫌いなわけではありません。
   *Betsu ni sore ga **kirai na wake** dewa arimasen.*
   It doesn't mean that I particularly hate it. (See also II.)

3. After verbs and adjectives in the dictionary or **nai**-form

   日本語を学ぶわけは日本語で漫画を読みたいからです。
   *Nihongo o manabu **wake** wa Nihongo de manga o yomitai kara desu.*
   The reason I learn Japanese is that I want to read comics in Japanese.

4. After verbs and adjectives in the **ta**-form

会社を辞めたわけは言いたくありません。
*Kaisha o yame**ta wake** wa iitaku arimasen.*
I don't want to tell you why I quit the company.

犬がうるさかったわけが分かりました。
*Inu ga urusakat**ta wake** ga wakarimashita.*
I understand why the dog has been barking.

II. IDIOMATIC USE

1. Followed by the linking verb **da/desu** to mean 'that's why . . .'

それで遅れたわけですね。
*Sore de okure**ta wake desu** ne.* (after verbs and adjectives in the *ta*-form)
That's why you were late, isn't it?

それでは大変なわけだ。
*Sore dewa **taihen na wake da**.* (after (adjectival) nouns + *na/no*)
If that is the case, it will of course be difficult.

それでみんな集まっているわけですね。
*Sore de minna atsumatte **iru wake desu** ne.* (after verbs and adjectives in the dictionary form)
That's why they are all gathering, isn't it?

そういう事情で消極的だったわけですね。
*Sōiū jijō de **shōkyokuteki datta wake desu** ne.* (after (adjectival) nouns + *datta*)
You have a good reason to have been passive under such circumstances.

2. Followed by the negative linking verb (**dewa nai**) to mean 'it does not necessarily mean that . . .'

あなたに賛成するわけではありません。
*Anata ni sansei suru **wake dewa arimasen**.* (after verbs in the dictionary form)
It doesn't mean that I quite agree with you. (I almost disagree.)

私はやりたいわけではありません。
*Watashi wa yaritai **wake dewa arimasen**.* (after adjectives in the dictionary form)
It doesn't mean that I want to do it. (I'd like to cancel it if allowed.)

あなたに賛成しないわけではありません。
*Anata ni sansei shinai **wake dewa arimasen**.* (after verbs in the *nai*-form)
It doesn't mean that I don't agree with you. (I sort of agree with you.)

私はやりたくないわけではありません。
*Watashi wa yaritaku**nai wake dewa arimasen**.* (after adjectives in the *nai*-form)
It doesn't mean that I don't want to do it. (I sort of want to do it.)

あなたが悪いわけではない。

*Anata ga warui **wake dewa nai**.* (after adjectives in the dictionary form)
It doesn't mean that you are wrong. (You are almost right.)

必ずしもあなたの提案に同意したわけではありません。

*Kanarazushimo anata no teian ni dōi shi**ta wake** dewa arimasen.* (after verbs in the *ta*-form)
I don't necessarily agree to your proposal.

私たちはずっと無関心な／だった わけではありません。

*Watashi tachi wa zutto **mukanshin na/datta wake** dewa arimasen.* (after (adjectival) nouns + *na/no/datta*)
We are/were not necessarily indifferent throughout.

3. After a verb in the dictionary form, followed by ***ni wa ikanai*** meaning 'have to do . . .'

あなたがしないなら私もするわけにはいきません。

*Anata ga shinai nara watashi mo suru **wake ni wa ikimasen**.*
If you don't do it, I shouldn't either.

4. Followed by verbs in the ***nai*-form** + ***ni wa ikanai*** meaning 'have to do . . .'

彼女を手伝わないわけにはいきません。

*Kanojo o tetsudawa**nai wake ni wa ikimasen**.*
I should not keep from helping her. (I have to help her.)

5. Followed by ***ga nai*** to mean 'there is no reason for. . . .'

彼女とうまくやっていけるわけがない。

*Kanojo to umaku yatte ike**ru wake ga nai**.* (after verbs in the dictionary form)
There is no way to get along with her.

漢字の試験がやさしいわけがない。

*Kanji no shiken ga yasashii **wake ga nai**.* (after adjectives in the dictionary form)
The kanji test cannot be easy.

私が幸せになれないわけがない。

*Watashi ga shiawase ni nare**nai wake ga nai**.* (after verbs and adjectives in the *nai*-form)
I am sure to become happy.

一人で寂しくないわけがない。

*Hitori de sabishiku**nai wake ga nai**.* (after adjectives in the *nai*-form)
Of course I feel lonely when I'm alone.

新しいものが本当のわけがない。

*Atarashii mono ga hontō **no wake ga nai**.* (after (adjectival) nouns + *na/no*)
What is new cannot be true.

wo を → See **o**.

wo motte をもって → See **o motte**.

wo tōshite を通して → See **o tōshite**.

ya や [PARTICLE]

and . . . (and the like), or, as soon as

The particle *ya* follows a noun to list examples. It can also follow a verb in the dictionary form, meaning 'as soon as. . . .'

1. After nouns

   高齢者や子供を大切にすべきです。
   Kōreisha ya kodomo o taisetsu ni subeki desu.
   You should care for old people and children (or the weak).

   私は歌舞伎や能は観ません。
   Watashi wa kabuki ya nō wa mimasen.
   I don't watch Kabuki or No plays. (or such traditional plays)

   → See also *to*, *to ka*, *yara*, and *mo*.

2. After verbs in the dictionary form

   地震が起こるや私は慌てて飛び出した。
   Jishin ga okoru ya watashi wa awatete tobidashita.
   As soon as the earthquake occurred, I jumped out in a hurry.

   → See also *to*.

yara やら [PARTICLE]

. . . and . . . , and so on, what with, wonder

The particle *yara* follows nouns, verbs, and adjectives and is used for randomly listing them as examples, mainly when one is complaining. (→ See *toka* and *ya*.) It also follows question words, forming indefinite pronouns like 'someone' and 'somewhere,' just as the particle *ka* does. (→ See *ka*.) When it follows a sentence, it just obscures the specificity of the statement, meaning '. . . or something like that.'

1. After each of nouns

   部屋の中は本やらCDやら服やらでごちゃごちゃです。
   Heya no naka wa hon yara shīdī yara fuku yara de gochagocha desu.
   My room is a jumble of books, CDs, and clothes.

残業やら出張やらで家にほとんどいない。
Zangyō yara shutchō yara de ie ni hotondo inai.
What with overtime work and (what with) business trips, I'm almost always away from home.

2. After verbs and adjectives in the dictionary form or *nai*-form

腹が立つやら悲しいやらで何も言葉が出ない。
Hara ga tatsu yara kanashii yara de nani mo kotoba ga denai.
What with anger and sadness, we're left speechless.

行くやら行かないやらでもめました。
Iku yara ikanai yara de momemashita.
We had a trouble with (deciding) to go, not to go, etc.

3. After interrogative words (+ particle)

だれやら怪しい人物がうろついている。
Dare yara ayashii jinbutsu ga urotsuite iru.
Someone suspicious is prowling about.

どこやらでお会いしましたね。 *Doko yara de oai shimashita ne.*
I remember we met each other somewhere.

4. At the end of a sentence (with *no*)

いつできる(の)やら。 *Itsu dekiru (no) yara.*
I wonder when it will be completed.

yaru やる [AUXILIARY VERB]

to do something for the benefit of one's subordinate

The auxiliary verb *yaru* can be used instead of the auxiliary verb *ageru* when the action is done for one's subordinate. (→ See *ageru <auxiliary verb>*.)

弟に本を読んでやりました。 *Otōto ni hon o yonde yarimashita.*
I read a book for my little brother.

yaru やる [VERB]

to do, give

Yaru is an informal version of the verb *suru* or *ageru* but can be a verb with distinct meanings. When *yaru* is used instead of *ageru*, the receiver of an item or service is implied to be the speaker's subordinate, and its usage may sound affectionate or rude depending on the context.

1. *Yaru* used to mean *suru* 'to do'

どうやったらいいのか分かりません。 *Dō yattara ii no ka wakarimasen.*
I don't know how to do it.

キャッチボールでもやりませんか。 *Kyatchi bōru demo **yarimasen** ka.*
Won't you play catch with me?

宿題でもやろうかな。 *Shukudai demo **yarō** kana.*
Shall I do homework or something?

→ See *suru.*

2. *Yaru* used to mean ***ageru*** 'to give'

犬にえさをやって下さい。ないています。
*Inu ni esa o **yatte** kudasai. Naite imasu.*
Give food to the dog. It's barking.

この服は弟にやります。
*Kono fuku wa otōto ni **yarimasu**.* (sounds affectionate)
I'll give these clothes to my little brother.

こんなものお前にやるよ。
*Konna mono omae ni **yaru** yo.* (sounds rude)
I'll give such a thing to you.

(Some people use *ageru* for feeding an animal.)

何か買ってやろうか。
*Nani ka kat**te yarō** ka.* (speaking to a very intimate person or a child)
Shall I buy you something good?

→ See *ageru.*

3. *Yaru* used to mean specific actions

In addition to meaning 'to do,' *yaru* can also mean 'to do business' or can be used to express some meanings understood by the speaker and the listener.

店はまだやっていますか。 *Mise wa mada **yatte** imasu ka.*
Is the store still open?

一杯やりませんか。 ***Ippai yarimasen** ka.* **Won't you have a drink?**

うちの者をやります。 *Uchi no mono o **yarimasu**.*
I'll send my subordinate to you.

やるならやれよ。 ***Yaru** nara **yare** yo.*
Beat me if you want to. (or shoot, kill, etc.)

yasui やすい [AUXILIARY ADJECTIVE]

(be) easy to (do), (be) liable to (do), (be) apt to (do)

The auxiliary adjective *yasui* follows a verb in the combining form to mean 'to be easy to do. . . .' The resulting form patterns like adjectives. To express the opposite notion, use the auxiliary adjective *nikui*. (→ See *nikui*.)

1. Used as a sentence predicate

   私は風邪にかかりやすい。 *Watashi wa kaze ni **kakariyasui**.*
   I am prone to catching colds.

   この携帯は扱いやすい。 *Kono keitai wa **atsukaiyasui**.*
   This mobile phone is easy to handle.

2. Used as a prenominal modifier

   彼は親しくなりやすい人です。 *Kare wa shitashiku **nariyasui** hito desu.*
   He is a man who is easy to make friends with.

3. Used as a complement

   彼は飲むと怒りやすくなる。 *Kare wa nomu to **okoriyasuku** naru.*
   He is apt to get angry after he drinks.

yo よ [PARTICLE]

(. . .), you know, (. . .), I tell you

Yo is a sentence-final particle, which emphasizes the statement. It is often used in colloquial speech and implies that the speaker is kindly telling the listener what he/she might not know and trying to call his/her attention. It sounds friendly when expressing permission, invitations, or agreements but might sound very imposing when expressing prohibition or disagreement.

> 「今日は天気がとても悪いですよ。」「そうですか。」
> *"Kyō wa tenki ga totemo warui desu **yo**." "Sō desu ka."*
> **"The weather is very bad today, I tell you." "Really?"**

> 「本田さんも行きますよ。」「そうなんですか。」
> *"Honda san mo ikimasu **yo**." "Sō na n desu ka."*
> **"Mr. Honda is going too, I tell you." "Is he?"**

> ぜひパーティーに来て下さいよ。 *Zehi pātī ni kite **kudasai yo**.*
> **By all means please come to our party, I'm asking.**

→ See also *ne*.

yō 用 [NOUN SUFFIX]

suitable for, for (. . . use)

Yō follows a noun and indicates the purpose of some item. It is optionally followed by *no* when there is a noun after it.

> この本は初心者用です。 *Kono hon wa **shoshinsha yō** desu.*
> **This book is suitable for beginners.**

家庭用(の)耕耘機はありますか。 ***Katei yō (no)*** *kōunki wa arimasu ka.*
Do you have a farm tractor for home use?

登山用(の)靴は買いましたか。 ***Tozan yō (no)*** *kutsu wa kaimashita ka.*
Did you buy shoes for mountain climbing?

(y)ō よう [VERB SUFFIX]

volitional form formative

Yō or just *ō* is a verb suffix that creates a volitional form. The volitional form of a verb can be created by replacing the final *ru* of a *ru*-verb and the final *u* of an *u*-verb with *yō* and *ō*, respectively. (→ See Volitional form under Verbs.) The volitional form expresses the speaker's volition. When used at the end of the sentence, it enthusiastically and informally expresses one's volition, meaning either 'I will do . . .' or 'Let's do. . . .' In polite/neutral contexts, it is better to use its polite counterpart, the combining form + *mashō*. (*Mashō* was historically derived from *mase* (the front part of *masen*) and this suffix, *mase* + *(y)ō*.) Negative volition is expressed by the *nai*-form followed by *de okō* or *de iyō* or by the dictionary form followed by *no o yameyō*. For describing one's will, intention, and plan, *(y)ō to omou* is used. For expressing attempt, *(y)ō to suru* is used.

1. Affirmative

   映画を見にいこう。 *Eiga o mi ni* ***ikō***. **Let's go and see a movie.**

   クーラーをつけようか。 *Kūrā o* ***tsukeyō*** *ka.*
   Shall I turn on the air conditioner?

   この店で買い物をしようよ。 *Kono mise de kaimono o* ***shiyō*** *yo.*
   Let's do our shopping in this shop, shall we?

   私がしましょう。*Watashi ga* ***shimashō***. **Let me do it.**

   いっしょにしましょう。 *Isshoni* ***shimashō***. **Let's do it together.**

2. Negative

   今日はずっとねないでいよう。 *Kyō wa zutto nenai de* ***iyō***.
   Let's try not to sleep today.

   あの人を相手にしないでいましょう。
   Ano hito o aite ni shinai de ***imashō***.
   Let's refuse to deal with that man.

   あまり飲まないでおきましょう。 *Amari nomanai de* ***okimashō***.
   Let's not drink too much.

   台風なのでドライブに行くのをやめよう。
   Taifū na node doraibu ni iku no o ***yameyō***.
   Let's not go for a drive because a typhoon has come.

3. **(Y)ō to omou**

もっと努力しようと思います。 *Motto doryoku **shiyō to omoimasu.***
I would like to put more effort (into it).

来月から日本語のコースを取ろうと思っています。
*Raigetsu kara Nihongo no kōsu o **torō to omotte imasu.***
I'm thinking of beginning a Japanese course next month.

4. **(Y)ō to suru**

うそをつこうとしました。でもできませんでした。
*Uso o **tsukō to shimashita.** Demo, dekimasen deshita.*
I tried to lie, but I could not.

出かけようとした時山田さんが来ました。
***Dekakeyō to shita** toki, Yamada san ga kimashita.*
When I tried to go out, Ms. Yamada came in.

yō da ようだ [PREDICATIVE PHRASE (CONJECTURE)]

to seem to, to be likely to

Yō da or *yō desu* can follow a clause to express conjecture. (→ See also *darō, mitai da, rashii <conjecture>,* and *sō da.*) The predicate before *yō* ends in the dictionary form, the *ta*-form, or the *nai*-form, but (adjectival) nouns must be followed by *no* or *na* rather than by *da* in the non-past affirmative context.

1. After nouns + **no**

彼は留守のようでした。 *Kare wa **rusu no yō deshita.***
He seemed to be out. (because there was no answer)

2. After adjectival nouns + **na/no**

彼は大丈夫なようです。 *Kare wa **daijōbu na yō desu.***
He seems to be all right. (because I heard no bad news)

彼は病気のようだ。 *Kare wa **byōki no yō da.*** **He seems to be sick.**

3. After (adjectival) nouns + **ja nai, datta,** or **ja nakatta**

彼は練習が嫌だったようです。 *Kare wa renshū ga **iya datta yō desu.***
It appears that he did not like practicing.

4. After verbs and adjectives in the dictionary form

彼は外国へ旅行に行くようです。
*Kare wa gaikoku e ryoko ni iku **yō desu.***
He looks like he will travel abroad. (because he is carrying his suitcase)

その試験はやさしいようです。 *Sono shiken wa yasashii **yō desu.***
The examination seems easy. (since many people passed it)

5. After verbs and adjectives in the *nai*-form

彼女はそのことを何も知らないようです。
Kanojo wa sono koto o nani mo shiranai yō desu.
She seems to know nothing about it.

石川さんはあまりゴルフをしたくないようです。
Ishikawa san wa amari gorufu o shitakunai yō desu.
It seems that Mr. Ishikawa doesn't really want to play golf.

6. After verbs and adjectives in the *ta*-form

彼女は入学試験に合格したようです。
Kanojo wa nyūgaku shiken ni gōkaku shita yō desu.
It seems that she passed the entrance examination.

彼の今日の戦績は厳しかったようです。
Kare no kyō no senseki wa kibishikatta yō desu.
His record today seems to have been poor.

yō da ようだ [PREDICATIVE PHRASE (RESEMBLANCE)]

to look like, such as, like, as, such . . . as, that appears . . . , to the effect, so as to
. . . , so that . . .

Yō da or *yō desu* can follow nouns and the particle *no* and express resemblance
or simile. The sentence is often accompanied by the adverb *marude* 'as if . . . /
as though. . . .' (→ See *marude*.) In fact, *yō* is an unsubstantial noun and creates
a new adjectival noun following another noun and *no* or a clause. Thus, the
resulting form is another adjectival noun, which can be followed by *na* when
placed before another noun, or by *ni* when used as an adverb. Being followed
by *na*, it forms a modifier for a noun, meaning 'like . . .' or 'appears. . . .' Being
followed by *ni*, it creates a phrase that expresses the manner of an action, specifying the desired outcome, meaning 'so as to . . .' or 'so that. . . .' (→ See also
yō da <*conjecture*>, *yō ni iu*, *yō ni naru*, *yō ni suru*, *ni*, and *tame ni*.)

1. After nouns followed by *no*

山田さんは天使のようです。 *Yamada san wa tenshi no yō desu.*
Ms. Yamada is like an angel.

あのプードルはまるで猫のようだ。
Ano pūdoru wa marude neko no yō da.
That poodle looks just like a cat.

あのテレビタレントはまるで女のような男だ。
Ano terebi tarento wa marude onna no yō na otoko da.
That TV personality is a man exactly like a woman.

この町は高いビルが多くて，まるでマンハッタンのようです。
*Kono machi wa takai biru ga ōkute, marude **Manhattan no yō desu**.*
This town has many tall buildings, and it is just like Manhattan.

若い人は東京や横浜のような大都市に住みたがる。
*Wakai hito wa **Tōkyō ya Yokohama no yō na** daitoshi ni sumitagaru.*
Young people want to live in big cities like Tokyo and Yokohama.

かつて日本人は蜂のように働くと言われた。
*Katsute Nihonjin wa **hachi no yō ni** hataraku to iwareta.*
It was once said that the Japanese worked like bees.

彼女はまるで魚のように速く泳げます。
*Kanojo wa marude **sakana no yō ni** hayaku oyogemasu.*
She can swim as fast as a fish.

いつものように家を出ましたが遅刻してしまいました。
***Itsumo no yō ni** ie o demashita ga chikoku shite shimaimashita.*
I left home as usual, but I ended up being late.

フランクのようにギターをうまく弾いてみたい。
***Furanku no yō ni** gitā o umaku hiite mitai.*
I'd like to play the guitar as well as Frank.

2. After demonstrative adjectives **kono, sono,** or **ano**

そのようなことを聞きました。 ***Sono yō na** koto o kikimashita.*
I heard something like that.

あのような美しい着物はかなり高いです。
***Ano yō na** utsukushii kimono wa kanari takai desu.*
Such a beautiful kimono as that is quite expensive.

このようにお願いできますか。 ***Kono yō ni** onegai dekimasu ka.*
Could you do it like this?

3. After adjectival nouns + **na/no**

スミスさんは独身のようなことを聞きました。
*Sumisu san wa **dokushin no yō na** koto o kikimashita.*
I heard such a thing as Mr. Smith is single.

田中さんはお酒は嫌いなようなことを言っていました。
*Tanaka san wa osake wa **kirai na yō na** koto o itte imashita.*
Mr. Tanaka said something like he does not like alcohol.

好きなようにしてけっこうです。 ***Suki na yō ni** shite kekkō desu.*
You can do as you like.

本当のように見せかけているのです。
***Hontō no yō ni** misekakete iru no desu.*
They are making it look like a true item.

4. After verbs and adjectives in the dictionary form, **nai**-form, or **ta**-form

もっと役に立つような機械を買いなさい。
Motto yaku ni tatsu yō na kikai o kainasai.
You should buy machines that are more useful.

彼女は会社を辞めるようなことを言っていました。
Kanojo wa kaisha o yameru yō na koto o itte imashita.
She said that she might quit the company. (I heard so.)

この辺ではあまり見ないような人だね。
Kono hen de wa amari minai yō na hito da ne.
That person isn't the sort we see around here, is he?

この間食べたようなケーキだよ。
Kono aida tabeta yō na kēki da yo.
This is a cake like the one we ate the other day.

5. After clauses

Yō ni is often used with a clause that describes one's purposes, often expressed by potential verbs that indicate the desired state, especially when the main clause expresses requests, suggestions, and one's intentions.

私にも操作できるように使い方を説明して下さい。
Watashi ni mo sōsa dekiru yō ni tsukaikata o setsumei shite kudasai.
Please explain how to use it so that I can operate it.

電車に間に合うように駅までタクシーで行きましょう。
Densha ni maniau yō ni eki made takushī de ikimashō.
Let's go by taxi to the train station so that we can catch the train.

私にも分かるようにもっとゆっくり日本語を話して下さい。
Watashi ni mo wakaru yō ni motto yukkuri Nihongo o hanashite kudasai.
Please speak Japanese more slowly so that I can understand it.

あなたが幸せになるように祈っています。
Anata ga shiawase ni naru yō ni inotte imasu.
I wish you happiness. (I hope you will be happy.)

試験に落ちないようにもっと勉強しなきゃ。
Shiken ni ochinai yō ni motto benkyō shinakya.
I have to study more so as not to fail the exam.

その計画はあなたが思うようにはうまくいかないでしょう。
Sono keikaku wa anata ga omou yō ni wa umaku ikanai deshō.
That plan will probably not work as well as you expect.

先に述べたように契約期間は三年です。
Saki ni nobeta yō ni keiyaku kikan wa san nen desu.
As mentioned before, the term of the contract is three years.

yō ni iu ように言う [PREDICATIVE PHRASE]

to tell/ask (somebody) to (do something)

When *yō ni* follows verbs in the dictionary form or *nai*-form and precedes a verb such as *iu* 'to tell,' *tanomu* 'to request,' *onegai-suru* 'to beg,' and *kōshō-suru* 'to negotiate,' the sentence indicates what the person denoted by the subject noun is requesting or commanding someone to do.

1. After verbs in the dictionary form

   昨日彼女に今日の三時にここへ来るように言いました。
   Kinō kanojo ni kyō no san ji ni koko e kuru yō ni iimashita.
   Yesterday I told her to come here at three o'clock today.

   彼に手伝ってくれるように頼みましたか。
   Kare ni tetsudatte kureru yō ni tanomimashita ka.
   Did you ask him to help you?

   先生に論文を読んでくれるようにお願いしてみます。
   Sensei ni ronbun o yonde kureru yō ni onegai shite mimasu.
   I'll try asking the professor to read my paper.

   食事をつけるように旅行会社に交渉します。
   Shokuji o tsukeru yō ni ryokō gaisha ni kōshō shimasu.
   I will negotiate with the travel agency so that they can provide meals.

2. After verbs in the *nai*-form

   彼にあまり飲まないように言いなさい。
   Kare ni amari nomanai yō ni iinasai.
   Tell him not to drink too much.

yō ni naru ようになる [PREDICATIVE PHRASE]

to become able to do . . . , to start to . . . , to stop to . . .

When *yō ni* follows verbs in the dictionary form or *nai*-form and precedes the verb *naru*, it expresses some change in one's behavior or ability. In this case, the preceding verb is occasionally in the potential form or denotes states or events that the speaker does not have control over, or the preceding clause expresses a natural result. The alternative form of . . . *nai yō ni naru* is . . . *naku naru.* (→ See also *naru*, *yō da* <resemblance>, and *yō ni suru*.)

1. After verbs in the dictionary form

   息子は最近早く起きるようになりました。
   Musuko wa saikin hayaku okiru yō ni narimashita.
   My son has started to get up early in the morning lately.

息子は最近早く起きられるようになりました。
*Musuko wa saikin hayaku okira**reru** yō ni narimashita.*
My son became able to get up early in the morning lately.

2. After verbs in the *nai*-form

母は最近，文句を言わないようになりました。
*Haha wa saikin monku o iwa**nai** yō ni narimashita.*
My mother stopped complaining recently.

The above sentence can be rephrased as:

母は最近，文句を言わなくなりました。
*Haha wa saikin monku o iwa**naku** narimashita.*

yō ni suru ようにする [PREDICATIVE PHRASE]

to make sure that . . . , take care that, try to (do) . . . , make it a rule to (do) . . .

When *yō ni* follows verbs in the dictionary form or *nai*-form and precedes the verb *suru*, it expresses the speaker's intention to make some efforts to achieve some goal or wish expressed by *yō ni*. When it is in the *te iru* form, as in *yō ni shite iru*, it expresses that one is habitually making such efforts. (→ See also *suru*, *yō da* <resemblance>, and *yō ni naru*.)

1. After verbs in the dictionary form

あす九時までにここに来るようにして下さい。
Asu ku ji made ni koko ni kuru yō ni shite kudasai.
Please make sure that you come here by nine tomorrow.

この頃は早寝早起きをするようにしています。
Kono goro wa hayane hayaoki o suru yō ni shite imasu.
Recently, I have been trying to go to bed early and get up early.

毎日漢字を三つ覚えるようにします。
Mainichi kanji o mittsu oboeru yō ni shimasu.
I'll make it a rule to learn three kanji every day.

2. After verbs in the *nai*-form

待ち合わせ時間に遅れないようにして下さい。
*Machiawase jikan ni okure**nai** yō ni shite kudasai.*
Please make sure that you won't be late for our appointment.

yori より [PARTICLE]

than, (not) . . . but, from, since, (out) of

The particle *yori* means either 'from' or 'than.' When it means 'than,' it follows nouns, verbs, and adjectives to create a comparative sentence. In the latter case, it is often followed by *mo* for emphasis.

1. Following nouns, to mean 'from'

   香港行きの飛行機は３番ゲートより出発します。
   *Honkon yuki no hikōki wa **san ban gēto yori** shuppatsu shimasu.*
   The plane for Hong Kong departs from Gate 3.

   (When meaning 'from,' *yori* may be replaced by *kara*.)

   開会式は十時より始まります。 *Kaikaishiki wa **jū ji yori** hajimarimasu.*
   The opening ceremony will be held starting at ten.

   → See also *kara*.

2. Following nouns, to mean 'than'

   日本語は英語よりもずいぶんむずかしいですね。
   *Nihongo wa **Eigo yori mo** zuibun muzukashii desu ne.*
   Japanese is much more difficult than English, isn't it?

   あの特急の方がこの電車よりも早く着きます。
   *Ano tokkyū no hō ga kono **densha yori mo** hayaku tsukimasu.*
   That special express will arrive earlier than this train.

   今日は帰りはいつもより遅くなります。
   *Kyō wa kaeri wa **itsumo yori** osoku narimasu.*
   I'll be home later than usual today.

   → See Comparisons.

3. After verbs and adjectives in the dictionary form, to mean 'than'

   今日は家でテレビを見るより外へ出かける方がいい。
   *Kyō wa ie de terebi o **miru yori** soto e dekakeru hō ga ii.*
   It's better to go out than watch TV at home today.

   こうするよりほかに方法がない。 *Kō **suru yori** hoka ni hōhō ga nai.*
   There is nothing else to do but this.

   同じ物なら高いより安い方がいいに決まっています。
   *Onaji mono nara **takai yori** yasui hō ga ii ni kimatte imasu.*
   If they are the same, naturally the cheap one is better than the expensive one.

   わずかなお金でもないよりはましです。
   *Wazuka na okane demo **nai yori** wa mashi desu.*
   Even a small sum of money is better than none.

4. After verbs and adjectives in the *nai*-form, to mean 'than'

   待つ間何もしないより雑誌でも読む方がいいです。
   *Matsu aida nani mo shi**nai yori** zasshi demo yomu hō ga ii desu.*
   Even reading a magazine is better than doing nothing while waiting.

この本は読まないより読んだ方がいい。
Kono hon wa yomanai yori yonda hō ga ii.
It would be better to read this book than not.

安くないより，安い方がいい。 *Yasuku **nai yori**, yasui hō ga ii.*
It is better to be cheap than not to be cheap.

5. After verbs in the **ta**-form, to mean 'than'

その専門雑誌は思ったよりやさしかったです。
Sono senmon zasshi wa omotta yori yasashikatta desu.
That technical journal was easier than I thought.

→ See also *hō* and *hodo*.

yoroshii よろしい [ADJECTIVE]

all right, okay

Yoroshii is a formal counterpart of the adjective *ii* 'good,' and thus used in a variety of constructions. It is a formal word, but for giving permission to one's superior, *kekkō* is more appropriate than *yoroshii desu*. However, for seeking permission from one's superior, *yoroshii desu ka* is most appropriate. (→ See also *kekkō* and *temo/demo ii*.)

1. After noun + **de**

「それでよろしいですか。」「はい，けっこうです。」
*"**Sore de yoroshii** desu ka." "Hai, kekkō desu."*
"Would it be all right?" "That will do."

「駅に行くのにこの道でよろしいですか。」「はい，大丈夫です。」
*"Eki e iku no ni kono **michi de yoroshii** desu ka." "Hai, daijōbu desu."*
"Can I just (go straight) on this street to go to the train station?" "Yes, sure."

2. After interrogative word + **demo**

いつでもよろしいですよ。 ***Itsu demo yoroshii** desu yo.*
Any time will be all right.

どちらでもよろしいです。 ***Dochira demo** yoroshii desu.* **Either will do.**

→ See *demo* <particle>.

3. After verbs in the **te**-form (+ **mo**)

コピー機はいつ使ってもよろしいです。
*Kopīki wa itsu tsukat**temo yoroshii** desu.*
You may use the copying machine at any time.

「もう帰ってよろしいですか。」「いえ，まだだめです。」
*"Mo kaet**te yoroshii** desu ka." "Ie, mada dame desu."*
"Is it all right if I go home now?" "No, not yet."

「ここでたばこを吸ってもよろしいですか。」「ここは禁煙です。」
"Koko de tabako o sutte mo yoroshii desu ka." "Koko wa kin'en desu."
"Is it all right if I smoke here?" "This is a no-smoking area."

バス停までついて行ってもよろしいですよ。
Basutei made tsuite itte mo yoroshii desu yo.
I'd be glad to accompany you to the bus stop.

→ See *temo ii / demo ii.*

4. After verbs in the **ta**-form + **hō ga**

辞めた方がよろしいですよ。 *Yameta hō ga yoroshii desu yo.*
It would be better to stop it.

→ See *hō ga ii.*

5. In conditional **ba**-form

よろしければこの会に参加しませんか。
Yoroshikereba kono kai ni sanka shimasen ka.
If you feel like it, wouldn't you like to join this meeting?

→ See *ba.*

zaru o enai ざるを得ない [PREDICATIVE PHRASE]

cannot help (doing), cannot help but (do), to be obliged to (do), to have no choice
but to (do)

Zaru o enai is used right after the initial part of the *nai*-form, and means that
there is no choice.

この条件では監督になる契約をあきらめざるを得ない。
*Kono jōken dewa kantoku ni naru keiyaku o **akiramezaru o enai**.*
**I am obliged to give up signing a contract to be the manager on this
condition.**

あれには笑わざるを得ませんでした。
*Are ni wa **warawazaru o emasen** deshita.*
I could not help laughing at that.

彼らには協力せざるを得ない。 *Karera ni wa kyōryoku **sezaru o enai**.*
We have no choice but to cooperate with them.

(Note the irregular initial part of *suru* is *se* before *zaru*.)

zenzen 全然 [ADVERB]

(not) at all, (not) in the least, (not) a bit, (not) anything, entirely, completely, very
much

Zenzen is an adverb used with verbs and adjectives in the negative form, expressing total negation and meaning '(not) at all.' However, some verbs like *chigau* 'to differ' can be used with *zenzen* even when it is in the affirmative form. More and more Japanese have started to use *zenzen* with other kind of affirmative predicates to mean 'very much' or 'quite.' (→ See also *mattaku*.)

1. Used with verbs in the negative form

   日本語は少し話せますが全然書けません。
   *Nihongo wa sukoshi hanasemasu ga **zenzen kakemasen**.*
   I can speak a little but cannot write in Japanese at all.

   そのことについては全然知りません。
   *Sono koto ni tsuite wa **zenzen shirimasen**.*
   I know nothing at all about it.

   ボスの言ったことは全然気にしていません。
   *Bosu no itta koto wa **zenzen** ki ni shite **imasen**.*
   I don't care a bit about what my boss said.

2. Used with adjectives in the negative form

   この本はぜんぜん難しくありませんよ。
   *Kono hon wa **zenzen** muzukashi**ku arimasen** yo.*
   This book is not difficult at all.

3. Used with adjectival nouns and a copular verb in the negative form

   このアパートはぜんぜん不便じゃありません。
   *Kono apāto wa **zenzen fuben ja arimasen**.*
   This apartment is not inconvenient at all.

4. Used with affirmative predicates

   あなたの言うことは彼の言うことと全然違います。
   *Anata no iu koto wa kare no iu koto to **zenzen** chigaimasu.*
   What you say is entirely different from what he says.

   そのジャケット全然いいですね。 *Sono jaketto **zenzen ii desu** ne.*
   Your jacket is very nice, isn't it?

   「元気ですか。」「全然元気です。」 *"Genki desu ka." "**Zenzen genki desu**."*
   "How are you?" "I'm very well."

zu ni ずに [ADVERBIAL PHRASE]

without (doing), not (do something) but (do another thing)

Zu ni is a slightly formal counterpart of *nai de*. (→ See *nai de*.) *Zu* is an old negative suffix that is still commonly used in modern Japanese and can replace *nai* in the *nai*-form of verbs, so *tabenai* can be *tabezu*. The verb *suru* is irregular, and its *zu*-form is *sezu*. The *zu*-form of the irregular verb *kuru* is *kozu*.

最後まであきらめずに頑張って下さい。
*Saigo made **akiramezu ni** ganbatte kudasai.*
Do your best and don't give up to the last.

彼は宿題もせずに遊んでいた。
*Kare wa shukudai mo **sezu ni** asonde ita.*
He was playing without having done his homework.

銀行からお金を借りずに済みそうです。
*Ginkō kara okane o **karizu ni** sumisō desu.*
It looks like we'll manage without borrowing money from the bank.

わざわざ東京まで行かずに済みました。
*Wazawaza Tōkyō made **ikazu ni** sumimashita.*
I didn't have to make a special trip to Tokyo.

チケットを見せずに会場に入ることはできません。
*Chiketto o **misezu ni** kaijō ni hairu koto wa dekimasen.*
You cannot enter the hall without showing the ticket.

Compare the following sentences:

チケットを見せながら会場に入ってください。
*Chiketto o **misenagara** kaijō ni haitte kudasai.*
Please enter the hall showing the ticket.

チケットを見せて会場に入ってください。
*Chiketto o **misete** kaijō ni haitte kudasai.*
Please show the ticket, and enter the hall.

→ See also *nagara, te,* and *nai de.*

Appendices

APPENDIX 1

List of Common Adjectival Nouns

abekobe no あべこべの contrary, opposite

aimai na 曖昧な ambiguous, vague

akiraka na 明らかな obvious, clear

an'i na 安易な easygoing

anraku na/no 安楽な/の comfortable, easy

anzen na 安全な safe, secure

asahaka na 浅はかな thoughtless, shallow, silly

atarimae no 当たり前の natural, ordinary

aware na 哀れな poor, pitiful, miserable

ayafuya na あやふやな vague, ambiguous, uncertain

azayaka na 鮮やかな bright, vivid, skillful

baka na 馬鹿な foolish, silly, stupid

bakudai na 莫大な great, huge, enormous, vast

ban'nō no 万能の almighty, omnipotent

barabara no ばらばらの broken up, in pieces, loose

batsugun no 抜群の distinguished, outstanding, unrivaled

benri na 便利な convenient, useful

betsu no/na 別の/な another, different

bimyō na 微妙な delicate, subtle

binbō na 貧乏な poor

binkan na 敏感な sensitive

binsoku na 敏速な quick, prompt

bōdai na 膨大な huge, vast, enormous

buji na 無事な safe

bukakkō na 不格好な awkward

bukimi na 不気味な weird, uncanny,

bukiyō na 不器用な awkward, unskillful, clumsy

bunan na 無難な passable

bungakuteki na 文学的な literary

burei na 無礼な rude, impolite

busaiku na 不細工な not good-looking

buzama na 無様な shabby, awkward

byōdō no/na 平等の/な equal, even

byōki no 病気の sick, diseased

byōteki na 病的な morbid

chakujitsu na 着実な steady

chikaku no 近くの near, close

chimitsu na 緻密な precise, minute, elaborate

chinpunkanpun na ちんぷんかんぷんな nonsensical, incongruous

chiteki na 知的な intellectual, intelligent

chōhatsuteki na 挑発的な provocative

chokkaku no 直角の right-angled

chūjitsu na 忠実な faithful, loyal

chūko no 中古の secondhand, used

chūnen no 中年の middle-aged

chūritsu no 中立の neutral

chūshōteki na 抽象的な abstract

chūtohanpa na 中途半端な half-done, lukewarm

daiji na 大事な important, valuable, precious

daijōbu na 大丈夫な all right, safe

daisuki na 大好きな very favorite

dame na 駄目な no good, impossible, hopeless

detarame na でたらめな inaccurate, random

dokudanteki na 独断的な arbitrary, dogmatic

dokushin no 独身の unmarried, single

dokusōteki na 独創的な creative, original

dokutoku no/na 独特の/な peculiar, unique

dōtokuteki na 道徳的な moral

dōyō no 同様の the same, similar

enman na 円満な happy (of relation)

fuan na 不安な uneasy, anxious, worried, restless

fuantei na 不安定な unstable, unsteady, precarious, insecure

fuben na 不便な inconvenient

fuchūi na 不注意な careless

fūgawari na 風変わりな strange, odd, quaint, queer, eccentric

fuhitsuyō na 不必要な unnecessary, needless

fui no 不意の unexpected

fujiyū na 不自由な inconvenient, physically handicapped

fukahi no 不可避の inevitable, unavoidable

fukai na 不快な unpleasant, disagreeable

fukakai na 不可解な incomprehensible, mysterious

fukaketsu no/na 不可欠の/な indispensable, essential

fukakujitsu na 不確実な uncertain, unreliable

fukakutei no 不確定の indefinite, unsettled

fukanō na 不可能な impossible

fukanzen na 不完全な imperfect, incomplete

fukeiki na 不景気な depressed (of economy)

fukigen na 不機嫌な ill-humored, ill-tempered, displeased, sullen

fukisoku na 不規則な irregular

fukitsu na 不吉な ominous

fukō na 不幸な unhappy, unfortunate, unlucky

fukōhei na 不公平な partial, unfair

fukuzatsu na 複雑な complicated, complex

fumajime na 不真面目な insincere, frivolous

fumei no 不明の not clear, obscure, unknown

furi na 不利な disadvantageous, unfavorable

fushigi na 不思議な strange, mysterious

fushizen na 不自然な unnatural, forced

futsū no 普通の usual, common, normal, ordinary

fuyō na/no 不要な/の unnecessary, needless

fuyukai na 不愉快な unpleasant, disagreeable, displeased

gehin na 下品な vulgar, mean, coarse

genjitsuteki na 現実的な realistic

genkaku na 厳格な strict, stern

genki na 元気な energetic, lively, healthy

genmitsu na 厳密な exact, strict

gensei na 厳正な strict, rigid, fair

gensōteki na 幻想的な fantastic, dreamy

gōin na 強引な forcible

gōka na 豪華な deluxe, gorgeous, grand

gokaku no 互角の even, well-matched

gōman na 傲慢な haughty, arrogant, insolent

gōsei na 豪勢な luxurious, grand

gutaiteki na 具体的な concrete, definite

gūzen no 偶然の accidental, casual, chance

hade na 派手な showy, bright, gaudy, high (of life), loud (of color)

hanayaka na 華やかな bright, brilliant, gorgeous, showy

hankōteki na 反抗的な rebellious, defiant

hantai no 反対の opposite, reverse, contrary

hanzatsu na 煩雑な complicated, troublesome, complex

hayari no 流行の fashionable, popular, prevailing

heibon na 平凡な commonplace, ordinary

heiki na 平気な composed, indifferent

heikinteki na 平均的な average

heisei na 平静な calm, quiet, composed, serene

heiwa na 平和な peaceful

hen na 変な odd, queer, strange

heta na 下手な unskillful, awkward, clumsy

hidari no 左の left (of direction)

higeki no 悲劇の tragic

higenjitsuteki na 非現実的な impractical, unreal, fantastic

hihanteki na 批判的な critical

hijō na 非常な remarkable

hikaeme na 控えめな moderate, temperate, reserved, modest

hikanteki na 悲観的な pessimistic, gloomy

hikyō na 卑怯な cowardly, unfair, unmanly

hima na 暇な not busy, not engaged, free, leisure

himitsu no 秘密の secret

hinjaku na 貧弱な poor, scanty

hinpan na 頻繁な frequent, repeated

hiretsu na 卑劣な mean, base, cowardly

hisan na 悲惨な miserable, tragic

hisashiburi no 久しぶりの after a long interval or separation

hiteiteki na 否定的な negative

hitsuzenteki na 必然的な inevitable

hitsuyō na 必要な necessary, indispensable

hōfu na 豊富な abundant, plentiful

hogaraka na 朗らかな cheerful, merry

honki no 本気の serious, earnest

honmono no 本物の real, true

honoka na 仄かな dim, faint, slight

hontō no 本当の true, real, actual

hyōjunteki na 標準的な standard

idai na 偉大な great

igai na 意外な unexpected, surprising

ijō na 異常な unusual, abnormal

imaichi na いまいちな not-so-great, lacking something

inken na 陰険な sly, crafty, cunning

ippan no 一般の general, universal, common, ordinary

iroiro na/no 色々な/の various

jimuteki na 事務的な businesslike

jiyū na/no 自由な/の free, liberal

jōbu na 丈夫な durable, firm, tough

jōhin na 上品な elegant, graceful, refined

jōnetsuteki na 情熱的な passionate, ardent

jōtō no 上等の excellent, of good quality

jōzu na 上手な expert, good (of technique)

jūbun na 十分な enough, sufficient

jūnan na 柔軟な soft, flexible, supple

junboku na 純朴な simple and honest, unsophisticated

jūyō na 重要な important

kakubetsu no 格別の special, exceptional

kandai na 寛大な generous, large-hearted, broad-minded

kandōteki na 感動的な impressive, moving

kanemochi no 金持の rich, wealthy

kanjin no/na 肝心の/な important, main, essential

kanpeki na 完璧な perfect, complete, faultless

kanshin na 感心な admirable, praiseworthy

kantan na 簡単な simple, brief, easy

kanzen na 完全な perfect, complete

kappatsu na 活発な lively, active

kasuka na 微かな faint, dim, slight

kawaisō na 可哀相な poor, pitiful

keishikiteki na 形式的な formal

keisotsu na 軽率な rash, hasty, careless, thoughtless, imprudent

keizaiteki na 経済的な economical

ken'aku na 険悪な hostile

kencho na 顕著な remarkable, noticeable, outstanding, striking

kenkō na 健康な healthy

kenmei na 賢明な wise

ken'yakuteki na 倹約的な thrifty, frugal

kenzen na 健全な sound, healthy

ketteiteki na 決定的な decisive, definite

kiken na 危険な dangerous, risky, perilous

kimyō na 奇妙な strange, queer

kinkyū no 緊急の urgent, pressing

kinodoku na 気の毒な poor, pitiful, unfortunate, sorry

kirei na 綺麗な pretty, beautiful, lovely

kiyō na 器用な skillful, handy

kōdai na 広大な vast, immense

kogirei na 小ぎれいな neat, trim

kojinteki na 個人的な individual, personal, private

kokumei na 克明な minute, detailed

kokusaiteki na 国際的な international

kōkyū na 高級な high-class

kōhei na 公平な fair, impartial, disinterested

kōman na 高慢な conceited, haughty, arrogant

kōsei na 公正な just, fair, impartial

kyakkanteki na 客観的な objective

kyokutan na 極端な extreme, radical

kyōretsu na 強烈な severe, intense

kyōryoku na 強力な powerful, strong

kyūkyoku no 究極の ultimate, final

majime na 真面目な eanest, serious, honest

makka na/no 真っ赤な/の deep red, crimson, scarlet, downright (of a lie)

makkura na/no 真っ暗な/の pitch-dark

makkuro na/no 真っ黒な/の coal-black, deep black

māmā no まあまあの not so bad, so-so

mame na まめな diligent, hardworking

manzoku na 満足な satisfactory, sufficient

mare na/no 稀な/の rare, unusual

maroyaka na まろやかな mild (of taste)

massao na/no 真っ青な/の deep blue, azure, pale

masshiro na/no 真っ白な/の pure-white, snow-white

massugu na まっすぐな straight, upright

matomo na/no まともな/の honest, normal

mazumazu no まずまずの not so bad, fairly good

mechakucha na 滅茶苦茶な unreasonable, nonsensical

mechamecha na 滅茶滅茶な broken to pieces, spoiled

meihaku na 明白な clear, evident, obvious

meikai na 明快な clear, lucid, explicit

meikaku na 明確な clear, distinct

meirō na 明朗な bright and cheerful

meiryō na 明瞭な clear, distinct, plain

meiwaku na 迷惑な troublesome, annoying

mendō na 面倒な troublesome, annoying

menmitsu na 綿密な minute, detailed

michi no 未知の unknown

migi no 右の right (of direction)

migoto na 見事な splendid, excellent, skillful

mijime na 惨めな miserable, wretched, pitiable

mijuku na 未熟な immature

mikaiketsu no 未解決の unsolved, unsettled, pending

miryokuteki na 魅力的な attractive

mitei no 未定の unfixed, undecided, unsettled, pending

miwakuteki na 魅惑的な charming, fascinating, attractive

mokuzō no 木造の wooden, made of wood

monoshizuka na 物静かな quiet (of person)

monozuki na 物好きな curious

mōretsu na 猛烈な violent, wild, fierce

moromoro no もろもろの all kinds of, various

mottomo na 尤もな reasonable, natural

moyori no 最寄りの the nearest

mubō na 無謀な rash, reckless

mucha na 無茶な extravagant, absurd, reckless

muda na 無駄な useless, wasteful, fruitless

mugai no/na 無害の/な harmless

mugen no 無限の infinite, limitless, endless

muimi na 無意味な meaningless, senseless

mujaki na 無邪気な innocent, simple (of mind)

mujitsu no 無実の innocent

mukanshin na 無関心な indifferent, unconcerned

mukō no 無効の invalid

mukuchi na 無口な taciturn, reticent

mumei no 無名の unknown, obscure (not famous)

munō na 無能な incompetent, incapable

muri na 無理な impossible, unreasonable (of request)

muryō no 無料の free of charge

musekinin na 無責任な irresponsible

mushinkei na 無神経な insensitive, inconsiderate

mutonchaku na 無頓着な indifferent, unconcerned

muyō no 無用の useless, of no use

muzai no 無罪の innocent, not guilty

muzan na 無残な merciless, cruel

muzei no 無税の tax-free, duty-free

nadaraka na なだらかな gently sloping

nagoyaka na 和やかな calm, peaceful, friendly

naisho no 内証の secret, private

nama no 生の raw, uncooked, undercooked

namaiki na 生意気な audacious, cheeky, saucy, impudent

nami no 並の ordinary, common, average

nameraka na 滑らかな smooth, fluent

nankai na 難解な hard to understand or solve, knotty

nigiyaka na 賑やかな lively, cheerful, merry, busy (of street)

nin'i no 任意の optional, voluntary

nise no 偽の false, fake, counterfeit, imitation, sham

nōritsuteki na 能率的な efficient

nyūnen na 入念な elaborate, careful

ōbō na 横暴な tyrannical, oppressive

odayaka na 穏やかな calm, mild, gentle, moderate

ōgesa na 大げさな exaggerated

ōhei na 横柄な arrogant, haughty, insolent

okiniiri no お気に入りの favorite, pet

onken na 穏健な moderate

onkō na 温厚な gentle, mild-mannered

omo na 主な main, chief, principal

omowaseburi na 思わせぶりな coquettish, suggestive

oroka na 愚かな foolish, silly, stupid

ōyake no 公の public

ōzappa na 大ざっぱな rough, loose

pikapika no ぴかぴかの glittering, gleaming, twinkling

rakkanteki na 楽観的な optimistic, easygoing

raku na 楽な easy, comfortable

rakutenteki na 楽天的な optimistic, easygoing

ranbō na 乱暴な violent

ranzatsu na 乱雑な untidy, in disorder

reigai no 例外の exceptional

reikoku na 冷酷な cruel, heartless

reisei na 冷静な calm, cool (of attitude)

reitan na 冷淡な cold (of attitude)

rekishiteki na 歴史的な historical, historic

rikō na 利口な clever, wise, smart, intelligent

rinji no 臨時の temporary, extraordinary

rippa na 立派な splendid, great, superb

rironteki na 理論的な theoretical

risōteki na 理想的な ideal

riseiteki na 理性的な rational, reasonable

rokotsu na 露骨な frank, outspoken, plain, open

rongai no 論外の that is out of the question

ronriteki na 論理的な logical

ryōshinteki na 良心的な conscientious

saiai no 最愛の one's dearest, one's beloved

saiaku no 最悪の the worst

saidai no 最大の the biggest, the greatest

saigo no 最後の final, ultimate, last

saihate no 最果ての the farthest

saikin no 最近の the latest, recent

saiko no 最古の the oldest

saikō no 最高の highest, best, supreme

saikyō no 最強の the strongest

saishin no 最新の the newest, the most up-to-date

saishinshiki no 最新式の the newest-style

saisho no 最初の first, original

saishō no 最小の the smallest, minimum 最少の the least

saitei no 最低の the lowest, the worst

saiteki no 最適の the most suitable, the best suited

saizen no 最善の the best
samazama na 様々な various, diverse
sasayaka na ささやかな tiny, little
sawayaka na 爽やかな fresh, refreshing
seidai na 盛大な splendid, grand, magnificent
seihantai no 正反対の directly opposite
seijitsu na 誠実な sincere, honest, faithful
seijō na 正常な normal
seikaku na 正確な exact, accurate, precise, correct
seiketsu na 清潔な clean, pure
seimitsu na 精密な minute, precise
seiryokuteki na 精力的な energetic, vigorous
seishiki na 正式な formal, regular, official
seitō na 正当な just, fair, lawful
sekkyokuteki na 積極的な positive, active
senmei na 鮮明な clear, distinct, vivid
senmon no 専門の professional, expert, technical
sensai na 繊細な delicate, sensitive, exquisite
sen'yō no 専用の exclusive, private
setsujitsu na 切実な urgent (of a problem), earnest (of a request)
shinayaka na しなやかな flexible, supple
shinchō na 慎重な careful, discreet
shinken na 真剣な earnest, serious
shinriteki na 心理的な psychological, mental
shinsetsu na 親切な kind, kindly
shinmitsu na 親密な intimate, friendly, close
shinpai na 心配な worried, anxious
shirafu no しらふの sober
shita no 下の located below
shitoyaka na しとやかな gentle, graceful
shitsurei na 失礼な impolite, rude
shizen na/no 自然な/の natural
shizuka na 静かな quiet, calm, silent
shōjiki na 正直な honest
shōki no 正気の sane
shōkyokuteki na 消極的な passive, negative
shōsai na 詳細な detailed, full, minute
shukanteki na 主観的な subjective
sōdai na 壮大な grand, magnificent, imposing
sōgōteki na 総合的な synthetic
sokuseki no 即席の instant, impromptu, extempore
somatsu na 粗末な humble, plain, miserable
son na 損な disadvantageous, thankless
sonota no その他の other (attributive use only)

sotchoku na 率直な frank, candid, open
sōtō no/na 相当の/な considerable
sozatsu na 粗雑な sloppy
suichoku no 垂直の perpendicular, vertical
suihei no 水平の level, horizontal
suki na 好きな favorite
sunao na 素直な obedient, yielding
suteki na 素敵な nice, splendid, wonderful, charming
tabō na 多忙な busy
taihen na 大変な terrible, serious, difficult (→ See also Appendix 3.)
taikutsu na 退屈な boring, tedious, monotonous
taira na 平らな flat, level, smooth
taisetsu na 大切な important, precious, valuable
takumi na 巧みな skillful, clever, dexterous
takusan no たくさんの a lot of, enough
tanjun na 単純な simple, simple-minded
tanki na 短気な short-tempered, quick-tempered
tan'nen na 丹念な painstaking, carefully made
tanpaku na 淡泊な indifferent, light (of color or taste)
tanteki na 端的な frank, straightforward
tappuri na/no たっぷりな/の full, ample, enough
taryō no 多量の abundant, copious
tashika na 確かな definite, certain, sure, undoubted
tegaru na 手軽な handy, simple, light
tegoro na 手頃な handy, reasonable (of price), moderate, convenient
teichō na 丁重な courteous, polite, respectful; 丁低調な low-tones, inactive
teikiteki na 定期的な periodical, regular
teinei na 丁寧な polite, courteous
teizoku na 低俗な vulgar
tekido no/na 適度の/な moderate, temperate
tekikaku na 的確な precise, accurate, exact
tekisetsu na 適切な suitable, appropriate, proper, fitting
tekitō na 適当な suitable, appropriate, proper, irresponsible
ten'nen no 天然の natural (of resources)
tetsugakuteki na 哲学的な philosophical
tetteiteki na 徹底的な thorough, thoroughgoing, exhaustive
tōku no 遠くの far

tokubetsu no/na 特別の/な special, extra, particular, exceptional

tokui no/na 得意の/な strong (of ability), in one's line

tokusei no 特製の specially made

tokushu na 特殊な special, particular, peculiar, unique

tōmei na 透明な transparent, clear

tonchinkan na とんちんかんな inconsistent, irrelevant

toshishita no 年下の junior, younger

toshiue no 年上の senior, older, elder

tōzen no/na 当然の/な natural, reasonable, expected

tsūkai na 痛快な extremely delightful, incisive

tsūretsu na 痛烈な bitter/severe

tsūsetsu na 痛切な keen, serious

ue no 上の up, upward, upper

ukatsu na 迂闊な careless

wagamama na 我が儘な selfish, egoistic, spoiled

waridaka no 割高の rather expensive

yabo na 野暮な unrefined, boorish

yakkai na 厄介な troublesome, annoying, burdensome

yobun na 余分な extra, spare, surplus

yōi na 容易な easy

yokei na 余計な extra, unnecessary, uninvited, unwanted

yōki na 陽気な merry, cheerful, bright, gay

yosōgai no 予想外の unexpected

yowaki na 弱気な timid, weak-minded

yūbō na 有望な promising, hopeful

yūdai na 雄大な grand, magnificent

yūdoku na 有毒な poisonous, toxic

yūeki na 有益な profitable, beneficial, instructive

yūfuku na 裕福な rich, wealthy, well-off

yūga na 優雅な elegant, graceful, refined, polished

yūgai na 有害な harmful, injurious, noxious

yūigi na 有意義な significant, meaningful

yukai na 愉快な pleasant, enjoyable, delightful

yūkan na 勇敢な brave, courageous

yūkō na 有効な effective, valid

yūmei na 有名な famous, well-known, noted

yūnō na 有能な able, capable

yūri na 有利な profitable, advantageous

yuruyaka na 緩やかな gentle (of slope), slow (of flow)

yūryoku na 有力な influential

yūsei na 優勢な superior, predominant

yūshū na 優秀な excellent, superior

yūsō na 勇壮な brave, soul-stirring

yutaka na 豊かな wealthy, rich, abundant

yūutsu na 憂鬱な gloomy, depressed, melancholy

yūzai no 有罪の guilty

zan'nen na 残念な regrettable, regretful, disappointing

zankoku na 残酷な cruel, brutal, heartless, merciless

zentai no 全体の whole

zetsubōteki na 絶望的な hopeless

zettai no 絶対の absolute, unconditional

zeitaku na 贅沢な luxurious, extravagant sumptuous

zuii no 随意の optional

<Derived from loanwords>

anrakkī na アンラッキーな unlucky

derikēto na デリケートな delicate

fasshonaburu na ファッショナブルな fashionable

furendorī na フレンドリーな friendly

furesshu na フレッシュな fresh

gōjasu na ゴージャスな gorgeous

hai na ハイな high-spirited

hansamu na ハンサムな handsome

hebī na ヘビーな heavy

hotto na ホットな hot

kūru na クールな cool

naisu na ナイスな nice

raito na ライトな light (not heavy)

rakkī na ラッキーな lucky

shinpuru na シンプルな simple

sumāto na スマートな smart

<Derived from mimetic words>

betabeta no ベタベタの sticky

dorodoro no どろどろの muddy

furafura no ふらふらの dizzy, unsteady

gatagata no ガタガタの rickety

kachikachi no カチカチの hard

pikapika no ピカピカの shiny

subesube no すべすべの smooth (of skin)

yoreyore no よれよれの shabby

<Ends with *taru*>

danko taru 断固たる firm, decisive, resolute

dōdō taru 堂々たる stately, imposing, grand, splendid, majestic

jikuji taru 忸怩たる bashful, shameful

kizen taru 毅然たる resolute, firm

rekizen taru 歴然たる obvious, evident

santan taru 惨憺たる pitiful, wretched, miserable, terrible, horrible

sōsō taru 錚々たる eminent, outstanding, conspicuous

<Ends with *to shita*>

aoao to shita 青々とした fresh and green

bakuzen to shita 漠然とした vague, obscure

dōdō to shita 堂々とした stately, imposing, grand, splendid, majestic

hirobiro to shita 広々とした extensive, roomy, spacious, commodious.

kizen to shita 毅然とした resolute, firm

konton to shita 混沌とした chaotic, disorderly

rin to shita 凛とした dignified

tantan to shita 淡々とした unconcerned, indifferent, cool

kansan to shita 閑散とした quiet, dull

kōryō to shita 荒涼とした desolate

APPENDIX 2

List of Common Adjectives

abunai 危ない dangerous
adokenai あどけない innocent, childish
akai 赤い red
akarui 明るい bright, cheerful
akippoi 飽きっぽい changeable, capricious
amai 甘い sweet, superficially optimistic, not strict
aoi 青い blue, pale, green (of traffic signal)
arai 荒い rough, coarse
asai 浅い shallow
atarashii 新しい new, fresh, up-to-date
atatakai 暖かい warm (informally *attakai*)
atsui 暑い, 熱い hot 厚い thick
awatadashii 慌ただしい busy, hurried
ayashii 怪しい suspicious, doubtful, uncertain
buatsui 分厚い thick, bulky
chīsai 小さい small, low (of volume) (*chīsa na* is a prenominal variant form)
chikai 近い near, close
darashinai だらしない untidy, sloppy, loose, slovenly
darui だるい tired
dekai でかい big, large
erai 偉い great
fukai 深い deep, profound, close (of relation)
furui 古い old (not used of humans)
fusawashii 相応しい suitable, suited, fit, proper
futebuteshii ふてぶてしい sulky, impudent
futoi 太い fat, bold
hanahadashii 甚だしい gross, too much
hateshinai 果てしない endless, limitless, boundless, everlasting
hayai 速い fast, quick, rapid, speedy, prompt 早い early
hazukashii 恥ずかしい shy, bashful
hidoi ひどい cruel, harsh, heavy (of rain), bad, severe (of sickness)
hikui 低い low, short (of height)
hiroi 広い wide, broad, spacious, vast
hitoshii 等しい equal, identical, same
hosoi 細い thin, slender
ichijirushii 著しい remarkable, striking
ii いい good, nice, fine, right, suitable (→ See also *yoi*.)
isamashii 勇ましい brave, bold

isogashii 忙しい busy
itai 痛い painful, sore
iyarashii 嫌らしい disagreeable, indecent, lascivious
kanashii 悲しい sad, sorrowful
karai 辛い salty, hot (of taste)
karui 軽い light, slight (of illness)
kashikoi 賢い smart, clever, wise
katai 堅い, 固い stiff, tight, hard
kawaii 可愛い lovely, cute, tiny
kayui 痒い itchy
kewashii 険しい steep, grim, stern
kimochi warui 気持ち悪い disagreeable, unpleasant (*kimoi* as slang)
kimuzukashii 気むずかしい hard to please
kīroi 黄色い yellow
kitanai 汚い dirty, foul, nasty
kitsui きつい hard, severe, tight
kōbashii 香ばしい aromatic, good-smelling
komakai 細かい small, trifling, trivial, minute, detailed, thrifty
konomashii 好ましい desirable, agreeable
kowai 怖い, 恐い afraid, fearful
kudoi くどい wordy, lengthy
kurai 暗い dark, gloomy
kuroi 黒い black, dark, tanned
kurushii 苦しい painful
kusai 臭い stink
kuyashii 悔しい regrettable, frustrating
kyōmibukai 興味深い interesting
magirawashii 紛らわしい confusing, ambiguous, misleading
marui 丸い round, circular, globular, spherical
mazui まずい not good, not proper, awkward (of situation)
mazushii 貧しい poor, needy, scanty
memagurushii 目まぐるしい rapid, fast-moving
mendōkusai 面倒くさい troublesome, reluctant (*mendoi* as slang)
mezamashii めざましい remarkable, striking
mezurashii 珍しい rare, unique, unusual, uncommon
migurushii 見苦しい ugly, mean, indecent, disgraceful
mijikai 短い short, brief
minikui 醜い ugly

mittomonai みっともない disgraceful, shameful, indecent, shabby

monosugoi もの凄い great, terrible, terrific, awful, dreadful, amazing

monotarinai 物足りない unsatisfied, unsatisfactory

moroi もろい fragile, frail

mottainai 勿体ない too good to throw away

munashii 空しい empty, vain, fruitless

muzukashii 難しい difficult, troublesome

nagai 長い long

nai 無い there is not, does not exist

narenareshii 馴れ馴れしい in an over-friendly manner

nebai ねばい sticky

nebarizuyoi 粘り強い tenacious, persevering

nemui 眠い sleepy, drowsy

nibui 鈍い dull, slow, blunt, dim (of light)

nigai 苦い bitter, sour (of face)

nikui にくい hateful, hard (to do)

noroi のろい slow, dull

nukui 温い warm

nurui ぬるい lukewarm, tepid

ōi 多い many, much, numerous, frequent (predicative use only)

oishii 美味しい delicious, tasty, good (of food)

okashii 可笑しい amusing, funny, strange, wrong, crazy, improper

ōkii 大きい big, large, loud, tall (*ōki na* is a prenominal variant form)

omoi 重い heavy, serious (of illness)

omoigakenai 思いがけない unexpected

omoshiroi 面白い interesting, amusing, enjoyable

oshii 惜しい regrettable, pitiful

osoroshii 恐ろしい fearful, terrible, horrible

otonashii 大人しい obedient, tame, well-behaved, quiet

sabishii 寂しい lonely

samui 寒い chilly, cold (of the weather)

sawagashii 騒がしい noisy, loud, boisterous

semai 狭い narrow, small

shibui 渋い sober (of color), tasteful, refined

shimeppoi 湿っぽい humid, damp, moist, wet, tearful

shitashii 親しい friendly, familiar

shitsukoi しつこい persistent, insistent, importunate, heavy (of taste)

subarashii 素晴らしい wonderful, excellent, marvelous, splendid

subayai 素早い quick, swift

sugasugashii すがすがしい refreshing

sugoi 凄い great, dreadful, terrible, horrible, fierce, ghastly (also an adverb as slang)

sukunai 少ない a few, a little

surudoi 鋭い sharp, acute, piercing, keen, shrewd

suzushii 涼しい cool (of the weather)

tadashii 正しい correct, accurate, right

takai 高い tall, high, expensive

takumashii 逞しい robust, sturdy, stout

tanoshii 楽しい pleasant, delightful, enjoyable

tarinai 足りない lacking, insufficient, foolish

tōi 遠い distant, far

tondemonai とんでもない terrible, awful

tsumaranai つまらない boring, dull, worthless

tsumetai 冷たい cold, icy

tsurai 辛い bitter, hard, painful

tsuyoi 強い strong, tough, powerful

umai 上手い good (of technique) 旨い delicious

ureshii 嬉しい glad, happy

urusai うるさい noisy, annoying, bothering, troublesome (*uzai* as slang)

usui 薄い thin, light (of color)

utagawashii 疑わしい doubtful, questionable, suspicious

utsukushii 美しい beautiful

wabishii 侘びしい desolate, lonely

wakai 若い young

warui 悪い bad, stale, sick

warugashikoi 悪賢い cunning, crafty

wazurawashii 煩わしい troublesome, annoying

yakamashii 喧しい noisy

yarinikui やりにくい hard to do, hard to get along

yasashii 易しい easy 優しい kind

yasui 安い cheap 易い easy (to do)

yawarakai 柔らかい soft

yayakoshii ややこしい complicated, complex, tangled

yoi 良い good, fine, sufficient (→ See also *ii* and *yoroshii*.)

yorokobashii 喜ばしい happy, glad, joyful

yoroshii 宜しい all right, good, allowable (→ See also *ii* and *yoi*.)

yowai 弱い weak, frail

yurui 緩い loose, loose-fitting, gentle (of slope), slow (of curve)

zūzūshii 図々しい impudent, audacious, cheeky, shameless

APPENDIX 3

List of Common Adverbs

amari 余り (not) very much

ato de 後で later

bochibochi ぼちぼち so-so, slowly

chanto ちゃんと neatly, properly, punctually, correctly

chōdo ちょうど just now, precisely

chotto ちょっと a little, a bit, a moment

dōyara どうやら probably (with *rashii* or *yō da*)

dōzo どうぞ please

dōmo どうも indeed

hotondo ほとんど almost, hardly, seldom (with a negative)

hyotto shitara ひょっとしたら possibly, by (some) chance

isoide 急いで in a hurry

itsumo いつも always, usually

kanarazu 必ず certainly, without fail, invariably

korekkiri これっきり for this once, once and for all

māmā まあまあ so-so

masaka まさか by no means, on no account, never

mazu まず to begin with, first of all

mō もう already, (by) now, soon, yet (in questions)

mochiron もちろん of course

moshikashite もしかして possibly, by (some) chance

nonbiri のんびり free from all care

sakki さっき a short while ago

sekkaku せっかく specially, with considerable trouble

sorosoro そろそろ slowly, little by little, soon

shibaraku しばらく for a while, for the time being

shitagatte 従って accordingly, therefore, thus

sukkari すっかり completely, perfectly

sukoshi 少し a little, a bit, a moment

sukoshimo 少しも (not) at all

susunde すすんで willingly, voluntarily

tabun たぶん probably, perhaps, maybe (used with *darō* or *to omoimasu*)

taihen 大変 very (much) (→ See also Appendix 1.)

takusan 沢山 a lot (→ See also Appendix 1.)

tatoe とても even, no matter

tokidoki 時々 sometimes

tokuni 特に especially, in particular

tonikaku とにかく anyhow, anyway, in any case

totemo とても very, really, (not) by any means

tsui つい unintentionally, by mistake

tsuini ついに finally, at last

yagate やがて before long, soon

yoku よく often, well, hard

yukkuri ゆっくり slowly, without hurry

zehi ぜひ by all means

zenzen ぜんぜん (not) at all, completely, very much

zettai 絶対 absolutely, by no means

zuibun ずいぶん fairly, very much, for a long time

zutto ずっと all the time

APPENDIX 4

List of Common Counters

bai 倍 times (multiplicative number)
ban 番 No. (number or ranking)
banme 番目 (ordinal number)
dai 台 vehicles or machines
doru ドル dollar
en 円 yen
fun 分 minutes
gatsu 月 ordinal month (of the year)
hai 杯 cups or glasses
hiki 匹 small animals, fish, worms, or insects
hon 本 long objects like sticks, bottles, etc.
ji 時 o'clock
jikan 時間 hours
ka 日 days (of the month, from the second to the tenth)

kagetsu ヶ月 months (as the unit)
kai 回 times (frequency) 階 floors
kiro キロ kilometers, kilograms
ko 個 objects of small, round, or non-specific shape
mai 枚 thin or flat objects like paper, boards, slices, etc.
nen 年 years (as the date and unit)
nichi 日 days (for one day or more than ten days, or for days of the month after the tenth)
nin 人 persons
sai 才 years old
satsu 冊 books, volumes
shūkan 週間 weeks

Pronunciation of some counter phrasess

1. HOURS (*jikan* 時間)

1 *ichi jikan*	6 *roku jikan*
2 *ni jikan*	7 *nana jikan, shichi jikan*
3 *san jikan*	8 *hachi jikan*
4 *yo jikan*	9 *ku jikan*
5 *go jikan*	10 *jū jikan*

2. MINUTES (*fun, pun*)

1 *ippun*	6 *roppun*
2 *ni fun*	7 *nana fun*
3 *san pun*	8 *hachi fun, happun*
4 *yon pun*	9 *kyū fun*
5 *go fun*	10 *jippun, juppun*

3. CUPS OR GLASSES (*hai, bai* 杯)

1 *ippai*	6 *roppai*
2 *ni hai*	7 *nana hai*
3 *san bai*	8 *hachi hai*
4 *yon hai*	9 *kyū hai*
5 *go hai*	10 *jippai, juppai*

4. LONG OBJECTS LIKE STICKS, BOTTLES, ETC. (*hon, bon* 本)

1 *ippon*	6 *roppon*
2 *ni hon*	7 *nana hon*
3 *san bon*	8 *hachi hon, happon*
4 *yon hon*	9 *kyū hon*
5 *go hon*	10 *jippon, juppon*

5. DATE (OF THE MONTH) (*ka* 日)

1 *tsuitachi*	6 *muika*
2 *futsuka*	7 *nanoka*
3 *mikka*	8 *yōka*
4 *yokka*	9 *kokonoka*
5 *itsuka*	10 *tōka* (what day of the month is *nan nichi*)

6. DAYS (AS A UNIT) (*nichi, ka* 日)

1 *ichi nichi*	6 *muika*
2 *futsuka*	7 *nanoka*
3 *mikka*	8 *yōka*
4 *yokka*	9 *kokonoka*
5 *itsuka*	10 *tōka* (how many days is *nan nichi*)

7. MONTHS (AS A UNIT) (*kagetsu* ヶ月)

1 *ikkagetsu*	6 *rokkagetsu*
2 *ni kagetsu*	7 *nana kagetsu*
3 *san kagetsu*	8 *hachi kagetsu*
4 *yon kagetsu*	9 *kyū kagetsu*
5 *go kagetsu*	10 *jikkagetsu, jukkagetsu*

8. KILOGRAMS OR KILOMETERS (*kiro* キロ)

1 *ichi kiro*	6 *rokkiro*
2 *ni kiro*	7 *nana kiro*
3 *san kiro*	8 *hachi kiro*
4 *yon kiro*	9 *kyū kiro*
5 *go kiro*	10 *jikkiro, jukkiro*

9. SMALL, ROUND, OR NON-SPECIFIC OBJECTS (*ko* 個)

1 *ikko*	6 *rokko*
2 *ni ko*	7 *nana ko*
3 *san ko*	8 *hachi ko*
4 *yon ko*	9 *kyū ko*
5 *go ko*	10 *jikko, jukko*

10. PERSONS (*nin, ri* 人)

1 *hitori*	6 *roku nin*
2 *futari*	7 *nana nin, shichi nin*
3 *san nin*	8 *hachi nin*
4 *yo nin*	9 *kyū nin, ku nin*
5 *go nin*	10 *jū nin*

11. YEARS OLD (*sai* 才, 歳)

1 *issai*	6 *roku sai*
2 *ni sai*	7 *nana sai*
3 *san sai*	8 *hassai*
4 *yon sai*	9 *kyū sai*
5 *go sai*	10 *jissai, jussai*

12. BOOKS, VOLUMES (*satsu* 冊)

1 *issatsu*	6 *roku satsu*
2 *ni satsu*	7 *nana satsu*
3 *san satsu*	8 *hassatsu*
4 *yon satsu*	9 *kyū satsu*
5 *go satsu*	10 *jissatsu, jussatsu*

13. SMALL ANIMALS (*hiki, biki* 匹)

1 *ippiki*	6 *roppiki*
2 *ni hiki*	7 *nana hiki*
3 *san biki*	8 *hachi hiki, happiki*
4 *yon hiki*	9 *kyū hiki*
5 *go hiki*	10 *jippiki, juppiki*

14. BIRDS, RABBITS (*wa, ba* 羽)

1 *ichi wa*	6 *roku wa, roppa*
2 *ni wa*	7 *nana wa, shichi wa*
3 *san wa, san ba*	8 *hachi wa, happa*
4 *yon wa, yon ba*	9 *kyū wa*
5 *go wa*	10 *jippa, juppa*

APPENDIX 5

List of Common Verbs

Irregular Verbs

kuru 来る to come

suru する to do, perform various actions, be in some state

Ru-verbs that end with *iru*

abiru 浴びる to be bathed

akiru 飽きる to get bored

chigiru ちぎる to tear

dekiru できる to be able to (do), to complete

ikiru 生きる to live

iru いる to be, exist, stay

kanjiru 感じる to feel

kariru 借りる to borrow, rent

kiru 着る to put on

miru 見る to see, look, watch

mochiiru 用いる to use

niru 似る to resemble 煮る to boil

nobiru 伸びる to lengthen 延びる to be put off

ochiru 落ちる to fall, come down, crash

okiru 起きる to get up, wake up

shinjiru 信じる to believe, trust

tariru 足りる to be sufficient

tojiru 閉じる to close 綴じる to bind

wabiru 詫びる to apology

Ru-verbs that end with *eru*

ageru あげる to give, raise, do (something) for others

akeru 開ける to open

akirameru あきらめる to give up

amaeru 甘える to behave like a spoiled child

arawareru 現れる to appear, turn up, come in sight

ataeru 与える to give

atatameru 温める to warm

awateru 慌てる to be confused, be hurried

butsukeru ぶつける to bump, to hit

dakishimeru 抱きしめる to hug

dekakeru 出かける to go out, set out

deru 出る to go out, come out, leave, graduate, appear

eru 得る to get, obtain

fueru 増える to increase

fukeru ふける to grow old, indulge

fukureru ふくれる to expand

furueru ふるえる to shiver, shudder

fuseru 伏せる to put one's face down

haeru 生える to sprout

hageru 禿げる to become bald

hajimeru 始める to start, begin, commence

hameru はめる to insert

hanareru 離れる to separate

haneru 跳ねる to bounce

hareru 晴れる to clear up

hazureru 外れる to be out of joint

hieru 冷える to grow cold

hikaeru 控える to make a note, reserve

hikiukeru 引く受ける to undertake

hirogeru 広げる to spread, expand, widen

hiromeru 広める to popularize

hoeru 吠える to bark, howl

horeru 惚れる to fall in love

ireru 入れる to put in, insert

itameru いためる to damage, hurt

kaeru 変える to change

kakeru かける to gallop, hang, call up

kakureru 隠れる to hide

katamukeru 傾ける to bend

katazukeru 片付ける to put in order

kazoeru 数える to count

kigaeru 着替える to change one's clothes

kikoeru 聞こえる to be heard, be audible

kimeru 決める to decide

koboreru こぼれる to spill

koeru 肥える to get fat, 越える go over

kogeru 焦げる to burn, scorch

kotaeru 答える to answer

kowareru 壊れる to break down, get out of order

kumiawaseru 組み合わせる to put (something) together

kuraberu 比べる to compare

kureru くれる to give, give a profit by an action (to me)

kuwaeru 加える to add

kuzureru くずれる to collapse

machigaeru 間違える to make a mistake

mageru 曲げる to bend

makaseru 任せる to put something in somebody's hands

makeru 負ける to be beaten, be defeated

matomeru まとめる to gather (something) together, sum up

mazeru 混ぜる to mix, blend

miageru 見上げる to look up

mieru 見える to be seen, be visible, appear (come)

miseru 見せる to show, let (somebody) see

misuteru 見捨てる to forsake, desert

mitomeru 認める to admit

mitoreru 見とれる to be lost in admiration

mitsukeru 見つける to find

mitsumeru 見つめる to gaze

mochiageru 持ち上げる to lift

moreru 漏れる to leak

motareru もたれる to lean

motomeru 求める to ask for (something), demand

mukaeru 迎える to welcome

mukeru 向ける to turn (something1) toward (something2)

naderu 撫でる to pet

nagameru 眺める to view

nagareru 流れる to flow

nageru 投げる to throw

nameru 舐める to lick

naraberu 並べる to put (something) side by side

nareru 慣れる to become accustomed

nebokeru 寝ぼける to be half asleep

neru 寝る to sleep, go to bed

nigeru 逃げる to run away

noberu 述べる to describe

nogareru 逃れる to be freed

noseru 乗せる to give (somebody) a ride

nukeru 抜ける to fall out

nureru 濡れる to get wet

oboeru 覚える to memorize, learn (by heart)

oboreru おぼれる to be drowned

oeru 終える to finish

okureru 遅れる to be late, be delayed

oreru 折れる to break in two, give in

osaeru 押さえる to press down

oshieru 教える to teach, tell

osoreru 恐れる to fear

sageru 下げる to lower

sakeru 裂ける to tear, 避ける to avoid

sameru 冷める to get cold, 覚める wake up

semeru 責める to blame, 攻める attack

shibireru しびれる to become numb

shimeru 閉める to close (a door) 締める to tighten 占める to occupy

shiraseru 知らせる to let (somebody) know (something)

someru 染める to dye

sonaeru 備える to equip

soroeru 揃える to put in order

susumeru 進める to carry forward, 勧める to recommend

suteru 捨てる to throw away

taeru 耐える to endure

tameru 貯める to store up

taoreru 倒れる to topple down

tasukeru 助ける to help

tateru 建てる to build

tazuneru 尋ねる to ask, visit, call on

todokeru 届ける to bring (something to somebody)

tojikomeru 閉じ込める to lock up

tokeru 溶ける to melt

tomeru 止める to stop 停める to park

toreru 取れる to come off

totonoeru 整える to make (someting) neat

tsubureru つぶれる to be crushed

tsukareru 疲れる to get tired

tsukeru 付ける to turn on, light, attach

tsukekuwaeru 付け加える to add

tsumeru 詰める to pack

tsureru 連れる to be accompanied

tsutaeru 伝える to inform

tsutomeru 勤める to work 努める to try

ukeru 受ける to receive

uketsukeru 受け付ける to accept

umareru 生まれる to be born

umeru 埋める to fill up, bury

wakareru 分かれる to part 別れる to part, divorce

wakeru 分ける to divide

wareru 割れる to crack, split

wasureru 忘れる to forget, leave (something) behind

yakeru 焼ける to burn

yameru 辞める to quit, stop, retire, 止める to stop

yawarageru 和らげる to soften

yugameru 歪める to distort

U-verbs

amaru 余る to be left over

arau 洗う to wash

arawasu 表す to express 現す to appear

aru 有る to exist

aruku 歩く to walk

asobu 遊ぶ to play, amuse oneself

ataru 当たる to hit, strike

atatamaru 暖まる to warm oneself

au 会う to meet, see (a person)

ayamaru 謝る to apologize

chigau 違う to differ, be wrong

chijimu 縮む to shrink

chikazuku 近づく to come soon, draw near, approach

chikau 誓う to swear

chirakasu ちらかす to scatter

chiru 散る (leaves) to fall

daku 抱く to embrace, hug

damaru 黙る to become silent, shut up

damasu だます to deceive

dasu 出す to let out, take out, post, hand in, pay

erabu 選ぶ to choose, select

fukumu 含む to contain, include

fukuramasu 膨らます to blow up, inflate

fukuramu 膨らむ to swell, expand

fumu 踏む to step on (something)

furatsuku ふらつく to totter, stagger

furikaeru 振り返る to look back

furishikiru 降りしきる to rain hard incessantly

furu 降る to fall (of rain or snow)

futoru 太る to grow fat

ganbaru 頑張る to do one's best, hold on, try hard

hagemasu 励ます to cheer up

hagemu 励む to work hard

hairu 入る to come in, go in, enter

hakaru 計る, 測る to measure, gauge

haku 履く to put on (shoes, trousers) 吐く to spit

hamaru はまる to fit in

hanasu 話す to speak, talk, tell, 離す to separate

harau 払う to pay

haru 貼る to paste, stick

hasamaru 挟まる to be pinched

hasamu 挟む to pinch

hashiru 走る to run, dash

hataraku 働く to work, labor, function

hatasu 果たす to accomplish (duty), keep (promise)

hayaru 流行る to be in fashion, be prevalent

hazusu 外す to take off, remove

heru 減る to decrease

hibiku 響く to echo, affect

hikaru 光る to shine, twinkle, flash

hiku 引く to pull, draw, minus, reduce a price 弾く to play (the piano, guitar)

hipparu 引っ張る to pull

hiraku 開く to open

hiromaru 広まる to spread, come into fashion

hiyasu 冷やす to cool (something)

hohoemu 微笑む to smile

horobosu 滅ぼす to destroy (enemy), ruin

horu 掘る to dig

iku 行く to go

iru 要る to need

itadaku いただく to receive, be given (a humble verb)

iu 言う to say, tell, speak

kaburu かぶる to put on (one's hat)

kaeru 帰る to go back, come back

kakomu 囲む to enclose, surround, encircle

kaku 書く to write

kakusu 隠す to hide, conceal, keep (someting) a secret

kamu かむ to bite, chew, crunch

kanashimu 悲しむ to feel sad, grieve

kasu 貸す to lend

katsu 勝つ to win

kau 買う to buy

kawaru 変わる to change

kayou 通う to commute

kazaru 飾る to decorate

keru 蹴る to kick

kesu 消す to turn off, erase, extinguish

kiku 聞く to hear, listen, ask

kimaru 決まる to be fixed, be decided

kiru 切る to cut, switch off

kobosu こぼす to spill

komu 混む to get crowded, get jammed

korobu ころぶ to fall down, tumble

korogaru ころがる to roll

korosu 殺す to kill

kōru 凍る to freeze

kubaru 配る to distribute

kurikaesu 繰り返す to repeat

ma ni au 間に合う to be in time, catch (a train, bus, etc.)

magaru 曲がる to turn (a corner), curve, bend

mairu 参る to go, come (as humble verb), admit one's defeat

majiru 混じる to be mixed, mingle

makasu 負かす to defeat

maku 巻く to wind, bandage 撒く to scatter 蒔く to sow

mamoru 守る to defend, guard

maneku 招く to invite, beckon

masaru 勝る to surpass, excel

masu 増す to increase

matomaru まとまる to be united, come to an agreement

matsu 待つ to wait

mawaru 回る to turn, spin, to take a roundabout way

mawasu 回す to turn, rotate, spin (something)

mayou 迷う to get lost, be puzzled

meiru 滅入る to feel gloomy

mekuru めくる to turn over (pages)

mimamoru 見守る to keep one's eye (on somebody)

minasu みなす to regard

minoru 実る to bear fruit or crops

modoru 戻る to be back

momu 揉む to massage

morau もらう to be given, receive

mōshikomu 申し込む to make an application

motarasu もたらす to bring about

motsu 持つ to hold, have, possess

mukau 向かう to leave (for some place)

muku 向く to face (to some direction) 剥く to peel

muragaru 群がる to flock

musaboru 貪る to devour

musu 蒸す to steam

musubu 結ぶ to link,

nagasu 流す to flush

nageku 嘆く to feel sad, grieve

naguru 殴る to punch, knock (somebody)

naku 泣く to cry, weep

nakunaru 無くなる to be gone, run out 亡くなる to pass away

nakusu 無くす to lose 亡くす to lose (of a person's death)

narabu 並ぶ to stand in a line

narasu 鳴らす to sound, ring (something)

narau 習う to take lessons, learn

naru なる to become, consist

nayamu 悩む to worry

negau 願う to wish, hope

nejiru ねじる to twist

nemuru 眠る to sleep

nerau 狙う to aim (at something), watch (for a chance)

neru 練る to elaborate, knead

nesugosu 寝過ごす to oversleep

netamu ねたむ to envy

nigiru 握る to grasp, grip, seize

nigoru 濁る to become muddy

nijimu にじむ to blot

nikumu 憎む to hate

niou 臭う to smell

niramu にらむ to glare (at somebody)

nobasu 伸ばす to lengthen 延ばす to postpone

noboru 登る to climb 上る to rise

nogasu 逃す to miss (a chance)

nokoru 残る to be left, remain

nokosu 残す to leave (something) (behind)

noku のく to step aside, go out of the way

nomu 飲む to drink, eat (soup), take (medicine)

noru 乗る to ride, get on, board

nozoku 除く to remove 覗く to peep

nozomu 望む to wish, hope

nugu 脱ぐ to take off

nukidasu 抜き出す to pick out, select, extract

nuru 塗る to paint

nusumu 盗む to steal

nuu 縫う to sew, stitch

ochitsuku 落ち着く to calm down

odorokasu 驚かす to surprise

odoroku 驚く to be surprised

oitsuku 追いつく to catch up

okasu 犯す to commit (a crime)

okonau 行う to do, perform (an action)

okoru 怒る to get angry

okosu 起こす to wake up (somebody)

oku 置く to put, place

okuru 送る to send, see off

omoidasu 思い出す to remember, recollect, recall

omoitsuku 思いつく to hit upon

omou 思う to think

orosu 下ろす to withdraw (savings)

oru おる to be, stay 折る to break (a stick)

osamaru 収まる to settle down

osou 襲う to attack

osu 押す to push, press

otosu 落とす to drop (something)

ōu 覆う to cover, veil

ou 追う to chase

owaru 終わる to be over, end

oyogu 泳ぐ to swim

sagaru 下がる to go down, step back

sakarau 逆らう to disobey

saku 咲く to blossom, tear

samasu 冷ます to cool

sasayaku ささやく to whisper

sasu 刺す to prick 指す to indicate

sawagu 騒ぐ to make a noise

sawaru 触る to touch

semaru 迫る to draw near

shaberu しゃべる to speak, chat

shibaru 縛る to tie

shiboru 絞る to squeeze

shikaru 叱る to scold

shimaru 閉まる to be closed, be shut

shimekiru 締め切る to close (subscription)

shimesu 示す to show, indicate, illustrate

shinu 死ぬ to die

shiru 知る to know

shizumu 沈む to go under water, feel depressed

sorasu そらす to change topic on purpose, turn one's eyes away

sosogu 注ぐ to pour

suberu 滑る to slip, slide

sukuu 救う to save, rescue

sumasu 済ます to finish

sumu 住む to live, reside

susugu すすぐ to rinse

suwaru 座る to sit down, be seated

takuramu 企む to plot, conspire

tamerau ためらう to hesitate

tamesu 試す to try, test

taru 足る to be enough

tasu 足す to add

tasukaru 助かる to be saved

tataku 叩く to beat, clap, knock, tap

tatamu たたむ to fold (up)

tatsu 立つ to stand up 発つ to leave

tobasu 飛ばす to fly (something), skip

tobiagaru 飛び上がる to jump up

tobikomu 飛び込む to dive

tobu 飛ぶ to fly

todoku 届く (hand) to reach, to be delivered

todomaru 留まる to stay, remain

tojikomoru 閉じこもる to keep oneself indoors

tokasu 溶かす to melt (something), comb

toku 解く to untie, solve

tomaru 止まる to come to a stop, run down 泊まる to stay (overnight)

toru 取る to take, take off, remove

tōru 通る to pass, go through

tōsu 通す to show (somebody) into (some place), make way for (somebody)

totonou 整う to be prepared

tsubusu つぶす to crush, squash, break, kill (time)

tsukamu つかむ to grasp, grip

tsukau 使う to use, handle, spend (money)

tsukkomu 突っ込む to dive, ask a sharp question

tsuku 着く to arrive 付く to stick

tsukuru 作る to make, cook, manufacture

tsumamu 摘む to pick (something) up with fingers

tsumaru 詰まる to be choked up, be at a loss for words

tsunagu つなぐ to connect

tsuranuku 貫く to penetrate, carry through

tsuru 吊る to hang, suspend 釣る to fish

tsutsumu 包む to wrap, pack

tsuzuku 続く to continue, follow

ugokasu 動かす to move, operate (something)

ugoku 動く to move

ukagau 伺う to call at one's house, ask

uku 浮く to float

umidasu 生み出す to produce

umu 生む to give birth

uramu 恨む to bear a grudge

uranau 占う to foretell

uridasu 売り出す to put (something) on the market

uru 売る to sell

utau 歌う to sing

utsu 打つ to hit, shoot

utsuru 移る to move (to another place) 映る/写る to be reflected

wakaru 分かる to understand, know, recognize

wakasu 沸かす to boil (water), heat (the bath)

warau 笑う to laugh, giggle, grin, chuckle

waru 割る to break, split (a hard thing)

wataru 渡る to cross

yaku 焼く to burn, tan, grill, broil, roast, bake, barbecue, toast

yakudatsu 役立つ to be useful

yakusu 訳す to translate

yaru やる to do, give (informal)

yasumu 休む to take a rest, be absent

yobu 呼ぶ to call, invite

yomu 読む to read

yoromeku よろめく to stagger, totter, stumble

you 酔う to get drunk, get sick (in a bus), get seasick

yowaru 弱る to become weak

yurusu 許す to permit, forgive

yusuru 揺する to shake

yuzuru 譲る to hand over, make way (for somebody)

U-verbs that end with *iru*

furishikiru 降りしきる to rain hard incessantly

hairu 入る to enter

hashiru 走る to run

iru 要る to need
  (*iru* [いる to be] is a *ru*-verb)

kiru 切る to cut
  (*kiru* [着る to wear] is a *ru*-verb)

nejiru ねじる to twist

shiru 知る to know

U-verbs that end with *eru*

heru 減る to decrease

kaeru 帰る to go back, come back
  (*kaeru* [変える to change] is a *ru*-verb)

keru 蹴る to kick

neru 練る to elaborate, knead
  (*neru* [寝る to go to bed] is a *ru*-verb)

shaberu しゃべる to speak, chat

suberu 滑る to slip, slide

Suru-verbs made of Sino-Japanese compounds

* These nouns form verbs when followed by *suru*. The meanings of both the noun and the verb are listed below.

anki 暗記 memorization, to learn something by heart

annai 案内 guidance, to guide

anshin 安心 relief, to feel relieved

baibai 売買 buying and selling, to buy and sell

baishō 賠償 compensation, to compensate

bakuhatsu 爆発 an eruption, a burst, an explosion; to erupt, burst, explode

bankai 挽回 recovery, to recover

bekkyo 別居 living apart, to live apart

benkai 弁解 an excuse, to make an excuse

benkyō 勉強 study, to study

bōbi 防備 defense, to defend

bōchō 膨張 expansion, to expand

bōhatsu 暴発 an accidental discharge of a gun, to go off accidentally

bōkyaku 忘却 forgetfulness, to forget

bōmei 亡命 seeking refuge abroad, to take refuge abroad

bōraku 暴落 a heavy fall, to drop sharply (of prices)

bōtō 暴騰 a sudden rise, to go up sharply (of prices) 暴投 a wild pitch, to throw a wild ball

bottō 没頭 devoting oneself, to devote oneself

bunkatsu 分割 division, to divide

bunretsu 分裂 division, to be divided

bunseki 分析 an analysis, to analyze

busō 武装 armament, to equip an army

chakuseki 着席 taking one's seat, to be seated

chiryō 治療 medical treatment, to cure

chochiku 貯蓄 savings, to save money

chōsa 調査 an investigation, to investigate

chōsei 調整 adjustment, to adjust

chūi 注意 attention, to pay attention

chūmoku 注目 notice, to take notice

chūmon 注文 an order, to order

dōi 同意 agreement, to agree

dokusho 読書 reading books, to read books

eijū 永住 permanent residence, to live permanently

eisha 映写 projection, to project on the screen

eiyaku 英訳 an English translation, to put into English

enchō 延長 extension, to extend

engo 援護 backing, to back up

enjō 炎上 destruction by fire, to be destroyed by fire

enki 延期 postponement, to postpone

ensei 遠征 an expedition, a playing tour; to go on an expedition, make a playing tour

enshū 演習 an exercise, to carry out exercises

enshutsu 演出 dramatic presentation, to produce

ensō 演奏 a performance, to play (a musical instrument)

enzetsu 演説 a speech, to make a speech

eshaku 会釈 a bow, to make a bow

etoku 会得 learning, to learn

etsuran 閲覧 public reading, to read

fuchaku 付着 adhesion, to adhere

fukujū 服従 obedience, to obey

fukusei 複製 reproduction, to reproduce

fukusha 複写 a copy, to copy

fukushū 復習 a review, to review 復讐 revenge, to revenge

fukuyō 服用 taking medicine, to take medicine

fusoku 不足 a lack, an insufficiency, to lack/ be insufficient

genshō 減少 decrease, to decrease

gokai 誤解 a misunderstanding, to misunderstand

gōkaku 合格 passage, to pass

gōkei 合計 the total/sum, to total/sum up

haaku 把握 a grasp, to grasp

hahei 派兵 sending troops, to send troops

haichi 配置 a disposition, to put something in position

haifu 配布 distribution, to distribute

haiken 拝見 having the honor of seeing, to have a look (a humble verb)

haiki 廃棄 scrapping, to scrap

haishi 廃止 abolition, to abolish

haishutsu 排出 a discharge, to discharge

haitatsu 配達 delivery, to deliver

hakai 破壊 destruction, to destroy

haken 派遣 dispatch, to dispatch

hakkō 発行 publication, to publish

hakkutsu 発掘 excavation, to excavate

hametsu 破滅 ruin, to go to ruin

hanbai 販売 a sale, to sell

handan 判断 a judgment, to judge

hangeki 反撃 a counterattack, to counterattack

hangen 半減 a half reduction, to reduce by half

hanpatsu 反発 a rebound, to bound back/be offended

hanran 反乱 a rebellion, to rebel 氾濫 flood, to flood

hanron 反論 a counterargument, to object

hansha 反射 reflection, to reflect

hantai 反対 an objection, to object

hantei 判定 a judgement, to judge

happō 発砲 firing a gun, to fire a gun, 発泡 foaming, to foam

happyō 発表 an announcement, a presentation, to announce/present

haretsu 破裂 a burst/an explosion, to burst/ explode

hasshin 発進 a start, to start 発信 sending a signal, to send a signal

hassō 発送 sending out, to send out

hatan 破綻 a failure, to fail

hatchaku 発着 arrival and departure, to come and go

hatchū 発注 an order, to place an order

hatsubai 発売 sale, to sell

hatsubyō 発病 being taken ill, to come down with a disease

hatsuiku 発育 growth, to grow (of a body)

hatsumei 発明 an invention, to invent

hatsumō 発毛 growth of hair, to grow (of hair)

hatsuon 発音 a pronunciation, to pronounce

hattatsu 発達 development, to develop

hatten 発展 development, to develop

heigō 併合 annexation, to annex

heikō 平行 being parallel, to be parallel, 並行 going abreast, to go side by side

heisa 閉鎖 closing, to close down/lock out

heiten 閉店 closing shop, to close shop

henji 返事 a reply, to make a reply

henka 変化 a change/a variation, to change/ vary

henkaku 変革 a change/reform, to change/ reform

henkan 返還 return, to return 変換 conversion, to convert

henkō 変更 an alteration, to alter

henkyaku 返却 return, to return/give back

hensai 返済 a repayment, to repay

hensei 編成 organization, to organize

henshin 変身 transformation, to transform oneself 返信 a reply, to answer a letter

henshū 編集 editing, to edit

hensō 返送 sending back, to send back 変装 a disguise, to disguise oneself

hihan 批判 a criticism, to criticize

hihyō 批評 a view/a criticism, to view/ criticize

hinan 非難 blame, to blame 避難 refuge, to take refuge

hinin 否認 a denial, to deny

hinpatsu 頻発 frequent occurrence, to occur frequently

hinshutsu 頻出 frequent appearance, to appear frequently

hirei 比例 a proportion, to be in proportion

hitei 否定 a denial, to deny

hōchi 放置 leaving as it is, to leave something as it is/leave somebody alone

hodō 補導 guidance of a delinquent, to guide (of a delinquent)

hōfuku 報復 revenge, to take revenge

hogo 保護 protection, to protect

hojū 補充 supplementation, to supplement

hokan 保管 safekeeping, to have something in one's custody

hokyō 補強 reinforcement, to reinforce

hokyū 補給 supply, to supply

hōmon 訪問 a visit, to visit

hōnichi 訪日 a visit to Japan, to visit Japan

hōnin 放任 noninterference, not to interfere

honrō 翻弄 trifling, to trifle

honsō 奔走 running about, to make every effort

hon'yaku 翻訳 a translation, to translate

hōrō 放浪 wandering about, to wander about

horyū 保留 reservation, to reserve/withhold

hōryū 放流 discharge (of water)/release of fish, to discharge/release fish

hosei 補正 correction, to correct

hoshō 保証 a guarantee, to guarantee 保障 security, to secure 補償 compensation, to compensate

hōshutsu 放出 emission, to emit

hōsō 放送 broadcasting, to broadcast

hosoku 補足 supplementation, to supplement

hossoku 発足 a start/an inauguration, to start

hoyō 保養 convalescence, to take a rest for one's health

hōyō 抱擁 a hug, to hug

hoyū 保有 possession, to possess

hozon 保存 preservation, to preserve

hyōgen 表現 an expression, to express

hyōji 表示 an indication, to indicate

hyōka 評価 evaluation, to evaluate

idō 移動 movement, to move

imi 意味 meaning, to mean

insatsu 印刷 printing, to print

jama 邪魔 a disturbance, to disturb

jikkō 実行 action, to carry out

jitsugen 実現 realization, to put into practice

jōei 上映 putting a movie on the screen, to put a movie on the screen

junbi 準備 preparation, to prepare

kaifuku 回復 recovery, to be recovered

kaiketsu 解決 solution, to be solved

kaishi 開始 beginning, to begin

kaiten 回転 rotation, to rotate

kakutoku 獲得 acquisition, to acquire

kandō 感動 impression, to be impressed

kangei 歓迎 welcome, to welcome

kankei 関係 relation, to relate

kanri 管理 administration, to administer

kanryō 完了 finishing, to finish

kansei 完成 completion, to be completed

kansha 感謝 thanks, to thank

katsudō 活動 activity, to be active

keiken 経験 an experience, to experience

keisan 計算 calculation, to calculate

keizoku 継続 continuation, to continue

kekkon 結婚 marriage, to get married

kenkyū 研究 research, to research

kensa 検査 examination, to examine

kensetsu 建設 construction, to construct

ketsugō 結合 union/combination, to be united/to combine

kettei 決定 determination, to be determined

kibō 希望 hope, to hope

kinshi 禁止 prohibition, to prohibit

kinyū 記入 writing, to write down

kioku 記憶 memory, to memorize

kiroku 記録 a record, to record

kitai 期待 expectation, to expect

kōdō 行動 action, to act

kōfun 興奮 excitement, to get excited

kōgi 抗議 a protest, to protest 講義 a lecture, to lecture

kōkai 後悔 a regret, to regret

konran 混乱 confusion, to be confused

koshō 故障 a breakdown, to break down

kotei 固定 fixing, to fix

kurō 苦労 difficulty, to have difficulty

kyōiku 教育 education, to educate

kyoka 許可 permission, to permit

kyōryoku 協力 cooperation, to cooperate

kyōsō 競争 competition, to compete

maibotsu 埋没 burying/embedding, to be forgotten/be buried

maishin 邁進 going forward, to go forward

maisō 埋葬 interment, to inter

maizō 埋蔵 lying under the ground, to bury

man'en 蔓延 a spread, to spread

manryō 満了 expiry, to expire

manzoku 満足 satisfaction, to be satisfied

massatsu 抹殺 liquidation, to liquidate

meichū 命中 a hit, to hit the mark

meiki 明記 specification, to specify

meirei 命令 an order/a command, to order/ command

meimei 命名 naming, to give a name

meiwaku 迷惑 an annoyance, to be annoyed

menjo 免除 exemption, to exempt

menkai 面会 receiving a caller, to receive a caller

menseki 免責 exemption from responsibility, to exempt from responsibility

mensetsu 面接 an interview, to have an interview

menshoku 免職 dismissal, to dismiss (from office)

menzei 免税 exemption from taxation, to exempt from taxation

metsubō 滅亡 ruin, to be ruined

mikkō 密航 a secret passage, to steal a passage

mikkoku 密告 betrayal, to betray

mippei 密閉 making airtight, to make airtight

mippū 密封 sealing up, to seal up

miryō 魅了 a charm, to charm

missetsu 密接 being close, to be close

mitchaku 密着 adhesion, to adhere

mitsubai 密売 illicit sale, to sell illicitly

mitsuryō 密漁 poaching, to poach

mitsuyaku 密約 a secret promise, to make a secret promise

mitsuyu 密輸 smuggling, to smuggle

mitsuzō 密造 illicit manufacture, to manufacture illicitly

miwaku 魅惑 fascination, to fascinate

mokudoku 黙読 silent reading, to read silently

mokuhi 黙秘 silence, to keep silent

mokunin 黙認 silent approval, to permit tacitly

mōsō 妄想 a fantasy, to be lost in fantasy

musō 夢想 a fancy, to fancy

nyūgaku 入学 entrance into a school, to enter a school

nyūjō 入場 admission, to be admitted to (a hall)

nyūkai 入会 becoming a member, to become a member

rachi 拉致 taking a person away, to take a person away

raihō 来訪 somebody's visit, (somebody) to visit

rainichi 来日 a visit to Japan, to visit Japan

raiten 来店 coming to a store, to come to a store

randoku 乱読 random reading, to read at random

ranpatsu 乱発 an overissue, to overissue

ranritsu 乱立 standing crowded, to be flooded (with candidates)

ransha 乱射 random shooting, to shoot at random

rakka 落下 a fall, to fall

rakuba 落馬 a fall off a horse, to fall off a horse

rakudai 落第 failure (in an exam), to fail an exam

rakusei 落成 completion (of building), to complete

rakushō 楽勝 an easy victory, to win an easy victory

rakutan 落胆 a discouragement, to be discouraged

raretsu 羅列 enumeration, to enumerate

reibō 冷房 air-conditioning, to air-condition

reigū 冷遇 a cold treatment, to treat coldly

reihai 礼拝 worship, to worship

reiji 例示 illustration, to illustrate

reishō 例証 illustration, to illustrate

reitō 冷凍 freezing, to freeze

reikyaku 冷却 cooling, to cool

reizō 冷蔵 refrigeration, to refrigerate

rendō 連動 gearing, to work together

rengō 連合 union, to unite

renkei 連携 cooperation, to cooperate

renketsu 連結 connection, to connect

renko 連呼 repeated calls, to call repeatedly

renkō 連行 taking somebody to a police station, to take somebody to a police station

renmei 連名 a joint signature, to put a joint signature 連盟 a league, to league

renpa 連覇 holding a championship, to hold a championship for years

renpai 連敗 consecutive defeats, to lose consecutive games

renpatsu 連発 running fire, to do something in rapid succession

renraku 連絡 contact, to make contact

renritsu 連立 an alliance, to ally

rensai 連載 serialization, to be serialized

rensen 連戦 a series of battles, to fight a series of battles *renshō* 連勝 consecutive victories, to win consecutive victories

renshū 練習 a practice/an exercise, to practice/do one's exercise

rensō 連想 association (of ideas), to associate

rentai 連帯 solidarity, to stand together

renzoku 連続 continuity, to continue

ribetsu 離別 a separation, to separate

ridatsu 離脱 a secession, to secede

rihan 離反 an estrangement, to be estranged

rikai 理解 understanding, to understand

rikisetsu 力説 an emphasis, to emphasize

rikisō 力走 a sprint, to sprint

rikkyaku 立脚 being based on something, to be based on something

rikon 離婚 a divorce, to divorce

rindoku 輪読 reading in turn, to read in turn

rinichi 離日 leaving Japan, to leave Japan

rinin 離任 leaving one's position, to leave one's position

rinseki 臨席 attendance, to attend

rinsetsu 隣接 adjoining, to adjoin

rinyū 離乳 weaning, to be weaned

risan 離散 dispersion, to disperse

rishoku 離職 leaving one's job, to leave one's job

rishū 履修 completion (of a course), to complete (a course)

risshō 立証 a proof, to prove

risshoku 立食 a stand-up meal, to eat standing

ritō 離党 a secession from a party, to leave a party 離島 an isolated island, to leave an island

riyō 利用 utilization, to utilize

rōhi 浪費 a waste, to waste

ronpa 論破 refutation, to refute

ronshō 論証 demonstration, to demonstrate

ronsō 論争 a dispute, to dispute

rufu 流布 circulation, to circulate

ruisui 類推 analogy, to know by analogy

ryōgae 両替 exchange (of money)/money changing, to exchange/change (money)

ryokō 旅行 a trip/travel, to make a trip/travel

ryōri 料理 cooking, to cook

ryōshō 了承 approval, to approve

ryōshū 領収 receipt, to receive

ryūchi 留置 detention, to detain

ryūdō 流動 fluidity, to be fluid

ryūgaku 留学 studying abroad, to go abroad to study

ryūho 留保 withholding, to withhold

ryūhyō 流氷 floating ice, (ice) to float

ryūi 留意 attention, to pay attention

ryūki 隆起 a bulge, to bulge

ryūkō 流行 a fashion, to be in fashion/be popular

ryūnen 留年 a repeat of a year (in school), to repeat a year (in school)

ryūnin 留任 remaining in office, to remain in office

ryūnyū 流入 an inflow, to flow in

ryūshutsu 流出 an outflow, to flow out

ryūtsū 流通 circulation, to circulate

ryūyō 流用 diversion, to divert

saibai 栽培 cultivation (of crops), to cultivate

sakusei 作成 making out, to make out

sanka 参加 participation, to participate

sanpo 散歩 a walk, to take a walk

sansei 賛成 approval, to approve

seichō 成長 growth, to grow up

seikatsu 生活 a life, to make a living

seisaku 制作 manufacture, to manufacture

seizon 生存 survival, to survive

sekkin 接近 an approach, to approach

senkyo 選挙 an election, to elect

sentaku 選択 choice/selection, to choose/ select 洗濯 washing, to launder

sesshoku 接触 contact, to come into contact

setsumei 説明 an explanation, to explain

setsuritsu 設立 foundation/establishment, to found/establish

setsuyaku 節約 an economy, to economize

settoku 説得 persuasion, to persuade

shazai 謝罪 an apology, to apologize

shindō 振動 vibration, to vibrate

shinpai 心配 anxiety, to be anxious

shinpo 進歩 progress, to make progress

shinrai 信頼 trust, to trust

shippai 失敗 a failure, to fail

shiteki 指摘 pointing out, to point out

shiyō 使用 use, to use

shōhi 消費 consumption, to consume

shōkai 紹介 introduction, to introduce

shōtai 招待 invitation, to invite

shori 処理 management, to manage

shoyū 所有 possession, to possess

shuchō 主張 insistence, to insist

shūgō 集合 a gathering, to get together

shukuhaku 宿泊 lodging, to stay/lodge

shuppan 出版 publication, to publish

shuppatsu 出発 departure/starting, to depart/start

shūryō 終了 end, to come to an end

shusseki 出席 attendance, to attend

shūtoku 習得 acquisition, to acquire

shutsugan 出願 an application, to apply

sokutei 測定 measurement, to measure

sonkei 尊敬 respect, to respect

sonzai 存在 existence, to exist

sōdan 相談 consultation, to consult

sōji 掃除 cleaning, to clean

sotsugyō 卒業 graduation, to graduate

sōzō 想像 imagination, to imagine

suisen 推薦 recommendation, to recommend

tassei 達成 achievement/attainment, to achieve/attain

teisei 訂正 correction, to correct

tenji 展示 exhibition/display, to exhibit/put (something) on display

tōchaku 到着 arrival, to arrive

tōjō 登場 coming on stage, to make an entrance 搭乗 embarkation, to board

tōron 討論 a discussion/a debate to discuss/debate

tsuikyū 追求 pursuit, to pursue

tsūyaku 通訳 interpretation, to interpret

undō 運動 exercise, to take exercise

unten 運転 driving/operation, to drive/operate

wakai 和解 reconciliation, to be reconciled

wankyoku 湾曲 a curve, to curve

waribiki 割引 a discount, to discount

wayaku 和訳 translation into Japanese, to translate into Japanese

yakudoku 訳読 oral translation, to orally translate

yakushin 躍進 rapid progress, to make rapid progress

yakusoku 約束 a promise, to promise

yobō 予防 prevention, to prevent

yōbō 要望 a demand, to demand

yochi 予知 foreseeing, to foresee

yogen 予言 prediction, to foretell

yoken 予見 foreseeing, to foresee

yokuatsu 抑圧 oppression, to oppress

yokusei 抑制 restraint, to restrain

yokushi 抑止 deterrence, to deter

yōkyū 要求 a demand, to demand

yōnin 容認 admission, to admit

yōsei 要請 a request, to request 養成 training, to train

yōsetsu 溶接 a weld, to weld

yoshū 予習 preparation (of lessons), to prepare lessons

yosō 予想 expectation, to expect

yosoku 予測 a forecast, to forecast

yotei 予定 a schedule, to schedule

yoyaku 予約 booking/reservation, to book/reserve

yōyaku 要約 a summary, to sum up

yūdō 誘導 guidance, to guide

yūkai 誘拐 abducting, to abduct

yunyū 輸入 importation, to import

yūri 遊離 separation, to separate

yūsen 優先 priority, to take priority

yusō 輸送 transportation, to transport

yūsō 郵送 sending by mail, to send by mail

yūshō 優勝 a victory, to win the victory

yushutsu 輸出 exportation, to export

yūtai 優待 preferential treatment, to give preferential treatment

yūzū 融通 accommodation, to accommodate somebody with money, etc.

zaigaku 在学 being in school, to be (enrolled) in school

zōdai 増大 enlargement/increase, to enlarge/increase

zōka 増加 an increase, to increase

Transitive/Intransitive pairs

INTRANSITIVE

agaru 上がる to go up

aku 開く to open

ataru 当たる to hit

butsukaru ぶつかる to bump

deru 出る to go out

fueru 増える to increase

hairu 入る to go in

hajimaru 始まる to begin

hanareru 離れる to separate

TRANSITIVE

ageru 上げる to raise

akeru 開ける to open

ateru 当てる to hit

butsukeru ぶつける to bump

dasu 出す to let out

fuyasu 増やす to increase

ireru 入れる to put in

hajimeru 始める to begin

hanasu 離す to let go

hazureru 外れる to come off

hieru 冷える to grow cold

hirogaru 広がる to spread

kaeru 帰る to go back

kakureru 隠れる to be hidden

kawaru 変わる to change

kieru 消える to be put out

kikoeru 聞こえる to be heard

kimaru 決まる to be decided

kireru 切れる to be cut

koboreru こぼれる to spill

kowareru 壊れる to break down

magaru 曲がる to bend

matomaru まとまる to be united/arranged

mawaru 回る to go round

mazaru 混ざる to be mixed

mieru 見える to be seen

michiru 満ちる to become full

mitsukaru 見つかる to be found

moreru 漏れる to leak

mukeru 剥ける to peel

muku 向く to face

naku 泣く to cry

nakunaru 無くなる to be lost

narabu 並ぶ to be lined up

nokoru 残る to be left over

nobiru 伸びる to grow long

nobiru 延びる to be postponed

noru 乗る to ride/get on

nukeru 抜ける to fall out

ochiru 落ちる to fall

okiru 起きる to get up

oreru 折れる to break in two

oriru 下りる to get down

owaru 終わる to be over

sagaru 下がる to go down/off

sameru 冷める to get cold

shimaru 閉まる to be closed

tamaru 貯まる to be saved up

tasukaru 助かる to be rescued/helped

tatsu 立つ to stand up

tobu 飛ぶ to fly

tokeru 溶ける to melt

tomaru 止まる to stop

toreru 取れる to come off

tsuzuku 続く to be continued

tsuku 付く to be lighted/be attached

tsumaru 詰まる to be packed

tsunagaru 繋がる to be connected

tsutawaru 伝わる to be transmitted

umareru うまれる to be born

yakeru 焼ける to bake/be burned

yasumu 休む to take a rest

waku 沸く to be boiled

wareru 割れる to be cracked

hazusu 外す to remove

hiyasu 冷やす to cool

hirogeru 広げる to spread

kaesu 帰す to let go back

kakusu 隠す to hide

kaeru 変える to change

kesu 消す to put out

kiku 聞く to hear

kimeru 決める to decide

kiru 切る to cut

kobosu こぼす to spill

kowasu 壊す to break

mageru 曲げる to bend

matomeru まとめる to unite/arrange

mawasu 回す to turn/rotate

mazeru 混ぜる to mix

miru 見る to see

mitasu 満たす to fill

mitsukeru 見つける to find

morasu 漏らす to let leak

muku 剥く to peel

mukeru 向ける to turn

nakasu 泣かす to move . . . to tears

nakusu 無くす to lose

naraberu 並べる to line up

nokosu 残す to leave

nobasu 伸ばす to lengthen

nobasu 延ばす to postpone

noseru 乗せる to give a ride

nuku 抜く to pull out

otosu 落とす to drop

okosu 起こす to wake up

oru 折る to break off/fold

orosu 下ろす to take down

oeru 終える to finish

sageru 下げる to lower

samasu 冷ます to cool

shimeru 閉める to close

tameru 貯める to save up

tasukeru 助ける to rescue/help

tateru 立てる to put up/ stand

tobasu 飛ばす to let fly

tokasu 溶かす to melt

tomeru 止める to stop

toru 取る to remove/take

tsuzukeru 続ける to continue

tsukeru 付ける to light/attach

tsumeru 詰める to pack

tsunagu 繋ぐ to connect

tsutaeru 伝える to tell

umu うむ to give birth/produce

yaku 焼く to bake/burn

yasumeru 休める to give a rest

wakasu 沸かす to boil

waru 割る to crack

APPENDIX 6

List of Selected Nouns

Nouns made of verbs in the combining form

• *Ru*-verbs

akirame 諦め resignation
amae 甘え tendency to be dependent on others like a spoiled child
hage 禿げ being bald, baldness
hajime 始め beginning
hare 晴れ fine weather
hazure 外れ outskirts, losing number
kangae 考え thought, idea, opinion
kanji 感じ feeling, sense
katazuke 片付け clearing something away
kigae 着替え spare clothes
koge 焦げ burned part
kotae 答え answer
kumiawase 組み合わせ combination
make 負け lost game
matome まとめ summary
motome 求め claim, request, demand
mukae 迎え welcoming
nagame 眺め view
nagare 流れ flow
nare 慣れ experience repeated, expertise
okure 遅れ delay, time lag
osae 押さえ weight, control
oshie 教え lesson, doctrine, teachings
osore 恐れ fear, anxiety
shirase 知らせ news, notice
sonae 備え preparation
susume 勧め advice, suggestion
tasuke 助け help, aid
tsure 連れ companion
tsukare 疲れ tiredness
tsutome 勤め work, duty
uke 受け popularity, defense
uketsuke 受け付け reception desk
umare 生まれ birth
wakare 別れ parting

• *U*-verbs

amari 余り rest, surplus
asobi 遊び playing, pastime
atari 当たり strike, hit, success

chigai 違い difference
chikai 誓い vow
fukumi 含み hidden meaning, implication
hagemashi 励まし encouragement
hanashi 話 talk, conversation, story, consultation, speech
hashiri 走り run
hataraki 働き work, action, function
hayari 流行り fashion, vogue
hibiki 響き sound, ring
hikari 光 light, twinkle, flash
hiraki 開き gap, difference
hohoemi 微笑み smile
iki 行き going
kaeri 帰り going back, coming back
kanashimi 悲しみ sorrow, sadness
kashi 貸し loan
kachi 勝ち win, victory
kazari 飾り decoration, ornament
kimari 決まり settlement
kōri 氷 (サ) ice
koroshi 殺し killing
kurikaeshi 繰り返し repetition
machigai 間違い mistake
magari 曲がり turn, bend
maki 巻き roll
mamori 守り defense, protection
maneki 招き invitation
matomari まとまり settlement, consistency
mawari 回り rotation, round
mayoi 迷い delusion, perplexity
minori 実り crop, harvest
mōshikomi 申し込み application, subscription
muki 向き direction
musubi 結び conclusion, close
nagashi 流し sink
nageki 嘆き sorrow, grief
narabi 並び row
nayami 悩み worry
negai 願い wish, hope
nemuri 眠り sleep, slumber

nerai 狙い aim
netami ねたみ envy, jealousy
nigiri 握り grasp, sushi
nioi 匂い, 臭い perfume, smell
nobori 上り up train, inbound train
nokori 残り rest, what is left
nozomi 望み wish
nusumi 盗み theft
odoroki 驚き surprise
okonai 行い behavior, act
omoi 思い thought, feelings
ōi 覆い cover
ochitsuki 落ち着き presence of mind
owari 終わり end
sasayaki ささやき whisper
sawagi 騒ぎ disturbance, brawl, fuss
shimekiri 締め切り deadline, closing
sukui 救い a rescue
susugi すすぎ rinse
tameshi 試し trial, test
tashi 足し a supplement
tatami たたみ folding, tatami mat

tomari 泊まり lodging
tōri 通り street
tsukai 使い errand
tsukkomi 突っ込み digging (into a matter)
tsukuri 作り structure, construction
tsumami つまみ picking up with fingers, a knob, an hors d'oeuvre
tsunagi つなぎ connection, filling up the gap
tsuri 釣り fishing, angling
tsutsumi 包み package
tsuzuki 続き sequel
ugoki 動き movement, trend
ukagai 伺い visit, inquiry
uki 浮き buoy, aloat
uranai 占い fortune-telling
urami 恨み ill feeling, grudge
uridashi 売り出し beginning to sell, bargain sale
warai 笑い laughter, sneer
yasumi 休み rest, day off, holiday
yomi 読み foresight, reading

Compound nouns with verbs in the combining form

kaerimichi 帰り道 one's way back (home)
kaimono 買い物 shopping
nomimono 飲み物 something to drink, a drink
norimono 乗り物 means of transportation
tabemono 食べ物 something to eat, food
yakiniku 焼き肉 roast meat
yomimono 読み物 something to read, reading material